NEW ENGLAND STATE POLITICS

NEW ENGLAND
STATE
POLITICS

★

BY DUANE LOCKARD

★

PRINCETON, NEW JERSEY
PRINCETON UNIVERSITY PRESS
1959

❖

The Library of Congress catalog entry for this book
appears at the end of the text

❖

DUANE LOCKARD has combined a scholarly and
political career. He has taught at Yale and Wes-
leyan and is now an associate professor of government at Connecticut College, New London,
Connecticut. In 1954 he was elected to the Connecticut State Senate, serving from 1955 to 1957.
His greatest interests were constitutional reform,
municipal home rule, and the party primary.
Though he has now returned to the campus, he
has continued his general political interests and
activities, and serves as chairman of the New London Citizens Action Committee. Mr. Lockard has
written articles in the field of law, politics, and
political science. This book is the result of seven
years of research, involving over one
thousand interviews.

❖

Printed in the United States of America
by Princeton University Press, Princeton, N.J.

TO BEVERLY

PREFACE

———————————— ★ ————————————

W<small>HEN</small> I began work on this study of New England state politics some seven years ago, little did I realize the magnitude of the task being undertaken. I soon discovered the paucity of published materials on the politics of individual states. For my own state, Connecticut, the task was not quite so formidable, since I had participated sufficiently in its politics to acquire some understanding, but comparative analysis demanded considerable familiarity with all six New England states. I learned a great deal by reading all I could find on New England politics, but I still had a long way to go. Had it not been for the kindness of almost a thousand people interviewed in the ensuing years of research, this book would have been impossible to write. Governors, judges, administrators, lobbyists, party leaders, hundreds of legislators, and dozens of newspaper reporters took time out to deal patiently with my questions. Several visits to each of the states were devoted mainly to interviews, and during the period from 1955 to 1957 I was a member of the Connecticut Senate, where I combined an official with an investigative role. Part of the interviews were relatively systematic in that I set a pattern of questions which I put to the legislators of a given state, particularly in regard to their personal conception of the roles they played as legislators. Other interviews were less systematic in that I encouraged people to range far and wide in discussing the politics of their state. To avoid omitting the name of anyone who gave me valuable information, I refrain from listing all those who gave me interviews. This is no indication of lack of gratitude; I am deeply grateful to them all.

I wish to express my appreciation to the Ford Foundation Fund for the Advancement of Education for granting me a Faculty Fellowship for the academic year 1955-1956, during which time much of the research and interviewing was accomplished. The Social Science Research Council granted me a fellowship for the spring term in 1957, during which time a first draft was written. Connecticut College kindly provided several research grants for various expenses incurred, ranging from newspaper clipping services and travel costs to student typing aid. Professor Allan P. Sindler of Yale read the manuscript and made many helpful criticisms of the early chapters, and Mr. Donald Craig read several chapters and contributed much in his criticisms of style. Professor V. O. Key, Jr. of Harvard has contributed more to this work than he probably realizes: he started me off on the project when he supervised my dissertation on Connecticut politics while he was at Yale. He corrected more faults than I like to remember, and in his various works on state politics he has both established the highest standards of scholarship and set forth the lines for investigation that others must inevitably follow. I also had the benefit of consultation with him at several stages of the evolution of this work. And Miss R. Miriam Brokaw, Managing Editor of Princeton University Press, has been an unfailing source of help in matters large and small that beset an author enroute to publication day. I must make it clear, however, that no faults of this work are to be attributed to either the institutions or the individuals who contributed so much to it. All errors of fact or interpretation are my sole responsibility.

Finally, I want to thank my wife, Beverly, and my daughters, Linda, Janet, and Leslie, for patience and aid beyond the call of duty. A book in preparation can be a most unwelcome guest in the home; this was no exception. My wife's editorial assistance was invaluable; indeed the book might be better if I had accepted even more of her suggestions. Linda and Janet laboriously read proof with me when pleasures beckoned but were put aside. Leslie, who is not much older than the idea for the book, did her bit by putting up with a preoccupied father.

W.D.L.

November 15, 1958
Connecticut College
New London, Connecticut

CONTENTS

———————— ★ ————————

CONTENTS

MAPS AND CHARTS

Drawn by R. Williams

NEW ENGLAND STATE POLITICS

CHAPTER 1

———— ★ ————

ABOUT NEW ENGLAND:
AN INTRODUCTION

THERE are two New Englands. Most outlanders think of only one of them when New England comes to mind. The image is of a quaint, quiet, and very reserved community; a place of picturesque stone fences, charming village greens, and of nasal-toned, eloquently laconic Yankees. There is still such a New England, an important facet of the total character of the region, but it has for some time been declining before a newer New England. The older New England in its prime was largely an agricultural society, but the rocky soil proved more productive of stone fences than of grain. Transportation to the West brought in grains at a price that even the most industrious Yankee could not meet. Since in general New England is not blessed with rich stores of mineral resources, there was only one direction in which the area could go—toward industry—and it went with a flourish. In the process a newer New England was fashioned.

Industrialization created a demand for labor, a demand greater than the deserting farm population could supply. So the mill owners brought the needed "hands" from Europe and French Canada to tend their machines. Soon the birth registry began to record fewer Calebs and Nathaniels and more Patricks, Anthonys, and Pierres. In time, imposing Catholic churches took their places alongside stately Congregational buildings. Cities grew too large for the town-meeting system to govern any longer; the democratic atmosphere of the town meeting gave way to machine politics. In ghettos reserved for the non-Yankee newcomers political clubs sprang up to plan and maneuver as adroitly as the men who met in Tom Dawes's garret in pre-Revolutionary Boston to caucus before town meetings, much to the displeasure of John Adams. Eventually the cities could not contain their teeming numbers and sprawling suburbs surrounded every city. In small towns adjacent to the cities the once relatively isolated Yankees found challengers to their political hegemony.

There is no *strict* division in area between the two New Englands. Each element is intermixed with the other in nearly every part of the region. However, more of the old New England is to be found north of the Massachusetts border and more of the new in the three southern states. Both elements are significant in both areas, but the old New England is more powerful in the north. Industry is not so concentrated; agriculture is more important in the economy and life of the communities. The small independent town remains a live social unit. In the other three states 43 per cent of the people live in cities with more than 50,000 population; if we include the immediate regions around these cities (formally, the "standard metropolitan areas") they then contain 68 per cent of the three-state population. The proportion of ethnic minorities is much greater in the southern portion; there, about four out of six of those employed work in manufacturing.

The social and economic patterns of upper and lower New England are sufficiently different to have produced distinctly different political systems, but there are enough similarities within the region as a whole to make comparisons possible. Regionalists may argue whether New England actually constitutes a "region" in the strictest sense of the term, but for present purposes this debate is irrelevant.[1] Notwithstanding the changes wrought by the last century particularly, there are many elements of a common heritage operative in all the New England states.

There are, for example, considerable similarities in the governmental structures of these states—similarities not shared in general

---

[1] The debate about the nature of New England has a long history, but in essence the dispute concerns the apparent heterogeneity of economic and social patterns between the northern and southern sections of the area and the all-too-customary tendency to neglect this fact in the glib generalizations so often made about New England. See, for example, George Wilson Pierson, "The Obstinate Concept of New England: A Study in Denudation," 28 *New England Quarterly* 3-18 (Mar. 1955). Also on the skeptical side is Howard L. Green, "Hinterland Boundaries of New York City and Boston in Southern New England," 31 *Economic Geography* 283-301. See the comments made in the articles on "The Withering of New England" by Oscar Handlin and Howard Mumford Jones in 185 *Atlantic Monthly* 49-53 (Apr. 1950). In *The Case for Regional Planning With Special Reference to New England* the Directive Committee on Regional Planning of Yale University took the position that for all practical purposes of regional planning New England could be called a region. New Haven, 1949, Ch. 4.

with the rest of the forty-~~nine~~ ^town^ states. The town meeting and the concomitant emphasis on town autonomy are peculiar to New England. Only with the greatest reluctance, however, have these states adopted the home-rule movement whereby the municipality is freed of controls by the state legislature. This, in part at least, is the product of another peculiarity of New England government—the tendency to give legislative representation to every town. The practice of town representation in at least one house of the legislature has been deemed a substitute for home rule. Also significantly, town representation has helped make New England legislatures the largest in the country.[2] County government is relatively insignificant, and accordingly political organization over most of New England tends to be localized within the individual town rather than based on the county as in most of the rest of the country. The wave of disaffection with political parties which swept the country in connection with the Muckraker and allied reform movements of the first decades of this century had relatively less effect in New England than in the West. The anti-party spirit, which spawned the Non-Partisan movement in the prairie states and the non-party practices of many Western states, was a far less effective force in New England's political development. This is a partial explanation of the greater powers of parties in New England. And, finally, the constitutions of the New England states are both ancient and in general fairly brief and simple—at least by comparison.[3] The six New England constitutions were adopted earlier than those of any of the other states. (The dates of adoption in New England range from 1780 for Massachusetts to 1843 for Rhode Island.)

These elements of a common background and the fact that there is a territorial division between upper and lower New England combine to make the area a fascinating laboratory for the study of state

[2] The lower houses of New Hampshire, Connecticut, Vermont, and Massachusetts are the four largest in the country and constitute four of the six such houses in excess of 200 members. Massachusetts and Maine do not have representation for every town, but the other four states do. For non-New Englanders some explanation of the "town" may be in order. The total area of the New England state is divided into towns which are not only geographic units but which have governments with broad powers. They have powers that in most states are allotted to the county as well as those given to ordinary local governments.

[3] Only the Massachusetts constitution comes near the average for length of state constitutions, with some 28,700 words. Thirty-seven states have constitutions longer than any of the New England states and the three briefest are in New England: Vermont, Rhode Island, and Connecticut.

politics. In the three northern states one-party systems prevail and in the remaining three states there is competition between the two major parties. Party competition in Connecticut and Massachusetts is brisk, and there is actually more competition in Rhode Island than the data of Table 1 would indicate, but the reader will have to accept that fact on faith for the moment.[4] In any event Table 1 illustrates the general demarcation between one- and two-party politics in the area.

TABLE 1

The Party Tendencies of the New England States, 1930-1956

State	Mean Republican percentage of the vote for governor	Number of Republican majorities for governor	Number of elections producing change of party control of governorship
Vermont	65.5%	14 of 14	0
New Hampshire	55.6	14 of 14	0
Maine	54.7	10 of 14	3
Massachusetts	50.2	6 of 14	7
Connecticut	50.1	5 of 12	7
Rhode Island	44.6	2 of 14	3

The study of one- and two-party states within the context of one region provides an opportunity to make a comparative analysis concentrating on the variations between the two types of political system. It is a general assumption that two-party competition results in a more salutary political atmosphere, but surprisingly little research has been devoted to testing this hypothesis. Various scholars have reported on the politics of individual states and have made generalizations about, for example, the political patterns of one-party states, but little has been done to make direct comparisons between the two types. In one sense this is not surprising, for the political conditions of the South, where one-partyism is most prevalent, are so strikingly different from the conditions in a state like New York or Connecticut, a fact which demonstrates the difficulty of working with *all* the states as a frame of reference. Comparing Connecticut and Mississippi is possible in some respects, but the

[4] See Chapter 7 for an analysis of Rhode Island parties.

limits of valid comparison are soon reached. Thus the rationale of a regional comparative analysis of state politics: it reduces the uncertainties and variables to more manageable proportions.

To test the hypothesis that two-party politics is in some sense more democratic, more responsible, or more rational than one-party politics, it is necessary to go beyond the party organizations as such. To restrict one's view to elections, campaigning, and intra- or inter-party maneuvering on the hustings is inadequate. Some broader perspective is necessary. Part of that perspective can be supplied by looking at the legislative process. In the one-party states, for instance, the factions of the dominant parties are of great significance, for in essence they supply virtually the only means of organized opposition to the holders of power at any given moment. In the two-party states the role of the party's leadership (both in and out of the legislature) is an important determinant of the party's role, whether great or small. Legislative politics reveal much about these telling characteristics of the two types of party system. The legislature accordingly becomes an obvious source for the examination of a whole political system.

In the ensuing treatment of New England state politics I have sought to describe the political parties as best I could.[5] I have then studied the legislative politics of each state in recent decades to try to observe the political system in operation. In the end I have drawn some tentative conclusions about New England state politics. Whether these conclusions are applicable to other parts of the country I leave to others to decide.

---

[5] I am fully aware of the almost infinite complexity of the broad matrix of forces that make a political system what it is; I can only plead that I have done my best to ferret out the relevant elements of the broad historical, social, economic, and constitutional forces that have made the politics of each state what it is. I have not attempted a systematic effort to treat New England's contribution to national politics, a topic beyond the scope of this comparative analysis of state political systems.

CHAPTER 2

──────── ★ ────────

VERMONT: POLITICAL PARADOX

VERMONT is a land of political paradox. It is conservative, but it has a liberal strain. It has a one-party system, but it lacks many of the common attributes of one-partyism: there is little bitterness, almost no outright corruption, and the extent of popular political participation is not particularly depressed. Early in its history Vermont was liberal, even radical, in belief and action; later it abruptly turned to marked conservatism and in this century it has by fits and starts been both conservative and liberal in its public policies.

It is not enough to say in explanation that Vermonters are cussed and independent people who do things in their own way regardless of what course others may take. It is not enough to say, but it is one of the things that must be said. The Vermont tradition of independence is as sedulously and seriously nurtured among Vermonters as is the tradition of any state—far more than most. What this tradition implies cannot be reduced to a few sentences, and yet the importance of the tradition demands that a suggestion of its elements be attempted.

Prominent among the lures to attract tourists to Vermont is the theme of "Vermont unspoiled," an island of the past where the habits, sights, sounds, and smells of industrial progress are absent, leaving an unsullied land for the enjoyment of today's all-embracing leisure class. As usual what the promoters say does not quite conform with reality; yet there is considerable truth in it. Vermont is a kind of capsule of the American past. It is relatively isolated and it has retained many of the virtues of a simpler past era. As nineteenth-century American orators sang the praises of self-reliance, thrift and independence, and a fierce sense of freedom, so must an unbiased present-day observer of Vermont identify these traits as typically Vermont. Not all Vermonters share these traits equally, of course; yet the spirit of Vermont certainly evokes the feeling that these virtues are meaningful. They are more than slogans for politi-

8

cal campaigns and sermons; they are elements of a past that shape the present political direction of the state.

What evidence of the survival of Vermont tradition can be found today? Dorothy Canfield Fisher stoutly maintains that tradition continues to have an influence, and cites as evidence the resistance of the state to the hysterical reaction to Communism found so commonly in other states. She quotes a fellow Vermonter that "Anybody who tries to bore from within in Vermont is going to strike granite."[1] When legislation restricting civil rights was presented in the Vermont legislature, it was turned down as unwanted "witch hunting." The brief story of one or two of these proposals will illustrate.

In 1953 Charles A. Plumley, a 77-year-old veteran of eighteen years in the United States House of Representatives, apparently decided that Vermont was in danger. Perhaps he was unhappy in his political retirement and wanted some excitement; for whatever reason, he urged that Vermont censor her school textbooks to cull out those of subversive nature. Accordingly a neighbor of Plumley's introduced a bill into the Vermont House of Representatives to implement the former Congressman's ideas. The bill called for an appointive board to survey all textbooks and to withdraw any that had "subversive or disloyal" content (neither of these terms being defined).

Plumley had several texts in mind that he wanted exorcised. He contended that Vermont was a "testing ground for the Communists," citing as an item of evidence that Alger Hiss had a home in the little town of Peacham. Late in March a move was started to get Plumley to address a joint session of the General Assembly, but several leaders blocked this, one calling it "an effort at back-door lobbying." The newspapers failed to take up the cry and demand censorship; most of them were critical of the bill. The teachers were opposed, and there was considerable popular opposition to the bill as an invasion of the powers of locally elected school boards. Yet the same kind of opposition to such legislation had been heard in many other states where it became law. Teacher opposition, the desire for local autonomy, and the uncertainties of such vaguely worded law having failed to halt censorship elsewhere, many Vermonters thought the

[1] *Vermont Tradition, The Biography of an Outlook on Life*, Boston, 1953, p. 397. But see the dissenting point of view in Miriam Chapin's article "Vermont: Where Are All Those Yankees?" 215 *Harper's Magazine* 50-54 (Dec. 1957).

bill might pass. The Appropriations Committee of the House ended the speculation in late March when it voted 14 to one against the bill. (The Education Committee had passed it on to Appropriations without recommendation.) The House itself made it final when only 11 affirmative votes could be mustered against the 202 "nay."[2] Only one member, the bill's sponsor, got up to support it, and the House turned a deaf ear to his warning of danger as well as to his plea that a similar law worked well in New York. The reporting member of the Appropriations Committee said they would not put "the stamp of approval on $1,000 for this witch hunt."[3]

Nor has Vermont accepted legislation to restrict the Communist party from the ballot, although the proposal has been made. A bill was presented in the 1951 session of the General Assembly to deny a place on the ballot for any party "directly or indirectly" associated with Communist, Fascist, or other un-American principles. After the Judiciary Committee had amended the bill, it passed in the House without a roll-call vote and without much debate. The Senate Judiciary Committee, however, returned an unfavorable report, and after extensive discussion—there was no disagreement—the bill was unanimously rejected. Said one member of the Senate Judiciary Committee, "If the spirit of liberty should vanish in the United States, and our institutions should languish, it could all be restored by the generous store held by the people in this brave little state of Vermont." The words were not his own, but those of that famous Vermonter, Calvin Coolidge, yet the spirit of the remainder of his speech was in keeping with the quotation. Vermont, going her own way, was not ready to join other states in this form of restriction on liberty as she understood it.[4]

The late Bernard DeVoto once commented that Vermont is essentially Calvinist and that "there are more Yankees left in Vermont than anywhere else."[5] Both socially and politically Vermont is dominated by the small-town and country Yankee. A third of the population lives in towns of less than 2,500 and a greater proportion of

[2] See the *Burlington Free Press*, Mar. 31, 1953.
[3] *Ibid.*
[4] See Dorothy Canfield Fisher, *op.cit.*, pp. 400-402. See also the *Journal of the Senate of the State of Vermont*, 1951, pp. 434-435 (Apr. 23, 1951).
[5] "How to Live among the Vermonters," 173 *Harper's Magazine* 333-336 at p. 334 (Aug., 1936). DeVoto is also responsible for the remark that to Vermonters the difference between ten and eleven cents is not negligible—it is one cent.

the people live on farms than in any other New England state (21.5 per cent in 1950). Vermonters are fond of pointing out that there are more cattle than people in the state, a fact confirmed by the Census Bureau. Vermont, like some of the hill regions of the South, has been a reservoir from which the industrialized cities of the nation have drawn their population; in the first decade of this century two-thirds of Vermont's towns lost in population and in the second decade three-fourths of them declined.[6] Vermonters and ex-Vermonters debate the consequences of this emigration, some contending that it has drained off the ambitious and enterprising, others denying this. Dorothy Canfield Fisher says, "In a Vermont family which had two sons and three daughters, those who moved West were not necessarily the more energetic ones, the brainier ones. Sometimes they were. Sometimes they weren't. It seems to have been a question whether 'they felt to.' Some did. Some didn't."[7] Without entering a family quarrel on what is at best a moot point, one can observe that there was little infusion of new blood and new ideas and that at least some adventurous and energetic types deserted the marginal farms of the hillsides. Hence there was more and more relative isolation of the state from the new developments in more urban parts of the country.

There was some new blood, and non-Yankee blood at that. But the influx of the Irish, the French-Canadians, and the Italians to Vermont was meager compared with that in the neighboring states. These newer groups have come to have a minor political role, but the dominance of the Yankee has been unshaken thus far. The Yankee community retains a conservatism of pre-industrial and pre-urban America, but with an added touch of Yankee spirit of the special variety spawned by the cantankerous beginnings and development of Vermont.

Vermont, remember, began as an independent republic and remained one until 1791, when it deigned to ratify the Constitution and petition Congress for admission to the Union as the fourteenth state. A frontier spirit pervaded Vermont's first (1777) constitu-

---

[6] Harold F. Wilson, *The Hill Country of Northern New England*, New York, 1936, pp. 368-370. The relative decline of the state is indicated by the fact that it began with five members in the United States House of Representatives and now has only one.

[7] *Op.cit.*, p. 284.

11

tion, as liberal as any constitution of the period. In addition to the usual rights granted the people, Vermont added abolition of slavery and universal manhood suffrage. In rejection of the conservative argument that a second house of the legislature was necessary to represent property, the constitution provided a unicameral legislature. With the constitution went a political spirit to match—Vermont in that day was radical. Ethan Allen and Irishman Matthew Lyon were typical of their era. Lyon, publisher of a "rabidly republican sheet called the *Scourge of Aristocracy*,"[8] was in Congress when he was prosecuted under the Alien and Sedition Acts for his attacks on President John Adams. Convicted and imprisoned, he was still in jail when reelected to Congress by a good margin against four opponents.[9]

The 1777 constitutional prohibition of slavery in Vermont was prophetic of a significant theme in Vermont politics. As hill people they had no need for slavery—as was true even in hill country of the South—and having no seaports they were not tempted by the lucrative slave trade. Although the state rejected the old Federalist party for the Jeffersonians, the slavery question was among the reasons for the abandonment of Democratic ties even before the Civil War. By 1856 the anti-slavery feeling was so deep in Vermont that John C. Freemont, candidate of the newly born Republican party, won the state by a margin of nearly four to one.[10] At this point in time a man named Abraham Lincoln joined the party with some hesitancy, which presumably proves beyond all doubt the legitimacy of Vermont's Republicanism—to be "more Republican" than Abraham Lincoln ought to be evidence enough. And as the twig was bent, the tree has been inclined.

Vermont Republicanism

In every presidential, congressional, and gubernatorial campaign in Vermont from 1856 to today the Republican candidates have

[8] Earl Newton, *The Vermont Story, A History of the People of the Green Mountain State, 1749-1949*, Montpelier, Vermont, 1949, p. 119.

[9] *Ibid.*, p. 120.

[10] Antipathy to slavery was not just the penchant of a militant few in Vermont; it appears to have been a widely held conviction. Candidates urging the strongest anti-slavery positions won elections regularly, and the response of the people to the Civil War was enthusiastic. Enlistments were plentiful, and apparently the state lost more than its share of wounded and dead. "In proportion to population," says Earl Newton, "Vermont gave the lives of more of its sons to the Union cause than any other state." *Op.cit.*, p. 126.

12

without exception been successful.[10a] Almost everyone will recall that in 1936 Vermont was one of only two states (the other being Maine) to remain Republican against the Roosevelt landslide, but fewer people will remember that in 1912, when another Roosevelt was on the war path, Vermont was similarly one of two states to give the Republican nominee a plurality (along with Utah). Such a record of Republican consistency places Vermont in the list of indisputably one-party states. Although the Democratic party musters a larger vote in Vermont than does the Republican party in most Southern states, this fact does not really mean much, for up to the present at least the Democrats in Vermont are more notable for their persistence than for their ultimate political significance.[11]

To categorize the state as one-party requires no feat of analysis or research. What is far more difficult is to describe with any accuracy *what kind of one-party system it is*. There is in fact a wide range of differences in the actual political systems of the various one-party states. In some there is a relatively continuous two-factional alignment where the two factions assume something loosely akin to the role of parties in a two-party state. In others there is one continuous faction and a more or less disconnected opposition faction. In still others there is multi-factionalism where it is every-man-for-himself. To illustrate the difficulty of assessing Vermont as a Republican one-party state, consider these two recent efforts at appraisal. Ranney and Kendall, after a brief discussion of the background of Vermont politics, say: "All this sounds very much like the 'multifactionalism' characteristic of many of the southern one-party states. During the Progressive era a half-century ago . . . Vermont politics became bifactional for a time; but the Progressive faction and the old-guard faction eventually merged, and multifactionalism (or the 'absence of machine politics,' as Vermonters prefer to say) has been characteristic of the state's politics ever since."[12] Coleman Ransone presents an entirely different picture of the state's politics. He says: "Of the

[10a] Although true when written, this was changed by the 1958 election. A Democrat actually won election to the U.S. House seat. See p. 45 below.

[11] Between 1900 and 1954 in gubernatorial elections, for example, Republican candidates in Vermont have received an average of 69.8 per cent of the major party vote. North Carolina and Tennessee are the only Southern states with comparable second-party strength, according to the figures presented by Alexander Heard in his book, *A Two Party South?* Chapel Hill, North Carolina, 1952, Ch. IV and particularly pp. 66-67. In several of the Southern states there is often no Republican candidate at all, a form of supine cooperation that the Vermont Democrats never offer their adversaries.

[12] Austin Ranney and Willmore Kendall, *Democracy and the American Party System*, New York, 1956, p. 193.

states in the one-party group, Virginia and Vermont seem to have the clearly defined dual-factional structure. In Virginia the Byrd and anti-Byrd forces give the Democratic Party two fairly definite wings and the same is true in Vermont where the Proctor and anti-Proctor forces make up two wings of the Republican Party."[13]

Which of these contradictory views of Vermont Republican politics is accurate? The evidence suggests that the bifactional alignment is more nearly descriptive of the realities of Vermont politics, but even this must be taken with caution. The conservative Proctor organization has clearly been the most dominant force in Vermont politics for many generations, but to compare this group with the Byrd machine in Virginia is at best doubtful, since the differences between them are so striking. The Byrd machine is tightly knit; it has discipline; it has considerable control over local and county offices; and there is a definite carry-over of organizational strength into the legislature.[14] None of these things is true of the Proctor organization.

The organization built around the Proctor family, prominent in the marble industry of the state, has existed so long that it has been many things in the course of its history. Prior to the Progressive revolt of the second decade of this century, there seems to have been a real machine with local outposts and considerable internal discipline and control. It is difficult to be certain exactly how powerful the organization was in those earlier years, but subsequently it has been a relatively loose and flexible organization, able to meet rebellious elements with compromise. Serious challenges have been infrequent, partly because the organization restricted its area of control. One may speculate that had the organization tried to maintain a complete control of Vermont politics from the top to the bottom the antagonism aroused would have defeated it in time. Organization power is considerable but its leaders have not overplayed their hand.

Notwithstanding that Vermont is and has been a predominantly

[13] Coleman B. Ransone, Jr., *The Office of Governor in the United States*, University, Alabama, 1956, pp. 31-32.

[14] See V. O. Key's analysis of Virginia politics in his *Southern Politics in State and Nation*, New York, 1949, Ch. 2. Through a state board of compensation the machine in Virginia "fixes the compensation of the principal county officials and makes allowances for the salaries and expense of their offices" (at p. 21). To say the least, this facilitates discipline.

agricultural state, the Proctor organization has been based much more on industrial than upon agricultural power. The Proctor dynasty had its origins with Redfield Proctor, who came to the state after the Civil War to operate a failing marble company. He built up his company and with judicious combinations with other organizations produced a quasi-monopolistic control over the state's main extractive industry.[15] Three other Proctors have been governor since Redfield Proctor's day, the latest being Mortimer Proctor, who served from 1945 to 1947.

The early ascendancy of the Proctor family was attributable not only to the importance of the marble industry in the state but also to the unusual qualities of leadership of such men as Redfield Proctor and Fletcher Proctor, who followed him in command. Other rising industrial groups cooperated with the Proctors, but the place of the marble industry in the economy of the state enhanced the Proctor family position. More recently other economic interests have moved up in importance and accordingly have taken a more active part in politics. The machine-tool industry, with which both Senator Ralph Flanders and the recent governor, Joseph Johnson, are associated, has muscled its way into a prominent position. It may now be somewhat anachronistic to call the conservative faction the "Proctor organization," since the family no longer dominates it. The Proctors are still with the faction, however, even if they are not the guiding spirits, and the general continuity of ideological orientation and the political methods employed are sufficiently unchanged to make the term reasonably accurate. It is in any event still used in political discussion in the state.

The Proctor organization has most of the time controlled access to the highest political offices in Vermont. A definite ladder of advancement has provided an opportunity to examine the political dependability as well, perhaps, as the abilities of those who sought the governorship. The customary route to the top includes service in the House or in the Senate (or both), then election to the lieutenant governor's chair before running for governor. Of the ten governors who served between 1925 and 1958, eight had been in the House before becoming lieutenant governor, an office each held in the terms

[15] See Robert C. Gilmore's brief history of the rise of the Proctor family's economic and political power in his "The Vermont Marble Company, 1869-1939," xiv *New England Social Studies Bulletin* (Dec. 1956), pp. 11-20, and (Mar. 1957), pp. 14-20.

immediately preceding his service as governor.[16] Money for campaigning, some organizational support in various counties, and usually newspaper support have helped put the Proctor candidates over. No doubt the seeming inevitability of the ladder of ascendancy helped the regular candidates, since to some extent a kind of legitimacy seemed to attach to the regular promotion of those coming along.[17]

Most Proctor-faction governors have been conservatives of the "do-nothing" school. Representative of the business and financial interests of the state, they want to keep government costs, government regulation, and service functions at the lowest reasonable levels. The atmosphere of the state legislature, for reasons I will try to explain later, is well suited to this kind of negative approach. It is true that some Proctor governors have worked for progressive legislation on occasion, but for the most part a placid "low-pressure" politics and government has seemed to be the goal. In earlier times they opposed factory inspection, regulation of child labor, workmen's compensation, and other "progressive" measures of this sort.[18] More recently, Governor Johnson's opposition to public distribution

[16] Five of these eight had also served one or more terms in the Senate, and several had been either president pro tempore of the Senate or speaker of the House.

[17] This ladder of ascendancy has gained a certain popular acceptance comparable to the previously held notion that candidates must be rotated between the eastern and western parts of the state. This came to be called the "Mountain Rule," under which for 90 years prior to 1928 no two successive candidates could come from the same side of the mountain. In short no governor could succeed himself, and open battles for access to power were not so likely since the battles were settled within either region then due for the office. In 1928, however, John W. Weeks, then 74 years old, broke the rule and ran to succeed himself. His success surprised commentators, who thought it impossible to break so iron-clad a rule. The main point of Weeks's opponent's campaign was that east-west alternation rule should not be broken, but it failed to overcome the popularity of Weeks, sometimes called the "Al Smith of Vermont." (The description left much to be desired by way of parallel. Virtually their only similarities were their low origins.) See the *New York Times* commentary on the election, Sept. 12, 13, and 23, 1928. The east-west division of the party continued for some time after Weeks's success. Many still cite it as a line of demarcation, but as subsequent election data indicate, the division, so far as one is perceptible, is now more north-south. Observers of the legislature also report the tendency of members to think of themselves as northern and southern respectively. See Oliver Garceau and Corinne Silverman, "A Pressure Group and the Pressured: a Case Report," 48 *American Political Science Review* 672-691 (Sept. 1954) at p. 689.

[18] See Winston A. Flint, *The Progressive Movement in Vermont*, Washington, D.C., 1941, Chs. 8 and 9. Flint also points out, however, that one Proctor governor (Allen M. Fletcher) did support a factory inspection law and other labor legislation.

of the St. Lawrence Seaway electrical power in the 1957 session of the General Assembly (thereby helping to defeat the proposal objected to by the utilities, who, of course, wanted to distribute it themselves) is illustrative of the present-day attitudes of the conservative governors.[19]

Opposition to the Proctor candidates has been sporadic, weak, and usually disorganized. Opponents are often found, but, lacking money and organizational support, their ratio of success to failure has been discouraging to the ambitious. There has been a considerable number of challenges of gubernatorial candidates, but proportionately fewer challenges of congressional candidates, as Table 2 indicates. Note that in the gubernatorial races there has been a challenger in 17 of the 21 contests between 1916 and 1956, even though in five of these races the opposition was unable to center on any single candidate to carry the opposition banner. In some instances the opposition has conceivably missed opportunities to win because of inability to settle on one candidate, as in 1950, when the two opposition candidates drew more votes than Emerson, the Proctor candidate, although the latter won with a plurality of the vote.[20]

TABLE 2

Primary Contests in the Republican Party in Vermont, 1916-1956

	Governor	Senator	Represent-ative
Number of contests	21	17	29
Number with incumbents running	7	12	22
Number with incumbents uncontested	1	8	13
Number with two candidates	12	5	8
Number with one candidate	4	10	17
Number with more than two candidates	5	7	4

There have been only three relatively brief periods when the anti-Proctor or more liberal faction has posed a successful opposition— from 1910 to 1915, during the depression period from 1936 to

---

[19] Innumerable examples could be cited, but one more will suffice. Governor Emerson, a Proctor man who was lieutenant governor under Governor Gibson (1947-1950), cast a tie-breaking vote in the Senate to defeat a Gibson proposal to have public-health units travel around the state to check the health of school children.

[20] Emerson had 43 per cent of the vote, Stacey 35, and Bove 22.

1940, and again between 1945 and 1950. In the first of these periods the opposition did not win the governorship but scared the organization into passing some unwanted legislation, including the party primary law.[21] In the depression the present Senator, George Aiken, was elected governor with the backing of the Farm Bureau Federation and other dissident elements who opposed the Proctor group. Although his program was not particularly radical in character, some of his proposals were sufficiently liberal to win him the enmity of the Proctor organization, with the result that it opposed him when he sought election to the Senate in 1940. Notwithstanding the opposition of most of the state's newspapers and the Proctor organization, Aiken beat Ralph Flanders in the primary.[22] Once in the Senate, Aiken compiled a relatively liberal voting record, much more liberal than that of Flanders, who had to wait six years for his opportunity to enter the Senate.[23]

During the war years the Proctor organization reclaimed the governorship, but the liberal wing returned with a vengeance in 1947. Mortimer R. Proctor, the fourth of the Proctor dynasty to hold the office, was seeking reelection in 1946, and since the custom had already grown up that no man who asked for a second term would be denied it, his success was generally conceded. He of course had the backing of his faction and considerable newspaper support, but he faced a formidable adversary. Young, liberal, energetic, and outspoken, Ernest W. Gibson, son of Vermont's late U.S. Senator, had just returned from the South Pacific where he had been wounded during long service as an army colonel. Gibson, as the anti-Proctor candidate for governor, campaigned against the "line of succession" rule to which he had to be an exception to win, for he had not served the usual apprenticeship in the House, Senate, and lieutenant governor's chair. He also made a vigorous attack on Mortimer Proctor's administration, which one opposition paper had called "a Study in Still Life."[24] Lacking money and organized support, but with farm group help, he won the governorship.

[21] See Flint, *op.cit.*, p. 105.

[22] See Earl Newton, *op.cit.*, pp. 254-255.

[23] The AFL-CIO Committee on Political Education reported in a pamphlet, "Voting Records of Senators and Representatives, 1947 through 1954," that Aiken had cast 19 "right" votes and 9 "wrong" ones in their view. Flanders on the other hand was credited with 9 "right" votes and 19 "wrong" ones.

[24] See Earl Newton, *op.cit.*, p. 255. Gibson's father had likewise done battle with

Once in office Gibson proceeded to get enacted a legislative program that is the clearest evidence that Vermont's is not purely a conservative outlook. About the best comparison with Gibson would be Connecticut's liberal postwar governor, Chester Bowles. Although Bowles was perhaps a bit more outspokenly liberal, he was on the whole less successful in getting his programs enacted than his Vermont counterpart. Gibson overcame objections to the extension of certain federal aid programs for the state, a move which surprised some people in view of the state's indignant refusal in 1936 to permit a federal highway in the state financed by the New Deal and in view of the fact that some Vermont farmers got out their guns to resist the building of federal dams in their pleasant valleys.

Federal aid programs had been used in Vermont before Gibson's proposals were made, but his success in overriding the objections to further federal aid was a notable event. After a battle, he got through a minimum salary law for teachers,[25] established a teachers' retirement fund, increased state aid to education by $1 million, improved the administration of the state welfare law, and overcame the sheriffs' objections to the creation of a State Police Department. Perhaps even more surprising was his success in getting a state income-tax law passed. The need for new taxes was apparent, but if anything was to be done, according to the industrial and more conservative elements, it ought to be done by a sales tax. Instead, Gibson won acceptance of an income tax with relatively liberal deductions.[26]

Prior to his service in the army, Gibson had served briefly in the U.S. Senate to fill out the term of his late father. His seat happened to be near that of a Senator from Missouri later to become President of the United States. President Truman later remembered his old friend by appointing him to the Federal District Court bench in

the Proctors, and had won. In 1934 he had gone to the Senate after several terms in the House, but he had to overcome the opposition of the Proctor organization. The elder Gibson had also been among the dissidents in the days of the Progressive Party of Theodore Roosevelt.

[25] I vividly recall my own frustrating and unsuccessful efforts to get a minimum-salary law through the Connecticut General Assembly in the 1955 session. The effort foundered on the rock of local prerogatives. Why the same argument did not doom the Vermont bill is hard to comprehend. Perhaps the deplorably low salaries prevalent in Vermont then and the modest request for a $1,500 minimum explain Gibson's success.

[26] For a brief résumé of Gibson's accomplishments see Melvin S. Wax, "Vermont's New Dealing Yankee," 168 *The Nation* 659-660, June 11, 1949.

1950 before his term as governor expired. Had he not accepted President Truman's offer, Gibson might well have changed the pattern of Vermont politics considerably; with the donning of judicial robes, his political influence virtually disappeared. Following Gibson, two conservative, generally uninspired, and more typical governors have restored the customary peace and tranquillity expected of Vermont politics.

What are the respective sources of strength of the Proctor and the anti-Proctor groups? In terms of interest-group backing, we have noted the importance of manufacturing and marble interests in the Proctor faction. Farm groups and apparently the newer elements moving into the state, many of them concentrated in the southern part of the state, have been the main backing of the liberal wing at least *within the party*. But the liberal wing has also drawn strength in primaries from the Democrats, since in effect Vermont has an open primary in which a person may choose whichever party primary he prefers on primary election day.[27] In an election which clearly pits a more liberal against a more conservative candidate the Democratic voters are frequently found to be voting in the Republican primary for the liberal candidate. Democratic statewide candidates are almost never challenged and therefore participation by Democrats in their own party's primary is normally very light. The turnout for the Democratic primary between 1930 and 1954 averaged about seven per cent of the turnout for the Republican primary, with the highest percentage being 11.7 per cent. Below is listed the Democratic turnout as percentages of the Republican primary vote totals since

1940: 9.7%	1946: 3.7%	1950: 5.6%
1942: 7.9	1948: 3.7	1952: 7.6
1944: 6.1		1954: 7.4

1940. In the middle two elections, in other words, the participation in the Democratic primary fell off; the assumption is that many of

[27] Vermont law provides that "A person voting at [a] primary shall indicate to the ballot clerk his party choice, and such ballot clerk shall give him a ballot of such party and no other." (*Vermont Statutes*, Revision of 1947, Ch. 13, Sec. 168.) Apparently some effort is made to keep local caucuses for the nomination of members of the lower house somewhat more restricted to party members. Caucus check lists are required, for example, and a certificate must be filed stating party affiliation. (See *Vermont Statutes*, Ch. 15, Sec. 235-236.) These rules do not apply to the state primary, however.

these people were voting for Gibson. In Winooski and Burlington, both normally Democratic, Gibson alone won more votes in the 1948 primary than all the Republican gubernatorial candidates combined could win in 1950, 1952, or 1954. It cannot be proved, of course, but Gibson's 90 per cent of the vote in the Republican primary in Winooski suggests some Democratic participation.[28]

The Proctor forces have their greatest strength in three northern counties, the anti-Proctor forces in three southern counties, as Figure 1 indicates. This is at least the present distribution of strength, to judge from five recent gubernatorial campaigns in which the two groups had clear contests going. Going back to Aiken's gubernatorial victories, one cannot discover any similarity between his areas of strength and the areas of greatest strength for more recent anti-Proctor candidates. In more recent campaigns, however, the anti-Proctor candidates have consistently done better in the three southern counties of Bennington, Windsor, and Windham. These same three southern counties are among the most heavily industrialized in the state and, as the southernmost counties, they have also received a considerable influx of newcomers into the state. It is likely, although not certain, that these are factors which have made these counties more liberal in outlook. The three Proctor counties (Orleans, Lamoille, and Washington) are more rural and sparsely settled.[29] Rutland County, which shares many of the same charac-

[28] Professor Andrew E. Nuquist of the University of Vermont tells this story of his campaign against Congressman Plumley in 1946, to illustrate the Democratic voting in Republican primaries. At a pre-election meeting held by the League of Women Voters at which both Republican and Democratic candidates spoke, the Democratic Congressional candidate told the audience to vote for Nuquist. "I haven't a chance of winning and I wish you would vote for Nuquist in the primary," he is reported to have said. His remarks showed more realism than party loyalty, perhaps, but the implicit invitation for Democrats to vote in the Republican primary tends to confirm the statistical inference. (From an interview with Professor Nuquist, Apr. 27, 1957.)

[29] It may seem to be a kind of contradiction to say that three primarily rural counties have supported the Proctor faction, and yet to contend that the Farm Bureau and farmer support have been important elements in the anti-Proctor camp. This is nevertheless the fact, for under the guidance of Arthur Packard the Farm Bureau in Vermont has been—in contrast to its conservative orientation in other states—a liberal element; the support of the organization in effect, although not always in outright commitment, has gone to the liberal wing. The Bureau is not the only farm organization in the state, of course, and there has always been considerable conservative farm support for the Proctor faction. Moreover, according to some observers, the three Proctor counties mentioned have been dominated by conservative politicians with some pro-Proctor organization.

teristics of the three anti-Proctor counties, is also the home of the Proctor family, and it is the one county which has consistently divided its vote nearly 50-50 between the two factions.

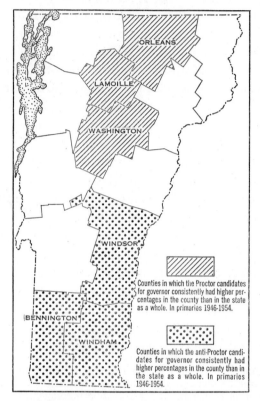

1. Proctor and Anti-Proctor Areas of
Greatest Strength (1946-1954)

Since Vermont is the most one-party-dominated state north of the Mason Dixon Line, it is interesting to compare the operations of Vermont's Republican party with the tactics of the Democratic party in the Southern states. Such a comparative analysis is possible thanks largely to the pioneering study of Southern politics made by Professor V. O. Key, Jr. In the course of his work, Key has singled out several leading characteristics of one-party politics in the South; it is useful to apply his generalizations about the South to states like Vermont. He says, for example, that in the South there is a tendency to emphasize personalities instead of issues in running for office. Under these conditions there is considerable dependence upon localism—a personal appeal that pays off through heavy "home town" support, or, as he calls it, "friends and neighbors." There is also a tendency to invite demagoguery as the appeal to personality overshadows the issues.[30]

The general avoidance of issues in a one-party system is perhaps the consequence of the lack of any pressure to focus on issues. A two-party system provides two continuously distinct groups of politicians aiming at the exclusion of the opposition from power. Undoubtedly they would find it just as useful to avoid issues as any other politicians, but the pressure of the opposition party in campaigns often forces them to take some kind of position. Certainly there are successful politicians in two-party states who consistently avoid taking clear stands on questions of public policy, but such evasion is less common and more risky in the two-party than in the one-party states. In the latter states the very vagueness of political alignments puts little pressure on politicians to espouse particular policy positions; emphasis on personality seems to predominate.

In most Republican primaries in Vermont not a great deal of attention is given to issues. The only exceptions are the rare campaigns when men like Aiken and Gibson have staged battles against Proctor candidates; then there is battling on policy questions, sometimes quite vigorously, as in Gibson's campaigns of 1946 and 1948. But these campaigns remain the exceptions; in most, there is a Proctor candidate who apparently has no great desire to conduct either a vigorous campaign or, when elected, a vigorous administration. On the whole, the attitude seems to be, the less said about issues the better. Even if gubernatorial candidates did want to discuss policy more conspicuously, the public would not have a clear chance to hold any factional group responsible for their actions, since there is very little carryover of factional alignments into the legislature. This is not to say, however, that there is a virtually complete absence of policy discussion, as seems to be the case in some Southern states. In all campaigns from 1946 to 1954 there was some semblance of

[30] V. O. Key, *op.cit.*, Ch. 14, "The Nature and Consequences of One-party Factionalism." Key's points are reduced here to very brief statements which are elaborated on somewhat as the discussion ensues. For a concise restatement of Key's conclusions on this by Key's chief aide in his Southern politics undertaking, see Alexander Heard, *op.cit.*, pp. 10-13.

anti-Proctor opposition, and thus there was at least some attention to policy matters, even though not enough to bestir any great public attention.[31]

In the Southern multifactional states, according to Key, localism plays an important role in deciding primary elections. Where personality is emphasized above policy, the contacts of the candidate with the people take on an exaggerated importance. Since his connections are greatest in his own home area the candidate is likely to pull a very strong local vote. In two-party areas this is not so important for the obvious reason that the traditional and policy orientations of the voter with his party will override his attachment to the local candidate. To the extent, therefore, that the factions take on some of the attributes of a party system within a party, the pull of localism is likely to be less persuasive since voters react to the factional alignment as well as to personality.

How important is localism or "friends and neighbors" in Vermont? It has some effect, to be sure, but nothing like the patterns of the multifactional parties in the South. Localism shows up in the home counties of most candidates in recent elections, but equally or more important is the bifactional division in the party between 1946 and 1954. Vermont counties only infrequently give any gubernatorial candidate an overwhelming margin of their vote. In gubernatorial primaries between 1946 and 1954 there were eight instances of counties casting as much as 75 per cent of their vote for one candidate. Significantly, in six of those eight cases the favored candidate was a local boy. Yet in each of these six cases the "friends and neighbors" pull was reinforced by factional pulls—that is, the candidate was from the area in which his faction had its greatest strength.

The limited scope of "friends and neighbors" in Vermont is illustrated by the 1946 gubernatorial primary. That year Mortimer Proctor carried his home county with 53 per cent of the vote, but his home county vote was not as high as in two northern counties where the Proctor strength has traditionally been great—there he won 55 and 59 per cent of the vote. In 1952 in a two-man contest that pitted the two factions against each other there appears to be considerable localism, but note that this general distribution of strength coincides with the factional areas as illustrated in Figure 1.

[31] There is, for example, far less attention to issues in Maine than in Vermont in the average election.

Emerson's 87 per cent of the vote in his home county is therefore not just a local endorsement, but both that and a continuance of habitual Proctor faction attachments.[32]

Has the one-party system of Vermont invited demagogic appeals? In general, no. In some cases extravagant claims may be made and efforts to appeal to emotional reactions certainly crop up, but with no greater and probably a lesser frequency than in some two-party states. Relatively mild demagogy is subtly preached on Catholicism, but this is more an inter- rather than intra-party conflict and in any event it is not signally important. In Vermont, unlike the South, there is no emotionally disturbing "problem" like the Negro question on which to base rampant demagogy.

Furthermore, the tendency toward bifactionalism creates a political atmosphere in which the appeal to demagogy is neither so necessary nor so fruitful as it is in a multifactional situation. Stunts such as campaigning with a hillbilly band or "the red galluses" showmanship of Georgia's Gene Talmadge have not turned up in Vermont. Some of this sort of extreme effort to attract attention does occur in Maine's Republican party, but Maine tends to have a much more multifactional arrangement within the dominant Republican party than is true in Vermont.

Key also makes the point that in Southern politics there is frequently favoritism in matters of contracts and other governmental dealings with money. Where the factions are in today and out tomorrow with virtually no concern for the next candidate who represents the group (if indeed the group continues its existence in any form), there is an invitation to take the attitude of "getting while the getting is good."[33] Although there is certainly some fast and loose playing with state money and favors in the two-party states,

---

[32] The suspiciously minded may be wondering whether the chance location of Proctor and anti-Proctor candidates in fact shaped the areas of strength of the two factions—thus making the actual alignment not that of faction but of "friends and neighbors." Such is not the case. Candidacies over the period 1946 to 1956 have been widely scattered geographically and the general alignments along factional lines have remained. In 1954, for example, both candidates were from the *same* county and three of the four highest anti-Proctor counties were the three southern counties of Bennington, Windham, and Windsor; similarly, the Proctor candidate had his greatest margins in the three northern Proctor counties notwithstanding that he *lived* in Windsor County in the south, where his percentage of the vote was slightly *less* than it was statewide.

[33] See Heard, *op.cit.*, p. 11, and V. O. Key, *op.cit.*, p. 305.

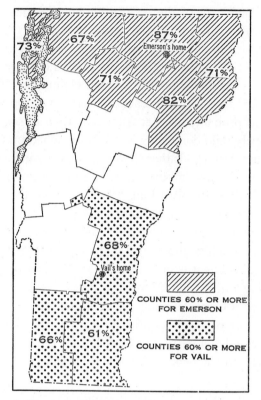

2. Vermont "Friends and Neighbors" Influence,
1952 Republican Primary for Governor

disorganized and "atomistic" one-party politics is a heady invitation to play the boodle game. In Vermont, whether for reasons of
greater bifactionalism or for other reasons of a cultural nature—no
one can say which factor is the more important with absolute certainty—there is remarkably little boodling.[34]

Perhaps the most widely recognized feature of Southern politics
is the restricted size of the electorate. Much misinformation is
bandied about on this score, but the general impression of a low

[34] "The late William Allen White . . . refused at first to believe that there was
not corruption in a party so long in power. He admitted later, however, after a
study of conditions in Vermont, that the state was so small and everyone seemed
to know so much about his neighbor's business that graft was practically impossible." Robert W. Mitchell, "Unique Vermont," 60 *American Mercury* 336-340
(Mar. 1945) at p. 339. This may have been White's view of the reason for the
lack of corruption, but I doubt its validity. Size per se is no bar to the corrupt, as
many a small-town treasurer has proved.

level of participation is supported by the facts. Key points out that in gubernatorial primaries in the Southern states between 1920 and 1946 the range of participation among all citizens over 21 years of age varied from 11.6 per cent average in Virginia to 42.8 per cent in North Carolina.[35] In none of the upper New England states, all more or less one-party in their politics, is there this great degree of limitation on the electorate.

In Vermont there is somewhat less voting participation than in most states; in 1940 and 1948 Vermont ranked 33 and 31 among all the states in the proportion of the adult population participating in the presidential elections of those years.[36] In those two elections Vermont not only surpassed the states of the South in voting turnout but also "outvoted" Maryland, Arizona, Kentucky, Maine, and Oklahoma. Reasonably close to the Vermont ratio of voters to non-voters were the figures for such states as Michigan, Pennsylvania, and Washington.[37] In contests for state officers, the proportion of adults voting fluctuates between the presidential and off-year elections, reflecting the higher enthusiasm of presidential campaigns. The average percentage of the adult population voting for governor in off-year elections between 1930 and 1954 was 40.6 per cent, and in presidential years, 59.3 per cent.

Presumably one of the important reasons why voting lags in Vermont is the fact that it is a one-party state where Republican nominees, after all, have won all statewide offices from time immemorial. However, the general feeling that all is done when the primary is over is by no means so strong a feeling in Vermont as it is in the South. Indeed many liberals in the state staunchly claim that the degree of popular participation would be increased considerably if the poll tax were removed as an implicit barrier to voting in state and national elections in Vermont. Under the law, strictly speaking, the payment of poll taxes is not a requirement for voting in state or national elections, but it is demanded prior to participation in town meetings. There are supposed to be two voting lists—one for town meetings and local elections, another for state and national elections.

[35] Key, *op.cit.*, p. 504. In the cases of North Carolina and Tennessee, Key uses the general election rather than the primary as his gauge, since general election figures are more indicative.

[36] See *The Political Almanac*, 1952, compiled by George Gallup and the staff of the American Institute of Public Opinion, New York, 1952, pp. 84-85.

[37] *Ibid.*

But non-payment of the town and state poll taxes—which can comprise a considerable burden when the $5 per adult state "old age tax" is added to local levies amounting to as much as $15 per adult —can actually become the ground for denial of the right to vote in general elections. Legally, non-payment of the poll tax is supposed to be a bar only to town-meeting participation, but if embarrassing questions about the tax are asked at the time of the general election, some voters are said to prefer non-voting to the alternative of digging up perhaps $40 to pay the tax for husband and wife. Liberal opponents of the tax claim that many are thus disenfranchised and argue that the avowed purpose of the law is to keep the indigent from voting. Governor Gibson in his first formal message to the General Assembly asked repeal of the poll tax, disapproving of "payment of the poll tax as a requisite for a right to vote in town or village meetings. This tax deters many people from ever exercising their right to vote. Yet only so long as the right to vote is used by large numbers of people will this State and this country survive as a democracy."[38] It is difficult if not impossible to say how much the tax decreases voting participation, especially since payment of the tax is now also a prerequisite to getting a driver's license, but undoubtedly it keeps some voters away from the polls.

Again unlike the South, participation in the Vermont primary is lighter than in the general election. In all Southern states except North Carolina there are normally more voters in the Democratic primary than in the general election, ranging from a slightly greater number in Virginia's primary to more than ten times as many in South Carolina.[39] In Vermont only about half as many people vote in the Republican primary as in the following general election.[40] There is usually a smaller vote for the ultimate Republican gubernatorial candidate in the general election than the combined Republican candidates got in the primary, however, a fact presumably reflecting two different things—the participation of some Democrats in the Republican primary and the feeling that the election is over

[38] See his Inaugural Message, Jan. 9, 1947, *Journal of the Senate of the State of Vermont*, 1947, p. 724.

[39] See the table showing averages for all the Southern states in Coleman Ransone, *op.cit.*, p. 17.

[40] Between 1930 and 1954 in thirteen gubernatorial races the average participation in the Republican primary amounted to 53.2 per cent of the total participation in the general election.

once the Republican primary is over. Yet the latter feeling is by no means so strong as it obviously is in the South. There the idea of a one-party system is not only accepted; it is applauded as a necessary *method* for the accomplishment of an important purpose, namely, the exclusion of the Negro from politics. In Vermont one-partyism is not cultivated as a system for any particular reason, and indeed it appears that many staunch Yankees have a sense of guilt that the state does not conform to what is an accepted American pattern, the two-party system. Furthermore, if Vermont Republicans went to sleep after the primary as South Carolina Democrats do they would wake up the morning after election with a Democratic governor. It is significant that the state in the South with the highest percentage of Republican votes for governor is also the state with the highest interest in the general election as compared to the primary. Indeed the percentages for the proportion of the minority party vote and the proportion of primary to general election voters in North Carolina and Vermont are nearly identical.[41]

In some respects the operation of Vermont's one-party system bears resemblances to one-party politics in the South, but the differences are perhaps even more striking than the similarities. One of the most important differences is the role of the Democratic party as the minority in Vermont. By and large the Republicans of the South have not offered the kind of resistance that Vermont Democrats have. The minority's role in Vermont politics has *some* importance at least.

Vermont Democrats: The Persistent Few

High on the list of never-accept-defeat politicians of this country are the Vermont Democrats. Without victory in a national or state-wide election since 1856,[41a] they continue to put up candidates and run campaigns. Since the first primary election in 1916 the Democrats have never once failed to make a nomination for any statewide office in any election, regular or special. Usually not more than a corporal's guard participates in the primary since there have been

[41] Ransone cites the fact that North Carolina and Vermont had exactly the same percentage of minority vote for governor (in the general election) between 1930 and 1950: 68.5 per cent. The total participation in the dominant party's primary as a percentage of general election turnout—for the same years—were 54.4 per cent for North Carolina and 56.0 per cent for Vermont. *Op.cit.*, p. 17.

[41a] See fn. 59, p. 45 below.

virtually no contests for these nominations. Of course, no plausible reason can be offered as to why there ought to be any significant contest over who is to be the next defeated Democratic candidate for congressman or governor, and indeed some of the nominees have seen no reason to make even a token campaign against the Republican nominee. One Democrat, in fact, recently accepted a nomination *on the condition* that he would not be expected to campaign. Still, the Democrats get a respectable share of the vote and within the last few years have come astonishingly close to actually winning the governorship. In 1952 and 1954 the Democratic candidates got 43.4 and 47.7 per cent of the vote for governor, and the Republican plurality in the 1954 election was whittled down to just over 5,000 votes out of about 114,000 cast.[42]

Some new developments may be underway in the Vermont Democratic party and therefore in Vermont politics as a whole.[42a] As Vermont slowly changes its character—even Vermont is not entirely immune to the national trend toward industrialization and urbanization—the Democrats seem to grow in strength. Between 1940 and 1950 the urban population of the state grew by 12 per cent, the rural non-farm population by 22 per cent, but the rural farm population *declined* by 23 per cent. The Census Bureau defines as urban all localities over 2,500 in population; most of the urban population in Vermont lives in localities relatively near the defined minimum. In fact only three of Vermont's cities exceed 10,000, and together these three cities (Rutland, Barre, Burlington) have only 16.7 per cent of the state's population. Vermont is not suddenly becoming a highly urban society by any means, but the trend away from agriculture and toward the factory is apparent, and it certainly has political consequences.

It is politically significant that even in isolated Vermont about one-quarter of the population is either first- or second-generation

[42] Perhaps some of the Democratic vote in 1954 can be explained by the fact that the party ran a farmer for governor, which the Republicans have not done for many decades. Frank E. Branon, the Democratic nominee, is not only a small farmer but a respected, quiet, Vermont-like man, even if an Irish-Catholic. During the campaign a Connecticut Democrat, Senator Patrick Ward, went to Vermont to help Branon's campaign. Senator Ward is a fiery speaker and a devoted union man (an official of the United Automobile Workers) and he had some of Branon's backers biting their nails for fear Ward's vigorous speeches would backfire. Vermont Democratic campaigning is understandably more placid than Senator Ward's.

[42a] See p. 45 below.

30

foreign-born.[43] While this is a lower proportion of "foreign stock" (meaning the foreign-born, their children, or children born of mixed foreign and native parents) than is to be found in any of the other New England states, it is still not a negligible factor. About half the foreign-born population of the state comes from neighboring Quebec, most of whom are French-speaking Catholics. Indeed the proportion of Catholics in the state is fairly high, even though we tend to think of Vermont as purely Yankee. One calculation places the Catholic population of the state at 30 per cent of the total.[44]

In Vermont as elsewhere the French-Canadians and the Irish have generally preferred the Democratic party. Accordingly, the leadership of the Democratic party has been largely Irish with occasional French-Canadians in high positions. In the Democratic delegations of the General Assembly Irish and French names predominate, but few such names are to be found among the Republicans. As Table 3 indicates this distinction between the parties was true fifty years ago as it is now. On the slates for statewide offices, however, not many French names are to be found. There

TABLE 3

Ethnic Minorities in the Vermont Legislature, 1900 and 1950*

| | 1900 | | | | 1950 | | | |
| | Republicans | | Democrats | | Republicans | | Democrats | |
	#	%	#	%	#	%	#	%
Total representation	196	100	48	100	222	100	22	100
Irish names	1	0.5	8	16.7	3	1.3	7	31.8
French-Canadian names	1	0.5	2	4.2	7	3.4	3	13.6
Other	194	99.0	38	79.1	212	95.3	12	54.6

* Identification of the ethnic origin of names is admittedly not an infallible process, but the magnitude of the difference between the two parties is great enough to offset marginal errors.

Irish and Yankee names predominate. In 1954, for example, three Irish and four Yankee names were to be found on the Democratic slate of seven.

Since most Irish and French-Canadians are Catholic, it is inter-

[43] See E. P. Hutchinson, *Immigrants and Their Children, 1850-1950*, New York, 1956, p. 29.
[44] *The Official Catholic Directory*, New York, 1957, p. 335.

esting to see the distribution of Catholics in the legislature. There were, for example, 14 Catholics in the lower House of the General Assembly in 1900 and 12 of them were Democrats. By 1955 the number of Republicans listing themselves as Catholics had increased somewhat, but the proportion of Democratic Catholics had increased proportionately even more.[45]

The significance of the "foreign-stock" population in elections is suggested by Figures 3 and 4, illustrating the counties with high proportions of "foreign-stock" population and the highest percentages of Democratic vote for governor in 1954. The correlation is not so precise as the maps may suggest—the ethnic factor is one among many elements that influence voting. Yet the fact that the six northern counties with the largest French-Canadian population are also the ones with the greatest Democratic vote is significant.[46]

If it is correct that the Democrats are destined to play a new role of competition in Vermont politics, their organization may accordingly have to be altered. In general the organization of the Democratic party in Vermont has been more nominal than real. At the top there have been a handful of politicians who held the reins and controlled the situation without much interference from the rank and file, the latter being few and scattered. The primary interest of the organization has been national patronage, when the Democrats are in power in Washington, and many leaders have apparently had no particular concern beyond getting lined up for patronage. Since there is little reason to desire a statewide office nomination except to attract attention for patronage purposes, the Vermont Democratic party therefore resembles some of the southern Republican parties—a paper organization existing only at the top.

[45] In the 1955 session the religious preference information given by each member shows the following breakdown by party (excluding three House members and one senator who gave no religious preference):

| | REPUBLICANS | | DEMOCRATS | |
	Protestants	*Catholics*	*Protestants*	*Catholics*
Senate	20	2	0	7
House	213	6	12	12

[46] Notice in the maps the use of 1930 census data. This is made necessary by the fact that in the regular censuses since that year the data for "second-generation" population have not been made available on a county basis. The 1930 data are not as inaccurate as one might imagine, however. Here we seek only to know the relative concentration of the second-generation population. The 1930 figures, we may presume, are a reasonable indication of the present trends, since immigrants are inclined to locate near others of their ethnic extraction.

There are, of course, some areas of considerable Democratic strength, and in these the Democratic organizations are alive. In Winooski, an industrial town in Chittenden County, the Democrats sometimes win as much as 80 to 90 per cent of the vote for governor. Similarly in Burlington, St. Albans, Bennington, and Barre and a few scattered areas there are Democratic organizations, but considering the state as a whole there is very little effort to reach down to the community level with the organization. Contrasting the Republican and Democratic methods of selecting delegates to the respective state conventions, one observer said this: "The Republicans hold caucuses in virtually every town; in many towns, however, no one troubles to hold a Democratic caucus, partly because there are not enough interested Democrats and partly because an unknown

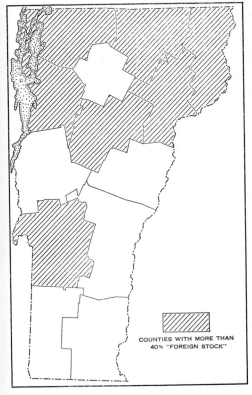

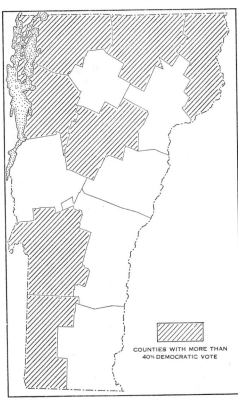

COUNTIES WITH MORE THAN 40% "FOREIGN STOCK"

COUNTIES WITH MORE THAN 40% DEMOCRATIC VOTE

3. Vermont Foreign Ethnic Group Concentration as of 1930 Census

4. Vermont: 1954 Election for Governor, Counties with More than 40 Per Cent Democratic Vote

Democrat has little chance of bucking the Democratic organization at the state convention."[47]

Reflecting the geography of Democratic strength in the state, the main source of leadership in the party has come from Chittenden County, the site of the state's largest city and an area of considerable industrial development with large French-Canadian and Irish minorities. Such leaders as Robert Larrow, city attorney for Burlington, J. Edward Moran, long the mayor of Burlington, and Russell Niquette, a member of the General Assembly from Winooski since 1937, all come from Chittenden County and all are important functionaries of the Democratic party. There are leaders from Rutland, Bennington, and Barre, who run for office and assume importance from time to time, but the major strength still appears to reside with such old-timers as Moran, who has been active for more than thirty years. (Both he and Larrow have run for governor.) One other leader in the party deserves mention—Leonard W. Morrison, former state tax commissioner. Morrison, a Bennington attorney with unusual talent in the taxation field, has carried out a successful career notwithstanding the disadvantage of his Roman Catholic and Democratic party background. After several years as city attorney in Bennington, he went to the legislature in 1945 and was made secretary of an Interim Commission on State Government and Finance. His knowledge of fiscal policy was put to good use in the next session when he led the battle for the passage of Governor Gibson's income tax bill. His mastery of the details of taxation was such that after an hour-long speech on the income tax in the House he was applauded generously. Before Gibson's retirement from politics, he appointed Morrison state tax commissioner and none of Gibson's successors dared remove him. Some observers say this is a tribute to his ability as well as to his political position. Firing him would have been bad politics, it is said, since his ability is widely recognized. Morrison was being considered as a candidate for governor in 1958, but this was forestalled in March of that year by Governor Johnson, who unexpectedly appointed him to the Superior Court bench. (He was the first Democrat so honored since 1902.) The governor denied he was trying to help the Republican party by this appointment, but a good many skeptics remained unconvinced.

[47] Paul T. David, Malcolm Moos, Ralph M. Goldman, *Presidential Nominating Politics in 1952*, Baltimore, 1954, Vol. II, p. 63.

Although many past and present Democrats have been staunch conservatives, more recently the Democrats have been turning toward a somewhat more liberal position. They have often cooperated with the liberal wing of the Republican party, and in both 1952 and 1954 there is reason to believe that the liberal Republicans not only gave Branon their votes, after the primaries of those years, but otherwise assisted him in campaigning against Governors Emerson and Johnson. Some observers believe that some sort of basic realignment could come to Vermont politics with the liberal Republicans giving up the effort to fight in the Republican party, where they have been losing consistently since 1950, and turning toward the Democratic party. Of course, the traditional loyalty to the Republican party of most Vermonters, liberal or otherwise, constitutes a formidable barrier to such a union, but in the judgment of some observer-participants it is within the realm of possibility.

The Vermont Legislature: Low-Pressure Politics

The atmosphere of the Vermont General Assembly is much like that of a town meeting, an institution with which most of its members are thoroughly familiar. There is a similar unpredictability about the outcome of legislative contests characteristic of the town meeting at times, and the general attitude of easy give-and-take must seem familiar to town-meeting-trained legislators. Vermont legislators consider fewer bills in a session (about 500 to 600) than those of any other New England legislature, and they appear to go about their task with a more leisurely approach than any of their neighbors. Partisanship is virtually absent, since there are usually too few Democrats to make it worthwhile to argue in partisan terms. By outward appearances at least the decisions are made on the floor of the House and Senate after open discussion. Similarly, committee executive sessions are most of the time open to press and public. In Vermont to exclude the press from a committee session (routine procedure in most states) is to create a news story of mildly rebuking tone.

Perhaps this atmosphere is what might be expected in a state where politics is usually low pressure and where the factional lines in the dominant party are not rigid. The factional distinctions between the Proctor and anti-Proctor forces, as noted above, do not reach down into the local town organizations in many areas, and in the choice of local legislators the factional divisions are usually entirely ignored. Disputes do develop and at times can become very bitter, but in the normal course of a session a much more peaceful air prevails than obtains in most state legislatures.

Three major factors have great bearing on the manner of operation of the General Assembly. First, farmers are numerous in both Houses. In the Senate during the 1955 session 11 members out of 30 were farmers; in the House 91 members of 246 listed themselves as farmers. No other group even approached the size of the farm bloc. (Small business operators, retired people, and housewives comprised the next most numerous groups.) In view of the apportionment of the House, the size of the farm bloc is no occasion for surprise, for in the House each town is entitled to one representative and, regardless of size, gets no more than one. As of 1950 the 16 largest towns (which includes all those over 2,500 population) have 36.6 per cent of the population of the state but only 6.5 per cent of the House representation. On the other hand the 19 towns with less than 200 people have 7.3 per cent of the representation in the House but less than one per cent of the state's population.

There is a greater equality of representation in terms of population in the Senate, which, according to the Constitution, is to be apportioned by population, with none of the 13 counties having less than one member. As of the 1950 Census this meant that each group of 12,500 people should have one senator, but two counties have senators for 3,328 and 6,275 people respectively. The largest district, Orange County, has 17,027 people with one senator, but no other counties deviate seriously from the average.

A second factor of significance, although hardly unique among American state legislatures, is that usually about half the membership is new to the legislative halls and to the special brand of confusion that prevails there. In the sessions from 1949 to 1955 there was an average freshman membership in the House of 49.7 per cent. The Senate usually has a more experienced group to work with, but even there the proportion of newcomers is relatively high. In the same four sessions an average of about one-quarter of the senators had seen no previous experience, and another quarter of them were serving in the Senate for the first time after House experience.[48]

[48] To be more exact, an average of 22 per cent of the senators in the period 1949 to 1955 were new to the legislative process, and 27 per cent were new to the Senate

The implications of this lack of continuity of service are serious. Legislative work can be demanding and intricate, and experience in grappling with all manner of problems can serve to improve the legislative output as well as to make the legislators wary enough not to be sold a bill of goods through simple innocence. In short it is significant that in the 1955 session in Vermont there were only six members of the Senate who had been serving there in 1951. Even though Vermont's legislative operations are less hectic than those of most of her neighbors, and even though many bills are local in nature (whether to allow fishing in "Ticklenaked Pond") or of a homely nature familiar to most Vermonters (whether to discontinue the bounty paid upon the delivery to the town clerk of porcupine ears), there remain many serious questions of policy demanding greater experience and knowledge even if not more finesse. (The porcupine or fishing problems may be very time-consuming and the pressures in a sense may be terrific, but the need for technical insight is much less than that required on a bill involving revision of the tax code, or overhauling the administrative structure of the state.)

In general the less familiar a legislator is with parliamentary procedure and the occult language of statutes, the less likely is he to know what he is doing or, more important, what someone is trying to do with him. Even granting that a Vermonter can be stubborn, he is not immune to being made the pawn of a clever operator. It is true that at times, out of confusion and a vague feeling of not knowing what is going on during a battle over a piece of legislation, the members will just vote "no" on the general ground that what is not done now can always be reconsidered another day without harm to anyone. The trouble with this assumption, of course, is that inaction can indeed be harmful. The confusion that may be temporarily resolved by a negative vote does not therefore produce "neutral" results. Rather, it plays into the hands of those who would stop action, and can often be positive in its ultimate connotations.[49]

---

after serving in the House—or an average of 49 per cent new to the ways of the Senate.

[49] Some mitigation of the problem of inexperience is found in the fact that the total volume of legislation is relatively small and that the committees are forced to bring out their bills in a fairly short time. As a result of the rule that bills must be reported out within fifteen days unless excused by the House or Senate, there is a fairly steady flow of the legislation to the floor rather than a bunching up of

A third factor of extreme importance is the lack of Democratic strength in the General Assembly. In recent sessions the number of Democrats in the Senate has been as low as one, and in the House fewer than 20 out of 246. As a result there is remarkably little partisan feeling in the General Assembly. Surprisingly, Democrats are given committee chairmanships on the basis of experience and ability. In the 1955 House, Russell Niquette of Winooski, a Democratic member of the House for eight terms, was made chairman of the Judiciary Committee and another Democrat who had served seven terms was made vice-chairman of the Education Committee. Four of seven Senate Democrats were chairmen of committees that session. Frank Branon, Democratic candidate *for both governor and state senator* in 1954 (but successful in the latter race only) was made chairman of the Conservation and Development Committee. Neither Branon's nor any other of the committees over which Democrats presided was a crucially important one (with the possible exception of the House Judiciary Committee). But that they as minority party members got any chairmanships at all must be nearly unique among state legislatures.[50]

Party-line divisions are infrequent or nearly non-existent in the legislature, but intra-Republican party schisms cannot be said to supplant party divisions. From time to time factional alignments do arise, but the usual situation is more fluid and unstructured. Groups appear to form, disperse, and reform with ever-changing composition depending upon the question before the house. Only when external political situations (such as sharp factional cleavage in a gubernatorial primary) or when an aggressive program sponsored by a governor precipitate factional conflict does the normally fluid situation give way to any degree of consistent factional an-

---

bills toward the end of the session. This naturally facilitates the handling of bills in a more rational manner.

[50] As is the practice in most states, the speaker of the House makes the committee assignments and designates the chairman for each, and in the Senate the lieutenant governor, the president *pro tempore* with one other senator act as a committee to choose the committees. Politically there is no pressure to appoint Democrats. Appointments are made with some regard for seniority (although that rule is not rigidly adhered to), ability, and prestige. Branon, for example, is well liked among legislators of both parties, and granting him chairmanship of a committee was taken as a matter of course. While visiting the Vermont legislature in 1955, I sat in on an executive session of the Agriculture Committee and found that Branon was deferred to more than any other member present—although all the others were Republicans.

tagonism. One may search most session roll-call votes in vain for clear and consistent patterns of factional division. Relatively few questions are brought up for roll-call votes, of course, but even when heated controversy breaks out—such as during the governorship of Governor Gibson—it is hard to identify the group alignments.

On particular bills, divisions along conservative-liberal lines appear from time to time. The activities of certain interest groups—representative of industry and farm groups, for example—often lead to divisions that are more or less the conflicts of farmer against industry. But the consistent urban-rural conflict, so common in the lower three states of New England, is virtually unknown in Vermont. For the relatively small urban areas with even smaller legislative representation to argue their case on such a basis would be the poorest possible tactics.

The relatively open and free discussion of issues by legislators and the lack of any single source of consistent control should not lead to the conclusion that there is indeed no leadership in the General Assembly. Leadership can come from the governor or from others outside the legislature. There is also a legislative leadership comprised of three overlapping groups within the legislative body: the county delegation chairmen, the chairmen of committees in each House, and the formally elected officers—speaker, president *pro tempore*, and the lieutenant governor. The effectiveness of any of these leadership elements will depend on a number of factors: the abilities and the prestige of the leaders, the general political situation prevailing at a given moment, and the nature of the questions up for consideration. If the factional antagonism is high—as, for example, in the administration of Governor Gibson—the leadership of these inner groups is less crucial than when the situation is not structured by factionalism. Similarly, the nature of the question at hand affects the power of these groups. A farm bill to provide for control of a cattle disease could lead to such divisions among both leaders and farmer legislators that the "formal" leadership groups would have virtually no influence. On a question of an appropriation or a tax issue or even on labor legislation the leaders may be able to talk and maneuver their way to adoption of their program.

Apparently it was the action of but a handful of leaders who blocked the proposed invitation of former Congressman Plumley to speak to the General Assembly on his censorship bill in 1953. The newspapers appeared to have assumed he would be invited, but within a few days of their assertion that he *would* address the legislature, they suddenly announced that he would not. Two legislative leaders were quoted to the effect that they did not deem it necessary or proper to invite him. Those interested in the proposal could have raised the matter of the invitation through a simple resolution, but the opposition of the select few was sufficient to head off any such action.

There are several very important interest groups that contribute leadership of a sort to the legislature. The Farm Bureau, as we have observed, is strong in Vermont and has played a considerable political role. In supporting the liberal faction it has not restricted itself to the campaign for governor but naturally plays a role in legislative policy-making. Nor does it limit itself to farm issues there; tax policy, highway questions, public utilities control, and other such issues come within its ken. The Farm Bureau contingent in the legislature is large enough to be decisive at certain times. Oliver Garceau and Corinne Silverman call the Bureau the "most powerful organized group in the state."[51]

Often opposed to the Bureau is the Associated Industries of Vermont, comprised of some 450 different manufacturing and other business concerns as of 1951, representing about half the state's payroll.[52] In a general way this group is aligned with the Proctor faction, although the AIV, as it is customarily called, does not enter gubernatorial campaigns to the same extent that the Farm Bureau does. Within the legislature the AIV has many powerful friends in most sessions. In 1951 several key members of the legislature were either members of the AIV or had been appointed to committee chairmanships more or less at the behest of AIV's able lobbyist and executive vice-president, Theodore ("Ted") Kane. The lieutenant governor (a manufacturer) and the speaker of the House (vice-president of the Proctor family's Vermont Marble Company) were dependable allies. Five important committee chairmen were either

[51] "A Pressure Group and the Pressured: A Case Report," 48 *American Political Science Review* 672-691 (Sept. 1954) at p. 680. This article presents a clear and convincing analysis of the Vermont General Assembly during the 1951 session. My own interviewing of Vermont legislators corroborated many points made in this article.

[52] *Ibid.*, p. 672.

AIV members or (in one case) had been made chairmen with Kane's assistance.[53] Access to influential members in key positions is insufficient to guarantee complete success to AIV, however, for there is considerable antagonism toward business in general among Vermont legislators, notwithstanding the Republicanism of the state. One legislator told me that he usually could trust information given to him by lobbyists, "but I never trust anything the AIV tells me until I check it for myself." According to Garceau and Silverman, Mr. Kane never assumed that "business could call the tune, even with relation to labor. This, be it noted, was not because labor was strong, but because business interests remained essentially weak. Farm leaders were characteristically Bull Moose progressive on business issues, disliked bankers for the record, distrusted big business and Wall Street to notable political advantage."[54]

Largely as a consequence of the open distrust of business interests AIV must play a cautious back-stage role. In 1951 they were interested in a bill concerning the extension of workmen's compensation coverage to silicosis. After securing postponement of this law for several years, they were now ready to consider it, but they did not want to take the chance of having the situation get out of hand to the extent that a too-inclusive bill might be substituted for their own version. Having helped place some of their men in crucial committee positions, and with friends as speaker of the House and lieutenant governor, they proceeded to clear their program with the governor, who suggested that certain changes might be necessary to head off trouble. Accordingly, negotiations were carried on with the representatives of the CIO. Some "horse trading" between the two interests produced an agreement for labor to abandon its demands for improved unemployment compensation benefits and for AIV to stop its demands for tightening unemployment benefit eligibility.

Labor has but a handful of dependable last-ditch supporters. Why then would AIV feel the necessity to strike any kind of bargain with labor under these circumstances? In the judgment of Garceau and Silverman they were ready to negotiate because they felt uncertain of the outcome if the half-dozen legislators sympathetic to labor should get up on the floor and stir up a fight. Uncertainty that such a situation could be safely controlled led to the extra-legislative

[53] *Ibid.*, p. 673.
[54] *Ibid.*, p. 677.

negotiations. Two legislators sat in on most of these negotiations. One was "the AIV-picked chairman of the House Commerce and Labor Committee"[55] and the other was a representative from the town of Barre, the home of many granite workers who were demanding that silicosis be listed as an occupational disease. These two legislators "rose on the day of debate [in the House] and announced that both industry and labor thought the bill should pass. They sat down, the vote was taken, and an occupational disease bill passed the House. The Senate also noting that [the two House members] urged the bill, granted its approval and the bill became law."[56]

The behind-the-scenes procedures employed by the AIV are, of course, not unusual. Effort to get friendly committee chairmen, clearing a proposal with the governor, off-stage negotiation with other interest groups, legislators speaking in the chamber reflecting the wishes of the group—all these tactics are relatively commonplace legislative procedures. What is striking about the situation in Vermont is that the conservative business group felt so uncertain about its position in this nominally conservative state. To a certain extent the 1951 session presented an unusual set of circumstances in that a very liberal and successful governor had just left the scene, and his followers still retained some sense of loyalty to him and his ideas. Indeed shortly after the passage of the occupational disease bill the theretofore unstructured and factionless situation in the General Assembly gave way to sharp factional alignments as the Farm Bureau group rose against what they thought was an effort by Governor Emerson to undo Governor Gibson's programs of the previous years. In short the success of the AIV was in part possible because of the absence of tightly drawn factional lines.

In many if not most sessions the factional lines do not get drawn with as much sharpness as they were during Gibson's time or in the 1951 session after the midway point. The amateur legislators of Vermont are often led by unseen operators who, unknown to the legislators, maneuver legislation through to ultimate approval. From their interviewing in 1951 Garceau and Silverman emerged with the impression that there was an "extremely low level of recognition of interest-group activity. Although every representative interviewed knew of the Vermont Farm Bureau, more than a third have never

55 *Ibid.*, p. 678.
56 *Ibid.*, p. 678.

heard of the Associated Industries of Vermont, and only a few more had any notion that the interests in Vermont were organized. One-third of the representatives had never heard of Arthur Packard, for a generation the president and lobbyist for the Farm Bureau, and about two-thirds of them were unable to identify the lobbyists for either the AIV or the CIO. Even fewer were able to recall more than one issue in which these groups had been interested."[57]

Vermont, I began by saying, is a political paradox. Here is one of the most curious of all these paradoxes. Vermont prides itself on being a land of stubborn independence of attitude, with a generally conservative turn of mind, cut off from the mainstream of national development along industrial and urban lines. But there is a liberalism in Vermont policy that is unexpected under these circumstances. More confusing still is the apparent fact that the rugged individualists who came to the legislature can be led by unseen manipulators. What looks like a friendly town meeting turns out to be a confused but nevertheless often carefully managed forum. What rational explanation can be offered?

The foremost factor here would appear to be the governor and the factional groups supporting him. In a relatively wide-open situation where there are no party organizations that lay down even a general pattern for legislators to follow, the governor as the most visible public official and the one with the greatest prestige has a distinct advantage. What he chooses to make of this potential power depends on his personality and political outlook. A Proctor faction governor is unlikely to seek earth-shaking policy changes; the maintenance of *status quo* is often his prime goal. If the opposition faction, led largely by the Farm Bureau element, fails to pull itself together to propose counter-measures and to drive them through to enactment—which, of course, is difficult to do in the absence of clearly focused leadership in the governor's chair—then the conservative governor can take advantage of the "low-pressure" political situation and the amateur character of the legislature to achieve his prime goal of inaction. If, on the other hand, the governor is anti-Proctor, Farm Bureau oriented, the likelihood is that he will have a program requiring change in basic policies and necessary appropriations and taxes to sustain those new programs. The success of men like Aiken

[57] *Ibid.*, p. 685.

and Gibson suggests that a dynamic governor with a definite program and the support of Farm Bureau men can drive such a program through, notwithstanding the relative conservatism and comparative poverty of the state. The situation is not one of sheep-like legislators being led to whatever pasture the governor chooses. The amateurism of the legislators undoubtedly makes them look naïve and unaware of the forces at play in the legislature, and in this sense they can be led along to a kind of negativism through confusion. But underneath this the latent faction lines still lie ready to be exploited. That governors succeed in getting action or inaction is not therefore solely attributable to their charm or to bossing tactics employed on lost legislative souls. On the contrary, their success is dependent upon the emergence or failure to emerge of a factional pattern that makes sense in economic, historical, and political terms. The farmers have been numerically the most important element in Vermont politics, but the business groups with greater supply of money for political purposes and the relatively greater concentration of leadership have tended to dominate the Republican party and politics in general most of the time. The farmers' resentment of business interests led to the development of the anti-Proctor coalition led by the Farm Bureau element. At times the latter faction can frustrate the Proctor governors,[58] but the organized strength of the Farm Bureau element comes to the fore most decisively only when a governor friendly to it is in power.

At the base of the political operations of the Vermont legislature, then, rests the factional dichotomy of Proctor versus anti-Proctor, business versus farm groups. These factional groups do not always

[58] Garceau and Silverman discuss the defeat administered to Governor Emerson on tax policy and several departmental appropriations once the Farm Bureau faction had pulled itself together midway in the session in 1951 to defend former Governor Gibson's program. (*Ibid.*, pp. 679-681.) But the fact remains that the liberal faction at this point was stronger in the legislature than it has been subsequently; at that point the Gibson program was still fresh enough in memory to get organized support. The liberal faction has failed in several undertakings since that time, not having had a single governor of their persuasion. Most recently in 1957 a bill to allow the distribution of power from the St. Lawrence Seaway project by state and local government authority was defeated in a close vote in the Senate. The public utilities won this battle. It is true that Gibson had lost on a similar occasion in 1949, but his was a proposal to set up a Vermont power authority to distribute the power *if and when* the power became available. The tentativeness of his proposal helped to defeat it. Governor Johnson and the more conservative element in the legislature did not have too much difficulty defeating the proposal in 1957.

line up in opposition to each other. Even when the factional lines are apparently drawn, the situation often remains so confused that it is difficult to ferret out who is on which side—except for the leadership groups. But the emergence of these factional lines is often a decisive factor for the passage or failure of legislation. When there is no sharp division—which is to say when the Farm Bureau element is weak and not pulled together sufficiently to force the more conservative element to coalesce—the advantage goes to the conservatives, since in general they seek inactivity rather than a program requiring legislative enactment.

Should the future see the Democratic party grow to greater strength, this whole pattern may well be shifted. If Vermont continues to become more industrialized and more heavily urban in population, the Democrats may begin really to threaten on election day.[59] The pressure will be on the Republican party to cease being the loosely disorganized instrument that it is now. Not only will Democrats be denied committee chairmanships, one assumes, but the policy-making process in the legislature may well change sharply. The influence of the Democrats will be felt not only on the hustings and on election day but also during the ensuing months of the legislative session. In the meantime, the internal divisions of the Republican party are much more decisive and significant than any differences between the parties.

[59] The 1958 election proved to be the point at which the Democrats broke the dam and won a statewide election. Democrat William H. Meyer narrowly won Vermont's lone seat in the House of Representatives, and his running mate for governor, Bernard J. Leddy, apparently lost by 996 votes (he won 49.6 per cent of the vote). These are unofficial figures and the Democrats asked for a recount on the gubernatorial election.

Obviously the forces dimly perceived in the course of this chapter were at work in this election. These election results are, however, harbingers and not the consummation of fundamental change in Vermont politics. In time, I have no doubt, something approximating two-party politics will come to Vermont, but the general description of Vermont as a one-party system remains valid for the near future. Lacking organization and facing deeply traditional Republicanism, the Democratic party will be some time in achieving political parity.

CHAPTER 3

———————— ★ ————————

NEW HAMPSHIRE POLITICS: TRIUMPH
OF CONSERVATISM

IT MAY seem to the traveler that only the narrow Connecticut River separates New Hampshire from Vermont; in fact, a wide gulf divides them. They share some old Yankee traits and some geographical attributes, it is true, but the differences between the two states are striking. The scouring glaciers were kinder to the Vermont hillsides than to New Hampshire; in consequence agriculture has continued to be a mainstay of Vermont's economy, while in New Hampshire agriculture has increasingly given way to industry. The growth of manufacturing in New Hampshire has led to greater concentration in cities (57 per cent of the people live in urban places in contrast to 36 per cent in Vermont as of 1950), to more immigration, to greater Catholic-Protestant and ethnic rivalry. If the relative homogeneity of Vermont has helped make Vermont politics placid and low-pressure, the greater heterogeneity of New Hampshire has made its politics more tempestuous.

New Hampshire has been as plagued by official corruption as Vermont has been free of it. The people of New Hampshire have been subjected to peculation and bribery down through her history, beginning with a none-too-honest governor in 1741, Benning Wentworth. Governor of the colony for twenty-five years, Wentworth established more townships than "all his predecessors put together. . . . Distributing about two hundred tracts of land of generous proportions to various groups of persons, it was his practice in each case to reserve for himself a personally selected lot of five hundred acres. In less than twenty years he thus acquired, without expense to himself, one hundred thousand acres scattered over New Hampshire."[1] Corruption in late nineteenth-century New Hampshire— particularly with regard to bribery of public officials by railroad interests—was sufficiently notorious to make a dramatic setting for

[1] Federal Writer's Project, Works Progress Administration, *New Hampshire*, Boston, 1938, pp. 37-38.

46

the popular novels of the American author, Winston Churchill.[2] The extent of corruption in New Hampshire today is no match for the conditions which existed in the eighteenth and nineteenth centuries, but there are highly dubious practices still current that are hardly praiseworthy. The role in state politics of the race-track interests, for example, has often been criticized, and some other leading interests have also done considerable dealing under the table.

By comparison with the great industrial states, both New Hampshire and Vermont would have to be classified as conservative in outlook. But New Hampshire, somewhat paradoxically in view of its heavier industrialization, is really the more conservative of the two. While it is true that Governors Winant and Tobey of the 1920's and 1930's were relatively liberal, and that Tobey stood out as a liberal in the U.S. Senate, they are notable exceptions. More characteristic of New Hampshire politics are such men as Senator Styles Bridges and the far-to-the-right pronouncements of the ultra-conservative *Manchester Union*. Only New Hampshire of the three one-party states of New England has had anything to do with the witch-hunting of recent years. There the legislature authorized a fire-eating attorney general (a protégé of Senator Bridges, by the way) to search out subversion instead of laughing the proposition out of court as the Vermonters had done.

Vermonters can hardly be said to be profligate about government spending, but they do not seem to be as obsessed with that question as are their New Hampshire neighbors. This, of course, is more appearance than reality—there is probably no difference at all between the citizens of the two states in this respect. What has happened is that the powers-that-be in New Hampshire tend to convert *all* policy to questions of economy-in-government, for the obvious purpose of keeping taxes down and keeping a tight check-rein on the service and regulatory functions of government. Few states have so regressive a tax structure as that of New Hampshire—unlike her neighbor, which for all its reputed conservatism has an income tax with relatively liberal exemptions and moderately graduated rates.[3]

---

[2] See particularly *Coniston* and *Mr. Crewe's Career*, both of which are written in the Muckraker spirit of utter exasperation with the prevailing political bossism and corruption of the day. Churchill, by the way, did more than complain about the state of affairs; he was active in the Progressive movement and was that party's candidate for governor in 1912.

[3] One student of New Hampshire's tax structure found that at least 60 per cent

There are in short some unexpected characteristics of New Hampshire politics. In many respects it does not fit the patterns one might anticipate. One might reasonably expect it to be a state with considerable two-party competition, but in state politics a one-party atmosphere prevails. It might well be expected to be somewhat more liberal in policy outlook than its more Yankee and agricultural neighbor to the west. But it definitely is not. It seems to me that the characteristics of New Hampshire's party system go far to explain some of these discrepancies.

The Republican Party: Conservatives and Conservatives

Half a century ago the Republican party in New Hampshire was something to be reckoned with. Its top leadership was strong, arrogant, and almost unchallenged. Railroad interests along with timber barons and a few others had control over the party organizations, and local party barons held their fiefs at the grace of the leadership. Both top and bottom elements of the party performed mutual services in the best feudal tradition—votes from the bottom up and pay-offs and patronage from the top down—but there was no doubt that the dominant power rested with the leadership. Venality was common as rising economic interests maneuvered to protect and expand their investments. Frequently governors were mere pawns in the hands of party leaders and railroad magnates, although one governor (Charles Sawyer, 1887-1889) vetoed a bill favoring the Boston and Maine Railroad on the grounds that the bill had been bought. He said, "To my mind it is conclusively shown that there have been deliberate and systematic attempts at wholesale bribery of the servants of the people in the legislature. It matters not that both of the parties are probably equally guilty."[4] Shortly after this fiasco a bill passed to prohibit political spending by such

---

and possibly 72 per cent of the state's tax receipts were based on regressive taxes (i.e., taxes which do not reflect relative ability to pay). See Benjamin J. Katz, "The Case for Broad-Base Taxes," *Taxation in New Hampshire*, Durham, N.H., 1954, p. 18.

[4] William E. Chandler, "The Growth of Railroad Power in New Hampshire" (a pamphlet reprinting articles in the *Manchester Union* of Dec. 31, 1898 and Jan. 4, 1899) quotes the veto message of the governor, at p. 25. See also Chandler's "The Growth of the Use of Money in Politics," reprinted from the same newspaper for Dec. 24 and Dec. 28, 1898, and "New Hampshire, a Slave State" from the *Monitor* of Feb. 1891.

interests as the railroads; it was, however, repealed at the next session![5]

With the passage of time (*and* of a party primary law in 1909) the once sovereign Republican party organization went into decline. It has by no means withered away, but the function it serves is vastly different from that of the late nineteenth and early twentieth centuries. Power to reward and to discipline has been vastly curtailed by the greater freedom of the rebel to go his own way in an independent appeal to the voters in the primary.

The formal organization is now supposedly aloof until the primary decides who the party nominees are to be; this is not wholly true since the leaders of the party clique dominant at any particular time can help an aspiring candidate in the primary even if they cannot guarantee success. For example, in 1950 it was apparent that Senator Bridges was supporting his former administrative assistant, Wesley Powell, in an effort to defeat Senator Tobey. Bridges' alliance with the most conservative and usually the most dominant faction of the party made it possible for him to employ—in a quiet way—the strength of the organization in behalf of Powell. Even so, the support of Senator Bridges' faction, considerable campaign money from within and without the state, and the support of the ultra-conservative press were insufficient to unseat the colorful, bible-quoting, "Truman-Republican" Tobey.[6]

Following the decline of the old oligarchy a kind of bifactional division has developed in the New Hampshire Republican party. This has to be said with caution, however, for there is not much visibility or continuity to either faction. From time to time battles for nomination develop in which it is fairly clear that two factions have chosen sides, but at other times it is difficult to determine the alignment. Certainly the factions have nothing like the continuity and visibility to be found in the Byrd machine and its opposition faction in Virginia nor even the Proctor and anti-Proctor elements in Vermont. In fact, New Hampshire Republican factions have been divided to a considerable extent over questions of national policy. In the post-World War II era this is probably the result of the conflict between Senator Bridges and the late Senator Tobey, and more

[5] Chandler, "The Growth of Railroad Power in New Hampshire," p. 26.

[6] The vote was remarkably close, however: 39,203 to 37,893. The *Manchester Union* was accused of printing a Powell political leaflet as an editorial without identifying its source.

recently the Taft-Eisenhower schism. Yet though the source of friction has been extraterritorial, it certainly has had its internal impact.

For some time now the leadership elements of both factions have been of decidedly conservative hue—the distinction has been that of more-conservative versus the less-conservative. The Bridges element naturally takes the more right-wing position. Now that Owen Brewster of Maine has been defeated, Bridges has indisputable claim to being New England's most conservative senator. The odd thing is, however, that Bridges came into politics through the other camp. The son of a struggling Maine farmer, Bridges worked his way through the University of Maine, where he studied agriculture. He migrated to New Hampshire to work for the state agricultural extension staff and later worked for the state Farm Bureau Federation. His entry into politics was made under the sponsorship of a leader of the progressive Republican group in the state, wealthy Robert P. Bass, governor in 1911-1913. He served as private secretary to Bass in the days when the Winant-Tobey-Bass group was opposing the die-hard conservative group led by U.S. Senator George H. Moses. Tobey, as governor, appointed Bridges to the Public Service Commission in 1930. Odder still is the fact that at first the Governor's Council opposed the nomination for fear that Bridges was too opposed to public utilities. (Not too many years later the aging Senator George Norris, outraged at Bridges, stood on the floor of the Senate and called him "the one Member outstanding in the Senate of the United States who does exactly what the Power Trust of America wants done.")[7] While still allied with the Bass-Tobey element, Bridges beat the leader of the Old Guard, former Senator Moses, when the latter sought in 1938 to return to the Senate, having been ousted by a Democrat in 1932.

Notwithstanding the flag under which he entered the Senate, Bridges soon swung around to a decidedly conservative position, and ultimately assumed the position of leader of the Old Guard. His position is so secure that he seems almost invulnerable, although the material for attack seems readily available. A strong anti-Bridges article was published in *The Reporter* just before Bridges came up for election in 1954, at which time the magazine sent press releases and copies of the article to all ten New Hampshire daily newspapers.

[7] Douglass Cater, "Senator Styles Bridges and His Far-Flung Constituents," 11 *The Reporter* 8-21 (July 20, 1954) at p. 12.

Only one paper saw fit to use the release. Even granting that the writer was out to show Bridges at his worst, it would seem that an impending attack on a senator in a national magazine would rate mention in the state news columns. In due time at least six of the newspapers carried editorials in defense of the senator.[8]

There is no doubt that Bridges has a formidable political machine behind him. He built it up through patronage and innumerable contacts at home and around the country—and throughout the world too, if one accepts the stories about his associations with the "China Lobby." Nor is Bridges hurt much by the press of the state. The prime press lord of New Hampshire, William Loeb, publisher of the *Manchester Union Leader*, is among the senator's best friends and most influential supporters. Loeb, who bought the paper from the late Colonel Frank Knox, has a weapon of no small importance, not only because of its circulation (greater than all the other dailies in the state combined) but also because of his willingness to use it unashamedly to promote his views. An Eastern version of the late Colonel Bertie McCormick's *Chicago Tribune*, the *Union Leader* uses front-page editorials to wage political warfare much in the fashion of the nineteenth-century partisan press. On the fourth of July, 1953 Loeb sent the following telegram to President Eisenhower (and reprinted it as an editorial on the front page of the *Union*

[8] These editorials were reprinted in the *Congressional Record* for Aug. 19, 1954, attached to a rejoinder made by Bridges on the floor of the Senate. It is interesting to note that there is virtually no refutation of the various charges made by *The Reporter*, but rather a collateral attack on the magazine, its writers and editors, suggesting not very subtly that they were tinged with pro-Communism. Ten Senators got to their feet to defend the Senator from New Hampshire, and seven of them were prominent Democrats. See the *Congressional Record*, 83rd. Congress, 2nd. session, Aug. 19, 1954, pp. 15,182-15,190. Note also the reply to Senator Bridges' remarks by Max Ascoli, publisher of *The Reporter*, 11 *The Reporter* 2-6 (Sept. 23, 1954). In his reply Ascoli denies the truth of Bridges' assertion that Ascoli had been several times jailed "in Italy for Socialistic activities." Ascoli said: "The fact is that I have been jailed only once, and that most certainly not for 'socialistic activities.' This occurred on April 30, 1928, when, together with some other Italian anti-Fascist university professors, I was arrested, as far as I and my fellow prisoners could make out, for no other reason than a summons to repent or else. I was kept in jail about three weeks, and when released I was asked to write a letter to Mussolini in which I would announce my conversion to the Fascist faith. I did no such thing and was kept under strict police supervision from then until I left Italy in September 1931." Ascoli also notes in his rejoinder that Bridges took a statement from one of the former's books completely out of context, omitting a following sentence which completely altered the meaning of the quoted sentence. See the *Congressional Record* for Sept. 3, 1954, where Senator Herbert Lehman inserted Ascoli's reply.

51

Leader): SUGGEST THAT IF WANT PEACE AT ANY PRICE IN KOREA, YOU AND THE JOINT CHIEFS OF STAFF CELEBRATE THIS FOURTH OF JULY BY CRAWLING ON YOUR COLLECTIVE BELLIES BEFORE THE COMMUNISTS. . . . NO PRESIDENT IN THIS NATION'S HISTORY HAS SO DISHONORED THE UNITED STATES AS YOU HAVE. . . . Perhaps such shrillness of approach has limited the influence of his journal, but such audacity certainly must have *some* political significance.

Several former aides to Senator Bridges are now back in the state as leaders in the Bridges organization. Bert F. Teague, for example, contested an opening in the Second Congressional District in 1954 against Perkins Bass (son of the former progressive leader under whom Bridges made his start in politics) and lost to Bass by the narrow margin of 700 votes. Others of his protégés now active are Louis C. Wyman, attorney general and zealous investigator of Communists supposedly ensconced in New Hampshire's colleges, and Wesley Powell, three times a candidate for high office but never a winner.[8a] Although Senator Bridges took an ostensibly neutral position in the 1952 Taft-Eisenhower battle in New Hampshire, all his cohorts were out in support of the Ohio senator.[9]

The less-conservative element is perhaps less identifiable over any long period of time, but it has had some rather notable figures emerge from its ranks. John G. Winant, for example, successfully battled the entrenched leaders for nomination back in 1924, only to be turned back in an unconventional attempt to be renominated. Breaking with precedent he returned as governor for two successive terms (1931-1935). By the stodgy standards of his fellow governors he was virtually a radical. Even as a state legislator he fought for a 48-hour week for women in industry, for abolition of child labor, and for controls over public utilities. It is entirely possible that his stand for liberal issues prevented the election of a Democratic gubernatorial candidate during the depth of the depression when elsewhere in the country, and even in neighboring Maine, Democratic governors were winning in Republican states. Senator Tobey was in

[8a] He tried a fourth time in 1958 and won the Republican nomination for governor by a scant 29 votes. The nomination was contested by his opponent, former governor Hugh Gregg, although to no avail. Powell went on to win a narrow victory over the Democratic candidate, Bernard L. Boutin. Thus New Hampshire managed to resist the Democratic tide that swept Vermont and Maine over the dam in 1958.

[9] See Paul T. David, Malcolm Moos, Ralph M. Goldman, eds., *Presidential Nominating Politics in 1952, the North East*, Vol. II, Baltimore, 1954, p. 36 ff.

general of an equally liberal stripe. His tenure as governor (1929-1931) and his subsequent record in the Senate marked him as a renegade Republican, but his genuinely Yankee background, his flair as a public speaker, and his ability as a political organizer kept him alive politically alongside his astoundingly different colleague, Bridges. No Republican figure from this or any other faction of recent years has taken stands of such a liberal hue as Winant and Tobey.

Sherman Adams, who resigned under fire as President Eisenhower's first assistant, is probably the foremost example of the current type of "less-conservative" New Hampshire Republican. (Some Republicans think his role in the White House was downright radical, but as a New Hampshire politician he was scarcely radical by any standards.) Adams, born and raised in Vermont, came to Dartmouth as a student and returned to New Hampshire to stay in 1928. He first ran for public office as a Democrat, when he won a seat in the New Hampshire House in 1941. The next election he ran as both a Democrat and a Republican, but since he was elected by a Republican majority to be Speaker that session, the mantle of Democracy must have fitted him very loosely. In 1944 he went to Congress, only to resign in search of the governorship in 1946, which he failed to achieve. In his second effort (1948) he did become governor and made his fame as an originator of austerity budgets, the opponent of all new taxes, the initiator of a conservation-timber tax system, and finally as a successful administrative reorganizer.[10]

Although the policy distinctions between the two factions may not be overwhelming and although some candidates, particularly for lower-level offices, do not choose sides in all contests, the factions have at least served to reduce the primary contests to two-man contests to a considerable degree, as the following data on the Republican gubernatorial primary contests for 1930-1956 indicate:

[10] For a profile on Adams, see the *New York Times*, Nov. 25, 1952, p. 24. While still governor Adams took the stump to work for Eisenhower, and was among the leaders of the Eisenhower movement not only in his home state but in the country at large. While absent from the state working for Eisenhower's election, he made arrangements to have his salary docked for time away from the governor's desk. The sincerity of this salary-docking episode seems doubtful now in view of Adams's own admissions about his relations with industrialist Bernard Goldfine. But whether "cleaner than a hound's tooth" or not, he is a typical "less conservative" faction leader.

Number of contests	14
Number with only two contestants	10
Median percentage of vote to winner (all contests)	62.8%
High and low percentages winner's vote	89.0% and 45.0%

To judge from the statistical data alone, New Hampshire bifactionalism compares favorably with that of the three Southern states with the greatest degree of bifactionalism.[11] That the Republican party in New Hampshire tends to divide into two camps in backing gubernatorial candidates does not necessarily indicate that there is great continuity or visibility of the factions involved. It is true that contests for high office have not developed into an "every-man-for-himself" situation, where half a dozen or more highly fluid groups back their own men. But for lower offices—even contests for congressman—multiple-candidate races do at times develop, a fact which at least suggests a limited degree of organization and continuity in the two factions.[12] As subsequent discussion will illustrate, there is very little carryover of the factional alignments into the legislature.

The appearance of bifactional divisions in New Hampshire's Republican party implies the loss of a preeminent position of *the* Republican organization in the state. A once unified and powerful

[11] See Key, *op.cit.*, p. 17. Key's figures show that Tennessee, Virginia, and Georgia have median percentages of the total vote taken by the two top candidates respectively as follows: 98.7, 98.3, and 91.6. For New Hampshire the comparable figure is 100, since in 10 of 14 contests there were only two candidates.

[12] Some recent Congressional primaries illustrate this point. Notice that at one point there were eight candidates for the Republican nomination (1954). The tabulation below does suggest some bifactionalism, although less than at the gubernatorial level:

YEAR	FIRST DISTRICT			
	Incumbent running	Number of candidates	Per cent for winner	Per cent for top two
1950	Yes	1	100	—
1952	Yes	4	70	86
1954	Yes	2	73.5	100
1956	Yes	2	73	100

YEAR	SECOND DISTRICT			
	Incumbent running	Number of candidates	Per cent for winner	Per cent for top two
1950	Yes	2	90	100
1952	Yes	3	84	96.5
1954	No	8	39.8	77.6
1956	Yes	2	75.7	100

group lost its authority and was replaced by warring factions. Why? The reasons for decline are numerous, and to limit the causes to any one factor would be foolhardy. Yet the temptation to lay much of the responsibility for the decline of the old organization to the party primary law is very strong. To the extent that the primary opens new avenues to the aspiring politician hoping to move into the ranks of the influentials either within the party or in public office, the primary thereby cuts some of the ground from under the customary party organization. If the main route to power is through the leadership of the party, the organization *ipso facto* is powerful. But if a direct appeal to the voters really becomes an alternative route to power, the central leadership is certain to decline. It is patently true that the primary has not had a uniform impact on party organization around the country. In some states it appears that the primary has gone far to diminish organizational authority; in other states for various reasons the organization has managed to retain its authority in coexistence with the party primary.

V. O. Key, Jr. has probed more deeply than any other scholar I know the question of the impact of the party primary on party organizations. He concludes that the primary has indeed weakened the party organization, although he tempers this conclusion with admonitions about inferring too much from statistical data without an accompanying examination of the informal structures of parties.[13] He makes the likely assumption that the extent to which the party organization can find candidates to run under its label for minor offices is a reasonable index of the activeness or atrophy of the organization. A party that cannot get local candidates has obviously lost its contacts with local voters and locally influential people. In his investigation Key found that certain states which have limited the use of the primary (by restricting the number of officials subject to primaries or using indirect methods—a primary for delegates who nominate important officers, for example) have suffered no significant decline in the number of candidates for the state legislature; in other states where the primary is extensively used, on the other hand, there has been a marked decline. He compared the years 1908 (as a pre-primary year) and 1948 to see if there were any

[13] V. O. Key, Jr. *American State Politics, An Introduction*, New York, 1956, Ch. 6, "Atrophy of Party Organization: A Study of Legislative Nominations."

change in the proportion of candidates offered for the legislature. Reduced somewhat in scope, his finding are repeated below:[14]

Proportion of Legislative Seats Uncontested

	1908	1948
Connecticut	2.4%	4.8%
Indiana	1.0	5.0
Ohio	1.8	18.5
Missouri	1.4	21.4

Source: *American State Politics* by V. O. Key, Jr., p. 190. Used with the kind permission of the author and Alfred A. Knopf, publisher.

Indiana has made only limited use of the primary, and in Connecticut the primary did not even exist in 1948. The latter two states make full use of the direct primary. The difference between the two categories is striking. The comparison between New Hampshire and the first two states is even more striking, however. In 1908, the year before the primary law was passed in the state, some 2.1 per cent of the candidates for the lower House won election without a general election contest, but in 1950 the number of uncontested seats had increased to 59 per cent! Perhaps part of the explanation of the New Hampshire data is to be found in the size of New Hampshire's lower House, which has 400 members. By the reduction of the size of districts to very small proportions it might be expected that the number of lop-sided districts would be increased. Connected with this point is Key's observation that the tendency toward atrophy is greater in the minority than in the majority party, which is as one might expect, there being ample reason to be discouraged as a permanent minority.[15] In New Hampshire I found that the impact was somewhat greater on the Democrats than on the Republicans, but the difference is not very marked.

TABLE 4

Party Variations in the Number of Unopposed Candidates for the New Hampshire House of Representatives, 1908 and 1950

	1908		1950	
	Democrats	*Republicans*	*Democrats*	*Republicans*
Number elected	117	269	130	265
Number unopposed	2	6	66	167
Per cent unopposed	1.7	2.2	51	63

[14] *Ibid.*, p. 190.   [15] *Ibid.*, p. 193.

It is highly probable that the party primary did tend to reduce the effectiveness of the party organization and to invite factional schism. But how is one to explain why some one-party states develop bifactionalism and others multifactionalism? Each state seems to develop in its own way, responding to the peculiar accidents and personalities of its history. Thus in New Hampshire the standing organization was challenged by a Bull Moose group which had combined with reform elements who were unwilling to be Democrats but were anxious to chop down the old organization. The Bass-Winant-Tobey group took the torch from the Bull Moose insurgents when they gave up the battle. Thus the old organization faced a highly organized opposition before and for some time after the passage of the primary law. In a sense the field was occupied, a fact which may well have served to discourage stragglers from offering a third force alternative.

In a sense, too, multifactionalism is a luxury more easily afforded in a state with the minority party so far in the minority as to offer very little opposition. What often happens in a bifactional situation is that one element battles another for possession of and control over the state organization. Under such circumstances the formal organization may not amount to much, but that it is worth fighting for—as it is in New Hampshire—suggests that it is not meaningless as a political weapon. The existence of a potentially strong Democratic party in the state may therefore be reasonably cited as a factor to discourage multifactionalism.

The opposition offered by the Democratic party in New Hampshire is more formidable than is often recognized. It is true that in elections for senator and congressman the Democrats have seldom won, but in presidential elections the party has carried the state five times in this century. Ranney and Kendall classify New Hampshire (along with Maine and ten other states) as a "Modified One-Party State," and they indicate that the Democratic party has won six statewide elections in the period 1914 to 1954, having won at least 40 per cent of the votes for President, U.S. Senator, and Governor in 86.9 per cent of those elections.[16] One must, however, be some-

---

[16] Austin Ranney and Willmore Kendall, *Democracy and the American Party System*, p. 164. Such a system of classification, be it noted, brings Tennessee, Iowa, and Kansas into the same category. See also the somewhat different classification of Joseph A. Schlesinger, "A Two-Dimensional Scheme for Classifying the States according to the Degree of Inter-Party Competition," 49 *American Political Science*

what skeptical of such data. There is a marked difference between Democratic victories for presidential electors in the state and Democratic victories for state offices, as Figure 5 indicates. That the minority party usually gets more than 40 per cent of the vote is of some significance, but that in state elections it almost never gets 50 per cent is equally important, if not more so. The Republican party cannot afford to go to sleep entirely with a 40 per cent minority in the campaign, but Republican campaigners must also have it in mind that only *twice since 1874 have the Democrats won the governorship* (1912 and 1922).

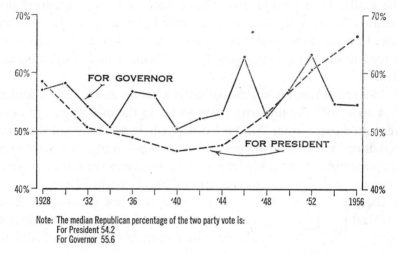

Note: The median Republican percentage of the two party vote is:
For President 54.2
For Governor 55.6

5. New Hampshire: Republican Percentage of Major Party Vote (1928-1956)

Significantly the Republicans of New Hampshire take nothing for granted in the general elections. This is illustrated by the fact that the primary is not considered *the* election as it is in some Southern one-party states. In several Southern states the total primary vote is as much as ten times the size of the general election vote. In New Hampshire the Republican primary vote is usually about one-third the size of the general election vote for Republican candidates.[17]

One interesting test of the stability of a bifactional system in a state is the extent to which localism figures heavily in primaries. The idea—as was set forth in the last chapter—is that the influence of

---

Review 1120-1128 (Dec. 1955). Probably where state politics are concerned the classification of New Hampshire by Coleman Ransone is more realistic. He puts it with 13 other states that have not chosen a minority party governor since 1930. (Vermont is the only other Republican state listed.) *Op.cit.*, p. 30.

[17] See Ransone, *op.cit.*, p. 17.

factional loyalty must not be very great when primary voters return inordinately high percentages for local candidates for no other apparent reason than that the candidate is local. In Vermont there is some localism, but it is sometimes hard to distinguish there between pure localism and regional attachments of voters to one of the two factions. Thus in a good many recent primaries localism and regional-factional alignments happened to coincide so as to exaggerate the vote for candidates from opposite ends of the state.

Localism has some effect on New Hampshire Republican primaries, although in recent factional battles the degree of exaggeration of local pluralities has not been really excessive. This is illustrated in a fairly typical primary held in 1954 for the U.S. Senate nomination. (See Figure 6). Norris Cotton, who won the nomination, is a middle-of-the-road candidate, more or less aligned with the "less-conservative" element. Wesley Powell represents the "more-conservative" faction. Robert Upton's alignment was not entirely clear, except that he definitely was not on friendly terms with the Bridges' element and did have some support from moderates. In Table 5 (as in Figure 6) notice that the tendency toward localism had an apparent effect beyond the big pluralities in the home counties. Powell, for example, got as much as one-quarter of the vote in only four counties: his home county and the three counties geographically contiguous to it.

TABLE 5

Percentages of Primary Vote for Republican Candidates
for Senate Nomination in New Hampshire, 1954

County	Cotton	Powell	Upton
Rockingham	21.1%	50.9%*	28.0%
Strafford	24.6	39.6	35.8
Belknap	33.2	19.8	47.0
Carroll	27.8	28.7	43.5
Merrimack	30.7	15.6	53.7*
Hillsborough	38.8	27.0	34.2
Cheshire	62.0	18.6	19.4
Sullivan	64.8	15.8	19.4
Grafton	77.0*	10.8	12.2
Coos	57.5	20.9	21.6
Total	40.6%	26.9%	32.5%

* Designates the home county of the candidate.

In contrast to Vermont's Republican factional regionalism, there is little if any tendency toward geographic alignment in the somewhat hazier factions of New Hampshire. In primaries where there is a fairly clear pitting of factional candidates against each other,

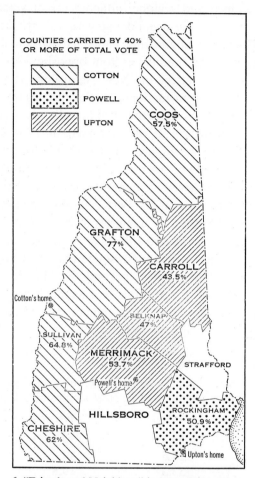

6. "Friends and Neighbors" in New Hampshire:
Republican Primary for U.S. Senate, 1954

there are no areas from which the candidates of a given faction consistently pull a heavy vote from election to election. In a last-ditch stand for renomination in 1950, Senator Tobey did not do well in some of the upstate places where Cotton did well in 1954. Indeed Senator Tobey carried only three counties in that contest (Hillsborough, which gave its local hero 64 per cent of its vote, and neighboring Cheshire and Sullivan Counties, which gave him only scant majorities).[18]

New Hampshire's particular kind of bifactionalism clearly produces a different kind of politics from that of Vermont. Among other differences, one can observe that there is a much less clear ladder of ascent for the aspirant for high office than in Vermont. Vermont has bifactionalism in which the dominant faction has been a fixed and consistent factor over a long period of time, and the opposition faction at best has been irregular and quite undisciplined. Although Vermont's Proctor organization is a far cry from the Byrd machine in Virginia, it does have a great deal to say about nominations to high office. One of the devices that permits the leadership to test the qualities as well as the attitudes of prospective high office holders is the ladder of ascent to which reference was made in the last chapter. In New Hampshire, however, there is no such required course of apprenticeship.

Most governors of recent decades have served in the legislature before venturing out for bigger game, but this is about as close as one can come to establishing the "pattern" in New Hampshire. Among the ten successive Republican governors who have served since 1924 only three had not served in either House of the legislature at some time before running for governor.[19] Half of these ten governors had and half had not been either speaker of the House or president of the Senate. Only two had held both legislative posts.

It is difficult to make unassailable generalizations about a state's politics on the basis of the careers of those who arrive at the topmost political offices. Most such generalizations can be disproved or at least made to seem too sweeping as experience in other states is brought out for comparison. Yet this much may be inferred from the career patterns in New Hampshire. First, as compared with Vermont, New Hampshire has more open contests for high offices, since the field is open to more serious contenders who have gained prominence outside the capital itself. Second, the first observation tends

---

[18] Tobey won that primary with just 50.6 per cent of the vote cast. In this same pattern was the 1956 gubernatorial primary between Lane Dwinell and Powell. Dwinell won 56 per cent of the vote this time, but the vote was reasonably close in all counties. In their home counties each candidate got 60 per cent of the vote, but only one other county had that high a percentage. Powell, however, carried only one county, but he did best again in the counties adjacent to his home county.

[19] Governors Spaulding (1927-1929), Bridges (1935-1937), and Gregg (1953-1955) were the only ones in this period who had not had legislative experience.

to corroborate the idea that Republican factions in New Hampshire are more fluid than those in Vermont, because no single faction has maintained its dominance long enough consistently to control access to higher office and thereby to give the sanctity of tradition to a practice that serves as a safeguard and a screening device.

New Hampshire Democrats: Party without Leadership

The most fascinating thing about the Democrats of New Hampshire is that a party able to win so many votes year after year is still unable to win elections. In Maine, where the Democratic percentage of the total vote is usually less, the Democrats have won gubernatorial elections more often.[20] Only one man since 1914 has won the governorship in New Hampshire on the Democratic ticket (Fred Brown, a former Boston Braves pitcher, who won in 1922). The same man later (1932) became the only Democrat to win popular election to the U.S. Senate since the passage of the Seventeenth Amendment. When one explores the possible reasons for this paradox, some interesting things emerge about the minority party in the Granite State.

Since the Democrats have won five presidential elections in New Hampshire in this century (1912, 1916, 1936, 1940, 1944) the question arises whether the state is like some Southern states in 1952 and 1956—where the lines of one-partyism were broken for the new conservatism of Eisenhower, just as the lines of New Hampshire conservatism were broken for Wilson and Franklin Roosevelt. Superficially the comparison is valid; both breakthroughs were based on national political questions that overcame state traditions. But there is a difference between the two situations in that the Democratic party in New Hampshire is no shadow party. It has an organization, even if not a very efficient one, and it garners a large proportion of the vote with great consistency. It is always a threat in state elections—not the kind of threat that Connecticut Republicans face, to be sure, but far more than the Florida Republicans can offer to the ruling Democrats there.

It requires no great effort to find out why the Democrats have won several presidential elections in New Hampshire and why they

[20] Ranney and Kendall (*op.cit.*) note that the Democrats have won at least 40 per cent of the vote in 55.5 per cent of the elections in Maine, but in 86.9 per cent of the elections in New Hampshire. Since 1932 the Democrats have won four gubernatorial elections in Maine, none in New Hampshire.

consistently get a large proportion of the vote in state elections. New Hampshire may still be thought of as a Robert Frost land of old Yankee qualities, but that picture is no longer entirely accurate. The old Yankees are outnumbered by newer ethnic elements. New Hampshire has too many manufacturing centers, too many large cities, to be like Vermont in its voting habits. Just as the national Democratic party during the New Deal - Fair Deal periods based its power upon the support of urban workers and ethnic minorities (along with other elements), so the Democratic party in New Hampshire has found the same elements to be its greatest source of strength.

That the strength of Democracy in New Hampshire is urban is easily demonstrated. One-half of the people live in twelve cities of over 5,000 population.[21] In the 1954 gubernatorial election the Democratic candidate got 45 per cent of the statewide vote, but won 56.2 per cent of the vote cast in the cities over 5,000 population. To put it another way, the Democrat got 63.7 per cent of his total vote from the urban areas in contrast to his opponent's 40.6 per cent. And yet the Democrat did not win in all these cities—he had majorities in only seven of the twelve.

Thus Democratic strength is centered in the cities of the state, but the extent to which the various cities support Democratic candidates varies widely. Perhaps by trying to isolate the significant characteristics of the cities that do produce Democratic majorities we may be able to identify more precisely the sources of Democratic strength. It seems to me that there are three salient characteristics of the more Democratic cities in the state: they have high proportions of foreign-born population, and more particularly of French-Canadian foreign-born, and also considerable manufacturing employment. Where all three factors occur simultaneously the cities are heavily Democratic; where they are relatively minor features and not concurrently present, the Republicans are likely to fare better.

There is considerable correlation between these social and economic data and the Democratic percentages won in the 1954 gubernatorial election. A more precise measure of the correlation can be

[21] The Census Bureau's definition of "urban" takes in more people, making the percentage 57.6 per cent. Cities over 5,000 have exactly 50.01 per cent of the people. Here reference is to only the 12 cities.

TABLE 6

Characteristics of New Hampshire's Cities over 5,000 Population

Towns	Percentage of foreign-born (1950)	Percentage of Fr.-Canadian born (1950)	Percentage of population employed in manufacturing (1950)	Percentage for Dem. cand. for gov. (1954)
Berlin	20.6%	15.4%	18.7%	59.7%
Manchester	17.4	8.5	20.7	63.8
Nashua	16.4	9.6	22.8	68.0
Somersworth	14.0	10.9	28.0	81.0
Claremont	13.9	7.6	18.8	51.2
Franklin	12.5	7.3	21.6	57.7
Laconia	10.4	6.2	12.7	42.4
Concord	10.0	2.8	10.7	32.8
Dover	9.9	3.1	18.0	46.6
Rochester	9.0	5.7	22.6	59.5*
Portsmouth	8.6	0.7	11.1	38.0
Keene	6.7	1.7	16.0	40.4

* Conceivably this high figure may be the consequence of the fact that a local man, John Shaw, was the Democratic candidate. Rochester does not normally have so high a Democratic percentage.

ascertained through a statistical process called rank correlation. It is unnecessary to go into the complications of the process; suffice it to say that if one ranked the towns according to descending percentages of, say, the proportion of foreign-born population, and then ranked them again according to descending percentages of Democratic vote, and both rankings were identical one would have a correlation coefficient of 1.0, or a perfect correlation. Lesser degrees of correlation may be stated as proportions of 1.0. Of the three criteria, the percentage of foreign-born has the lowest coefficient (.74); the percentage of French-Canadian-born produces a considerably higher coefficient (.87); and the proportion of the population engaged in manufacturing shows an even higher figure (.92).

What inferences may be safely drawn from these data? These are suggestive rather than conclusive indications of factors that influence voting, since manifestly there are many other variables with some effect on how voters make up their minds. But that such high levels of correlation are found for these factors suggests that the French-

Canadians of the state are strongly inclined toward the Democratic party, and that New Hampshire has not escaped the influence of the New Deal kind of appeal to the workingman. Economic status is a factor in voting behavior in the state which can be indicated by other means than those applied above. One such method is to check economic status directly against voting tendencies. I did this by comparing the rental value of homes in all wards of Manchester, New Hampshire's largest city, with the percentage of Democratic vote in the gubernatorial election discussed above. The two poorest wards voted 79.8 and 77.7 per cent Democratic, whereas the two wards of highest rental value voted 32.4 and 40 per cent Democratic. The correlation by ranking all wards was very high—a coefficient of .87.

These figures suggest why the Democratic party is able to maintain its large block of votes year after year, and they also suggest an explanation of why Roosevelt carried the state three times. The base for a national election victory was at hand if the support of some of the Republican regulars around the state was added to the urban Democratic vote.

The figures do not explain, however, why the Democrats cannot win state elections. Although there can be no absolute certainty about this question it seems to me that the leadership in New Hampshire is largely responsible for the party's failures.[22] The failures of the leadership seem to be associated with two factors: the very bitter internecine warfare between ethnic factions and the considerable number of leaders who seem inordinately fond of landing patronage positions—so fond that they seem to value patronage above party success.

It almost seems at times that the Democratic party in New Hampshire is composed solely of the French-Canadians and the Irish. There are small-town Yankee Democrats, however, and the fact that from time to time Democrats represent very small farming towns in the legislature is evidence to prove it. Indeed Dayton D. McKean, a former state Democratic chairman, has observed that there are "little enclaves of Democrats in New Hampshire who trace their political ancestry back to Andrew Jackson, although individually they may have no clear idea what it was that Jackson stood

[22] It can hardly be said that Republican governors have been so consistently brilliant that the Democrats are automatically excluded, even though some able ones may have at times blighted Democratic chances.

for."[23] However, the bulk of Democratic strength in the state is among the newer brands of New Hampshiremen, not with those who trace their ancestry back to the Revolution.

The Irish came before the French-Canadians, and the absence of a language barrier facilitated their early entry into political life. For whatever reasons they became Democrats for the most part, and in time some became leaders of the party. French-Canadians began to be imported in the late nineteenth century to work as mill hands, but they were slower to enter politics both for reasons of language and probably also because they are more clannish and less given to assimilation into the community. They came in vast numbers; it is estimated that the French-Canadian immigrants and their descendants now comprise as much as one-quarter of the total population. When they entered politics, they too came largely into the Democratic party.[24] In due course they demanded positions of leadership in some proportion to their numbers.

Some indication of the increasing role of Irish and French-Canadian politicians is given by Table 7, which estimates, by inspection of names, the number of each ethnic group to be found in the legislature. Whatever error inevitably creeps into such a process of identification is offset by the magnitude of the differences between the numbers present in 1900 and 1950.

Clearly the new groups had a much more pronounced impact on the Democratic party than on the Republican. By one calculation the

TABLE 7

Irish and French-Canadian Names in the 1901 and 1951
Sessions of the New Hampshire House of Representatives

	DEMOCRATIC					REPUBLICAN			
Ethnic group	Number		Per cent		Ethnic group	Number		Per cent	
	1901	1951	1901	1951		1901	1951	1950	1951
Irish	9	31	9.2%	23.8%	Irish	4	9	1.3%	3.4%
French-Canadian	5	51	5.1	39.2	French-Canadian	4	7	1.3	2.6
All others	84	48	85.6	27.0	All Others	292	249	97.4	94.0

[23] Quoted in David, Moos, and Goldman, *op.cit.*, p. 28.

[24] Penn Kimball in an article "Profile of the Spotlight State" in the *New York Times* Magazine (Mar. 9, 1952) says that French-Canadian Catholic Churches outnumber the Irish 8 to 5. His also is the estimate that a quarter of New Hampshire is French-Canadian in one degree or another.

leadership of the Democratic party as of 1951 was said to contain 41 persons of whom "14 were of French or French-Canadian descent, 13 were Irish, 9 were English, Scottish or native American of many generations, 2 were Jewish, one was mixed French and Irish, and one Polish and one Greek."[25] By contrast the membership of the Republican delegation to their National Convention of 1952 was said to contain 12 Protestants and 2 Roman Catholics (alternates: 9 Protestants and 4 Catholics).[26]

The rise of these new groups brewed up some vigorous internal struggles for control. McKean says that "every Democratic primary in New Hampshire is an Irish versus French-Canadian struggle."[27] This may be an exaggeration, but it is surely accurate for many elections. I checked one primary in which the two front-runners were an Irishman and a French-Canadian (contesting for the nomination to run against Senator Bridges in 1954) and I found a considerable degree of correlation between the proportion of French-Canadian born in various towns and the tendency to vote for the Frenchman. The coefficient of correlation was .70, but if we omit the home towns of the two candidates—Manchester and Laconia— the coefficient rises to .82. The Irish candidate from Manchester won his home town, winning 10 of 14 wards. The interesting point, however, is that he lost the city's most heavily French-Canadian wards by 79.5, 77.8, and 56.0 per cent respectively.

Antagonism between the ethnic groups in the party's leadership has undoubtedly reduced the effectiveness of the party organization. Apparently neither side exerts much effort if its own men are not the candidates, and indeed it has been said that the party seems to work better when a Yankee is the nominee. The success of Fred Brown in being the only Democrat in the last forty years to win the governorship and a place in the U.S. Senate at least suggests that this is a possibility.

Another factor that may have militated against the creation of a strong organization is the tendency for many Democratic leaders to be all too deeply enamoured of patronage for themselves. Several key figures in the recent past have been quite concerned with self-promotion. Neither the constitution nor the laws of New Hampshire

[25] David, Moos, and Goldman, *op.cit.*, p. 41.
[26] *Ibid.*, p. 39.
[27] *Ibid.*, p. 41.

prohibit a legislator from holding posts on administrative commissions and boards, many of which require bipartisan membership. Talking with some of the Democratic legislative leaders, I formed the impression that they were more concerned with their chances to land on some commission than with making a party record for the next election. In relatively recent years, Democratic legislators have taken positions on the liquor, racing, planning and development, and aeronautics commissions, among others.

Patronage seeking is, of course, a common preoccupation of the leadership of a minority party in any one-party state. It is sometimes virtually the only reason minority leaders choose to form any kind of organization, although this is—particularly in the South and to some extent in Vermont and Maine—more often associated with hopes for federal patronage than for state jobs. Job seeking from the majority party—particularly where there are jobs vesting control over franchises and rights to conduct businesses as in racing and liquor distribution—can have strange effects on the minority party. Only the fairly prominent are likely to get the positions, of course— that is, the ones who might contribute the most to the party. But the seeker is put in a position where he may have to bargain with the leaders of the majority party if he hopes to get an appointment. He may therefore bargain away a party gain for a personal gain. By such means do minority parties become the "captives" of the majority, particularly in large urban areas where the practice is often called the "double machine."[28] There is no clear evidence that the practice has gone that far in New Hampshire, but a sufficient number of Democratic leaders have put patronage before party to hinder the advancement of the party.

The New Hampshire General Court: Biggest
Legislature of Them All

New Hampshire people are very fond of extolling the virtues of the largest legislature in the country outside Congress. (In the English-speaking world, in fact, it is exceeded in size only by Parliament and Congress.) The New Hampshire House of Representatives, even since its reduction in size in 1942, has about 400 members. It is the

[28] That something approaching captivity on the part of Republican politicians occurs in Rhode Island is more certain, as I indicate in Chapter 6. There is no doubt that there were Democrats who were captive aids to the Republican boss of Connecticut, J. H. Roraback. See Chapter 7.

persistent belief of many that such size in itself guarantees popular control—that such a large body defies the efforts of "selfish" interests to "buy" their way. (Constant reference to "buying" votes of legislators is perhaps an unconscious harking back to the state's less-than-noble reputation for venality.) John Gunther in his travels preparatory to writing *Inside U.S.A.* was apparently impressed with this contention. He repeats the stock argument about the House: "Because the legislature is so enormous it is hard to control; the pressure groups can operate in the senate—membership twenty-four—to some extent, but the lower house is too unwieldy."[29]

Number 58 of the *Federalist Papers* turns this argument upside down, contending rather that ". . . in all legislative assemblies the greater the number composing them may be, the fewer will be the men who will in fact direct their proceedings." To maintain that large size gives a legislative body either immunity from or susceptibility to wire-pulling by a few seems dubious to me. I am inclined to think that the evidence tends to support the Founders more than it does Gunther, but there is also no assurance that a large legislature *per se* is easily manageable by the adroit few. As usual, as much depends upon the political circumstances within which the institution operates as on the formal structure. This much at least must be said: the inordinate size of the New Hampshire House did not make it immune in the nineteenth century to some adroit and effective management by outside political bosses. The House of the late nineteenth century was practically the same size as today, and from all descriptions its decisions were as often made across the street in the Eagle Hotel rooms of the railroad lords and Republican bosses as in the capitol building.

With the decline in power of the railroads and the bosses, has the locus of decision-making crossed the street to the capitol? I would not deny that the House can take the bit in its teeth and that it does from time to time do so, but such events are heralded as big news items of exceptional interest. The sources of outside influence are more numerous now than fifty or seventy-five years ago and they are far more subtle, but the influences are present and on the whole quite effective. The party machine is weaker and the members of the House are less committed to programs than in earlier times. The varied interests operate differently, perhaps, but they do operate. The

[29] John Gunther, *Inside U.S.A.*, New York, 1947, pp. 489-490.

"four hundred" are not so organized as to be able to function as a policy-making group. They are the medium through which decisions are made, but rarely are they the decision-makers.

What are the most basic influences on the General Court, as New Hampshire (as well as Massachusetts) calls its legislature? Three economic interest groups are very powerful—the race tracks, the public utilities, and the lumber-paper manufacturing interests. From time to time other interests exert influence—the other manufacturing interests and the Grange, for example—but in interviews with a dozen or more politicians of all shades of opinion in New Hampshire I got the same answer: that the first three interests mentioned were the most powerful. These varied economic interests are not the sole operators on the scene, however, for one must count the governor and the Republican party as significant factors in the policy-making process. From time to time one or more of the economic interest groups may be in cooperation with either the party or the governor or both, but each remains a separate source of power over the General Court.

To start from the least powerful and work to the most, let me discuss in order the party, the governor, and the interests. One keen observer of the legislature told me that there were about a dozen members of the House who were most influential and about thirty or forty others who from time to time exert some influence. Of these virtually all are Republicans. What does this mean? Is there much sense of party among the members? Compared with Vermont, the party in New Hampshire is a guide; compared with Connecticut or Rhode Island, it is a weak imitation of a leadership element. Table 8 gives data on the indices of cohesion of the parties during three sessions of the General Court. This measures the degree to which the party members vote together on issues.

Perhaps the most surprising thing about the figures in Table 8 is that there appears to be so much party influence in New Hampshire. For obvious reasons the legislatures of one-party states usually do not exhibit great party unity. The extent of cohesion in New Hampshire is high for the legislature of a state tending toward one-party-ism, but this is not to say that the cohesiveness of New Hampshire parties is comparable to that of the parties of the three states of southern New England. The party legislative caucus meets infrequently in New Hampshire and rarely is it decisive. The state party

TABLE 8

New Hampshire General Court: Party Indices of Cohesion*

	1931 Senate House Session		1937 Senate House Session		1951 Senate House Session	
Average Democratic index	83.0	58.0	28.2	40.0	89.0	69.0
Average Republican index	59.5	51.8	28.8	53.0	61.5	50.0
Per cent of party votes†	38.6	18.2	0.0	11.0	42.0	19.0
Per cent majorities agree‡	21.0	36.5	57.5	43.0	22.0	21.6
Total roll-call votes	57	11	33	37	31	37

* The concept of the "index of cohesion" refers to a measure of the degree of party membership cohesion in roll-call voting. The method was devised by Stuart Rice and is described in his *Quantitative Methods in Politics* (New York, 1928), p. 209. This indicates not only the proportion of the party voting together on a bill but the degree to which they were effectively united. A 50-50 vote is an index of zero; a 75-25 vote is an index of 50. The session averages take in all votes on which the majorities of each party took opposite stands.

† This is the percentage of the roll-call votes on which the two parties disagreed and on which at least 80 per cent of the members of each party stood together.

‡ This is the proportion of the roll calls on which majorities of both parties voted the same way.

chairmen are not important figures in the legislative halls of Concord. The respective party chairmen only infrequently appear and then do not in most cases carry great prestige.

Some better appreciation of the significance of the unity of the parties in New Hampshire can be gained by examining the issues on which the parties did tend to stand together and those on which the parties splintered. During the three sessions analyzed there were 206 roll-call votes taken in both Houses combined. Majorities of *both* parties voted the *same* way on 66 of these roll calls. This leaves 140 roll calls where some degree of party unity in opposition to each other was apparent; of these votes about half (67) were minor matters and the others were on policies of some statewide importance. Votes in the first category—on local bills, or fishing rights, etc.—are interesting as an indication of the extent to which party lines get drawn even where serious questions are not being raised, but in the second category the divisions suggest some kind of policy orientation of the parties which is not only desirable but necessary if the parties are to provide some element of responsibility to the electorate. Among the more important matters 45 of the votes concerned governmental regulatory activities or services—such as unemployment compensation, insurance and small loan regulation, for example—and 23 votes were on matters of taxation and appropriation. The remaining five dealt with election law or broad patronage policies.

Could the average voter have made sense of the party positions when these sessions were over? Could he have discerned a difference between the Democratic and Republican policy orientations? If he were very sharply perceptive of the nuances of politics he might, but the average citizen would be likely to miss the differentiation except perhaps on the grossest scale. The average observer would note that the Democrats rather consistently voted against tax increases of almost any type, and that the Republicans increased taxes only with the greatest reluctance. He might also have noted a general tendency for the Democrats to take a more pro-labor point of view on wages and hours, unemployment and workmen's compensation, but this is far short of the kind of uniformity of attitude prevailing on such questions in session after session in Connecticut, for example. There is in brief some distinction of a liberal-conservative sort between the parties, but it is at best a blurred and irregular distinction.

There is some tendency toward sectionalism in the voting of members of the House. I cannot discern any general tendency for sectionalism to pull legislators of *both* parties from one county together irrespective of party affiliation, but at times a bloc of legislators from one area or city will tend to vote together while the rest of the party goes its own way. In 1937, the Democrats from Hillsborough County (which contains the two largest cities, Manchester and Nashua) stood together to a much greater extent than their party as a whole. In the House the average Democratic index of cohesion for those votes on which the majority of the two parties disagreed was 40, but the Democrats from Hillsborough County had an average index of 75.5 on those votes, indicating almost twice as much unity as the party as a whole.[30]

[30] Conceivably this tendency for the city delegations to stand together may help account for the generally higher degree of Democratic than Republican party unity. This is no doubt a simple reflection of the similarity of attitudes among

These large city delegations are the result of the rather bizarre system of apportionment in New Hampshire. The upper limit on the membership of the House is 400, and the basic population number for which one representative is to be apportioned is 729. Thus either a town or a city ward with at least 729 population is entitled to a member in the House.[31] This system results in some very large delegations from certain cities—for example, Manchester, 57 members; Nashua, 24; Concord, 20. Yet the cities are somewhat underrepresented, regardless of these huge delegations. Indeed, the lower house in New Hampshire is at the middle of all states ranked according to the degree of malapportionment—i.e., roughly half are worse and half are better.[32] In the Senate apportionment is not by population or any governmental subunit, but by districts drawn according to the amount of direct taxes paid. New Hampshire is, as a matter of fact, the only state to retain this archaic method of apportionment. But the degree of malapportionment in terms of population equality is not extreme. Indeed, two recent students of apportionment say that only seven states have upper chambers with "fairer" representation.[33]

How important a figure is the governor in deciding policy in New Hampshire? His power is not comparable to that of some governors—those of Rhode Island or New York, for example—but the trend in New Hampshire is toward greater gubernatorial power. In part the increase in political authority for the governor is a reflection of the fact that governors now are usually accorded two terms, a fact which naturally enhances their position. It could be argued that the inverse is true too—that because they are stronger they can also

urban representatives. Nothing about the Democratic state leadership suggests that it has much to do with *inducing* this cohesion.

[31] Towns which have a population of less than 729 have periodic opportunities to elect a representative, and according to population size they are permitted to elect a member from one to four times in each five legislative elections. For city wards or towns with more than 729 people, the second representative is granted only for twice the base figure (or 1,458 people). For a discussion of the apportionment of both House and Senate in New Hampshire, see Robert B. Dishman, "A New Constitution for New Hampshire?" University of New Hampshire Public Administration Service pamphlet, Governmental Series No. 6, Apr. 1956, Chs. 3, 4. Mr. Dishman's discussion of the constitution leads into a broad and fairly comprehensive treatment of New Hampshire government; anyone studying New Hampshire government will find it indispensable.

[32] See Manning J. Dauer and Robert G. Kelsay, "Unrepresentative States," 44 *National Municipal Review* 371-375 (1955); New Hampshire's House is listed twenty-third among the lower chambers of the country.

[33] *Ibid.*

demand a second term. I have no desire to argue hen-and-egg here, for it matters not which causes which, the significant fact is that the governor is now in a stronger position since the inception of the two-term rule approximately dating from Governor Francis Murphy (1937-1941).

That the governor does not have to deal with strongly cohesive parties is in a sense a factor enhancing his power. If the Republican party were cohesive and the governor were only nominally its head, the situation would be very different, but with a relatively splintered party he has an advantage, for in part he operates in a power vacuum. One governor told me that with 120 new members of the House when he first became governor he was very anxious to get his program well along before the new ones began to learn the ropes. His chances of persuading a majority to accept his program were much better early in the session before the interest groups had fully moved into position and before the situation had become "structured."

The undoubted prestige of the governorship and the fact that the governor is the most "visible" element of the government give him an opportunity to bring public sentiment into play on his side. His use of public opinion is dependent upon many factors, not least the subject at hand and the nature of the opposing forces, but unless the situation has already crystallized too much around other forces the governor's efforts to arouse public support can be a significant element of political leverage. Governors meet and work with legislative leaders regularly. When I talked to legislators during a recent session, several referred to the House majority leader as someone whom the governor had "appointed." Similarly, the governor will on rare occasions appear before legislative committees to plead for his bills; this arouses the attention not only of legislators but also of the press.

Moreover, the governor can and does use the power of patronage to achieve his goals. Until 1950 there was relatively little in the way of a merit system in New Hampshire, and the great number of patronage openings gave ample leeway for use of jobs to manipulate policy. Since the inception of the merit system the potentialities of patronage have been narrowed somewhat but by no means removed. In this connection the institution of the Governor's Council should be mentioned. This hangover from colonial times remains in only three states—Massachusetts, Maine, and New Hampshire. In all three it has no particular purpose except to deal with patronage. In New Hampshire the Council is elected from districts; usually one member is Democratic and the other four Republican. Ostensibly the purpose of the body is to advise and consult with the governor about executive policy broadly. But in practice the Council is concerned only with the most insignificant administrative matters. I sat in on a Council session once where the topics taken up, among other minor matters, concerned approval of one $10 and another $39 expense request, and the granting of three $50 prizes to reward state employees for their submitted suggestions. The Council then listened to the comptroller's report on major requests for working funds from the departments for the next few weeks, approved this, discussed a minor appointment, and then adjourned. The Council in short is an elective Republican patronage approval body; no other visible reason for its continued existence has come to my attention.

New Hampshire has a short ballot for its top officials: the governor alone is elected (there is no lieutenant governor). In one sense this fact enhances the position of the governor, since he does not have to contend with elected administrative officials who may feel their own importance is equal to the governor's, both having come to office by the same elective route. This is often a problem in states where long lists of elective officials tend to diminish the authority of the governor. Since wide administrative power is but a form of political power, the short ballot undoubtedly contributed to the trend toward greater gubernatorial power.

Among the major economic interests, the most dramatic is the race-track lobby. In matters of concern to the race track, these lobbyists have an effectiveness to marvel at or shudder at, depending on one's point of view. A few years ago there was said to be free liquor provided by the race track for the benefit of the legislative membership. When a complaint was registered, the "track took the position that it had tried to cut off the liquor but that unnamed pressure forced it to keep the alcohol flowing."[34] Such liberality has been discontinued, I am told, but the success of the tracks seems undiminished.

Among the devices employed is that of giving jobs at the track

[34] John Strohmeyer, "Yankee Morals and the $2 Bet," 213 *Harper's Magazine* 38-42 (July 1956) at p. 40.

to some 30 or 40 members of the General Court; from them at least sympathy can be expected when bills come up for consideration. Unfavorable publicity about legislators' working at the tracks had no particular effect in New Hampshire, where, even after wide publicity, the working legislators increased from 33 to 44 between 1953 and 1955.[35] Employment at the tracks is used as political patronage for members and for political leaders who are not directly employed.

The track is actually run by something known as the New Hampshire Jockey Club, under the general direction of "Lew" Smith.[36] The legislative contacts of this organization are handled through a former attorney general, William Phinney. Naturally the track interests give liberally to charity, and they constantly emphasize not only that the pari-mutuel tax income for the state obviates the need for further forms of taxation but also that much of the money actually comes from "suckers" from outside the state. I talked with conservative farmer-legislators, who themselves do not frequent the track but who shudder at the thought of having to raise equivalent revenue from other sources.

The success of the track in turning the legislature to its way of thinking is indicated by the relative proportions of the total "take" going to the track operators and the state. The state of New Hampshire receives less than any of the other New England states on the pari-mutuel betting. New Hampshire's "take" is 5 per cent from each bet with 6½ per cent for the track (in contrast to a 7 per cent-7 per cent division in Massachusetts and a split of 7 per cent for the state and 6.5 per cent for the track in Rhode Island). To show their ability to keep down competition, the Jockey Club has been able to defeat dog-racing at least three times.

The impact of the tracks is never limited to the ovals where horses run, of course. Where the races are being run, there will be bookmakers who move in to affect if not corrupt law enforcement as well as law enactment. Senator Tobey as a member of the Kefauver Crime Investigating Committee came to grief during an interchange

---

[35] *Christian Science Monitor*, Nov. 3, 1955. Legislators are, however, forbidden to work at the tracks during legislative sessions.

[36] Dayton McKean identifies Smith as a "boss" who rules "quietly." He is, says McKean, "recognized by the politicians . . . as the boss, but he is scarcely known outside." The American Assembly *The Forty-Eight States, Their Tasks as Policy Makers and Administrators*, New York, 1955, p. 79. Some observers feel that the designation "boss" is too strong to apply to Smith, even though all I have met agree he has considerable influence.

with former Mayor William O'Dwyer of New York when he ignored the tendency of the gamblers to follow bettors wherever they may be. O'Dwyer asked why Tobey wasn't more concerned with trouble in his own backyard instead of pestering him. Tobey denied that there was any extensive bookmaking in New Hampshire, but the senator was wrong. Frank O'Neil, a reporter for the *Manchester Union Leader*, stated that some $30,000,000 was bet at the tracks by bookies in the state every year. "No one can challenge the statement," he said, "that there is a flourishing bookie business in operation throughout the State."[37]

If the horse-racing interests are relatively limited in their efforts to affect legislation, the other major interests are not. The public utilities, paper-manufacturing, and lumber interests have broader concerns. They must worry about the broad range of employer-employee relations, taxation, real estate, and specific regulatory actions aimed at their businesses (e.g., rate setting, water-pollution control, working conditions, etc.). Their success is not so stunning as that of the race track, but in the long run they are equally effective. Although there are relatively strong unions in some of the industries (such as the shoe and textile manufacturing plants) the union movement is not strong. Apparently the unions are reduced to bargaining, as in Vermont, with the manufacturing interests for concessions in legislation and not with legislators themselves. Many legislators could not identify a single labor lobbyist for me, although not one failed to identify lobbyists for the major interests opposed to the unions.

A great many aspects of New Hampshire politics tend to ease the way for the groups seeking legislative action in promotion of their business interests. The fact that the Republican party has a loose and uncertain bifactional structure in which state policy issues are rarely made the clear subject of controversy assists the special interests in getting their way. That the minority party has so many leaders as much or more interested in feathering their own nests as in promoting the Democratic party to a position of strength from which it might seriously compete for power with the dominant Republicans is likewise beneficial to the powerful economic interests. Democrats often spearhead the fight for these special interest bills. (For in-

[37] Quoted in the *New York Times*, Mar. 20, 1953, p. 20.

stance, it was the Democratic Minority leader in the House in 1955 who led the campaign for a lottery scheme to be set up in connection with sweepstakes horse races. The bill passed both Houses, but church group antagonism was so bitter that the governor vetoed the bill after having given some observers and participants the impression that he would sign it.) In short, the somewhat confusing and largely unstructured situation in the legislature plays into the hands of these economic interests.

One thing that does much to add to the confusion is the fact that the legislature is largely peopled by newcomers and amateurs and farmers down from the hills to earn $200 per session (the lowest legislative salary anywhere in the country). Both the House and the Senate face a huge turnover in every session. In recent sessions of the House the number of new members ranged from 120 to 175, or approximately from one-third to nearly one-half the membership. In the Senate, surprisingly, there is even less tenure, for in five recent sessions (1947 to 1955) I found that an average of only seven senators were holdovers from the previous session. (Even this is a considerable increase over the situation prevailing about fifty years ago, when at times there was not a single senator returned from earlier sessions—as was the case in 1895; in the 1899 and 1901 sessions only one member returned from the previous session.) Some House members stay in office for long periods, and one Democratic senator served from 1933 to 1947. Those who do stay achieve considerable influence over the others who are passing through on their way from oblivion to oblivion.

Evidence that the dominant economic powers and the political leadership are quite aware of the consequences of this turnover and of the extremely low pay (not only awareness but readiness to put those consequences to good use) is shown by this comment made to me by a former speaker of the House: "The low salary and the very large size of our House are good things. For in a way it makes it necessary to have a good many farm people and also retired people. Farmers and retired people are dependable. They're conservative. They offset the radicals we get from Manchester."

CHAPTER 4

────────── ★ ──────────

MAINE: PINE, POWER, AND POLITICS

IN FEW American states are the reins of government more openly or completely in the hands of a few leaders of economic interest groups than in Maine. Ironically it is the wealth of exploitable resources in Maine that produces this kind of economic-political power. While all significant economic interest blocs tend to move into politics in some degree—particularly when the economy falls subject to public controls of various kinds—the industries that depend on exploitation of removable resources have special reasons for moving into politics. The public has a stake in those resources which can override the claims of the property owner and therefore the entrepreneur has cogent reasons for finding ways to influence decision-making in this area. Such groups have never felt compelled to restrict their activities to the immediate area of concern, however.

Thus the abundance of timber and water power in Maine has indirectly created Maine's Number One Political Problem: the manipulation of government by the overlords of the companies based on these resources. More than three-quarters of Maine is in woodland and most of that terrain is owned by a few timber companies and paper manufacturers. In an earlier day, acquisition of this land led to some of the most ignoble politics this state has ever known; although present practices are not so corrupt as in the earlier times they are hardly laudable. Similarly, the developers of hydroelectric power—of which Maine has nearly as much potentially as any state east of the Rocky Mountains—moved into politics not only to secure rights to water-power sites but also to protect their investment from rate cutters, competition, and controls. These two groups, combined with the textile and shoe manufacturers, have done more than merely "influence" Maine politics; "control" is probably a more accurate term.

The efforts of these groups are not hampered by the fact that Maine is a one-party state. Competitive two-party politics does not necessarily make interest-group control impossible, but as a general rule it can be said to complicate the political situation enough to render such control more difficult. If only one party exists as a likely source of political control, the task of the group wishing to bend policy to its end is roughly speaking cut in half—only one organization need be catered to. Where a strong organization exists in the party to dominate the political decision-making channels, the chore of the group is to get some kind of "in" with the clique which runs the organization. But suppose a situation like that so common in the South prevails—where there is no strong organization of the dominant party but where a series of more or less discontinuous factions vie with each other for the offices and power positions of government?

That is in fact exactly the situation in Maine. Republican operations in Maine resemble in many respects the multifactionalism found in so many Southern states. It was not always so, for the Republican organization early in this century was a powerful and apparently arrogant coterie serving the needs of these important interest groups—pine, power, and manufacturing. That organization fell, or was torn apart in time, and multifactionalism took its place, and the key interests had to find ways to meet a new political structure. By describing the parties and the legislative operations of Maine I can perhaps throw some light upon methods employed to meet the particular problems of multifactionalism in the special forms it has taken in Maine.

Maine Republicanism: Multifactionalism

Maine is second only to Vermont in its constancy to the cause of Republicanism. Only once since there has been a Republican party have the presidential electors of the state voted for a Democrat; this was in 1912 when Teddy Roosevelt produced schizoid tendencies in Republican ranks. Only twice have the Republicans lost control of the legislature: in 1879 when the combined Democrats and Greenback parties took command and again in 1911 when the Democrats won undisputed control. In 1855 the first Republican candidate to run for governor won in a three-way race, and in the sixty-four gubernatorial campaigns since that time only nine Republican candidates failed to make the grade.[1] Republicans have comprised the lion's share of the state's delegations to Congress.

---

[1] Republican gubernatorial candidates lost in 1878, 1880, 1910, 1914, 1932, 1934, 1954, 1956, and 1958.

Recently certain scholarly efforts to categorize the states as to their political tendencies have resulted in the exclusion of Maine from the one-party states.[2] Maine is considered among the "strong Republican" states, but not really one-party. While one must grant that Maine is less Republican than Vermont, and less one-party than Mississippi, the total picture of Maine politics suggests that it *is* one-party, even though the Democrats may have won the governorship five times in the last quarter century. Only three of Maine's sixteen counties were Democratic in as many as three of the five presidential elections of the New Deal - Fair Deal era. Only six Democrats have served in the U.S. House of Representatives in this century and not one Democrat had been elected to the U.S. Senate since the passage of the Seventeenth Amendment until Edmund Muskie turned the trick in 1958.

Coleman B. Ransone notes that one common characteristic of the one-party state is that voters tend to focus on the primary as *the* election, since the crucial question is who will represent the dominant party in the general election. In the one-party states of the South the number of voters in the primary exceeds the number in the general election—often by as many as ten times. In New Hampshire, which Ransone lists among the one-party states where state politics are concerned, the average proportion of voters in the Republican primary is 33.5 per cent of the voters in the general election (total vote for the office of governor) for the period 1930 to 1950.[3] A similar calculation for Maine for the period between the initiation of the primary in 1912 and 1954 produces coincidentally precisely the same percentage: 33.5 per cent. (Using the same base period as the one Ransone employed for New Hampshire, 1930-1950, one gets an average of 32.3 per cent.

These data would seem to indicate that the people of Maine and New Hampshire do not think of their states as purely one-party. They do not consider the primary as the real decision-maker and thus ignore the general election as unimportant. But the fact that Maine voters show as much—or conversely as little—interest in the primary as the voters of New Hampshire weakens the distinction between them in terms of party tendencies. And, as subsequent dis-

[2] See Coleman B. Ransone, Jr., *op.cit.*, p. 10; and Austin Ranney and Willmore Kendall, *op.cit.*, p. 164.

[3] Ransone, *op.cit.*, p. 17.

cussion in this chapter will indicate, the politics of Maine is actually more like the one-party politics of the South than New Hampshire's.

The Republican tradition in Maine was founded on the slavery question and the Civil War. Prior to the Civil War, Maine had been predominantly Democratic, perhaps out of antagonism to the Federalist leaders of Massachusetts from which Maine won its independence when it became a separate state in 1820, and partly as a consequence of the frontier kind of community that Maine was in those early days.[4] From mid-century onward the prohibition question was important in Maine politics—mostly to the disadvantage of the Democrats apparently—but the question of rum was unneeded garnishing. Consistent Republican majorities would have come from waving the "bloody shirt" and shouting the campaign cry of "vote as you shot."

Maine is somewhat off the beaten path—it is the only state in the country which borders on only one other state—and as a result it has been less affected by the mobility of the American population, a factor which has undoubtedly served to "nationalize" the politics of many states. The traditional Republican alignment of Maine voters has therefore been protected by the relatively static character of the population. There have been new elements infused into the population of Maine, but the rate of growth has been slow. Between 1820 and the present the population of Maine has slightly more than doubled, while the population of the country as a whole has increased more than seventeen times. The comparative decline of Maine is indicated by the fact that it started off with eight Congressmen and now has only three.

Late in the nineteenth century a strong machine developed in the Republican party, led by and in behalf of the operators of the timber, railroad, and manufacturing interests, all of which were then expanding. The "ring" or machine managed the politics of the state through the convention, and whatever existing opposition elements there were did not offer much challenge. Grumbling about the highhanded tactics and the outright corruption of the machine grew in volume during the first decade of this century; this discontent unquestionably contributed to the sweeping Democratic victory of 1910. Republican victory margins had been decreasing throughout

---

[4] Between 1820 and 1855, when the Republican party came on the scene in Maine, Democrats won all but three of the annual gubernatorial elections.

the decade, and there was a growing disaffection with the machine on the part of many Republicans who were to become the Progressive party in the state in 1912.[5] Apparently the dissolution of the machine was well begun in that election, but the Democratic governor and legislature helped the process along by passing a direct primary act. With the abolition of the nominating convention the means of easy control over nomination—and hence to a considerable degree control over the whole political structure—was ended.

To attribute the decline of the machine to the primary would hardly be accurate, although it undoubtedly was a contributing factor. Even though the old machine has never been quite the same after the passage of the primary act, the signs of dissolution were on hand before the passage of the law. Nor could it be argued that the rise of the Progressive party was in any way related to the coming of the primary. Yet the rise of the Progressive party and the uneasy truce that brought these rebels back into the party were obviously significant contributing factors in the fall of the machine. In both Vermont and New Hampshire, as we have noted, the Progressive movement was more or less the origin of a second factional element that did battle with the Old Guard. In both cases there is a vaguely discernible line of development from the Progressives to the more liberal second factions of those states still existing today. The bifactionalism of those two states did not, however, develop in Maine.

Whatever the reason, the Progressives did not become the sole opposition faction. In the very first gubernatorial primary after the 1910 debacle there were three Republican candidates for the nomination; in the second (1914) there was only one candidate since the Progressives ran their own man, thereby giving the Democrats another victory; in 1916 there were four candidates seeking the Republican nomination. In the 1920's, at the height of the Insull empire's participation in Maine politics, some semblance of bifactional alignment appeared, but it was shortlived. The general trend has unquestionably been toward multifactionalism.

The existence of several shifting and uncertain Republican factions did not mean the extinction of the machine, however. It continues to exist and more often than not it manages to select favorites

[5] See Elizabeth Ring, "The Progressive Movement of 1912 and Third Party Movement of 1924 in Maine," *University of Maine Studies*, Second Series, No. 26, 1933, pp. 20-25.

in the primaries and quietly or publicly supports them through to eventual nomination. William F. Wyman, president of the Central Maine Power Company, is sometimes credited with being the boss of the Republican party in Maine, although I doubt the validity of the designation, if by "boss" one has in mind a political leader capable of delivering nominations and truly controlling his party.[6] Unquestionably Wyman and others before him in the history of the machine have exerted considerable power in the policy-making of the state, but their capacity to control nominations is not by any means invincible. The machine succeeded in quietly backing a conservative candidate in the 1956 gubernatorial primary but signally failed to stop the nomination of both the present U.S. Senators when they first went to Washington. Neither Senator Margaret Smith nor Senator Frederick Payne was in good standing with the machine, but both managed to win nomination over machine-favored men.[7]

The careers of both U.S. Senators well illustrate the kind of multifactionalism that Maine has. Mrs. Margaret Chase Smith first entered politics in 1940 when she ran for Congress to take the place of her deceased husband. That year she defeated four men for the nomination in the Second Congressional District. Typically, the opposition disappeared during her incumbency in the House and in three successive terms she was the only Republican candidate in the primaries. In 1948 she ran for the Senate—on the occasion of the retirement of Senator Wallace H. White—and won the nomination over three opponents, two of whom had been governor.[8] Her popularity was such that she won 52 per cent of the primary vote

[6] Dayton D. McKean, writing in the American Assembly report, *The Forty-Eight States, op.cit.*, quotes William H. Lawrence of the *New York Times* as saying that Wyman is "regarded as the political boss of the state," p. 79.

[7] The late Robert Braun of Portland was a predecessor to Wyman, and apparently exerted considerable influence through the machine. Braun, who died in 1953, had a hand in the economy of the state through his many directorships—banks, the state's largest department store, utilities, a paper company—and as chairman of Maine's largest textile manufacturing company. Naturally his economic power was not unrelated to his political power. He backed many a winner over the years—Horace Hildreth for governor among others—but he met with defeat too. In 1948 he backed Hildreth against Mrs. Smith and George D. Varney against Payne (for governor); both his favorites lost.

[8] Senator White had similarly run in a three-way contest in 1930 and thereafter had never had a primary opponent. Most of the Congressional candidates have had little primary opposition, but when an incumbent retires there is usually a relatively wide-open contest for the nomination. Significantly, similar practices are common in some Southern multifactional states.

notwithstanding the formidable opposition. Token opposition in 1954 came from an outspoken supporter of Senator McCarthy of Wisconsin, but Mrs. Smith won 83 per cent of the primary vote, and actually had a more difficult time in the general election when a better than usual Democratic candidate ran against her in a good year for Democrats in the state.

Senator Frederick G. Payne has been no favorite of the machine either. He ran unsuccessfully for the governorship in 1940 (second in a field of four) and in 1948 he defeated four other contenders and won the gubernatorial nomination, although he had only 35 per cent of the vote. During his two terms as governor he built up a considerable following in the state, the constancy of which was sorely tried by accusations directed at him concerning a liquor-purchasing scandal. He apparently convinced the voters that he had no responsibility for any favoritism that had been shown in the purchase of liquor for the State Liquor Commission, for he managed to defeat the machine-supported Senator Ralph O. Brewster in the 1952 primary. That there was a challenge to Brewster was somewhat unusual; that it should be successful was more surprising still.

Republican governors in Maine are usually given a second term without serious opposition from within the party. Since 1940, for example, only one incumbent has had any opposition in his second-term bid, and indeed until 1954 no Republican governor for forty years had failed to serve a second term. Even when it is fairly obvious that a governor is going to have at least a serious contest in the general election, there are no opposition candidates. The case of Governor Burton W. Cross illustrates this. First elected in 1952, Governor Cross had proved to be one of the most unpopular chief executives in many a year. A florist by trade, Cross had served in the legislature and appeared to have the virtues much admired in Maine—he was a conservative and an opponent of government spending; he built up a small surplus in the state treasury. But the very accomplishments of his administration were a threat to his political life. He had put through some administrative reforms and had knocked out pork-barrel procedure for road building, and, as so often happens, both programs made him many political enemies. His tendency to speak his mind when politically it would have been wiser to equivocate or be silent got him into trouble with the Aroostook County potato farmers through his denunciation of the potato price-support program. Several of his appointments had brought newspaper censure, particularly his appointment of a political aide to the Superior Court who was promoted to the Supreme Court within a few months. In short he had an unusual number of enemies within the party. But no opponent came forth to contest his renomination.

Had there been any continuous and active anti-machine faction, it surely would have sensed a chance to defeat Cross—or at least seen the possibility of capitalizing on his latent unpopularity. No ready-made nucleus for opposition existed. Factions spring up to support individuals and in most cases soon die out. However Maine does not have personal politics of the "every man for himself" type that prevails in Florida.[9] There the party organization is virtually non-existent, since each candidate—and usually there is a small crowd contesting the important offices—operates as a lone wolf without regard for the organization or candidates for other offices. In Maine there is an organization, even if not supremely powerful, which has to be taken into consideration by the prospective candidate. At the county and town level the Republican organization is an important asset for the candidate, and to smooth the way and get its cooperation, even some of the rebels go out of their way to support other candidates. Senator Smith, for example, works with the local party organizations as well as with her own *ad hoc* committees around the state. Her campaigns are well managed and in comparison with the awkward fumbling "Well, what do we do next?" atmosphere of Democratic campaigns they are marvels of smoothness. To accomplish this she depends upon county and town Republican chairmen to set up rallies, local tea parties, and receptions, and make other arrangements to get in touch with the voters. She and other semi-independent Republicans do not forget the party when cooperation is feasible and helpful to their own cause.[10]

The extent to which Maine compares with the Southern multifactional political arrangements depends, of course, on what part

[9] See Key, *Southern Politics*, Ch. 5.

[10] Most of the cooperative spirit comes forth in the general election rather than in the primary, although there is an occasional connection made between candidates in the primary as well. Maine, however, has nothing comparable to the Louisiana primary election "ticket system." Under the ticket system a slate of candidates for all major offices, and often many local ones, will be announced before the primary, and candidates run in tandem for mutual assistance. See Allan P. Sindler, *Huey Long's Louisiana*, Baltimore, 1956, pp. 273-282.

of the South one uses for comparison. To judge from statistical evidence and from V. O. Key's analysis of the Southern states, Maine appears to be somewhere in the middle—neither bifactional nor completely multifactional in the "every man for himself" manner. The following compilation incorporates primary data for the northern New England states into data presented by Key to illustrate the "extent to which the Democratic party divides into two party-like factions or veers toward a splintered factional system." Key lists "the percentage of the total vote polled jointly by the two high candidates for governor in the first Democratic primary":[11]

	*Median**	*High*	*Low*
Tennessee	98.7%	100.0%	76.0%
Virginia	98.3	100.0	82.8
Georgia	91.6	100.0	74.4
NEW HAMPSHIRE†	100.0	100.0	83.5
VERMONT	100.0	100.0	78.0
MAINE	84.0	100.0	56.0
North Carolina	77.4	100.0	54.0
Alabama	75.2	100.0	52.9
Louisiana	69.1	99.7	62.4
Arkansas	64.2‡	99.4	46.7
South Carolina	63.2	100.0	45.4
Texas	63.2	97.1	48.3
Mississippi	62.9	86.0	59.0
Florida	57.0	93.7	30.0

* Key's medians are based on primaries, 1920-1948. For Maine the period is 1912-1956, New Hampshire 1930-1956, Vermont 1930-1956.

† Maine, Vermont, and New Hampshire percentages are for Republican primaries.

‡ Key excludes from his calculations in Texas and Arkansas incumbent governors seeking a second term. If this is done in Maine, where the practice of granting an incumbent an uncontested second nomination is gaining ground, the median drops to 81.0.

Source: Southern Politics in State and Nation, by V. O. Key, Jr., p. 17. Used with the kind permission of Alfred A. Knopf, publisher.

Another interesting and revealing measure of the extent of multifactionalism can be seen below; the number of candidates running for the Republican gubernatorial nomination in Maine who received at least five per cent of the total vote is listed. (In five of these races there were stragglers who failed to get as much as five per cent of the vote; they are accordingly disregarded.)

[11] V. O. Key, *Southern Politics,* p. 17.

Number of Candidates in Republican Gubernatorial
Primaries in Maine, 1912-1956[12]

Number of primaries involving		Number of incumbents involved in each category
1 candidate	5	5
2 candidates	7	4
3 candidates	6	0
4 candidates	4	0
5 candidates	1	0

[12] Compare these data on Maine gubernatorial primaries with those presented on the one-party Southern states plus Vermont and New Hampshire by Coleman B. Ransone, Jr., *op.cit.*, p. 31. See also Key, *Southern Politics*, p. 411. If we exclude the five one-man primaries for Maine, the median number of candidates is three which compares with such Southern states as North Carolina, Alabama, and Georgia.

No trend toward greater or lesser degrees of multifactionalism is discernible in Maine. Except for the period in the 1920's when some degree of bifactionalism appeared to be developing, there is no particular difference in the extent to which the party contests are splinter fights or bifactional rivalries as between the earliest and the later periods. Generally speaking this is true of Congressional nominations as it is of gubernatorial contests, although there is possibly some tightening up of the contests for the Senate nomination. The wide-open race for the Senate nomination in 1948 suggests, however, that the multifactionalism of other aspects of the state's politics also affects Senate nominations.

Such personally oriented factions place the campaign emphasis on "personality" and "color" rather than on issues. Mrs. Smith's personal charm has unquestionably been an asset to her, and other candidates have used what might well be called a demagogic sort of appeal to attract attention. Owen Brewster, a descendant of the Mayflower Brewsters, was a leader in the Ku Klux Klan in the 1920's and promoted his own stock through the anti-Catholicism of the KKK.[13] He and others attracted attention through growling at the Insull utility interests that were expanding their operations in Maine. As "foreign" influences they were safe objects of attack, even though

[13] Brewster's affiliation with the KKK (which incidentally appears to have been stronger in Maine than anywhere else in New England) is mentioned by several commentators on Maine politics. See, for example, Lane Lancaster, "The Democratic Party in Maine," 18 *National Municipal Review* 744-749 (1929) at p. 748.

some of the attackers were notably unwilling or unable to do much in the way of curbing the influence of the hydroelectric power group.

More recently, the 1948 campaign of Neil Bishop for governor suggests the kind of antic-oriented political tactics so common in the South. Bishop sought the gubernatorial nomination as one of a field of five, and, while he was not demagogic in the sense that he would say anything, responsible or irresponsible, to gain attention, he nevertheless appealed to the voters in the same down-to-earth-but-away-from-the-issues manner associated with the hillbilly, guitar-playing politicians of the Southern hill country. Campaigning in a beat-up old farm truck, Bishop talked about haying, milking, barn repairs, and other mundane matters of rustic concern. He announced he was running for governor because his house had burned down and therefore he wanted to occupy the governor's mansion for a spell. He promised never to buy bottled milk; he would, he promised, install a cow in a shed behind the mansion. It is true that Bishop commented on other matters—he particularly deplored the high costs of government—but even a generous soul could not have called it a campaign on issues. Newspapers bewail the absence of issues in campaigns, but the banal still seems popular. One paper editorialized in 1948 that "Nobody is allowed to say anything that has the least to do with government or the office being sought. Those running for governor comment on how noble it is to dig clams, grow blueberries, teach school, and wait on table. Our senatorial aspirants touched on ancient Roman roads, winter sports. . . ."[14]

If Maine primaries highlight the personal factor to the neglect of issues, then one might expect a considerable degree of localism in the public reaction to candidates. Where contests are between established factions, the degree of "friends and neighbors" attraction ought to be less than where the factions are temporary and built around individual candidates, the assumption being that personal popularity will be greatest at home, and conversely that even local talent from the "wrong" faction will be ignored where factional lines are strongly adhered to. Such an hypothesis can be tested in Maine's gubernatorial and senatorial contests. The results of such checking indicate that in most primaries the "friends and neighbors" pull for local candidates is present to a remarkable extent. An early senatorial primary illustrates the extent to which localism

[14] See the *Lisbon Enterprise* (Maine) of October 28, 1948.

can affect a Maine Republican primary. In 1916 in a three-way contest for the senatorial nomination the candidates got the following percentages of the vote cast in the home counties of contesting candidates.

County	Fernald	Hale	Hersey
Androscoggin	81%*	11%	8%
Cumberland	34	62	4
Aroostook	8	12	80*

* Indicates the home county of the candidate. Hale won the nomination.

The 1932 gubernatorial race is another clearcut case of the "friends and neighbors" influence. There were four candidates who got as much as five per cent of the vote in the primary. Each candidate got the lion's share of his home county vote. Indeed the fifth candidate, who got only 3.7 per cent of the total vote in the state, collected 64 per cent of that vote in his home county and an adjacent county. The following statistics indicate the distribution of the vote in the respective home counties of the candidates:

County	Ames	Barrows	Carlton	Martin
Washington	75.6%*	6.6%	6.7%	10.3%
Penobscot	26.0	56.0	4.2	13.5
Sagadahoc	8.5	11.4	58.0*	20.4
Kennebec	10.9	23.7	16.6	48.4*

* The asterisk indicates the home counties of the candidates. The percentages do not add to 100.0 per cent by the counties since the fifth candidate got a small proportion in each of the counties. Martin won the nomination.

More recently, the 1956 Republican gubernatorial primary illustrates the continuing influence of "friends and neighbors" in Maine. From behind the scenes the key figures of the organization gave assistance to William A. Trafton, and it was enough to put him over. Conservative, from an impeccable family, and wealthy enough to afford a campaign against Governor Edmund Muskie that the party half expected to lose, Trafton was from the organization's point of view "The Ideal Man for Maine's Ideals," as he was billed around the state. Although the organizational backing was helpful to Trafton, the influence of localism was nevertheless present. The counties with the highest and lowest percentages for Trafton (with one exception) fall into place according to the geographic areas from which the candidates came. (See Figure 7.)

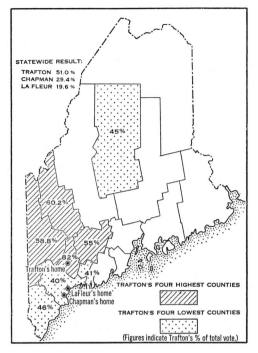

STATEWIDE RESULT:
TRAFTON 51.0 %
CHAPMAN 29.4%
LA FLEUR 19.6 %

45%

60.2%

58.8%   55%

.82%
Trafton's home   .41%
40%
LaFleur's home
Chapman's home
46%

TRAFTON'S FOUR HIGHEST COUNTIES

TRAFTON'S FOUR LOWEST COUNTIES

(Figures indicate Trafton's % of total vote.)

7. "Friends and Neighbors" in Maine:
Republican Primary for Governor, 1956

This is not to say that all elections follow the pattern set forth in the two cases above; there are some races in which an individual exerts such strength that he can overcome the local strength of individual candidates sufficiently to win pluralities in the other fellow's backyard. Mrs. Smith did this in 1948, for example, when she had a plurality of the vote in 14 of the 16 counties. Even though it is not always present to an extreme degree, the "friends and neighbors" attraction is far greater in Maine politics than in Vermont or New Hampshire, as the data presented in the two previous chapters indicate.

Interestingly, there is no well-established ladder of ascent to the governorship in Maine as there is in Vermont. Many who arrive at the governorship have served previously in the legislature, but a search of the records of Republican governors fails to show any consistent ladder. Of the eleven most recent Republican governors, nine had been in the House or Senate, four had served as president of the Senate (second in command in the state, there being no lieutenant governor), and only one had been speaker of the House. That gubernatorial candidates can move into the office without going through a specified apprenticeship tends further to corroborate the argument that Maine has personalized factions.

Although the state machine has slipped from its once great power and now finds itself being challenged by colorful figures who override the wishes of the organization, there are many local Republican organizations which retain their vitality and their ability to dictate local nominations. In a great many cases local nominations go completely unchallenged. That a local candidate has no opposition in the primary is not in itself proof that a powerful organization has overpowered all opposition so massively that it absolutely dictates nominations. It is possible that one candidate may be so popular that opponents hesitate to take him on or that public apathy is such that the primary has atrophied into this form of disuse. A third explanation might be that the uncontested nominations go to incumbents, who by custom are allowed at least a second chance. All these reasons for uncontested nominations are undoubtedly present in any given year in Maine, but the fact remains that the number of uncontested nominations is very high and that the organizations do not let the minority party have many areas by default through failure to put up any candidate at all. On the latter point, the contrast with local Republican organizations in New Hampshire is clear. There, as we indicated, the proportion of Democrats uncontested is high. In Maine this is not the case. In 1954, for example, there was a Republican nominated for every Senate seat and for every one of the county offices—even in Androscoggin County, where the Democrats have a fairly consistent majority control—and only eight of the 151 seats in the House of Representatives went by default.

Table 9 indicates the extent to which nominations are contested within the Republican party. Such a high proportion of uncontested nominations suggests local organization strength, notwithstanding the plausibility of other possible explanations. In the absence of corroborating evidence, the statistical proof would not be convincing, but discussions with many Maine politicians have brought evidence of the strength of many local organizations, even though they are not necessarily "bossed" in the sense that only one man

TABLE 9

Contests for Republican Nominations in Maine, 1954, 1956

	Senate		House		County offices	
	1954	*1956*	*1954*	*1956*	*1954*	*1956*
Number contested	21	21	72	48	32	30
Number not contested	12	12	71	98	77	41
Per cent not contested	36.4%	36.4%	49.6%	67.0%	70.5%	57.8%

handles the helm. (True, some are "bossed" in this manner, but it would appear that this is the exception and not the rule.)

There are from time to time very lively contests in local areas to challenge the local organizations, and on occasion there are upsets. An interesting instance of such an upset is the case of Jim Briggs of Caribou in upper Aroostook County in the far north country. Briggs, a young liberal Republican, opposed an incumbent member of the lower House of the legislature in the 1954 primary. The incumbent had the backing of the local organization and especially the support of a local Republican leader who operated a potato-starch factory. The campaign centered on the Republican leader, for Briggs chose to emphasize the question of the pollution of Maine's streams, and the potato-starch manufacturer was actually one of the polluters. When the votes were counted, Briggs claimed to have won by four votes, but this result was contested and submitted to the governor and Council where, as Briggs tells it, three of his votes and one of his opponent's were tossed out. This should have made him the victor by two votes, but the Council on a recount declared him the loser, 485 to 484. Briggs ran as a write-in candidate and won 58 per cent of the 2,067 votes cast. There being no Democratic candidate for the legislature in the district, Briggs figures he got most of the Democratic votes—perhaps some 300—and thus with Democratic help he upset the organization. The Caribou district got itself a liberal and independent Republican willing to do battle with the dominant economic interests of the state. More about Briggs later in the discussion of the legislature.

However much Maine's politics resembles the politics of the South, there is this difference between Maine and most of the South

—in Maine there is a second party strong enough occasionally to threaten the majority party for some high offices. Some of the consequences of the minority party pressure on the Republicans will be apparent in the following discussion of the Democratic party in Maine.

Democrats in Maine: Down Under
Down East

"Thirty-two-state central committeemen, a few score councillors, an occasional mayor, a sprinkling of rustic select men and assessors, and several thousand hereditary voters without a program and almost without hope—such is the party of Jefferson in the Pine Tree State."[15] This was the sorry assessment of Democratic assets in Maine as of 1929. The party's condition is better today than it was thirty-odd years ago, but its status as a minority party remains a fact—for the present at least. Republican enrollments preparatory to primaries are more than two times as great as the Democratic. In 1954, for example, 55 per cent of the registered voters signed up with the Republican party; 23 per cent chose the Democratic; and 22 per cent ignored both and remained independent.[16] Democratic strength is not so scant as these percentages might suggest, however, for their average percentage of the two-party vote for governor since 1900 (up to 1956) was 43.3 per cent. Since 1930, although there have been some lean years in this period, the Democratic average has been even higher—45.3 per cent, and it is worth repeating that since 1932 four of the 13 gubernatorial elections have been carried by Democratic candidates.[17]

It is conceivable that the Democratic proportion of the vote might on some occasions have been considerably higher but for the quaint

[15] Lane Lancaster, *op.cit.*, p. 744.

[16] The distribution was only slightly changed in 1956. The percentages were: Republican 51.6 per cent, Democratic 21.4, independent 27. Conceivably the decrease in Republican enrollment and increase in independents reflected an intention to desert the party to vote for Governor Muskie, the Democratic incumbent. See "State of Maine, Number of Registered and Enrolled Voters" for 1954 and 1956, Mimeo., Office of the Secretary of State.

[17] Since 1940 the Democratic percentage of the two-party vote has ranged between a low of 29.7 in 1944 and a high of 59.8 in 1956. The 1958 election came after this was written; therefore the numbers now become 14 elections of which 5 were won by Democrats. The percentage calculations above do not include the 1958 election for which only unofficial returns are available. Those indicate tentatively that the Democrat, Clinton Clauson, won 52.1 per cent of the vote for governor.

Maine custom of holding its state elections in September instead of November. In many states national Democratic party victories helped to carry Democratic governors and lesser officers to victory in presidential election years especially. This point has not been overlooked by Republican strategists, even though the potent argument that Maine could save some money by holding both elections at once has always sounded persuasive. During one recent legislative session the Republican national committeeman made a rush trip to Augusta to head off threatened passage of a constitutional amendment to consolidate the two elections.[18] According to one reporter's calculation, bills to change the election date have been debated thirty-five times in the legislature. In 1957, in a surprising turnabout, the legislature passed a constitutional amendment to do all the voting in November, and in a referendum the September election date was finally abolished.[19]

When on occasion a Democrat wins a high office in Maine it is clear that he did so with Republican votes, since the Republicans have on the enrollment lists more than a majority of the registered electors. Common sense would also indicate that many of those who do not bother to register with a party still vote Republican. Without intensive interviewing of voters it would be virtually impossible to ascertain how many "normal" Republican votes the better or successful Democratic candidates get. At best, however, it is likely to be a fairly small proportion of the total vote. What can be measured with greater accuracy is the pile of votes on which, so to speak, the Democrats stand to attract the winning margin from their adversaries. Or, to put the query another way, where do the Democrats attract enough strength in election after election to which the defectors' votes may be added?

There are some Democrats in every Maine community, even if no more than half a dozen. Some may indeed be remnants of the Jacksonian tradition still alive in scattered outposts, but such sur-

[18] All manner of reasons have been offered for not changing the election date— that it was good "publicity" for Maine, that Maine had always done it thus, and therefore ought to continue for tradition's sake, etc. Probably more important was the undeniable fact that the national party organizations were always ready to pour in some extra money for the early campaign in hopes of a victory to show some kind of trend, even though no one really believed the old slogan "As Maine goes, so goes the nation."

[19] See *New York Times*, Sept. 10, 1957. Some 61 per cent of those voting favored repeal.

viving Jacksonian traditionalists contribute little to the strength of the party. The greatest strength of the Democratic party in Maine today comes from two sources: from the French-Canadians and certain other "foreign-stock" groups, and from the urban workers. Second only to New Hampshire is Maine's concentration of French-Canadian first- and second-generation settlers.[20] More than a quarter of the people in Maine either were born abroad or one of their parents was (actually 27 per cent of the population as of 1950), and not quite four of ten of such "foreign-stock" people came from French-Canada. All told, the first- and second-generation French-Canadian population amounts to only ten per cent of the state's population, but if one adds to this an unknown quantity represented by third- or even fourth-generation French-Canadians, who still retain their ethnic community ties, this then constitutes a considerable proportion of the state's electorate. They do not vote as a bloc—no group this large could be expected to do so. But the fact remains that most of them have become Democrats.

Several facts about recent elections suggest the important contribution of the French-Canadian community to the Democratic cause. To begin with, the one county that has been most Democratic in this state, Androscoggin, is also the county with the highest proportion of French-Canadians. Most Democratic candidates for the legislature and county offices in the county are French-Canadian, a fact that reflects the heavy concentration of that ethnic group. Further suggestive evidence is to be found by ranking all the counties according to the proportion of French-Canadians, and then ranking the counties according to the percentage of Democratic vote. Such ranking based on the 1956 vote for governor produces a coefficient of correlation of .9 where 1.0 would mean that there was complete correspondence between the two rankings.[21]

In order to narrow down the French-Canadian factor somewhat it is possible to isolate the towns and cities with heavy French-Canadian concentrations and check their voting. There are 14 localities with over 2,500 population where the number of French-Canadian foreign-born exceeds five per cent, and in the 1954 election only one of them failed to produce a Democratic majority for governor. The exception was the city of Auburn, which to a con-

[20] E. P. Hutchinson, *op.cit.*, p. 43.
[21] See Chapter 3, pp. 63-64, for a brief explanation of this statistical method.

siderable extent is a suburban community of long-standing Republican tendencies. Significantly it has 5.5 per cent French-Canadian foreign-born, which ranks it well toward the bottom of the list of the 14 towns. By ranking the towns, a coefficient of correlation based on the 1954 gubernatorial vote was calculated similarly to that for the counties. Here the coefficient was .86. Listed in Table 10 are the percentages for the ethnic factor as well as election percentages.

TABLE 10

French-Canadian Population and Democratic Tendencies in Maine Cities

Towns	French-Canadian born as percentage of total population	Democratic percentage of two-party vote for governor*, 1954
Lewiston	15.8%	78.10%
Sanford	14.6	69.0
Biddeford	13.6	86.0
Winslow	13.1	79.0
Madwaska	12.7	78.0
Van Buren	12.5	77.8
Rumford	11.4	76.5
Mexico	7.6	68.0
Brunswick	7.1	63.0
Waterville	7.0	69.0
Augusta	6.2	54.8
Auburn	5.5	44.5
Westbrook	5.2	59.0
Saco	5.0	58.9

* The Democratic margin in these towns is somewhat higher than usual, but this was an unusual year in that a Democratic governor was elected. This fact does not affect the validity of the rank correlation analysis, but the unsuspecting should not imagine that there are many occasions when even these Democratically inclined towns produce such majorities as these.

Governor Muskie actually polled majorities in 247 localities as opposed to 238 for his opponent, Governor Cross. Except for some very small towns, where lopsided voting took place (for example, St. John Place in Aroostook County voted 55 to 8 for Muskie), the towns in this list contributed the heaviest Democratic majorities.

Other ethnic minority groups—such as the Irish and other smaller groups—have tended to be Democratic in Maine. There are exceptions to this rule: for example, the Canadians, other than those from Quebec, are inclined to be Republican. The Republican party has made no great effort to attract minorities, and indeed during the 1920's through indirect connections with the KKK repelled many of them.

Suggestion of the ethnic-group alignment can be seen if one checks the names of candidates for major offices. In the last two generations a great many of the Democratic candidates for major offices have been Irish or French-Canadian. (Such names as Lausier, Jullien, Dubord, Moran, and McGuillicuddy keep turning up.) It is also interesting to compare the proportions of identifiable Irish and French names among legislators according to parties, as does Table 11. This tendency for particular ethnic groups to divide along

TABLE 11

Ethnic Group Representation in the Maine House of
Representatives, 1900 and 1950

| | DEMOCRATS | | | | REPUBLICANS | | | |
| | *Number* | | Per cent of all *Democrats* | | *Number* | | Per cent of all *Republicans* | |
	1900	1950	1900	1950	1900	1950	1900	1950
Irish names	3	4	12%	16%	2	4	1.6%	.8%
French names	2	13	8	52	1	3	3.1	2.3

party lines also shows up in religious affiliations, as might be expected. In the 1955 session, when for the first time in the history of the state a Catholic governor had just been elected, 22 of the 24 Democratic members of the lower House were Catholic, as were all six Democratic senators.

The ethnic factor is not the only significant factor to observe in analysis of Democratic strength in Maine. Although the state is not as industrialized as lower New England, there is considerable manufacturing in the state, and in the industrial towns the Democratic party usually does well. In the town of Biddeford, for example, the very high proportion of Democratic vote (see the listing above) can be explained not only by the French-Canadian concentration but also by the fact that it is an industrial town. It is apparently not just a question of urbanization, for certain other cities which under other circumstances one might expect to be Democratic remain Republican strongholds—for example, Portland (population 77,600) and Bangor (population 31,500). Only one other city in the state with a population over 10,000 is as much a Republican stronghold as these two, South Portland, in which only five per cent of the population is employed in manufacturing (Portland has 7.4 per cent in manufacturing and Bangor 5.1 per cent). All the remaining nine cities with more than 10,000 population have larger proportions of manufacturing employees, ranging from 12.5 per cent in Augusta to 30.7 in Sanford. All these cities are more Democratic than the first three, an indication that even in far-off Maine the revolutionary impact of the New Deal has been felt.[22]

As might be expected of a minority party, there are large areas of Maine without any sort of meaningful Democratic organization. Former state Democratic chairman, John C. Donovan, says that at the beginning of the 1956 campaign only 123 of Maine's more than 400 towns had local party committees.[23] At present when the party seems to be undergoing something of a renaissance, there is more organization both at top and bottom of the party than is customary, but even so to compare it with the Republican party organization is difficult if not impossible. There is some kind of Republican organization covering the whole state, but in many areas the Democrats offer no candidates and cannot even scrape up delegates to go to conventions. Not long ago it was difficult to find members from some areas to serve on the state central committee.[24]

Perhaps the best indication of the sparseness of local Democratic organizations is found in the frequent failure to make even a token opposition effort to the Republicans. In 1948, for example, Republican candidates in half the legislative districts faced no Democratic opponents at all. In more recent elections as Democratic chances

[22] The ethnic factor is also involved here; I am not seeking to establish any one-factor explanation of voting tendencies. Both factors are apparently important elements in Democratic chances in the state. Indeed by ranking the towns according to percentages of Democratic vote in 1954 and comparing this ranking with rankings by French-Canadian population and manufacturing employment, I found no remarkable difference in the resulting coefficients: .77 for ethnic factor and .70 for manufacturing. But when I chose towns with very high concentrations of French-Canadians without regard to manufacturing, I got a much higher coefficient: .86. (See above, p. 97.)

[23] John C. Donovan, *Congressional Campaign: Maine Elects a Democrat*, New York, 1958, p. 3.

[24] Although it may well be atypical, a conversation I had with two Maine Democrats in one of the larger cities indicated a remarkable still-life quality about local Democratic organization. One told me in tones of awe and horror of the Republican machinery at work on election day. "You know what they do? They get a list of all Republicans and sit at the door of the polling place and check off Republicans as they come to vote." This is so routine a procedure in any organized party that their shocked reaction seemed amazing. Yet the two men, who professed to be "party workers," had never used so elementary a tactic.

have seemed improved there have been more Democratic nominees running, but even so 42 of the 1954 Republican candidates for the House (total membership, 151) had no opposition. In 1956, when Democratic hopes were higher still, no Democratic candidates were run in 20 districts. In certain counties the Democrats have so little organization (or so little hope—the two go together) that they fail to contest even one House seat in the county.[25] In 1954 Democrats contested 26 of 33 senatorial seats and only 51 of the 109 county offices up for election that year. In the county nominations the fact that they contested nearly half the offices is not as impressive as it appears, since 61 per cent of the Democratic nominees were running in six of the 16 counties, and again in some counties, Aroostook and Waldo, there were no Democrats running.

It is generally true of minority parties that the leaders and the subleaders are very much interested in national patronage and anxiously maneuver in anticipation of the day when their party controls Washington. Undoubtedly this is a factor which helps keep alive some sort of organization in some states where, in the absence of this outside hope, a byproduct of the federal system, there might be no party organization at all. But even if this goal does recruit some ambitious candidates, it also brings in people with divided interests; on other occasions it takes away the promising young performers who might, if they did not migrate to Washington, contribute something worthwhile to the local party. There is no clear evidence that Democratic politicians have sold out to the major party for state patronage in Maine, but the pull of national patronage during the long New Deal era undoubtedly weakened Democratic strength in Maine.[26]

[25] In Waldo, Lincoln, and Piscataquis Counties the Democrats contested only two of the eleven House seats at stake in those counties in 1954. See the discussion of Democratic disorganization in Philip S. Wilder, Jr., *Maine Politics, A Study of Responsible One-Party Government* (unpublished doctoral dissertation, Harvard University, 1951). Mr. Wilder's work treats both the historical and contemporary aspects of Maine politics.

[26] As Lawrence Pelletier has pointed out, another common burden for minority parties is borne by the Maine Democrats: because the party is weak it tends to stay weak. The actual contests are in the dominant party, which attracts newcomers and the young to participate, at least when there is no strong traditional bias toward one side or the other. Even forgetting social or business reasons for being with the majority party (and, although they cannot be measured very well, they are significant), the voting evidence indicates that many people who vote Democratic in the state register with the Republican party in order to participate in the primary. See David, Moos, and Goldman, *op.cit.*, p. 10.

One of the assets of the Democratic party, such a great proportion of the French-Canadians, is also the bane of the existence of the organization. Constant rivalries spring up between the French-Canadians, the Yankees, and the Irish. To nominate someone from any one of these ethnic groups is to produce grumbling from the others. At the state convention in 1952 a disgruntled delegate rose to complain of the distribution of the slate of delegates to the Democratic national convention. "The slate is lopsided," he said. "Let's divide this thing up among the different religions. The slate is, as I predicted, a packed house, and it sounds to me like a list of delegates to the Knights of Columbus convention."[27] Not all contests end as conflicts based on ethnic rivalries. An able Yankee candidate for Congress, Frank M. Coffin, defeated a French-Canadian opponent in the 1956 Democratic primary in the Second District, which contains Androscoggin County, the most French-Canadian area in the state.[28] Ethnic ties can be overcome by candidates of ability. Ethnic group rivalry remains a significant deterrent to the Democratic party in Maine, even though at present it appears to be at a minimum with a party leader who fits into none of the traditional ethnic niches. Governor Muskie, unquestionably the leader of the party in the state, is a Catholic, the son of a Polish-born tailor, and thus is able to circumvent some of the rivalries that might otherwise beset him.

There are some signs now, although they may be misleading, that the Democratic party is emerging from the cocoon which has encased it for a century. The leadership is better than it has been for generations. The candidates offered are such as to attract and not repel attention. Twice before in this century it has seemed that the Democratic party might pull within hailing distance of their Republican adversaries, but on each occasion the illusion proved false. In 1910 the Democrats were the beneficiaries of accumulated angry frustration with the ruling Republican machine which had become corrupt. Their sweeping victory of that year, which went so far as to give the Democrats the legislature as well as the governorship, resulted in some relatively liberal legislation, but they ran afoul of the prohibition enforcement problem and in 1912 the newly formed Progressive Party made a temporary agreement with the

[27] *Ibid.*, p. 21.
[28] On the Coffin campaign see Donovan, *op.cit.*

regular Republicans not to run a Progressive candidate.[29] Consequently the Republicans retook the governorship in 1912, and although the Democrats won the office in 1914 with a plurality of the vote (due to the fact that a Progressive candidate ran) the time for anything resembling two-party competition was not yet at hand. Nor had that time arrived during the early New Deal era when a Democrat won the governorship twice (1932 and 1934). Maine politics slipped back into its customary path in a short time.

The break-through of 1954 was also occasioned by unhappiness with the Republican party or, perhaps more accurately, with the gubernatorial candidate of the party. Governor Cross, for reasons already referred to, had become unpopular, and the state was undergoing a considerable economic slump. As usual the Republican party had a much better organization with far more money than the Democrats could raise. No individual contribution to the Democratic party exceeded $100 and the state organization reported expenditures of only $15,400 in contrast to nearly twice that amount reported by the Republican organization ($27,885).[30] The governor was supported by Senator Smith in many specific references, and Vice-President Richard Nixon cut short his vacation for a brief swing through the state to urge larger than ever Republican majorities to prove support for the Eisenhower administration. Notwithstanding this formidable opposition, the Democrats won the governorship and came closer to defeating Senator Smith than many observers had thought possible.

Three young and enterprising Democrats had much to do with this stunning upset: one as state chairman, one as gubernatorial and the other as senatorial candidate. Paul Fullam, a professor of history from Colby College, won 42 per cent of the vote against the very popular Mrs. Smith—in contrast to the meager 29 per cent garnered by the last Democrat to oppose her.[31] The 1954 campaign was conducted by Frank M. Coffin, a young Yankee lawyer from Lewiston. The Republican newspapers of the state had words of at

[29] See Elizabeth Ring, *op.cit.*, pp. 24-25.

[30] As usual, Republican contributions came in larger sums, many of them from outside sources. For example, the Republican report listed these contributions: John D. Rockefeller, Jr., $2,000; Nelson Rockefeller, $500; $200 from Mrs. Atwater Kent. All these data are from the files of the office of the secretary of state in Augusta.

[31] Professor Fullam died during the summer of 1955.

least faint praise for Coffin as a new departure for the Democratic party in the state. (There is virtually no Democratic press in the state.) By tremendous effort Coffin managed to get a skeleton organization working over most of the state, and in many urban areas, at least, had relatively successful machinery set up. He retained the party chairmanship after the election and proceeded during the interim between the 1954 and 1956 elections to build up a staff for the party headquarters and to recruit as many workers as possible. New publications were put out by the party and a renewed effort was made to get some kind of contact with the workers through citizen committees, questionnaires, and public meetings. An elaborate forty-page questionnaire was sent out to about 1,000 community leaders about the forthcoming Democratic platform for 1956. To measure the effect of such organizational and propaganda effort is next to impossible, but it undoubtedly assisted the party in 1956; if nothing else, it helped to bring Frank Coffin front and center in the party. Accordingly he was nominated and elected to Congress in 1956, the first Democratic member of Congress from Maine since the 1930's.[32]

Governor Edmund Muskie was the key figure in this Democratic resurgence. His background and political career are worth discussing briefly here, since they reveal some significant things about the politics of Maine—both about the character and role of the Democratic party in Maine and the position of a minority governor in a state government otherwise dominated by the opposition party. Lanky, lean, and lantern-jawed, Muskie is a political enigma. Although he speaks slowly and with a mild Down-East accent and is comparatively conservative, he is both a Democrat and a Catholic, traits which ought to have made him ineligible to be governor of Maine. Born of Polish-American parents in the town of Rumford, he worked his way through Bates College, where he was a member of Phi Beta Kappa and where he got some training for future political encounters by being a star on the debating team. (He challenged Governor Cross to debate him during the 1954 campaign but, not

[32] Coffin relinquished the state chairmanship when he went to Washington. In his stead John C. Donovan took the job. Donovan, professor of government at Bates College, is another young, active politician of the Muskie-Coffin type. As might be expected, not all the old-line Democratic politicians are delighted with these newcomers—Donovan's selection as chairman required some pushing by Muskie and Coffin—but since the 1954 victory relative harmony has prevailed in the party.

surprisingly, the challenge was never accepted.) From Bates, Muskie went on to Cornell Law School and graduated *cum laude*. The war intervened for four years; then, on returning from the South Pacific, where he served as a naval officer on a destroyer, he went to Waterville, opened a law practice, and in 1947 ran for the lower House of legislature. He won and in his second term in the House was made minority leader. He resigned his seat in 1951 to become state director of the Office of Price Stabilization during the Korean War.

Notwithstanding the fact that Maine was the one New England state with a flourishing Ku Klux Klan in the 1920's and that there has been much outspoken anti-Catholicism in the state, there was no public effort to attack Muskie on a religious basis. During the campaign some Republican politicians went to official court records to make photostatic copies of the papers by which Muskie's father had changed his surname from Marciszewski to Muskie, but no public use was ever made of this, presumably in fear that it might backfire.

Muskie's campaign was disarming to the Republicans. He went about looking, as the *Wall Street Journal* put it, "like a slightly fleshed-out brother of blue-blooded, lantern-jawed Senator Leverett Saltonstall of Massachusetts."[33] Nor did Muskie fit any of the boogey-man prototypes that Democrats are often described as being—he had served as a lobbyist for the Maine Central Railway in 1953, he took a generally conservative but constructive approach that emphasized Maine's particular problems, and he at least talked about possible solutions. He attacked Governor Cross for doing nothing to attract industries to the state to take up the slack left by fleeing textile mills. He discussed the problems of fisheries and lobster industries. His approach was cautious, not very partisan in phraseology, and calmly rational in tone.

The outgoing governor and legislature prepared a slipping stone for Muskie to step on when he was inaugurated. Soon after the September election a special session of the legislature was called. As a parting gesture the lame-duck governor sponsored and got passed bills to increase state employees' salaries, to raise the teacher retirement allowance, and to appropriate money for a new state office building. As might be expected, the Democratic legislators had a field day with their defeated colleagues. They particularly

[33] *Wall Street Journal*, Oct. 16, 1956.

criticized the unplanned spending of the "hastily called" session and rode the majority for the passage of a bill to eliminate a tax on cigars. Alluding to the pressure applied by the "inner circle of Republican wheels," one Democratic Senator rhetorically asked, "If Governor [Cross], who vetoed the tobacco-cigar tax repealer in 1953, felt that . . . [session of the] legislature had no right to subtract from the expected revenues of the [next] legislature, what has changed his mind? How can such legislation reasonably be classified as emergency legislation?"[34]

However adroit the Republican leaders while the reins were still in their hands, they began to lose control over the situation when Governor Muskie came on the scene. Their experience in dealing with a Democratic governor was, after all, limited—few Republican legislators had been active during the administration of the most recent Democratic governor. In his inaugural address the new governor asked for 37 pieces of legislation, and ultimately got 22 of them passed—not bad as gubernatorial batting averages go. At one point leading Republicans were quoted as saying that the reorganization of the Development Commission into a Department of Industry and Commerce, as proposed by Muskie, was utterly unnecessary, but before the battle was over the Republican leadership had conceded. In caucus, the Republicans were told that failure to pass the bill was handing the Democrats the next election on a platter. One Republican predicted that the party would be blamed for everything from the departure of a textile mill to the death of a chicken in Aroostook County.

The infamous Fernald Law, which for forty-five years had prohibited the transportation of electrical power out of Maine, was repealed at Muskie's urging. Increased appropriations for education and humane institutions were granted, and a bill was approved to provide a study of the state's government. There were notable failures too—particularly in the field of resources controls and labor legislation—but the achievements were nevertheless significant.

Maine has the "short ballot," which means that the only state official elected by the whole electorate of the state is the governor. The legislature appoints the heads of four major departments (state

[34] *Legislative Record* of the Special Session of the 96th Legislature, 1954, p. 36. Maine is one of the few states that provides a verbatim reporting of all legislative debate. No other New England state does so.

treasurer, attorney general, secretary of state, and commissioner of agriculture). Other department heads are chosen by the governor with the consent of the Executive Council. The Council itself is chosen by the legislature, thereby giving the Republicans not only a check on patronage disbursement but some control over administrative activities. Through the Council and the legislative appointment of certain department heads a governor of the minority party, and to some extent even a Republican governor, is held in check.[35] During his first term Muskie had several battles over appointments with his Council—all seven members of which naturally were Republicans—and in some cases he lost the appointment but won a victory in the sense that the Council made itself look "political" and the governor more or less "virtuous." In one instance of this sort Muskie sought to appoint a Republican to the State Milk Commission, but the Republican he chose, Obed S. Millett, had supported him in the campaign for governor and was therefore *persona non grata* to the Council. Confirmation was refused on the grounds that "if Mr. Millett could not be faithful to his political party, there might be some question as to his responsibility in a state job."[36]

Whether the present fair weather for the Democratic party represents just another brief interim between long dry spells or a real change in political climate no one can say with certainty.[36a] The Republicans have assisted the Democrats greatly in giving them this

[35] A study of Maine government made in 1955-1956 criticized the lack of executive power to control administration. "Top-level supervision of the 29 operating agencies is provided by 62 officials; five of them are elected by the legislature, 50 of them are named by the governor subject to the approval of the council (albeit most of them for longer terms than the governor's term), four of them are ex-officio commission members, and [three others by various means of selection]. . . . Thirteen of the board and commission members must by law be selected from special interest groups. Under the appointment arrangements described the governor can hardly be designated as the 'supreme executive' power of the state, the terminology of the state constitution notwithstanding." Public Administration Service, "Organization and Administration of the Government of the State of Maine, A Survey Report" (Submitted to the Governor and Executive Council, June 12, 1956), mimeo., p. 8. See also the critical commentary on the Executive Council in W. A. Newdick, "The Executive Council of Maine," unpublished master's thesis, University of Maine, 1951, in Maine State Library, Augusta.

[36] *New York Times*, Aug. 17, 1955.

[36a] The 1958 election, which occurred after this was written, would seem to indicate a transition to competitive parties may be in progress. Muskie won election to the U.S. Senate with 60.4 per cent of the vote (unofficial totals); Dr. Clinton A. Clauson won the governorship with 52.1 per cent; and two Democrats won house seats. Democratic membership in the house increased to 39 per cent of the total; in the Senate it became 38 per cent.

new chance—both through their neglect of state problems[37] and through bumbling in their relationships with a deceptively clever politician like Governor Muskie. Of necessity, however, attention is focused on the governor more than on his party, since he has with him no more than an oversized corporal's guard of Democrats in the legislature and the administration. In the long run increasing industrialization will tend to swell Democratic ranks, but at best this is a slow process. Maine's ambitious program for attracting industry to the state has had moderate success, but it cannot alter the economy of the state overnight. In the meantime, it is conceivable that able and aggressive Democratic leadership and Republican disorganization may permit a closer approach to a competitive two-party system than Maine has seen since the Civil War.

The Maine Legislature: The Power
of the Big Three

The politics of the Maine legislature revolves around the dominating roles of the most powerful interest groups in the state—power, timber, and manufacturing. There are other groups involved—the farmers, fishermen, labor, and the parties from time to time play significant roles—but the power of the Big Three economic interests is such that the other elements seem to fade into the background, or else at times they become appendages of the Big Three. When the power and timber interests were acquiring the rights and property they now control, many legislators became mere pawns in a game for high stakes, uncounted millions of dollars worth of power and timber. The nearly absolute power of these companies, when they were getting established, is of more than historical interest, for strong remnants of this kind of authority remain today.

Evidence of the power of the Big Three is not hard to find. Although Muskie had considerable success in passing his suggested legislation in 1955, his defeats came largely on matters of prime importance to the Big Three. He did not get a minimum wage of 75 cents for intra-state employees (although the Eisenhower Administration had accepted a one-dollar minimum for employees in

[37] This is the way the *Wall Street Journal* put it: "In recent years the Republican politicos of Maine, with exceptions, have not impressed voters that they care passionately for their state. They have behaved complacently in office, and have grabbed Ike's coattails on election day. They have proclaimed their adherence to 'internationalism' and 'liberalism,' letting local problems go wag." Oct. 16, 1956.

inter-state industry). He also failed to get a state labor relations commission and he got his proposed increases in unemployment insurance only after reduction. Proposals to broaden the exemptions on the sales tax and to institute a state income and corporate franchise tax were both refused. No improvement was made in the state's water pollution laws, and the utilities staved off a threat to their rate setting system. A longer look at some of the Big Three operations during the session is in order.

One glaring example of the effectiveness of the Big Three in the legislature is the hopeless inadequacy of the state's laws on water pollution. Maine's waterways are crucially important to her economy. They provide much-needed water to industries which Maine hopes to beckon to her cities. Since Maine's economy increasingly depends upon the tourist influx, pure and clear waters instead of fish-killing, unsanitary streams are necessary. The paper and potato-starch industries are most interested in the freedom to pollute streams, but they have allies in the municipal fathers who fear the cost of building sewage treatment plants and in the hydroelectric companies who do not want to jeopardize the manufacturing interests to whom their power is sold. The president of the Associated Industries of Maine gave a series of television talks on water pollution in November 1954 (presumably preparatory to the possible battle on the question in the forthcoming legislative session). He agreed that pollution was harmful and that it ought to be curtailed, but he strongly maintained that nothing should be done at the time to disturb any business that was then polluting streams. The chairman of the Maine Development Commission, which might be expected to balance off its interest in the recruitment of new industries with its concern for conservation of resources, appeared before a legislative committee in the 1953 session to *oppose* legislation against pollution. (It ought to be noted, however, that the chairman of the commission at that time was also listed as a lobbyist for the Central Maine Power Company and was its vice-president.)

Maine actually has a law against pollution (dating from 1945) but it is more amusing than effective. Four different classes of water are established by the law—running from "class A" in which no pollution is allowed to "class D" which are "primarily devoted to transportation of sewerage and industrial wastes without creation of nuisance."[38] One section of the pollution law exempts from the provisions of the law twelve major rivers of the state, a fact which led a weekly newspaper commentator to remark, "We have an 'anti-pollution law' on our books now. It says no mill shall dump its wastes in any river EXCEPT—and then it lists all the rivers in Maine that ever had a mill on them. This kind of legislation is what a state like Maine gets when it permits industry to take over its government. . . . Nobody is going to come right out and say he wants Maine to stink. It's like kicking your mother; you don't do it. Yet Maine Stinks."[39]

Hopes were high among the proponents of pollution law revision in the 1955 session. The governor put into his inaugural message a plea for action on the problem, asking for "reorganization of the water improvement commission to give increased representation to 'public' members having no direct connection with industry." It was true that the governor's position was a bit equivocal in that he also stated: "It is essential that our policy in this field be firm and progressive while avoiding damage to our industrial structure."[40] But he had asked for something to be done, and this was a hopeful sign.

Representative James Briggs of Caribou, who had campaigned on the pollution issue more than on anything else, took the lead in the anti-pollution drive. He exhibited a series of color photographs which showed a Maine river clogged with thousands of dead fish, killed by the waste discharged from a potato-starch plant. Flies were thick on decaying fish and on garbage dumped into rivers by municipalities. Armed with graphic illustrations, great reams of reports, and other information on the problem, as well as a dry but sometimes biting wit, Briggs introduced a "Clean Waters Act," which proposed to enforce anti-pollution measures over a period of several years. Two other bills on this subject were proposed: one introduced by the Democrats which proposed a more gradual elimination of pollution; and a committee revision of the Democratic bill, which actually opened up new pollution possibilities rather than restricting the practice. The latter bill extended the "grandfather clause" of the original act, by allowing pollution initiated before September 1955 (i.e., several months after the

[38] Ch. 79, *Revised Statutes of Maine.*
[39] *Fort Fairfield Review*, Apr. 8, 1953.
[40] *Maine Legislative Record of the 97th Legislature*, 1955, p. 44.

passage of the act) to be exempted from the required license provisions that would apply to new pollution added after that date.

A hearing that lasted two days was held on the bills. Fervent pleas for no action on pollution were backed up with the threat that anti-pollution legislation would "spell the disintegration and eventual death of most existing industries." The *Lewiston Daily Sun* replied to this charge in an editorial, saying, "That is pure poppycock, and the industry spokesmen know it. Other states have cleaned up their rivers and profited by it."[41] Briggs told the House on May 5, 1955 that the hearing had amply illustrated the public interest in the bill. ". . . Several hundred persons traveled at their own expense from every corner of our state to observe the proceedings and to give testimony. It is a little bit ironical in the light of this to note that the bill which received such overwhelming public support now receives the unanimous Ought Not To Pass stamp of the committee, while one testified for by a public utility official and two lobbyists, received a unanimous Ought To Pass from the same committee."[42] On the key vote, Briggs's Clean Waters Act was defeated 82-42, and it appeared that the bill opening the way to more pollution would pass instead. It did not pass, however, and the anti-pollution contingent left the session with the law no worse than when the session began, something of which they had by no means been sure in May.

Until 1955 Maine had on its statute books one of the oddest pieces of legislation in any state, the Fernald Law, which forbade the exportation from the state of any hydroelectric power. Passed originally in 1909 with the hope that it might attract industry because of the availability of power, the law ultimately became a fetter to the growth of the power industry, and its leaders therefore sought repeal in the 1920's. This was the heyday of the Insull empire's invasion of Maine. Prior to 1911, nearly all the electrical utilities in the state were home-owned, but gradually outside capital moved in and built up huge combines like the Maine Central Power Company. Sumner Pike (now chairman of the State Public Utilities Commission and one-time member of the federal Atomic Energy Commission) said of this process: "It happens that in this part of the State of Maine [meaning the area around Bates College, where he was

[41] Apr. 16, 1955.
[42] *Legislative Record*, 1955, p. 1684.

delivering a commencement address] one of the most fantastic examples of monopoly gone wild occurred when Samuel Insull of Chicago bought our power companies which sell electric current, then bought or built cotton or pulp mills to make sure that they would buy the current which he had to sell, and later bought banks to lend money to the mills so they could pay their power bills. This all, incidentally, with other people's money, not Mr. Insull's."[43] Powerful as were the Insull interests, they failed to get enough public support to pass a referendum repealing the Fernald Law in 1929, although some $200,000 were spent propagandizing for repeal.[44]

With the subsequent passage of the Federal Power Act, the utilities in Maine were glad the Fernald Law was on the books, for it apparently meant the Federal Power Commission had no jurisdiction over them, since they were by law intra-state concerns. Thus the power companies swung around to an opposite position; they now opposed time and again the repeal of the law and always with success until 1955. By that time, however, the previously solid front of the utilities had been breached—some of the companies were pleading for repeal, since the law interfered with their projects on the Canadian border where sales across the international boundary were necessary for economic production of power. Moreover the Federal Power Commission had found an "in" for examining the books of one of the companies on other grounds, so even the opponents of repeal had their stand weakened somewhat. Thus more through division within the ranks of the utilities than anything else, the law was repealed. One of the more colorful chapters of Maine's economic-politics had closed.

If the forces of the power companies were divided on the Fernald Law repeal in 1955, they were not divided on the question of property assessment for purposes of rate setting. At the tag end of the 1953 session of the legislature a bill was shunted through the legislature (without debate) to provide that in rate-setting cases before the Public Utilities Commission the rates would have to be set on the basis of "current value" and not "original cost minus depreciation." Obviously this makes a great difference in an age of inflation

[43] Quoted in Lincoln Smith, *The Power Policy of Maine*, Los Angeles, 1951, p. 78.
[44] *Ibid.*, p. 106. The referendum lost, 64,000 to 54,000.

when the replacement cost of a power dam might be two or three times its original cost. The state chairman of the Democratic party presented a brief at the 1955 hearing on a repeal bill, as did Sumner Pike, chairman of the Public Utilities Commission, but the lobbyists for the utilities were out in force both in the hearing and in the subsequent consideration of the bill in both Houses. The Committee on Public Utilities divided five to five on the question, but in roll-call votes the repeal movement failed when the two Houses failed to agree on a single bill.[45]

Even though the power and timber groups are the most powerful and certainly the most dramatic pressure groups in Augusta, they are not the only ones. Some 200 lobbyists register under Maine's weak lobbying law in the average session. The requirement that the lobbyist register and a prohibition of "contingent" fee lobbying (that is, the lobbyist is paid if he gets results, otherwise not) is virtually all the law does provide. A brief flurry about tightening the law came in 1955 but, after a hearing at which legislators talked about "breathing the free air of Maine" and not much else, the idea was abandoned.

Both the Farm Bureau and the Grange are active in Maine politics, concerning themselves with tax policy, roads, and other questions in addition to strictly agricultural problems. Notwithstanding the extensiveness of agriculture in Maine, the farm groups are not the key interest groups that they are in many other agricultural states—Vermont, for example. There is an active liquor and beer lobby, the former having been in difficulty recently with the scandal in the Liquor Commission over the purchase of "favored" brands for the state liquor stores. The beer lobby got itself into trouble in 1953 when several too-eager lobbyists practically leaned over the shoulders of senators debating and about to vote on a bill banning disposable beer bottles. Also conspicuously present when the occasion requires is the horse-racing lobby, which, while it is not so influential as its counterparts in Massachusetts, New Hampshire, or Rhode Island, still exerts considerable pressure on legislators from time to

[45] See *Legislative Record*, 1955, pp. 1,724, 1,998. The roll-call vote in the Senate to sustain current value was 27 to 5 (24 Republicans and 3 Democrats for and 2 Republicans and 3 Democrats against); in the House the vote on the key bill rejected the current value doctrine by 77 to 49 (55 Republicans against current value along with 22 Democrats; 47 Republicans and 2 Democrats for current value).

time. The racing season is brief in Maine, however, and the total income to the state from pari-mutuel betting is not large enough to make this an important source of political power.[46]

Labor has its contingent of lobbyists in Augusta, but interestingly they appear to do more negotiating with the lobbyists for industry than with the legislators themselves. This is similar to the situation in Vermont, and again it is not surprising that labor representatives conduct their business with the industrial leaders, since the latter have such great power in the legislature. Particularly important as a bargaining agent for industry is the Associated Industries of Maine. Labor can depend on some assistance from the Democratic minority in the legislature, but this is usually so small that it does not mean much. Labor is divided politically, however, with the old line AFL unions tending toward the Republican party, and the CIO unions toward the Democrats. Notwithstanding the general labor support of Muskie, particularly in his second-term campaign, not a great deal in the way of labor legislation was forthcoming from the two regular sessions of the legislature during his incumbency. At best, of course, Muskie's power to influence such legislation would not be great; the power of well-entrenched economic interests is too great to overcome in such a vital matter. Muskie's appeal to industry and his generally conservative position may have further hampered the chances for labor legislation.

Labor's power is contingent on its voting strength since its economic power, at least in a state like Maine, is not very great. If industrialization should continue in the state (twenty-five new industries came into the state in the first nine months of 1956 with a payroll of $11,000,000 annually) labor will undoubtedly acquire greater political strength. The opportunity for wielding that power may be somewhat greater than in some other states, since the apportionment of the legislature is not so heavily slanted against the urban areas as it is in many states. The apportionment favors rural areas to some degree, producing bitter complaints about the tendency for rural districts to hold on to their unequal advantage over the

[46] Maine collects around $700,000 from horse racing, or less than 1 per cent of its state income in contrast to five or six times that proportion collected in other New England states where racing is legal. See *State of Maine Budget Document,* 1956-1957, pp. 1, 5. For comparative figures on the various states, see *The Book of the States,* 1956-1957, p. 236.

cities.[47] Both the Senate and the House of Representatives are set up on a district basis, and it is therefore possible to get something near a fair apportionment through simple legislative action. It is at least a more conceivable change than in many of the states, where any substantial improvement must await the more difficult process of constitutional change.[48]

That the apportionment of Maine is somewhat warped in favor of the rural districts only facilitates the operations of the Big Three interest groups. The general conservativeness of Maine is strongest in the rural areas and small towns, which probably reflects in part the gradual loss of Maine's younger population to other areas where economic prospects are brighter. Whatever the basic causes, the legislators who come to Augusta every other winter reflect the conservatism of their constituents. Many of them arrive with the "take-it-easy" or "wait-awhile" mood so useful to the dominant interests; they arrive on the legislative scene ready to say no to large expenditures and to frown on governmental regulation. Not all of them have these views, of course, but the great majority appear to fit the description.

Among the legislators there is also invariably a sprinkling of direct representatives of the utilities, timber, and manufacturing groups. For example, in 1955 Robert Haskell, president of the Senate in that term, is vice-president of the Bangor Hydroelectric Company, the second largest power company in the state. Senator James Reid, attorney for the New England Telephone Company, was chairman of the Judiciary Committee that session. While there is no implication that these senators or others in roughly comparable but less

[47] See, for example, the pamphlet "Modernizing the Legislature" by Dwight E. Sargent, a collection of editorials from the *Portland Press Herald* of Dec. 1-30, 1954. See particularly the 7th in the series, where it is stated, "The 500,000 state-of-Mainers living in country districts are represented in the House by 97 legislators; the 400,000 urbanites by only 54. In many rural communities legislators represent no more than 2,000 to 2,500 voters, whereas in Lewiston they represent more than 8,000 each, and in Portland more than 10,000, a situation resulting from a constitutional provision limiting municipalities, regardless of size, to seven representatives."

[48] The present apportionment of the Maine legislature is not too bad as compared with the other states. Dauer and Kelsay in their analysis of the apportionment of state legislatures rank the Maine Senate 14th and the House 15th with the states having the greatest equality of voters per district at the top and those with the greatest disproportion at the bottom. By their calculations the ratio between the largest district and the smallest in the Maine Senate is 2.6 and in the House 4.7. The reapportionment of the 1955 session cut the latter figure somewhat, but the compromised bill did not alter the situation much. See Dauer and Kelsay, *op.cit.*, pp. 571-575.

spectacular positions used their official positions for illegal purposes, it remains true that they are on the spot to advise their colleagues about the intricacies of rate-setting practices, for example, which can be an extremely complicated question. Without improper action of any kind, such representatives are invaluable assets to their companies far beyond the votes they cast on bills.[49]

As we observed earlier in discussing the legislatures of Vermont and New Hampshire, the hand of the lobbyist is strengthened where the turnover of legislators is high. It is more than an assumption; it is a fact that it is easier both to convince and to confuse a greenhorn than a veteran legislator. In Maine the average session opens with about one half the members new to the game. In 1955 there were but 20 members of the 151-member House who had been there in 1951, only two sessions back. Interestingly nearly half—eight, to be exact—of the holdovers were Democrats, who seem to have more durability than the Republicans. This probably results from the fact that the Democrats tend to come from the multimember districts in one city while most Republicans come from single-member, multitown districts where the custom of rotation of the honor from town to town often prevails. Some members of the 1951 House had graduated to the Senate, but even so the Senate had only eight members who had been in the Senate two sessions ago. Twenty-six of the 33 senators had had some previous legislative experience, however, which is far more than the average for the House, where only 43 per cent of the representatives had had experience in 1951.[50]

The dominant economic interests are deeply involved in the operations of the Republican party. But the party is so loose an organization that it is not possible for the interests to gain control over the legislature just by getting control of the political organization of the party. The process is much more diffuse than that. But this fact should not rule out the framework of the Republican party as a relevant instrument of policy-making either in the legislature or in the

[49] I have no reason to believe that either of these senators ever behaved in any but the most ethical manner, but the fact is that some men of easy virtue in such positions do not find it possible to differentiate between their employer's welfare and the public welfare. During my tenure as a state senator and in the course of hundreds of interviews with other legislators I was often impressed by the dubious ambivalence of loyalties—or as Washington now phrases it "conflict of loyalties"— which led legislators to neglect their public trust for personal aggrandizement.

[50] The dean of the Senate is a Democrat, Jean C. Boucher, from the city of Lewiston. Boucher has been serving since 1933, an unusual record.

administrative structure of the state. On occasion it is possible for the leadership of the party—assuming the leaders themselves are reasonably in agreement—to appeal to the party spirit of the Republican membership of the legislature. A few times in a session this appeal will bear fruit, but repeated use is of no avail. Legislators chosen in primaries do not necessarily respond to a loose and disjointed state organization that has no particular means of disciplining them. There were rumors in 1955 of threats being made against non-conforming Republicans—threats that campaign assistance would be denied in the next election, for example. But the disciplinary power of the organization is so meager that discipline in the sense that it applies in Connecticut, for example, is out of the question.

The Republican membership of the legislature caucuses only infrequently, although the formal legislative leaders meet often with the governor, when he is a Republican, to discuss and decide legislative strategy. In the House a Republican policy committee comprised of 16 county delegation chairmen provides an element of leadership in conjunction with the majority leader and the speaker. As compared with the three states of southern New England, party leaders can do little to hold their party following in line on roll-call votes. This is not surprising since there is so much multifactionalism in Maine politics and so little discipline. As the data in Table 12 indicate, there are not many roll-call votes and not a great deal of unity in party voting on the Republican side, although on the Democratic side there is considerable unanimity.

TABLE 12

Party Cohesion in the Maine Legislature for Selected Sessions*

| | TOTAL ROLL CALLS | | NUMBER OF VOTES WITH MAJORITIES OPPOSED | | SENATE | | HOUSE | |
| | | | | | *Average index of cohesion for roll calls with majorities opposed* | | | |
YEAR	Sen.	House	Sen.	House	Repub.	Dem.	Repub.	Dem.
1931	†	7	†	3	†	†	38	45
1937	14	8	6	4	39	96.5	46.5	69
1951	11	12	7	9	24.7	94.	50.5	73.5

* The measure here is the "index of cohesion" explained in Chapter 3. See p. 71.

† In 1931 there were no Democrats in the Senate and therefore no calculations were made for the Senate in that year.

There are not many roll-call votes demanded in Maine, as Table 12 indicates, although it takes but one-fifth of those present to call for a show-down vote. Since roll calls are so sparse, no sweeping generalizations are feasible from the limited data.

There are at least some suggestive inferences to be made from these data, however. First, there is a greater unanimity among the Democrats than among the Republicans. This probably reflects the greater similarity among the hardy band of Democrats who manage to get into the legislature—most of them are urban representatives, whereas the Republicans are both urban and rural. Second, more than half the roll calls of these sessions (combining both the House and Senate votes) produced majorities of the two parties lined up on opposite sides of the question (55 per cent, to be exact). No doubt the relatively high incidence of majority-opposed roll calls reflects the Democratic tendency to demand a roll call only on an issue where they believe they can embarrass the majority. The brief résumé below of the kinds of issues on which the majorities of the parties took opposite sides confirms this, since the greatest proportions of the roll calls came on matters of taxation, always a distasteful task for a majority party to have to face. In this listing the votes in both the House and the Senate are combined, there being no particular difference in the distribution of issues between the two.

Issues on which majorities of parties opposed	Per cent of total majority opposed issues
Taxation	62.0%
Party organization or elections	13.8
Local questions	6.9
Welfare	3.5
Business regulation	3.5
Miscellaneous	10.3
	100.0%

In the last analysis the multifactionalism of Maine's Republican party has a considerable significance for the policy-making process. The kind of contests over policy which might be highlighted in open-party controversy in a two-party state simply slide by unnoticed or dissolve before campaign time. Even the opportunity to present opposing sides of a question, which is sometimes conceivable in a bifactional arrangement—such as that of Vermont or New Hampshire—is not present in Maine. The Democrats may in time pull themselves up by their own bootstraps to constitute a formidable opposition party, but they have not yet reached the stage where they can challenge the Republicans beyond an occasional gubernatorial victory. A Democratic governor's hands are tied so firmly by the governmental and political structure that his accomplishments are at best limited. Only when the opposition party can move into the legislative arena to affect basic policies will the predominant authority of the Big Three be successfully challenged.

CHAPTER 5

--- ★ ---

MASSACHUSETTS: THE STANDING ORDER
UNDER ATTACK

ALEXIS DE TOCQUEVILLE found it hard to understand how America got along without an aristocracy, but he was certain that one did not exist and that the development of one was unlikely. In this as in so many things he was dead right; not even the outraged C. Wright Mills calls our "Power Elite" an aristocracy.[1] The perquisites and preferments of noble birth have nothing to do with American political and social development. Short of inherited state-recognized status, however, the role of famous first families varies from place to place: in some states, family names do not mean a great deal; in others, first-family, blueblood status has great political significance. Probably none of these privileged groups has so conspicuous or well-heralded a place as the Boston Brahmins.

Indeed the seriousness of purpose, the power, and unquestioned accomplishments of the Brahmins may well have been obscured by the popular view of them gleaned from unending satirical literature at their expense. Bumbling, narrowminded, and foolish some of them may have been, but many others were not. The fortunes made by Massachusetts' first families in the days of the clipper ships, in the mills, and in shrewd industrial investments were put into trust funds to be preserved and multiplied. This money set the basis for power which a carefully nurtured sense of superiority and responsibility brought to fruition.

The once predominant position of the select few has declined as more and more compromises have to be made toward the newer elements who have risen to power. But no group which has as many banking, business, and political ties as the Massachusetts aristocracy is suddenly going to be without power. Cleveland Amory, who drew a shrewd portrait in *The Proper Bostonians*, denies that the political position of the old order is wrecked: "The Proper Bostonian

---

[1] *The Power Elite*, New York, 1956, p. 278-279.

maintains, for example, that he has lost all political influence. 'Look at Mayor Curley,' he says. The outsider looks and he sees Mayor Curley, but he also notices Governor Robert P. Bradford of Mayflower Ancestry, two Senators by the names of Leverett Saltonstall and Henry Cabot Lodge, and a battery of Coolidges, Codmans, Curtises, Parkmans and Wigglesworths, all of whom have been extremely successful in the political line."[2]

In politics it is no fortuitous accident that the first families are Republican. They are for the most part conservatives in the best sense of the word. As they provided leadership in the days when John Adams wrote the present state constitution and as they provided the leadership of the old Federalist party, so now they provide the backbone of the conservative leadership of the state. It is true that from time to time a few of the elect have taken up the cause of radicalism: for example, Brooks Adams in the 1917-1919 Constitutional Convention.[3] Another exception to the rule is Endicott Peabody, of sterling background, who was an All-American football player at Harvard, and who turned up as a Democratic member of the Governor's Council in 1955. But they *are* exceptions.

Powerful as the standing order may be through its prestige and interlocking directorates and family trusts, it lacks one element which its major opponents have in abundance—numbers. Even in a democracy numbers may not be an absolute necessity to political power, but numerical strength does also imply power.

The opposition to the standing order is represented by the Irish- and Italian-led urban masses in the Democratic party. The forte of this element is precisely numbers. They vastly outnumber not only the first-family elite but also the rural-Yankee-suburban elements that are allied with the first families. Indeed, if the Democratic party could actually muster all the potential might of the immigrant and second- and third-generation population, Massachusetts would long since have become a one-party Democratic state. Most of the worker-"foreign-stock"-Catholic population of the state is Democratically inclined, and Massachusetts is one of the most industrialized, Catholic, and non-Yankee states in the nation. On the strength of these facts the state has become a highly competitive two-party state. The

[2] Cleveland Amory, *The Proper Bostonians*, Boston, 1947, p. 345.

[3] John A. Hague, "The Massachusetts Constitutional Convention 1917-1919," 27 *New England Quarterly*, 147-167 (June 1954) at pp. 158-160.

character and quality of the Democratic leadership has much to do—as we shall see later in this chapter—with the fact that the fullest possibilities of the Democratic vote have not been realized; yet the significant thing is that the Democrats have a considerable vote and therefore comprise a formidable opposition party.

The kinds of interests that ally themselves with the two parties, the quality and outlook of the respective leadership cadres of the parties—these are important in understanding the politics of the state. But one other highly important element is necessary for understanding: that Massachusetts has become a two-party state. The parties are different in their composition and to a degree in ideology, and they are in sharp competition. That the opposition is always looking for an opening for an argument on which to base the next campaign—and the fear that they may make good at it—this ever-present pressure is often a decisive element in the process of policy-making in Massachusetts.

The Democratic Party: Liberalism in Moderation

The emergence of the Democratic party as a competitor in Massachusetts politics was a slow process. There as in other states of southern New England, the extent of industrialization and the heavy waves of immigration seem to have predestined the rise of the Democratic party. In all three states the percentage of the population either foreign-born or second generation born of foreign parents comprised more than two-thirds of the population in 1920 in contrast to slightly more than one-third as a national average.[4] Localized Democratic victories began back in the nineteenth century, but not until 1928 did the fullest political impact of immigration and industrialization appear.

The handwriting on the wall appeared in 1884 when an Irish-Catholic became mayor of Boston. This victory was not only the result of Boston's having become one of the largest enclaves of Irishmen anywhere in the world, but also the ultimate political harvest of the nearly unbelievable circumstances under which immigrant workers had had to live. In the nineteenth century starva-

---

[4] E. P. Hutchinson, *Immigrants and Their Children, 1850-1950*, New York, 1956, p. 27. The percentages were Rhode Island 70.7, Massachusetts 67.6, Connecticut 66.9, and the United States as a whole 38.4. Rhode Island and Massachusetts ranked one-two in the nation as to the proportion of "foreign-stock" (first- and second-generation people), North Dakota was third, and Connecticut fourth.

121

tion wages were the lot of most Massachusetts immigrant workers; only the highly skilled workman could gain anything like a decent living. Oscar Handlin points out that the employers of Boston could keep wages low because of the abundance of labor. In New York in 1860 workers were scarce and could earn $8.00 to $10.00 a week; their counterparts in Boston got only $4.50 to $5.50.[5] Company towns were organized by the owners of mills to house their workers, and the housing investment was made to pay since in many cases the workers were not paid in cash but in orders on the company store where goods were exorbitantly priced. It was not uncommon for textile workers to earn as little as $1.75 a week during the 1840's. "One Holyoke manager found his hands 'languorous' in the early morning because they had breakfasted. He worked them without breakfast and was gratified to find that they produced three thousand more yards of cloth each week."[6] Meanwhile in the counting house large dividends were being distributed to the owners—as high as 14 per cent in some textile mills. The coming of the Industrial Revolution is never easy on those whose labor brings it to fruition, and in Massachusetts it seems to have been a particularly painful process. The resentments thus created had far-reaching political implications.

The Democratic party was the beneficiary and its opponents the losers as a result of the antagonism aroused by industrial conditions. Apparently in anticipation of trouble, the mill owners in 1857 kept some of their "hands" from voting by making literacy a prerequisite of suffrage. Before the end of the century, however, Irish Democrats began winning mayoralty elections in isolated industrial towns here and there, and the Democratic party began winning occasional gubernatorial elections as well. In the three annual elections from 1890 onward the Democrats elected governors, partly due to deep division within the Republican party. In 1904 a more formidable

[5] Oscar Handlin, *Boston's Immigrants, 1790-1865*, Cambridge, 1941, p. 83. See also Handlin's graph on p. 91 where the inadequacy of wages of the average workman is contrasted with estimated minimal expenses for a family of four.

[6] Works Progress Administration, *Massachusetts*, Boston, 1937, p. 70. The catalogue of industrial horrors of the mid-nineteenth century is ghastly and nearly endless. In this period women worked an 80-hour week for as little as $1.25, of which 75 cents was taken for board. To show how extreme this was, consider the fact that skilled labor was then earning as much as $1.25 to $1.50 a day, which was said to have been only a minimal living for a family. See Albert B. Hart (ed.), *The Commonwealth History of Massachusetts*, New York 1930, Vol. 4, p. 418. Child labor was also common, although in 1867 Massachusetts did outlaw the employment of children under *ten years of age. Ibid.*, p. 419.

kind of Democratic victory occurred, an election won with the vigorous support of organized labor.

Beginning in 1910 the Democrats won five annual gubernatorial elections in succession. Part of this was due to the splitting off of the Bull Moose Progressives; this was particularly true in 1913 when David Ignatius Walsh became the first Irish Catholic to occupy the governor's chair. Walsh went on to the Senate in 1918 and the Republican party resumed its control of the situation until another Democrat from the western part of the state won the governorship— Governor Joseph B. Ely in 1930. Yet between 1900 and 1928 the median Republican percentage of the two-party vote for governor was 54.1 per cent.

The election of 1928 electrified the Democratic party in Massachusetts. The candidacy of Al Smith, one-time fish-market worker from the East Side of New York City, Irish Catholic, and a liberal of sorts, hit home with the Catholic-worker elements of the state. Since 1928, as Figure 8 indicates, the Democrats have had the edge in Presidential politics in the state, winning consistently until 1948. Between the 1928 election and President Eisenhower's victory in 1956, the median Democratic vote was 52.4 per cent. But a different picture emerges in the races for the governorship, where the Democrats have won eight of the fifteen elections with a median percentage of 50.3.

Why the difference between state and national Democratic success in Massachusetts? The quality and prestige of Republican candidates have much to do with this, but other factors are also involved. For one thing, the Democratic party in Massachusetts has never been able to present the united front that its opponents do; it is more divided geographically and its leadership has in general less prestige and less authority than the Republican leadership. The questionable behavior of some Democratic officials, grave enough to involve several jail sentences for Congressmen, ex-governors, mayors, and others, has not enhanced the party's chances.[7]

Measuring the effectiveness of a political party organization in a two-party state is a difficult process. It is difficult enough in the one-

[7] The incarceration of former Governor, Congressman, and Mayor James M. Curley is a well-known story. Others like Congressman Thomas J. Lane have hardly been an asset to the party. Lane won renomination for Congress in 1956 two weeks after being released from the Danbury Federal prison, having been there after conviction for tax evasion. (See *New York Times*, Sept. 19, 1956.)

party states, but in the confused in-fighting of the two-party states it is very hard to decide how much credit or blame is to be assessed for the organizational factor. If we compare the three states of lower New England, however, we find the Massachusetts party organizations are weaker than those of Rhode Island and Connecticut. But if we include other two-party states in the comparison, the Massachusetts parties seem a good deal stronger than those of most states.

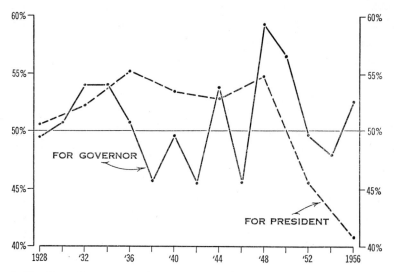

8. Two-Party State: Massachusetts Democratic Percentage of the Two-Party
for President and Governor (1928-1956)

If we draw an imaginary vertical line along which we place the party organizations of the two-party states from the least powerful at the bottom to the most powerful at the top, Massachusetts would probably be placed in the top quarter. It is hard to speculate about the placement of other states in such a spectrum since not much effort has been given to such analysis of state organizations, but it would seem that the organizations of New York, New Jersey, Pennsylvania, and Indiana would also be among the category of powerful parties.

The fact that the Massachusetts party organizations are weaker than those of her two neighbors to the south probably has a good deal to do with the party primary and its impact on the organization. Connecticut and Rhode Island ignored the pleas of the advocates of the primary so successfully that they were the last two states to adopt a primary in any form. Such long delay probably reflected the strength of the parties in those states, but the fact that there was long delay has tended further to enhance the power of the organizations, the only way up the ladder being through the organizations. Massachusetts was not far behind the innovators in taking up the primary in 1911. Some suggestion of the impact of the primary is seen in the increase in the number of uncontested seats in the legislature between 1908 and 1948. V. O. Key found that the number of single-member district seats that went by default increased from 19 per cent to 42 per cent.[8]

More than the primary has been involved in the gradual weakening of the party organizations of Massachusetts. This is suggested, if by nothing else, by the fact that the Democratic and Republican parties have not responded similarly under the impact of the primary. The Republican organization has in general withstood the winds of divisiveness that seem to blow from the primary, but the Democratic organization has been ripped apart by it. The Democratic organization is much less able to make its decisions stick, is more divided regionally, and more given to battles of personality.

The Democratic organization in fact seems at times to be nothing at all. Something called the Jefferson-Jackson Day Committee often has more money and apparently more power than the state committee itself. Personal organizations are numerous and various strong men often go their own way without regard for other candidates in a campaign. In a good many areas, particularly in the small Republican towns, there is no Democratic organization of any kind. In some smaller urban centers where there are Democratic majorities, the party organization may practically give way to labor groups who do most of the work of campaigning. The lack of constant contact between the central party and the local units has tended to result in the atrophy of some local units, and if the central organization has not atrophied it has certainly suffered badly from weakness born of internal division.

In truth the Democratic party seems to be two parties—a Boston

---

[8] Key, *American State Politics*, p. 190. In 1954 a total of 67 members of the House won by default, counting single-member and multiple-member seats together. Of these 43 were Democrats and 24 Republicans; that is, the Republicans put up 43 fewer candidates than they were entitled to and the Democrats 24. In all, 28 per cent of the seats were in effect uncontested, a somewhat lower figure than Key's, but he was calculating for *only* the single-member districts.

party and a western Massachusetts party. The largest single concentration of Democrats in Massachusetts is in Boston and its immediate environs. V. O. Key has analyzed the tendency of the Boston division of the party to control statewide nominations. The trend, as Table 13 (Key's table reproduced) indicates, has been toward a greater and greater proportion of the nominees for statewide office to be from the Boston area. "In the first decade of the century [prior to the enactment of a statewide primary law] only one out of four Democratic nominees for [statewide office] resided in Boston and vicinity. . . . By a slow but steady movement Boston Democrats after the introduction of the primary increased their proportion of the nominations to 82.9 per cent for the decade 1942-1952."[9] Key

TABLE 13

Trend in Residence of Democratic Nominees for
Statewide Office in Massachusetts, 1900-1952

Period	*No. of nominees**	*From Boston and vicinity†*		*Elected‡*	
		#	*%*	*#*	*%*
1900-1911	72	18	25.0	3	4.2
1912-1920	56	26	46.4	11	19.6
1922-1930	34	15	44.1	6	17.6
1932-1940	32	21	65.6	17	53.1
1942-1952	41	34	82.9	22	53.7

Source: American State Politics, by V. O. Key, Jr., p. 155. Used with the kind permission of the author and Alfred A. Knopf, publisher.

* Includes nominees for all statewide elective offices and for the United States Senate since 1916.

† Includes Suffolk County, Cambridge, Medford, and Somerville.

‡ That is, percentage of all Democratic nominees elected, not of those from Boston and vicinity only.

also points out that the shift in geographic location of the nominees, and with it the power in the state organization, was not a mere reflection of the changing location of the Democratic vote. "In fact," he says, "the division of the Democratic vote between Boston and vicinity and the rest of the state remained fairly constant."[10] In the period 1913-1920 as in 1942-1952 the average percentage of the Democratic primary vote from Boston and vicinity stayed at just over half the total vote, and the Boston and vicinity contribution to

[9] *Ibid.*, p. 154.   [10] *Ibid.*, p. 157.

the total general election vote stayed fairly constant at about one-quarter of the whole.

Boston is important to the Democrats, but the party must also depend on other large urban centers. This is illustrated by the results of Paul Dever's 1950 campaign for governor. There were seventeen cities of over 50,000 population in the state as of the 1950 census, comprising 50.2 per cent of the total population; from these Dever drew 64.4 per cent of his total vote. (His Republican opponent got 47.7 per cent of his vote from the same cities.) Democratic candidates count on losing heavily in the rural towns and in the many suburban towns, some of which have very large populations, and therefore the western cities are vitally important. It would seem that under these circumstances the party's leadership might have been anxious to get a few more outlanders on the ticket from time to time to let the hinterland know that Boston was still interested in something besides Boston. But in all the battles to provide a pre-primary convention to recommend statewide slates, the Democratic leadership was anti-convention. Governor Dever vetoed a pre-primary convention bill in 1951 after a Republican and Italian Democratic combination got it through the legislature.

Perhaps as a partial consequence of the Boston-versus-the-rest dichotomy in the Democratic party the state chairman has usually been an errand boy rather than a power in the party (in contrast with Connecticut, for example). He has virtually no patronage power, that being the province of the governor, and his tenure is usually brief, not relatively permanent as it tends to be in both Rhode Island and Connecticut. Note, for example, the year-long effort in 1955 to decide which of the two pretenders was the chairman. John C. Carr of Medford near Boston had presumably been elected by the 80-member state committee in 1952, but William H. Burke, a western Massachusetts onion farmer, contested Carr's position after being named chairman by a rump session of the committee. Ultimately the courts settled the question in Burke's favor, but even so he lasted only a year, being ousted by the 1956 convention and replaced by a former mayor of Somerville, John C. Lynch.

The chairmanship does not amount to much in any event, the real leadership being assumed by a few prominent officeholders or former officeholders. In the early days of the "new" Democratic party, such men as David I. Walsh and Joseph B. Ely, both from the western part of the state, and James Michael Curley of Boston were the actual leaders. Walsh and Curley fought each other for decades, although they never appeared on the ticket opposite each other. Walsh was the first Irish Catholic to become governor of the state (1916-1919); from there he went on to the United States Senate (1919-1947), where he remained with one brief interruption almost the rest of his life. Relatively liberal during his terms as governor, Walsh was a moderate in the Senate on all things except foreign policy, where his strong isolationism often put him in opposition to the British, a fact which only further cemented his relations with the Irish population of the state. Walsh was in many ways typical of the successful Massachusetts Democrat. Like Senator John Kennedy today, he was moderate enough to capture some Yankee support, which seems to be a necessity for long tenure. Such personal popularity does not carry with it control over the Democratic organization, however; it merely establishes the man as one among many leaders.

Curley is a different story—indeed he is a long story in himself. Politics has been his whole life from the time he emerged as a ward leader at the very beginning of this century until the present. Loved and hated with equal passion, seeking improvement for the down-trodden, using his charm and wit with a flourish, Curley was a hard man to beat. Adept at turning even adversity to his advantage, he has been one of the most colorful politicians of the century. Even two jail sentences and a court order to repay some $42,000 in misused funds did not ruin his career. Although there is some literary disguise involved, it is obvious that one of the best political novels of this decade—*The Last Hurrah*—is about Curley. Edwin O'Connor, the novelist, presents a highly sympathetic picture of a man who knew exactly what Irish aspirations were and also how to make the most of his Irish background, whether at a wake or in a public speech.[11] Curley was as adept as his fictional prototype, Frank Skeffington, in playing the role of the man dedicated to helping the un-

---

[11] Curley is quoted in *Life* (Sept. 10, 1956, pp. 120-138) referring to *The Last Hurrah* as "that book about me." He thought it omitted too many of his virtues. Not satisfied to leave his portrait to fiction, Curley went on to write his autobiography. He might well have left matters as they stood, for he boasts about all his feats, admirable and unscrupulous alike, with the inevitable result that the rather charming impression left by O'Connor is completely undone. Who doubts this judgment should read, *I'd Do It Again*, Englewood Cliffs, N.J., 1947.

derprivileged, but it was a role that he never succeeded in playing well much beyond the confines of his native Boston. Although Curley ran three times for governor, he made it only once. Nor did he fare any better when he sought to go to the United States Senate in 1936—he was defeated in that very Democratic year by "Little Boy Blue," as he called him: Henry Cabot Lodge. Yet Curley's power within Boston was sufficient to make him mayor for four terms, congressman for four terms, and a power in the state party for the better part of two generations. He continues to be popular with untold thousands of Boston people, a fact illustrated by his appointment (in his 83rd year) as a labor relations commissioner by Governor Foster Furcolo in 1957.

Comparisons between Curley and Huey Long were inevitably made during Curley's swashbuckling term as governor. One reporter said that "eighteen thousand state employees dare not speak out against the governor. . . . Camp followers are in charge of police departments, the state's educational system, civil service, public works, and all available judicial and administrative positions. The right to pardon criminals has been invested in Curley's controlled council and is exercised freely. With quick coups and an iron hand, he has usurped the power of all public officials and centered it in himself."[12] In retrospect, however, it is clear that Curley never had anything comparable to Huey Long's nearly undisputed power. If for no other reason, Curley's reign was too short to qualify him as a native dictator. The accusations, scandals, and rumors about his administration meant the end of Curley as a serious statewide candidate; he won statewide nomination twice again but never an election.

It is interesting to compare Curley with some of the more successful demagogues of the South. Like him, they play upon hatreds, fears, and insecurity. Bilbo and Rankin, for example, successfully appealed to Mississippi hill-country farmers with strong anti-Negro speeches; Curley talked to the Irish about the deprivations visited upon them by the rich Republicans who were the owners of the businesses for which they worked. He ranted about the Ku Klux Klan, an organization which never amounted to much in Massachusetts, but the Klan was anti-Catholic and therefore a good whipping boy. In his first campaign for governor (1924) he made

[12] Joseph F. Dineen, "The Kingfish of Massachusetts," 173 *Harper's Magazine* 343-357 (Sept. 1936) at p. 343.

an issue of supposed anti-Catholic discrimination against him. On several occasions when he spoke, a cross appeared burning on a nearby hillside, and when it would flash up Curley would say: "There it burns, the cross of hatred and not the cross of love, upon which Our Lord Jesus Christ was crucified, the cross of human avarice and hate and not the cross of Christian charity."[13] Some people charged at the time of these incendiary performances that Curley's own henchmen had set the crosses blazing, but no one could prove it. But Curley with devastating candor in his autobiography admits that they were self-arranged "stage props," and he went on to name two of his "fire-lighters."[14]

Demagoguery was as important to Curley as to any of the Southern Negro-baiters, but the significant thing is that he failed to make a success of it beyond the confines of his own vicinity. He could not build a statewide career on it as Long, Tillman, Talmadge, Bilbo, and many others did. That Massachusetts is a two-party state is unquestionably a factor in Curley's failure, although the animosities played on by the Southerners were different in degree and depth from those which Curley used.

Still, it was not by demagoguery alone that Curley carved out his niche in Massachusetts politics. His support of liberal-labor causes helped. He got a reputation for getting things done, for slicing through the barriers of red tape or tradition that restrained others. His boodling he turned to an asset by nourishing a legend that he was a modern Robin Hood. Tongue-in-cheek, he said in his autobiography that "Maladministration is intolerable when there are no civic improvements to show for a drained treasury."[15] His charm was such that he made a lasting impression on anyone he met. Many thousands apparently voted for him with the feeling that they "knew him personally."[16]

Curley has had no successor. Even granting that like Huey Long he was *sui generis*, it is significant that the Democrats who defeated him were cut from an entirely different pattern. Moderation and

---

[13] *Ibid.*   [14] See *I'd Do It Again*, p. 183.   [15] *Ibid.*, p. 125.

[16] Jerome S. Bruner and Sheldon J. Korchin, "The Boss and the Vote: Case Study in City Politics," 10 *Public Opinion Quarterly* 1-25 (spring 1946). They calculated by sampling methods that as many as 11,000 voters in Boston felt moved to vote for Curley for mayor in the 1945 campaign because they "knew him personally." P. 17. Curley died November 12, 1958, after this was written, and, true to pattern, a crowd estimated at one million people turned out for the funeral.

avoidance of the kind of demagoguery that carried Curley along have been the characteristics of such men as Maurice Tobin and John Hynes, for example, both of whom defeated Curley in races for the mayoralty of Boston.

Aside from Curley, who is a type apart, there seem to be two types of successful Democratic politicians in Massachusetts—the moderate man of honesty, prestige, and ability; the men of small attainment who employ the looseness of the organization and confusion of the electorate to ride into power on their eye-catching names. In the first category are men like Senator Kennedy, whose intellectual abilities, idealism, and unquestioned prestige have put him in the Senate at a tender age. The Kennedy family must be one of the richest in the state, able, for example, to give huge sums to charity.[17] The family association with the Democratic party is one of long-standing tradition. The senator's father, Joseph P. Kennedy, served as ambassador to England, and his grandfather, John F. "Honeyboy" Fitzgerald, was once a Democratic mayor of Boston. The family wealth no doubt accounts for the relatively conservative position in the party that most Kennedys have occupied—a position that the present Senator seems to come to naturally, as evidenced by the great support for him from the South in his dramatic bid for the vice-presidential nomination in 1956.

Foster Furcolo, elected governor in 1956, falls into the same general category—a moderate liberal with the good fortune to have both Italian and Irish ancestors. Although he ran in a primary against Thomas H. Buckley, a former state auditor with a well-known Irish vote-getting name, he won handily. When Furcolo was in Congress representing a district comprising Springfield, he attracted attention as a liberal and an able legislator. But along the way he took pot shots at the dangers to the Democratic party of the Americans for Democratic Action, a move not calculated to ruin him with the many Irish who later were to admire Senator McCarthy for his anti-Communist crusade. When Furcolo came to the governorship in 1957, one of his first actions was to request a state sales tax to cover the increasing costs of state government. This he did

---

[17] The family as of 1956 had given $2,609,000 to the archdiocese of Boston through the Joseph P. Kennedy, Jr. Foundation, established in memory of the senator's brother, who was killed as a navy flyer in World War II. See *Christian Science Monitor*, Feb. 10, 1956.

notwithstanding the anti-sales tax pledge of the Democratic platform on which he had been elected. Among the first to agree with his proposal was his Republican predecessor in office, Christian Herter.

The other type of successful Democratic politician has thrived on the party primary. The foremost stock-in-trade of these politicians is their name. Take the case of State Treasurer John F. Kennedy. Treasurer Kennedy is not related to Senator Kennedy, but the similarity of names has been the former's entree into politics. An obscure employee of a razor-blade company, he defeated the 1954 state convention endorsee in the primary. The Democratic State Committee "swallowed its astonishment" and supported him in the general election, saying his success was "typically American," adding that he had caught the "imagination and interest" of his fellow-citizens. His election, they added, would "afford proof that in Massachusetts democracy works and that Americans invariably draw their best talent for leadership from the rank and file of the people."[18] However "happy" the committee was with John Kennedy's success in 1954, they were unwilling to endorse him for reelection in 1956. The endorsement went to Clement A. Riley. Although still another Kennedy (J. M.) got in the race, John F. won again. Accused of trading on the name of the senator, the treasurer replied that, being older, he had had the name first. Apparently some voters actually do confuse the two people. A reporter once told me that on election day he had asked people on the street about the contest for treasurer and found some who told him something like this: "I don't know why the Senator wants to be treasurer too, but he's a good man and it's all right with me if he wants both jobs."

Hurley is another vote-drawing name traded on by aspiring nonentities. Since 1930 a highly confusing series of contests have been waged among such Hurleys as Francis X., Charles F., Joseph L., William E., and James M. As in open-substitution football, it may take even more than a score card to keep the players straight, a fact not overlooked by those who capitalize on the confusion.[19]

One of the best tests of a party organization is its ability to choose

[18] Quoted by Key in *American State Politics*, p. 216.
[19] The Republicans have had their problems with Charles L. Burrill and Fred J. Burrell, but the greater strength of the Republican organization has kept the situation more in hand than in the Democratic party. (*Ibid.*, pp. 162-163.)

candidates. Here the distinction between the Democratic and Republican organizations in Massachusetts is revealing. The data in Table 14 suggest that the Republicans are much more effective than the Democrats at ruling out nuisance challenges. Before the introduction of the pre-primary convention the Republicans had some troubles too, since the "word" could not be passed so authoritatively without a convention. Actually the Republicans had an "informal grass-roots" convention in 1952, even before the convention law was passed in 1954. Notice the sharp drop in number of Republican candidates between 1950 and 1952. The convention also trimmed the number of Democratic candidates somewhat, but far less than in the Republican party.[20]

TABLE 14

Contests in Democratic and Republican Primaries
for Statewide Offices, 1950-1956

OFFICE	DEMOCRATS Number of candidates				REPUBLICANS Number of candidates			
	1950	1952	1954	1956	1950	1952	1954	1956
Governor	1*	1*	2	2	6	1	1*	1
Lt. governor	5*	6*	1	3	5	1	1*	1
Sec. of state	8*	1*	1*	2*	7	1	1	1
Treasurer	1*	7*	3	5*	2	2	1	1
Auditor	1*	1*	1*	1*	2	1	1	1
Attorney gen'l.	4*	4*	1	2	5	1	1*	1*
U.S. Senator	–	1	3	–	–	1*	1*	–

* In all races where incumbents were involved the * appears.

Regional divisions and personality conflicts have not been the only sources of disharmony in the Democratic party; ethnic rivalries play their part too. The long-dominant Irish leadership of the party is being challenged more and more by emerging Italian leaders. As Table 15 indicates, the Irish now are and in the past have been the largest single element in the Democratic party's leadership, but the number of Italian leaders is constantly increasing. The proportion of Italians in the legislature increased vastly in the half century, while the proportion of Irish was unchanged. Italian Democratic

[20] Further evidence of tighter Republican control is found in analysis of Congressional contests. In 1954 there were eight Democratic contests for 14 nominations, including one for an incumbent's seat. The Republicans had three contests, two involving incumbents.

legislators, it will be remembered, bolted the party line to vote for the pre-primary convention in hopes of greater recognition for major offices. There has been no particular evidence that the Democratic leadership was swinging around to support more Italian candidates, unless the candidacy of Italian-Irish Foster Furcolo is a case in point. Even if the convention were to back more Italians, the concentration of Irish voters in the Boston area would very likely support popular Irish Democrats, who would surely file against them.

TABLE 15

Irish and Italian Names in the
Massachusetts House of Representatives, 1900 and 1955

	1900				1955			
	Republicans		*Democrats*		*Republicans*		*Democrats*	
	#	%	#	%	#	%	#	%
Total								
representation	165	100.0	71	100.0	113	100.0	127	100.0
Irish names	2	1.2	33	46.5	5	4.4	59	46.5
Italian names	0	0.0	0	0.0	5	4.4	22	17.3
Other	163	98.8	38	53.5	103	81.2	46	36.2

To summarize, several distinguishing characteristics of the Democratic party in Massachusetts seem to stand out prominently. First, the party organization is relatively loose, although not so splintered as to be entirely without effectiveness. As data to be presented subsequently indicate, legislative party members stand together with a fairly high degree of cohesion when compared with most state legislative party delegations. Second, the divisions of the party reflect the basic facts of geography and social composition. That is, the divisions are often between Boston and vicinity and the western part of the state, and along ethnic lines. Although the Boston area contributes a heavy share of the Democratic vote in both primaries and general elections, much of the strength of the party comes from other large urban areas and from the workers and immigrant or immigrant-descended families of the state. (See scatter-diagram of Figure 9.) Third, although it might seem that the heavy "foreign-stock" population and the heavy industrialization of the state would assure a relatively liberal Democratic party, the fact is that the party takes its liberalism only in moderation. This is presumably associated with

134

the strength of the Republican party, the merits and prestige of the candidates it offers, and with the outlander's dislike of big-city politicians. Up to the present, at least, the Democratic politicians who have fared best have been relatively moderate in outlook— Walsh, Dever, Furcolo, and Kennedy, for example. Fourth, the party has in the last twenty-five years emerged from second-class status to a place of equality with the Republicans. In recent years its success in winning the governorship has been matched by an

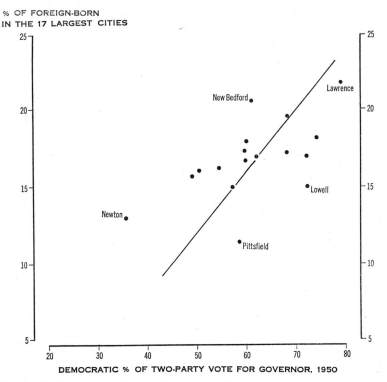

9. Foreign-Born Population and Democratic Vote in the Seventeen Largest Cities of Massachusetts, 1950

ability to carry most other statewide offices. It is true that only two Democrats have represented the state in the United States Senate in this century, but perhaps of even greater importance is the fact that the party since 1948 has been gaining strength in state legislature, where Democrats have been able to carry the House in four of five recent elections and to come very close in the Senate.[19a]

[19a] In 1958 a Democratic sweep finally gave the Democrats control of *both* houses of the General Court.

Massachusetts Republicans: Conservatism in Moderation

The story of Massachusetts Republicanism is one of graceful retreat on many fronts. Supreme and nearly unchallenged in the latter half of the nineteenth century, it began to have some competition as the immigrant waves poured in (up to as many as 100,000 coming into the state in one year).[21] The safe, comfortable conservatism of the age of industrial expansion was threatened not only by the Democratic vote at the polls but also by the split within the Republican party when the Bull Moose Progressive element began to make demands and to cause election losses. Indeed it was in great measure a consequence of Progressive pressure that a party primary law was passed in 1912 and that a constitutional convention was held to liberalize the framework of Massachusetts government.[22] The revised constitution was only superficially more liberal than its predecessor, but the old order was forced to make some concessions. The shift in orientation of the party did not come overnight, for Massachusetts Republicans of this era sent into national politics both Henry Cabot Lodge, Sr. and Calvin Coolidge, neither of whom will go down in history as radicals.

Still, the push was on, and the leadership was forced gradually to adapt the party credo and performance to the changing spirit of the times. Democratic victories after 1930 forced a more moderate kind of Republicanism to the fore, even though some diehards continued to agitate for a return to old virtues. Last-ditch conservatives like Basil Brewer, publisher of the *New Bedford Standard-Times*, rallied round Senator Taft in 1952 (Brewer's paper had supported Taft's candidacy in 1948 also), but the Eisenhower-Taft battle that was no battle in 1952 showed who controlled the Republican party in Massachusetts. In the Eisenhower camp were the vast majority of the big names of the party in Massachusetts, and accordingly Eisenhower carried about 70 per cent of the preference votes in the primary election.[23] Even conceding that there was more involved in the Eisenhower primary victory than rejection of ultra-conservatism—there were calculations then as later in the convention about who could win in November—this contest nevertheless showed

---

[21] See A. B. Hart, *op.cit.*, Vol. IV, p. 149.

[22] See John A. Hague, "The Massachusetts Constitutional Convention, 1917-1919," *op.cit.*

[23] See David, Moos, and Goldman, *op.cit.*, p. 84.

where the bulk of the party's present leadership and following stands. The moderate conservatism of Henry Cabot Lodge, Jr., Leverett Saltonstall, and Christian Herter is more typical of Republicanism in Massachusetts today than the philosophy of Basil Brewer. To say the least, the coming of the two-party system to Massachusetts had a profound effect on the Republican party.

Time has brought significant changes in the character of the organization, too; it has slipped from its one-time position of phenomenal power to a much weaker role. In the past the state convention did the nominating, and the powerful few were able without much interference to control the destinies not only of the party but of the state government. Such power no longer exists, but this does not mean that the organization has disintegrated entirely. As we have noted earlier, the Republican party organization is stronger than the Democratic in the state and stronger than most state party organizations around the country. It retains enough power to reward the faithful with promotion and to punish the recalcitrant by withholding promotion.

The methods of handling campaign finances by a party organization illustrate something of its strength. If the organization controls the purse-strings and not the individual candidate or his own personal committee, then it may be assumed that the organization counts, even if the payer of the piper may not call every tune. In the hard-fought campaign of 1954 most of the Republican money was spent by the state committee and little by organizations directly associated with the leading candidates. The reverse was true with the Democrats.

TABLE 16

The Candidate and the Organization:
Reported Campaign Expenditures in 1954

	Amount reported to secretary of state
Democratic state committee	$ 15,200
Murphy for governor committee	232,600
Furcolo for senator committee	49,600
Republican state committee	623,200
Saltonstall for senator committee	71,600
Herter for governor committee	85,400

Source: The League of Women Voters of Massachusetts, *Massachusetts State Government*, Cambridge, Mass., 1956, p. 331.

Roughly the same situation prevailed in the election of 1952.[24] Further evidence of the differences in the centers of gravity of the two parties is found in the manner in which money is handled within the organizations as such. The Republican party tends to collect money centrally and pass it down to the town committees for their use; in the Democratic party whatever is spent locally is usually collected locally too.[25] This is, of course, but a reflection of the greater centralization of the Republican party.

The position of the state chairman also seems to be stronger in the Republican than in the Democratic party, although in neither case does the chairman have the tenure and the power that he enjoys in Connecticut, for example. Far more power for directing the party appears to reside with the governor. Once a gubernatorial candidate is chosen he is usually conceded the power to decide whether the chairman is to be continued in power or replaced, much as the practice is, following presidential nominations.

Perhaps a good illustration of the difference in the Democratic and Republican organizations is the battle over the replacement of the state chairmen of the parties as the 1956 campaign began to get underway. In the Democratic party the affair could best be called a brawl all the way—at least as the press reported it, no doubt with some gleeful exaggeration. Statements and counter-statements to the press, accusations of falsehood mutually tossed back and forth, gave the dispute most of the elements of an Irish donnybrook, minus only the swinging of fists. There were threats of that too. While the Democrats were having their fracas, the heir apparent for the Republican nomination was carrying on a quiet war against the incumbent Republican chairman, but with a very different tone and with very different procedures. A dispatch to the *New York Times* illustrated the differences of approach. It noted that the Democrats had allowed the reporters in to hear their

[24] See the interesting and revealing article "Campaign Finance in Massachusetts," by Hugh D. Price in 6 *Public Policy* 25-46 (1955). The reported expenses of the Democratic and Republican state committees respectively were $441,491 and $1,058,501; similarly, Senators Kennedy and Lodge had various committees organized for their personal support and they spent respectively $350,292 and $58,266. See pp. 30, 37.

[25] *Ibid.*, p. 32. Price says that in 1952 "the local Republican committees relied almost exclusively on subventions from the state committee. The local Democratic committees were inactive in many communities, and the Democratic state committee reported no funds disbursed to any local committee." *Loc.cit.*

showdown on replacing their chairman; it then went on to describe the Republican methods: "Following a brief exchange of statements in the newspapers, a characteristic hush fell over the Republican headquarters. It has been the experience of political reporters in Massachusetts for years that the Republicans promote publicity, and hire press agents to carry out the program so long as it is favorable. Anything unfavorable is carefully thrashed out behind the closed doors of private social and dining clubs. The participants then walk out smiling at each other, each trying to ignore political knife handles protruding from their backs. So it was Tuesday night. . . . Reporters were barred from the meeting until after the balloting was finished. They were admitted in time to hear [the defeated chairman make] his valedictory."[26]

The chairman can exert a considerable influence in legislative matters which concern party policy in an organizational sense. The enactment of the pre-primary convention law was unusually important to the Republicans—desirous as they were of getting a better ethnic balance to their state tickets—and the following episode is an illustration of the effectiveness of the top leadership acting through the chairman.

During legislative consideration of the bill, one Boston newspaper reporter wrote that the bill "as now written follows exactly the pattern which Republican State Chairman Elmer Nelson laid down for the members of his party. The House has approved and the Senate went along with a minor, face-saving amendment offered by Senator Charles J. Innes of the Back Bay, Republican floor leader. Before the matter came before the Senate for its consideration, Innes was speaking of major amendments designed to make the proposed party conventions more democratic, small 'd.' However, he backed down and suggested only one amendment which will increase the number of delegates to the conventions by about 50 per cent. 'You have to bow to the majority,' said Innes after Republican Senators caucused and decided the pre-primary bill should be considered as a party measure. He had at first suggested that the bill

[26] *New York Times*, May 27, 1956. The defeated chairman's candor, an attribute that had helped him in trouble before, showed up in his parting remarks: "The chips are down now. We have lost three out of the last four elections for the House. Redistricting will be up next year and if it isn't Republican redistricting we'll be as long climbing back in again as the Democrats were. It took them 101 years." His fears were prophetic; in 1958 the Democrats did win power to redistrict.

should be amended to allow members of both parties to elect delegates to the convention which will indorse candidates."[27]

Table 14 shows how much more successful the Republicans were than the Democrats in making use of the pre-primary convention. When the whip cracked, those who had threatened primary contests actually did not initiate them. There was not a single convention nomination contested in 1954 and 1956 after the enactment of the law setting up the convention, and only one contest after the informal "grass roots" convention of 1952 (a convention held without benefit of legal sanction).[28] The Democrats had eight contests for statewide offices out of a possible 13 in the 1954 and 1956 primaries.

No doubt the Republican strategists who promoted the convention anticipated some such differential between the effectiveness of the parties in using the convention. The Democrats had a history of opposition to the convention, having got an earlier version of it repealed in 1937.[29] It was widely felt among Republicans that the solid Yankee slates they had been getting through their primary, reflecting the dominant element within the party, had become a detriment. In 1954 the slate was properly mixed, with two Jews, one Italian, and an Irish woman to accompany the three Yankees. The slate for 1956 was similarly "balanced": three Yankees, one French, one Italian, and one Jewish name.

How much effect the balancing of the tickets has had is hard to say. Some suggestion of the effect within the party, however, may be seen in the 1950 and 1952 primaries for state treasurer. There were two candidates for the office each time—indeed the same two— Fred J. Burrell and Roy C. Papalia. Burrell was an old-timer who had run in various primaries since 1919, having played the game

[27] *Boston Globe*, May 10, 1953. Instead of direct popular election of delegates the law finally provided for selection of delegates by local party committees, in the way that Nelson had suggested.

[28] Also illustrative is the fact that not since 1912 has there been a contest for delegates at large to a Republican national convention. Taft's followers threatened one in 1952 but such unseemly rebellion within the ranks was quelled before it came to an open primary contest. The Taft camp was given a couple of delegates at large; and thus compromised, the matter was dropped. See David, Moos, and Goldman, *op.cit.*, pp. 78-79.

[29] See Earl Latham, *Massachusetts Politics*, New York, undated, p. 27. Latham observes that in 1934 and 1936 when the law provided for the convention, the Democrats nominated "one Italian on what had been an all-Irish slate, and the Republicans put up Irish and French candidates."

of "Who's who?" in the typical Massachusetts manner. His "partner" had been Charles L. Burrill. Fred J. had had his successes and his troubles, once having been forced to resign when "the legislature initiated an inquiry looking toward impeachment proceedings. Banks had complained that to obtain deposits of state funds they needed to place their advertising through an agency designated by Mr. Burrell. The young treasurer denied any wrongdoing, and explained his resignation as an act of filial piety to save his aged mother from the pain of critical publicity."[30] Needless to say, it was Papalia whom the organization favored in both primaries, but this recognition could not be made so official in the first case, there being no convention to pronounce the benediction. In the 1950 primary Papalia got only 41 per cent of the vote, but in 1952, after the convention endorsement, he garnered 58 per cent.[31]

In general the composition of the Republican party is such that it requires some outside intervention to get non-Yankees to the fore on the state level, even though in local areas Swedes, Jews, or Italians may be the leaders. The actual proportion of Yankees in the state has declined to such a degree that a party trying to depend on them alone would be more ethnically pure than politically powerful.

More and more the Republican party is depending upon the middle class of all ethnic elements who are leaving the cities for the suburbs. This increasing dependence upon the suburbs is illustrated in the tendency of the party to draw its candidates from the eastern counties around Boston and not from western Massachusetts as it did early in the century. V. O. Key says this trend probably reflects the "movement of Yankees from Beacon Hill to the suburbs, but also it probably reflects a gain in capacity to win nominations by persons with a claim on considerable local concentrations of Republican voters."[32] Does this mean that in this two-party state there is something of the same "friends and neighbors" influence so common in the Southern one-party states? The analysis of the 1950 gubernatorial primary does not indicate that the "friends and neighbors" factor was decisive by any means, although it apparently has some

[30] Key, *American State Politics*, p. 162.
[31] See Chapter 12, "Ethnic Factors in New England Politics" for further analysis of the balanced ticket with specific reference to these campaigns.
[32] Key, *American State Politics*, p. 155.

TABLE 17

Trends in Residence of Republican Nominees for Statewide
Elective Office in Massachusetts, 1900-1952

Period	Total Nominees	From Boston		From eastern counties*		From western counties†	
		#	%	#	%	#	%
1900-1911	72	29	40.3	14	19.4	25	34.7
1912-1920	56	17	30.3	22	39.3	14	25.0
1922-1930	34	9	26.5	23	67.6	2	5.9
1932-1940	32	9	28.1	20	62.5	3	9.4
1942-1952	41	5	12.2	36	87.8	0	0.0

Source: American State Politics, by V. O. Key, Jr., p. 156. Used with the kind permission of the author and Alfred A. Knopf, publisher.

* Included in this category are nominees from Essex, Middlesex, Norfolk, Bristol, and Plymouth counties.

† This group of counties consists of Berkshire, Franklin, Hampshire, Hampden, and Worcester.

minor influence. The favored candidate was Arthur Coolidge; he won with a plurality of the vote (35.9 per cent) in a field of six candidates. Coolidge, from Middlesex County (near Boston), led in four of the five western counties as well as in four of the eastern counties, as Key describes them, losing Bristol County but adding Suffolk (most of which is Boston itself). While winning his own region (to suggest the possibility of "friends and neighbors") at the same time he won the regions most remote from his own territory. Only one of the candidates had anything like a locally restricted following, Clarence A. Barnes, from Bristol County. Barnes was a Taft man in 1952 and was considered a conservative candidate in 1950. He led in his own county and the Cape Cod, Martha's Vineyard, and Nantucket regions, which is not much of a victory since the population of these latter areas is negligible. The third major candidate, retired Admiral Louis Denfeld, also a Taft man in 1952, won 18.9 per cent of the total vote but he did not even win a plurality, let alone a majority, in his home county. He led in one western county and was a close second in his own county.

What do these facts suggest about the Republican organization? First, although the concentration of Republicans in the eastern suburban areas was an important contribution to Coolidge's victory, if he had not had substantial support in other areas far removed from the metropolitan area he probably could not have won. The blessings of the organization, although informally given, were more crucial than residence. Second, Barnes's success in his own region suggests something of a localized support, but the extent of it is limited at best. The fact that Denfeld, the second highest candidate, could not even win his own county also suggests something other

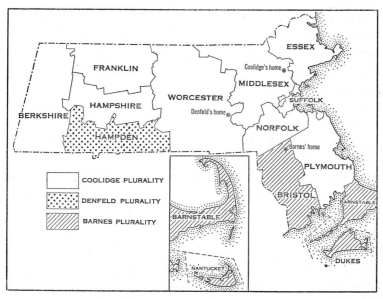

10. Massachusetts Republican Primary for Governor, 1950: Organization Strength over "Friends and Neighbors"

than a friendly local spirit to back a local man. All in all, effort to make the "friends and neighbors" explanation fit the facts will not work; other more persuasive forces were decisive.

There are three types of leaders who rise to positions of prominence in the party. The first is, of course, the Brahmin first-family type, who have contributed so much not only to the party but to the overall governance of the state. Second are what the vernacular refers to as "Swamp Yankees," those who are unmistakably Yankee but who lack social prestige and financial security. The third broad type are what Curley sometimes calls "the newer races," the Jews, Swedes, Italians, and even Irish who rise to positions of prominence on occasion.

First-family status is no prerequisite to a successful career in the Republican party, but it helps. The more successful Republicans of the last twenty years have all been of blueblood ancestry—Henry Cabot Lodge, Jr., Leverett Saltonstall, Robert Bradford, for example. Bradford, directly descended from William Bradford, who became governor of the Plymouth Colony in 1621, was governor from 1947 to 1949, having moved up from lieutenant governor's office from the previous term when he won election in an otherwise Democratic year. The successful careers of Lodge and Herter are well known. Perhaps no figure among the bluebloods in politics is more characteristic of the type than Leverett Saltonstall.

The Saltonstall ancestry traces back to the fourteenth century in England. The original American Saltonstall, Sir Richard, came to Massachusetts in 1630. The present senator is a wealthy man, the family fortunes having been made in railroad and real-estate speculation, mostly in the Midwest. Simple in his tastes, politically shrewd, he has through the years made himself an enviable record since he went to the General Court in 1923. After four terms he was speaker of the House, and in 1938 he beat Curley for the governorship. He entered the United States Senate in 1945.

A good party man, Saltonstall has been able to make the compromises that political expediency often requires; but he has taken an independent tack frequently enough to convince many voters that he is honest, conscientious, and dependable.[33] Although shy and early in his career a complete failure at speech-making, he gets along well in his personal relationships. One cannot help wondering how such a Yankee can draw votes from the Irish population of Boston as he does. In his last campaign in 1954 he was high man on the Republican ticket in Boston, running 16.8 per cent ahead of the average Republican vote in Boston for statewide offices; obviously a good many Democrats split their tickets for him. The only Irish member of the Republican ticket trailed Saltonstall by more than 30,000 votes in the city, notwithstanding the fact that Saltonstall was campaigning against Furcolo, whose Irish-Italian background was well known. Undoubtedly, Senator Kennedy's blunt refusal to endorse Furcolo had something to do with Saltonstall's large vote, but he has done well in Boston so many times that this factor is not the explanation of his success. Nor can his success be attributed

[33] On one occasion when a piece of boodle legislation was about to pass the House, over which he was presiding as speaker, Saltonstall took the gavel and left the floor in wrath. See Joseph F. Dineen, "Brahmin from Boston," 116 *New Republic* (Feb. 24, 1947) p. 14.

to the fact that he has found a Sullivan somewhere in his family tree which has entitled him to join the Charitable Irish Society.[34]

It is far more likely that his probity, the general efficiency of his administration, and his moderation in policy have been the main elements in Saltonstall's success in drawing votes from non-Republican sources. When he was governor he avoided condemnation of Roosevelt and even supported his foreign policy in several speeches. His record in labor matters was not that of a radical, but it was inoffensive enough to allow the CIO to support him in 1942. In the Senate he has been a moderate conservative, voting more conservatively than the bulk of the Democrats, to be sure, but more liberally than most of his fellow-Republicans. A record of Senate votes compiled by the AFL-CIO shows him below the average run of Republicans in the proportion of votes cast unfavorable to the desires of the labor group. The AFL-CIO tabulation of the votes of senators between 1947 and 1954 showed 36 Republicans who had been in office long enough to have cast at least 10 votes out of the 30 they took as an index of senatorial records. The median percentage of "wrong" votes among these 36 Republicans was 91 per cent, but Saltonstall's percentage was 85 per cent, lower than that of 23 of his colleagues. Interestingly he cast his "right" votes on questions of social welfare and domestic economic policy, not on labor matters.[35]

A second type of Republican of importance is the Yankee without high-born status, who has wealth or who for other reasons has made his way into a prominent position. A perfect example of this type is Sumner G. Whittier of Everett, northeast of Boston. A collateral descendant of the New England poet John Greenleaf Whittier, the present Whittier has sometimes been called a "swamp Yankee." Whittier is a young, affable, and energetic type, a former salesman who has advertised himself as a "three-decker Republican." The latter tag refers to his ownership of and residence in a three-story tenement which in the local patois has become a "three-

[34] John Gunther, *Inside U.S.A.*, has a brief sketch of Saltonstall's career from which some of my information is taken. See pp. 475-484.

[35] Committee on Political Education of the American Federation of Labor and the Congress of Industrial Organizations, "Voting Records of Senators and Representatives, 1947 through 1954." There were 11 other Republican senators in the listing who had cast less than 10 votes of the questions chosen. They are all excluded from these tabulations.

decker." This identification with the middle- and lower-income groups has been important to Whittier. He is popular with the party workers, so many of whom are middle-class suburban people. After serving in the state Senate, Whittier became lieutenant governor for two terms under Herter, and then sought the governorship in 1956. Some leaders were said to feel that he was too brash and too much a man of "three-decker" attitudes to be a proper Republican candidate for governor, but there was fear too that to deny him the endorsement of the convention would lead voters to conclude that "the GOP is a party of money which denies top honors to a 'three-decker candidate.' "[36] He was endorsed and without contest won the nomination. He failed, however, to defeat Furcolo in the general election.

Whether for reasons of social climbing, acquisition of wealth leading to conservative views, or disgust with occasional Democratic dishonesty, many of the foreign-stock groups in recent years have abandoned their usual association with the Democratic party. In addition, zealous efforts to attract such voters with balanced tickets and appointments of minority group leaders to patronage positions have put new faces and new names into the ranks of Republican leadership. For the most part the newcomers have not moved into the inner circle of leadership, but entry into even the outer circle was an exception to a long-established rule.

Among the most successful of the non-Yankees to move up in the party hierarchy is George Fingold, from the historic town of Concord. Fingold, who is a Jew, has been phenomenally successful in his three successive races for the office of attorney general. He sought but lost the Republican nomination for attorney general in 1950, coming in second of five (the other four being Yankees) with 30 per cent of the total vote to the winner's 35 per cent. In 1952 he ran uncontested in the primary with the backing of the informal pre-primary convention of that year. In that general election, running against an Irishman, he was the high man on the ticket, higher even than Eisenhower. His success may have been in part a result of charges of dishonesty leveled at his opponent, Francis E. Kelly, but his subsequent career disposes of any contention that his was a false victory. Victorious again in 1954, he was the lone Republican survivor of the Democratic sweep of state offices in 1956.

[36] *Christian Science Monitor*, Feb. 14, 1956.

There is no doubt that Fingold has been favored by Jewish voters in the state. Lawrence H. Fuchs presented evidence of this in his book, *The Political Behavior of American Jews.* Interviewing voters in the heavily Jewish Ward 14 of Boston, he found in the 1952 election that "of the 135 Jews who said they voted for Stevenson, at least 66.7 per cent crossed party lines to vote for George Fingold. . . ."[37] Still, this is in itself inadequate explanation of his success, for the proportion of Jews in the state is insufficient to count for that much. Fingold has won a reputation for efficiency and honesty on the job. He has the benefit of both Jewish support, as a "representative" of their ethnic aspirations, and of status derived from association with the elite of the state.[37a]

There are obvious similarities between the emergence of Fingold as a successful Republican and Furcolo as a successful Democrat. Both parties are beset with a similar problem: the leaders of the parties are being challenged by ethnic elements who feel they have been denied the opportunity to advance politically. The sharp differences in the character of the two-party organizations condition the manner of approach to the problem, of course. The Republicans lay down the line in the pre-primary convention to assert some control over those who would disrupt the party organization in a primary. In the Democratic party the non-Irish, non-Boston candidate comes to the fore by using the free-for-all tactics of the primary; in the Republican party the leadership arranges to put some ethnic representative on the ticket.

In short, the two-party organizations, although they operate under the same laws and seek to win elections from the same electorate, are remarkably different in approach and organization. This fundamental fact about Massachusetts politics will be further illustrated in the next chapter.

[37] Glencoe, Illinois, 1956, p. 142.

[37a] Fingold was in the campaign of 1958 as the party's candidate for governor, but suddenly on August 31 he died of a heart attack.

CHAPTER 6

———————————— ★ ————————————

LAWMAKING IN MASSACHUSETTS:
TRADITIONAL POMP AND POLITICAL
CIRCUMSTANCE

THE class distinctions implicit in the alignments of the parties of Massachusetts make for class politics of a sort in the legislature. The extent of these ideological differences, however, should not obscure one other basic fact about the General Court—that it remains one of the most orderly and well-conducted of our state legislatures. The battles of the parties and of liberal against conservative interests are fought out within a traditional framework that encourages rationality and democratic procedures. Before we measure the extent of party influence and examine the roles of various interests, it is necessary to say something about the procedures and, in a sense, the spirit of the institution.

Tradition is an important element of any democratic legislative body; habits of procedure once established are durable even beyond the point of utility at times. The traditional elements of Massachusetts legislative life are so ancient and august that one gets the feeling that the institution is even more tradition-oriented than those of other states. The General Court has an air of importance and decorum about it that resembles Congress or the House of Commons more than other state legislatures.

An illustration of tradition's role in the General Court is contained in the following tale of how the Senate handles the tabling of a bill. An oldtimer moved to table a bill and a newcomer asked whether, if he voted to table, he could later move to take it off the table. The president of the Senate answered affirmatively. His vote having been cast, the neophyte was told that not for two hundred years had anyone been so presumptuous as to move to take from the table what another had put there. The new member did not, of course, interfere with decorum.[1]

———

[1] This story was told me by James A. Travers, a reporter for the *Boston Record American*.

This atmosphere of reserve and decorum must unfortunately be set against other less admirable behavior. A *Life* photographer, for example, once caught one legislator giving another a "hot foot,"[2] and there have been instances of self-serving bills to grant large pensions for legislators, but such antics and borderline ethics seem to be the exception and not the rule. In general the competence, rationality, and efficiency of the Massachusetts General Court rank it with the best.

Along with two other New England states, Massachusetts uses a joint committee system, avoiding the waste of time involved in double hearings and separate House and Senate committee consideration of each bill. This works best when one party controls both houses, allowing one report to both houses after differences have been settled within the party family. In more recent years, when the Democrats have on occasion won the House, the operation of the joint committee system has been strained, but no insurmountable problems have arisen. The work load of the committees is tremendous. They have to consider literally thousands of bills every session under the Massachusetts system of "free petition," which means that any citizen can present a bill merely by getting the counter-signature of any member of the legislature, and such signatures are almost never refused. Unlike Congress and most other state legislatures the Massachusetts General Court does not permit bills to be killed by pigeon-holing them in committee; all bills must be reported out before the close of the session.[3] (In 1955 a total of 3,697 bills were introduced of which 933 were enacted.[4])

In 1954 Massachusetts made a faltering start on a legislative council to perform the function of general research on legislative problems. But the limits thus far placed on the council have kept it from performing the kind of role in analysis and recommendation on substantive policy issues that councils have come to assume in other states. The relative permanence of many legislative staff

[2] "Boston Hootfoot," 23 *Life* 34 (July 21, 1947).

[3] Thomas J. Wood says that in four successive sessions 7,400 bills went to committees and only two were not reported out. See his dissertation, "Distinctive Practices of the Massachusetts General Court" (unpublished), Harvard University, 1947. Mr. Wood's dissertation has an excellent analysis of the procedures of the General Court. See also Massachusetts League of Women Voters, *Massachusetts State Government*, Ch. 3, for a summary account of legislative procedure.

[4] The Council of State Governments, *The Book of the States, 1956-1957*, Chicago, 1955, p. 108.

workers[5] has perhaps not taken the place of council work, but the generally admitted excellence of the staff has been an important contribution to the efficiency and rationality of the General Court.

Although there are certainly exceptions, the general level of competence of the membership is high. The General Court has been the recruiting ground for higher office. W. E. Mullins, an able columnist and reporter for the *Boston Herald*, after commenting favorably on the talent in the 1953 session, went on to reminisce about the 1933 session which, he said, "produced more statesmen and prominent public servants of lesser distinction than any other in all the years." Along with Ambassador Lodge, Senator Salton-stall, Governors Herter and Dever, it also had in its ranks four future congressmen, eight judges, one state treasurer, and several others of lesser attainments.[6]

The salary of the General Court is not fabulously high ($4,500 a year), but with an added expense allowance it provides a considerable supplement to other income. Undoubtedly this has contributed to the fact that tenure is relatively high among the members. In itself tenure of course does not imply competence, and the high salaries which invite members to stay on is no guarantee that only the "better men" will come and stay, for this salary is as much an invitation to the hanger-on who seeks an easy berth as it is to the competent who could not afford to serve for a token salary. Among New England legislators, in fact, the average length of tenure of the Massachusetts contingent is slightly lower than that in Rhode Island, where the pay is still miserly ($5 a day!). Whatever the reasons, the average length of service of the Massachusetts House members as of 1952 was four years.[7] In the 1950 session 41 per cent of the members of the House had served four or more sessions (eight years), while only 27.9 per cent were in their first terms; this is in contrast to many if not most state legislatures, where about half the members are usually first termers.[8]

[5] In addition to the customary legislative reference work provided through the state library, there are House and Senate counsels and a separate staff for the Ways and Means Committee.

[6] W. E. Mullins, "This Is How I See It," *Boston Herald*, May 6, 1953.

[7] Corinne Silverman, "The Legislators' View of the Legislative Process," 18 *Public Opinion Quarterly* 180-190 (summer 1954) at p. 181.

[8] These calculations were made from data in Belle Zeller (ed.), *American State Legislatures*, New York, 1954, pp. 66-67. Among the New England states for the members of the lower Houses in office in 1950 the following percentages had served

Party Influence in the General Court

Those who last the longest among Massachusetts legislators seem to be those who can adapt themselves to the demands of their respective parties. Loyalty to the party and to its general ideological orientation, if not a *sina qua non* of longevity, seems nevertheless generally to accompany it.[9] Legislators adapt to the surroundings, and the role of party is such in Massachusetts that adaptation to it is nearly mandatory. While it is true that there are many issues on which the position of the party is of no particular consequence, on the questions of first importance—the structure and operation of the government, matters involving labor law, public welfare, and economic regulation—the role of the party is often decisive.

The party role in decision-making has been even greater since 1948 than it had been before; for since that time the Democrats have been winning the lower house with considerable regularity. Therefore, although Democrats managed to win the governorship about half the time since the beginning of the New Deal, the Democratic party had not controlled either house of the General Court. Nor had they since the Civil War, for that matter.[9a] The Democratic minority has been important, particularly since Democratic governors have come on the scene with some frequency, although their importance depended in part upon the chances for getting rebel Republicans to break the party lines and to vote with the minority. That the Democrats have also had control of the lower house when there is a Republican governor (e.g., the 1955 session) has raised party influences to a new level of significance.

The exclusion of the Democrats from majority control of the General Court has been the consequence of several different factors. In earlier times it was the simple result of constant Republican majorities with only a few notable Democrats winning the governorship, but even at such times the usual Republican attachments kept

four or more terms: Rhode Island, 51 per cent; New Hampshire, 23 per cent; Connecticut, 16.9 per cent; Maine, 12.6 per cent; and Vermont, 9.7 per cent.

[9] Duncan MacRae, Jr. discusses the problems of "job security" of the Massachusetts legislator in his article, "The Role of the State Legislator in Massachusetts," 19 *American Sociological Review*, 185-194 (1954). He concludes that "There is reason to believe that the more senior representatives tend to subscribe to a greater extent than do their juniors to standards characteristic of professional politicians, and to show high organization loyalty to the elective officers of their respective parties" (at p. 193).

[9a] The 1958 election broke with tradition; Democrats won both houses.

the legislature under Republican control. (This was true even in 1912 when many Bull Moose Progressives were elected.) Since the state has developed more competitive politics, the lack of Democratic success is attributable more to the concentration of Democratic votes in urban areas, where Democrats may win with huge but useless majorities while losing out in other areas, often by small margins.

There is a certain amount of gerrymandering, of which the Republicans are quite conscious and which they wish desperately to maintain. One recent Republican governor said in an interview that the most important thing for the Republican party in 1956 was to maintain control of the Senate. "If we lose that," he said, "we will be frozen out for good when the Democrats finish reapportioning in the 1957 session." Actually the degree of gerrymandering is not extensive at present. According to a recent analysis of apportionment of the legislatures of all the states, the Massachusetts Senate was the best apportioned of all the upper chambers in the country, and the House rank was eighth.[10]

To what extent do the parties significantly affect legislative policy-making in Massachusetts? Without trying to rank the states in any close fashion as to the degree of party control, we find that Massachusetts would have to be classed somewhere among the top half-dozen states. As subsequent chapters indicate, both Connecticut and Rhode Island have somewhat tighter party cohesion, but Massachusetts would come close after them, along with New York and Pennsylvania.[11] Table 18 indicates the extent of party cohesion in Massachusetts in three separate sessions between 1931 and 1951. Massachusetts is not among the states which require a roll-call vote on every issue before its passage, and therefore roll calls come only when there is real dispute, usually a dispute between the parties. The number of roll calls increased considerably between 1931 and 1951, but since there is no significant change in the degree of party cohesion this is probably the result of a greater volume of legislation and the greater party role in legislative matters referred to above.

[10] Dauer and Kelsay, *op.cit.*

[11] Malcolm E. Jewell has compared eight two-party states with respect to their party legislative cohesion. He found that Massachusetts, New York, and Pennsylvania were the states with the greatest apparent party cohesion. The other states he studied were Ohio, Illinois, Missouri, Colorado, and Washington. See his "Party Voting in American State Legislatures," 49 *American Political Science Review* 773-791 (1955).

Malcolm Jewell, in examining the 1947 session in Massachusetts, found a considerably higher proportion of votes on which the parties were opposed than in any of the sessions covered in the table, but this was probably the consequence of the time and circumstances, and it does not necessarily indicate that the three sessions studied here are atypical. The 1947 session was a particularly bitter one, in

TABLE 18

Party Cohesion in the Massachusetts General Court, 1931, 1937, 1951

	1931		1937		1951	
	Senate	*House*	*Senate*	*House*	*Senate*	*House*
Total number of roll calls	47	93	129	89	249	231
Parties on opposite sides (as %)*	80.9%	86.0%	81.4%	82.0%	78.3%	87.9%
Average Democratic index of cohesion†	84.0	86.3	94.5	82.1	77.3	78.3
Average Republican index of cohesion	59.4	58.4	63.4	66.0	63.9	78.6
Party votes (as %) of all roll calls‡	23.6%	47.6%	40.3%	47.2%	33.7%	61.3%

* The percentage of all roll calls on which majorities of each party took opposite sides.
† This is an average of the indices on all roll calls on which the parties took opposite sides.
‡ The percentage of all roll calls on which the parties disagreed and on which at least 80 per cent of each party voted alike.

which Governor Bradford pushed several more or less restrictive pieces of labor legislation, which aroused antagonism and party controversy.[12]

On what sorts of questions do the roll calls come? What kinds of questions divide the parties? Table 19 shows the distribution of all issues on which there was sufficient cohesion within *both* parties to produce opposing majorities of at least 80 per cent of the members of each party.

Perhaps the most notable thing about Table 19 is the high proportion of roll calls with tight cohesion for both parties on matters

[12] Jewell found that 93 per cent of the votes in both the House and the Senate had the parties opposed, and that on 38 per cent of the Senate votes and 40 per cent of the House votes both parties scored an index of at least 80 while in opposition to each other. (*Ibid.*, p. 776.)

concerning labor, taxation, appropriations, business regulation, and the broad category of health, welfare, and education. (Together these categories account for 43.9 per cent of all the party votes.) Although the parties, as one might expect, also diverged on matters of patronage and on questions of internal concern to the parties (e.g., elections and reapportionment), the broad categories of

TABLE 19

Issues Producing Party Cohesion in Massachusetts General Court, 1931, 1937, 1951*

	Number	*Per cent of all party votes*
Local matters	63	16.8%
Labor	48	12.8
Elections and reapportionment	45	12.0
Taxation	38	10.1
Appropriations	34	9.1
Business regulation	27	7.4
Civil service	22	5.9
Welfare, health, education	17	4.5
State administration	17	4.5
Judicial and legal	13	3.5
Legislative organization and procedure	12	3.2
National issues (resolutions to Congress)	8	2.1
Liquor and crime control	7	1.8
Other	23	6.3
	375	100.0

* Here both Senate and House roll calls are combined. In all there were 838 roll calls of which 375 produced "party votes."

statewide governmental policy accounted for a heavy proportion of the total. This corroborates the argument that the parties concern themselves with serious matters of policy and that they often present diametrically opposite views on them when the votes are counted.

It may occasion some surprise that there were so many roll calls on local questions. Those familiar with Massachusetts politics will know the major source of this friction—namely, Boston. Deep distrust of the urban masses long ago brought various forms of state control over Boston affairs (even including the appointment of the city's police commissioner by the governor). Increasing Democratic

majorities in the city have not persuaded the rural Yankees to release their grip. Therefore a good many votes are still cast along
party lines today on questions of the powers of Boston city government.

We have indicated a considerable degree of party influence in the
General Court; now the fascinating question arises, Why? The
problem of showing why the demonstrated cohesiveness occurs is an
elusive one. No simple categorical answer to the question is possible,
but at least three different factors appear to be involved: the closeness of party competition, ideological-interest differences between
the parties, the strength of the parties as influence organizations.

Close party competition in general induces party cohesion in the
legislature. Legislators are politicians; they want to win elections,
not only their own reelection but a general victory for their side.
Lifelong loyalties, as well as personal desires for promotion, patronage, or other preferential treatment, compel a legislator to think
of the party's position. In the close districts, of course, his own
reelection may be tied in closely with the chances of the gubernatorial candidate, who must in part run on his party's legislative
record. To the extent that the record of the party is an issue in
campaigns, the party must concentrate on making at least a reasonable record of legislative action. If there is no opposition party
strong enough to constitute a real threat in the next election—as in
the three upper New England states most of the time—there is not
much incentive to go along for the sake of the next election. The
competitiveness of Massachusetts politics is such that this is an
important consideration.

That party competition induces a certain amount of regularity
of party voting fails to explain the whole case, however. After all,
the national parties are competitive, but there is markedly less
cohesion in Congress than in the General Court. Undoubtedly competition is a necessary precondition to party cohesion, but whether
cohesiveness accompanies competition depends on other factors.
One of the most important of these is the nature of the respective
constituencies from which the parties draw the greatest number of
their legislators. Like-minded legislators will come from similar
districts and if a party's legislators are drawn from widely differing
constituencies the degree of cohesion will accordingly be less.

In Congress a Democrat may be an arch-conservative or an ultraliberal, and the same is true of Republicans, even though most of each party may fall into opposed categories. Apparently the most significant invitation to ignore the rest of the party lies in the nature of the constituency.[13] The same thing is true in the states, as Malcolm Jewell and others have shown. If the state has competitive parties and has rural-urban divisions that more or less correspond to the divisions between the parties, the chances are that the level of party cohesion will be high. But even if there is competition between the parties and the Democratic and Republican legislative parties are both composed of rural *and* urban elements the tendency is for the levels of cohesion to be lower.[14] In Massachusetts there is an ideological division between the parties reflecting the general urban-rural split, although in truth the split is more nearly urban versus rural and suburban regions.

The distribution of Republicans and Democrats in the House of Representatives in 1951 illustrates the point. The Democrats were predominantly urban; Republicans, rural and suburban. In that session almost nine out of ten Democratic members of the House were from urban-manufacturing towns. Indeed 74.4 per cent came from cities of over 50,000 population, and another 14.5 per cent came from smaller cities like Chicopee, Peabody, and Fitchburg.[15] Although some Republicans also came from these urban centers, the proportion was less than one-third of their total representation. The remainder came from small towns and suburban towns on the periphery of the large urban centers. Accordingly there is a greater area of policy agreement among Democrats than among the Republicans, because of the greater degree of similarity of constituencies from which the former group comes.

The strength of the party organization is another determinant of party cohesion in the legislature. If the organization is well-led, clearly identifiable, and powerful enough to give a boost to the career of the ordinary member of the party in the legislature, then the likelihood is that it can have a considerable influence on the way

[13] Regarding Congress, see Julius Turner, *Party and Constituency: Pressures on Congress*, Baltimore, 1951.

[14] See Malcolm Jewell, *op.cit.*, pp. 786-788.

[15] Even so the 1951 session had a somewhat smaller proportion of Democrats from urban districts than had been there in the previous session. In 1950 the Democrats won an unprecedented majority in the House and accordingly a greater number of members came from the smaller and surburban towns. Malcolm Jewell reports that in the 1947 session 87 per cent of the Democrats were from the largest cities, which does not take in as many cities as the above figures do, since there are 17 cities with over 50,000 population. (*Ibid.*, p. 786.)

members vote. Disciplinary action against the recalcitrant may be rare, but the fact that rewards and punishments are possible is a spur to regularity. In caucus the position of the leadership can be put across to the party membership, and on important questions a caucus is usually called in Massachusetts, although caucuses are less frequent than in Connecticut and Rhode Island.

It is interesting to observe in this connection that the degree of cohesion in the Democratic party is slightly higher than in the Republican. This is true despite the fact that the Republican party organization is manifestly more unified and powerful than the Democratic state organization. It would seem, *ex hypothesi*, that the Republicans with their more effective means of punishment and rewards ought to be able to force legislators into line more readily than the more splintered Democratic organization. To further complicate the situation a student of recent Massachusetts legislative operations, approaching the problem from a different angle, found the Republicans less given to consistency in their voting on questions of importance to the "organization" than the Democrats. On the other hand the Republicans, he found, tended to be more consistently "conservative" than were the Democrats "liberal."[16]

Why these seeming contradictions? First, to reiterate, the party organization is not the sole factor; its impact is one among many factors that influence the votes of legislators. For instance, I have pointed out that the two parties draw their popular strength from different elements of the society, and that these differences are observable in the kinds of legislative districts from which Republicans and Democrats come. The higher degree of Democratic unity is undoubtedly in part a consequence of the greater uniformity of Democratic districts than of Republican districts.[17] Furthermore, in

[16] Duncan MacRae, Jr., "Roll-Call Votes and Leadership," 20 *Public Opinion Quarterly* 543-558 (fall 1956). He used selected roll calls between 1947 and 1953 and checked the leaders of the House against non-leader members.

[17] In a detailed study of constituency-legislative behavior relationships in Massachusetts, Duncan MacRae showed that the Democrats chosen from "typically Republican" districts and Republicans from "typically Democratic" districts were more inclined to desert the position of the majority of their parties and vote with the opposition than those elected from districts more typical of their parties. Although MacRae does not make much of this point in his article, it appears from his data that more Republicans than Democrats were chosen from atypical districts, which tends to corroborate the position taken above regarding the lesser tendency of Republicans to maintain party regularity. See his article "The Relation between Roll-Call Votes and Constituencies in the Massachusetts House of Representatives," 46 *American Political Science Review* 1,046-1,055 (1952).

all three sessions for which roll-call analyses were made, Democrats held the governorship, a fact which undoubtedly was an incentive to party regularity to support "their" governor when he needed help on appropriations or other administration measures. It is harder to explain the apparent contradiction of a stronger Republican state party organization and a relatively lesser concern with "organizational" matters in roll-call voting. Duncan MacRae, who raises this point, says: ". . . It appears that the Republican party in the Massachusetts House of Representatives is relatively more concerned with 'ideological' aims—which we have described as 'conservatism'—than with gaining office or with organization loyalty *per se*."[18] Perhaps the best explanation is that a great number of Republicans who go to the legislature have a very definite "stake" in the community which makes their conservatism a natural position. Furthermore they are not likely to be quite so dependent as Democrats on political advancement for financial security and social status. Such a legislator may be far easier prey for a business interest group than is a typical Republican prey to a labor union. In the former case, employment opportunities may be offered as bait; in the latter no comparable bargaining tool is available. And if the less-well-fixed Democrat wants to remain in politics for a career, organizational loyalty may become a paramount consideration.[19]

[18] MacRae, "Roll-Call Votes and Leadership," p. 558.

[19] A glance at the occupational distribution of Democrats and Republicans in the House suggests that there are far more Democrats in the less-well-fixed category than Republicans. V. O. Key tabulated the occupations of the members of four recent sessions of the House and found that the proportion of businessmen was considerably higher for the Republicans and that the proportion of Democrats in the category of sales-clerical positions, for example, was more than three times that of the Republicans. See the data in the table below.

Occupational Distribution of Democrats and Republicans Serving in the
Mass. House of Representatives, 1945, 1947, 1949, 1951

OCCUPATIONAL CATEGORY	DEMOCRATS		REPUBLICANS	
	Number	*Per cent*	*Number*	*Per cent*
Professional	85	39.9	80	34.3
Business-managerial	49	23.0	94	40.3
Sales-clerical	47	22.1	16	6.9
Manual workers	13	6.1	5	2.1
Farmers	1	0.5	16	6.9
Local government	7	3.3	3	1.3
Unidentified	11	5.2	19	8.2
	213	100.0	233	100.0

Source: American State Politics, by V. O. Key, Jr., p. 262. Used with the kind permission of the author and Alfred A. Knopf, publisher.

Governors as Legislative Politicians in Massachusetts

Before turning to discussion of interest groups and their role in policy-making in Massachusetts, we must give some attention to the governorship as an important factor in the legislative process, the doctrine of separation of powers notwithstanding. Through his formal power as chief executive and his informal power as chief of the party the governor has to be considered the most important single person in making legislative decisions. The governor certainly does not always get his way—not by any means—and yet it is true that all actors in the legislative drama must turn to or contend with the governor throughout legislative struggles on significant bills.

The governor's legislative program, presented to the legislature early in the session, is the base point for all major legislative operations. This program, drawn from the platform of the campaign which elected the governor, is a powerful influence on his own party in the House and Senate. These two bodies may not agree with it— they may sometimes manage to scuttle it entirely (as they did Governor Furcolo's sales tax in 1957)—but for most members most of the time "their" governor's program is the starting point of their thinking. Since so many items of importance necessarily involve appropriations, the budget system is a controlling weapon in the hands of the governor. The governor's budget may not have any new items added to it by the legislature; if any new programs are to be submitted they must come through separate legislation with separately provided financing, a strong deterrent to independent programs.

In the course of the session a governor will have constant meetings with legislative leaders of his party, and with greater or lesser degrees of success will work out legislative strategy with them. Governor Herter, for instance, had dinner meetings with Republican legislative leaders at least once a week plus other occasional meetings as the situation seemed to demand.[20] As a consequence of the highly developed liaison between the governor and the legislature, there is a very low proportion of vetoes in Massachusetts—roughly half a dozen per session. Usually vetoes are sustained when used since a two-thirds majority is required to override them.

The chances of a governor's program depend of course upon his

[20] Interview, June 25, 1955.

party's position in the legislature. If the governor is a Republican, the likelihood of his having majorities in both Houses has in the past been very good. In 1955 Christian Herter had to work with a Democratic House of Representatives, the first time that had ever happened to a Republican. Customarily Democratic governors have had to contend with antagonistic majorities in both houses, and consequently their successes have come after more heroic struggles. Yet, whether Democrat or Republican, the governor has some special non-party tools to use for whipping up needed majorities for his proposals. Patronage, collateral support from interest groups, and pressure applied to the legislator interested in particular bills— all these are at hand to be used with more or less subtlety, depending on the man.

Patronage is perhaps the most important of these gubernatorial weapons. The often undignified scramble for patronage is a common enough practice among politicians, but in Massachusetts the open employment of patronage promises seems to play a significant role in the recruitment of extra legislative votes. Sometimes patronage benefits the member directly—the promise of a future job or agreement to throw contracts to the member for the hire of trucks by the state highway department. More frequently involved are jobs for supporters and constituents with which a member can mend his political fence. There are a good number of unclassified short-term jobs for which there always seem to be takers, and the member who gets the "credit" for passing most of these around gains in popularity—or at least so many members think. Legislators both of the governor's party and of the opposition can be heard in the halls of the State House complaining about the improper distribution of these small plums. One legislator in 1957 wrote an outraged letter to the press complaining that there were 27 veterans in his district for whom he had been unable to get even temporary state jobs, with the consequence that they were on relief, costing the taxpayer extra money.[21] As a Republican, the letter writer said, he would be "forced" into the position of advising these people to vote Republican the next time for "they well know that a Republican administration gave them work in the past." There is a limit to the number of such jobs to be passed out, and there are always bound to be some who get left out, but most governors reserve some of

---

[21] *Boston Herald,* Mar. 27, 1957.

these minor gratuities to bargain for votes as the session moves along.

Appointments which require approval do not go to the legislature in Massachusetts but to the Governor's Council. Thus the Council is involved in patronage, which is the one point at which it has any significant influence. The Council's role in administration is nil, although it supposedly acts as adviser to the governor on executive policy. With remarkable frankness Lieutenant Governor Whittier said in a 1956 speech that "the Governor's Council, which renders advice and consent to the governor according to law, has in truth small effect upon the actual management of the state."[22] The councillors do have the means of holding up the governor's appointments by refusing approval and thereby forcing their own choices to a limited degree. The legislator's position is weaker, but he can bargain with the legislative leaders of the governor's party on policy issues. The significance of patronage is suggested by the fact that some of the candidates for Republican floor leader in the House in 1957 were angry that their opponent, Frank S. Giles, had for three years been Governor Herter's "chief House patronage dispenser." Giles was criticized for continuing "in that job while actively rounding up support for his party leadership bid."[23]

Various pressure groups also come to the aid of a governor hard-pressed for votes to carry his program. Labor unions may collaborate to drum up votes in a close situation. Businesses have often allowed a governor a certain number of jobs in their firms to be passed along as encouragement to balky legislators. Even the race-track and liquor lobbyists have been known to work for seemingly unrelated issues on which the governor is having a hard time. They have, for example, sometimes backed a governor on his budget with presumably two different motives in mind: (1) it never hurts to have a governor somewhat indebted to your client, especially if it is a liquor wholesaler or a race-track operator; and (2) if the governor's budget does not call for any new or burdensome taxes on such vulnerable pastimes as betting and drinking, then it is safer to get

[22] *Christian Science Monitor*, Mar. 21, 1956. I attended a session of the Council in Mar. 1955; to judge from the agenda and the discussion, Mr. Whittier's statement certainly would not seem inaccurate.

[23] *Christian Science Monitor*, Feb. 11, 1956. Incidentally he got the job! The reporter went on to note that not only had Giles's activities made him Republican friends, but also his "key activity . . . had produced Democratic votes on many key roll calls."

the budget tucked away before someone gets bright ideas about new sources of revenue.

One final point about the governor's methods of getting his way with legislators. Through their legislative leaders, governors have been known to use the pork-barrel technique to push along highway bills, for example. By judicious promises about the timing and placement of highway projects, some legislators can be made to see particular bills in a new light. Moreover, general support for a bill which has been languishing in committee and which is of great significance to a particular legislator may be moved along or left to take its chances in the late session rush—depending, of course, on how the man interested in the bill looks at some of the governor's proposals. Surprisingly, however, there is relatively little use of local special legislation as bait to catch legislative support—far less than in Connecticut and Rhode Island. That is, the committee on local bills (considering bills to permit extra borrowing by a town, to permit some necessary charter change, etc.) very rarely promotes or allows to perish a legislator's bill depending on the voting of the member.

Interest Groups and Legislative Politics

One vital element of the legislative process is still missing—the interest groups. In the chapters on the one-party states of New England, there was more continuous discussion of them than has been necessary in covering Massachusetts. This is not to say that the various special interest groups have no importance in decision-making in Massachusetts—far from it, in fact—but their function is quite different from that of their counterparts in northern New England, where the political situation in the legislatures is more fluid. While it is not always a political vacuum into which the pressure group can move in those states, it comes much nearer to being a vacuum than in the southern states of New England. In Massachusetts, as in Rhode Island and Connecticut, the party organizations sit astride the channels through which all legislation must flow, a fact to which the pressure group must accommodate itself. In consequence, the role of the pressure group is not so imposing as in the one-party states. Interest groups have power, to be sure, but it is used differently and with different results.

One of the means by which interest groups have adapted themselves to the political facts of life in the Commonwealth is that many of them have become what might be called "built-in pressure groups." Their clientele are so aligned with one party or the other, and their interests so dominantly represented by the general position of one of the parties, that they come to be almost a constituent part of one party. In no case is the degree of affiliation comparable to the relationship between the Trades Union Congress and the British Labor party, where at times the two become nearly indistinguishable in the making of Labor party policy, but in Massachusetts (and again in Connecticut and Rhode Island) the ties are much closer than between the pressure organizations and the national political parties in the United States. Farm groups on the national level have not aligned themselves with either party, but in Massachusetts they are with the Republicans. Labor nationally is more sympathetic to the Democratic party and is much more helpful to it, but it maintains cordial relations with many Republicans and does not move into the inner councils of the Democratic party to the extent that it does in Massachusetts. In some areas the Democratic party in Massachusetts will leave to labor almost the whole job of campaigning for state candidates, and in many campaigns the money labor gives is a very crucial factor in the Democratic effort.

The interest groups expect some return for services rendered. They are often disappointed in the end, but both parties obviously make efforts to satisfy the needs of those interests on "their side." The close relationships of the "built-in" pressure group pay dividends when its party is in power, but when the opposition takes over the built-in group has its difficulties. The exigencies of a competitive party situation keep the built-in groups from being frozen out entirely. If the Republicans make a clean sweep of state government, they cannot afford to turn a deaf ear to all the entreaties of labor. Labor leaders may not have helped them get elected, and may in fact not be very helpful when they run for reelection, but there are too many workers who cast ballots to take too many chances with alienating them unnecessarily. Similarly, when the Democrats, although they have never managed a clean sweep of the governorship and both houses of the General Court, have a governor and control of one house, they do not ignore groups aligned with the Republicans.

Which are the most powerful groups in Massachusetts? To consider first those aligned with the Democratic party, the most significant are labor, the Catholic Church, and certain reform groups. According to a recent Republican floor leader in the House, he rarely had any direct contact with labor leaders. "They have been in my office once or twice during the session. And one of these visits was by my request."[24] Labor's contacts are primarily with the Democratic leaders, and they then depend upon their help in forcing the best compromise possible from the situation.

A good deal of foolishness has been written about the relationship between the Catholic Church and the Democratic party in Massachusetts. There is, of course, no denying that the Church is a significant factor in the Democratic party: so many Democratic voters, party leaders, and legislators are Roman Catholics that it could hardly be otherwise. But this has not by any means made Massachusetts into a theocracy. The area of interest of the Catholic Church does take in many matters of governmental concern—education is a prime example—but the range of problems in which the Church gets involved is limited. The late Cardinal O'Connell was said to have been influential in the General Court, although he never appeared there in person. His emissaries carried his messages concerning birth-control bills, the child-labor amendment, and a bill requiring blood tests before marriage. (Birth-control legislation got on the ballot through initiative action, but it was swamped by the voters.) Cardinal O'Connell was said to have had no use for James Curley, and indirectly he may have helped to defeat him in some of his campaigns; at least he went out of his way to make favorable comments about one of Curley's opponents, the late Maurice Tobin. The Cardinal's opposition was said to have accounted for the defeat of a lottery bill a few years back. Notwithstanding opposition by newspapers and Protestant ministers, the bill was gaining in strength and its passage seemed inevitable. Then at a crucial point the Cardinal gave an interview with newspaper reporters in which he blasted the lottery as "an out-and-out gambling machine" and "a source of corruption." "The effect of the interview," according to one reporter, "was quick and conclusive. Governor Curley, who had been thumping the tub for the measure, delivered the owlish judgment that 'public sentiment seems to be against the lottery bill.' Two hours later the House convened and legislators began arising

[24] In an interview with Charles Gibbons, then minority leader in the House and subsequently Republican state chairman, July 6, 1955.

in response to the roll call and announcing that they were switching their votes from yea to nay."[25] In all, 68 votes changed overnight, enough to defeat the bill. On a measure which involves "moral" values of this sort, there is no denying the influence of the Church, but its role is nonetheless limited since on broad issues of public policy it is more often silent than vocal.[26]

Although it has no great political power, one group aligned with the Democrats is a source of constant publicity for the liberal point of view, the Massachusetts Americans for Democratic Action. Small in numbers and at times tossed around even by leading Democrats, the ADA continues to make itself heard in Massachusetts even though it has nearly disappeared in many other states. Its members appear at legislative hearings to plead for bills and also make some effort to carry their message to the public. Their role, however, is probably more interesting than important.

Closely allied with the Republican party are the public-utility interests, the real-estate lobby, the Associated Industries of Massachusetts (the local version of the NAM), the Chamber of Commerce, the insurance companies, and the Massachusetts Federation of Taxpayer's Associations. All these groups have easy access to the leaders of the Republican party. Through shared opinions, campaign contributions, and at times common business connections, the lobbyists for these groups know they can present their arguments to attentive ears within "their" party, even as labor has similar access to the Democrats. In the normal course of events these business-oriented groups can also depend upon a bloc of votes in the Senate to forestall unwanted action. The nearest the Democrats have ever come to controlling this chamber was the even split of 1949-1950, but at other times the Republican majority is a last-resort safeguard for the conservatives.

It is true that a Republican governor will sometimes be ready to go further with high taxes, unemployment compensation, or welfare laws than the conservative elements, and he can also at times carry

[25] Jack Alexander, "The Cardinal and Cold Roast Boston," 214 *Saturday Evening Post* 10 (Oct. 4, 1941).

[26] One Catholic writer contends that the Church through its lay societies has not taken a sufficient interest in Boston politics. By ignoring its responsibilities the Catholic portion of society has allowed the moral level of public service to deteriorate, according to Katherine Loughlin. See her article "Boston's Political Morals," 43 *The Commonweal* 545-548 (Mar. 15, 1945).

the Senate Republicans with him, giving the conservative interests a defeat. When a Republican governor gets out of line with the conservative interests in this fashion, their lobbyists frequently appeal to a few relatively conservative Democrats for votes to bolster their dependable Republican element. One of the best examples of this process in recent years was the issue over amending the constitution in 1956. Democratic leaders were pushing for a graduated income tax (the state has an income tax, but it used a flat rate and is not "progressive" in the sense that it takes a bigger bite out of higher salaries). Backing the amendment with the Democratic leaders were the League of Women Voters of Massachusetts and the ADA. In opposition were the Greater Boston Chamber of Commerce and the Massachusetts Federation of Taxpayer's Associations, who, along with some other business groups, had propagandized the public at large against the plan. For a week before the convening of the joint session of the House and Senate where the amendment was to be considered these groups had been working on legislators, trying to line up anti-income-tax votes. They did well. Eleven Democrats joined 114 Republicans to defeat the amendment. (Four Republicans and 122 Democrats voted yes but an absolute majority was needed for passage, or 140 votes.) [27]

In 1949 the Democrats had just won their most amazing victory in capturing the House for the first time, gaining a tie in the Senate and electing a governor with a whopping majority. Several members introduced bills that put the conservative interests into a frenzy of self-protective activity. A Boston Democrat, for instance, introduced a bill to require the state to be a "self-insurer" in the workman's compensation program. Massachusetts firms, required by law to insure for workman's compensation, paid out some $191,000,000 in premiums to insurance companies for which in return the workers were making claims for only $101,000,000. "By contrast, Ohio's state-operated fund paid out over ninety per cent of the premiums collected." [28] After vigorous protest by the insurance companies, the bill was withdrawn, but Governor Dever proposed, at the behest of labor leaders, a state-operated compulsory sickness-insurance plan.

[27] See Edgar M. Mills's discussion in the *Christian Science Monitor*, May 15, 1956.
[28] Robert S. Allen (ed.), *Our Sovereign State*, New York, 1949, p. 49.

At this point, says one observer, "The insurance interests cast the last vestige of gentility to the winds. Their lobbyists tripled in number. Hundreds of insurance workers were furloughed and marshaled for service on Beacon Hill. In jammed committee rooms, they jeered and hooted supporters of the bill and applauded company spokesmen. These pressures again turned the trick and the governor's bill was axed."[29]

Such fanfare is not ordinarily resorted to by these groups; only extreme circumstances have called for such pyrotechnics. Usually, when the necessary votes cannot be marshaled from among Republican legislators, there are enough Democrats who are insurance men, or real-estate men, or small-business men to provide the margin of safety. Such behavior on the part of legislators indirectly in behalf of the "own" pocketbooks is not bribery and is not illegal, but it happens with disturbing regularity.

One group generally aligned with the Republicans nevertheless is variously aligned when necessary to promote its ideas, the Federation of Taxpayer's Associations. Its executive director, Norman F. MacDonald, has been known to urge drastic reduction of Republican as well as Democratic budgets. The free-spending tendency of the General Court at times is an open invitation to attack, since a good many nearly superfluous jobs seem to be created from time to time to satisfy demands for patronage. In the usual situation the Republicans are less guilty of this than the Democrats, and the main line of resistance rests with Republican money savers. It is with the latter that MacDonald makes his most fruitful contacts. His was the loudest of the voices in condemnation of the situation that ensued from the last days of the 1952 legislative session. At that time nearly 1,000 new jobs were created, a liberal pension was provided for legislators as well as a $1,000 pay raise, and 44 salaried state officers were voted lunch money and free transportation. Governor Dever vetoed 635 of the new jobs, but it took a special session to repeal the pensions, travel pay, and other emoluments voted for legislators. Undoubtedly the propaganda generated by MacDonald and his staff were significant factors in bringing full public awareness of what had happened during the session, and the general feeling among politicians is that Governor Dever lost the subsequent election by a

[29] *Ibid.*, p. 49.

narrow margin (14,400 votes out of almost 2½ million cast) in good part because of this skulduggery.[30]

There are other groups, some tied in with the parties and others unrelated. In an average session some 300 lobbyists register and subsequently report their expenses incurred for lobbying, running from $300,000 to $400,000 per session.[31] The biggest spenders are the business interests, as is customary, representing as they do so many different businesses with treasuries sufficient to hire able lobbyists. Labor spends relatively less, but its efforts are backed up with implicit (even if often unenforceable) threats to the political security of the politicians whom it approaches. The race-track interests also spend heavily, and one may wonder whether the sums reported actually account for the total outlays. In 1955, for example, they reported spending only $6,000, which may or may not be precisely accurate.[32]

There are several relatively powerful interest groups which do not align themselves strictly with either party—state employees, liquor interests, and veterans' groups, to name a few—but probably the most dramatic of these is the race-track element. High up in both the horse- and dog-track world are two brothers, Thomas and John Pappas, one of whom, in fair bipartisan spirit, is a Democrat and the other a Republican. Tom, the Republican brother, was an important fund raiser for President Eisenhower's campaign in 1956 and was listed euphemistically in newspaper stories at the time as a "wholesaler," which he is—a wholesaler of liquor (he is said to control about one-sixth of the Massachusetts market.)[33] Race-track betting is a big business, as important to budget balancers in government as to the race-track operators. In 1955, for instance, pari-mutuel betting in Massachusetts amounted to $134,600,000, of which the state received a tidy $10,700,000 in taxes (an equal sum went to track operators). Ten million may amount to only a meager proportion (about three per cent) of the total budget, but finding other equally large individual contributions is not easy.

The dog-racing and horse-racing tracks are so well established and so well fixed politically that there is scant likelihood that anyone

---

[30] On MacDonald, see J. R. Aswell and E. J. Michelson, "The Tightwad the Politicians Hate," 226 *Saturday Evening Post* 31ff. (Mar. 27, 1954).

[31] League of Women Voters of Massachusetts, *op.cit.*, p. 56.

[32] Cited from the records of the secretary of state by Latham, *op.cit.*, p. 71.

[33] Robert S. Allen, *op.cit.*, p. 44.

will have to face the task of finding alternative sources of income. Racing operations seem peculiarly dependent upon political good will, and the operators have hit upon the best method of making Massachusetts legislators happy—the distribution of race-track jobs through legislators and other officials. Since the demand for patronage is so intense in Massachusetts, the tracks have made some fast and influential friends. In Massachusetts, unlike Rhode Island and New Hampshire, the legislators themselves do not work at the tracks, but they do pass out race-track employment to constituents, perhaps to the extent of 85 per cent of all the jobs at the tracks. The clamor for these jobs became so intense that in 1954 the General Court passed a law "making it a crime for a public official to attempt to use his influence in landing a track job. While such a law could conceivably strike a blow at the patronage system, its practical use is simply to give it some order. As one legislator described it 'Now we can say "no" to some of our constituents without losing a vote.' "[34]

Official good will can be maintained in many ways—entertainment and yacht trips along with the patronage slice—but it takes somewhat subtler methods to keep the public in a good mood. Keeping adverse publicity out of the newspapers is, of course, highly important. One of the means to this end is the hiring of reporters as publicity agents on annual retainer fees. The judicious use of advertising, when the recurrent question of abolishing the race tracks comes up on a referendum, has undoubtedly helped to save the day. By assigning the tax returns from the tracks to old-age assistance race-track interests gain a neat propaganda advantage—the elimination of racing becomes a blow at grandmother! One Massachusetts observer, commenting on these publicity operations, said, "The horse and dog tracks fill the newspapers with heartrending pictures of a wispy-haired, sad-eyed old couple. Underneath is the caption: 'Make Their Last Years Secure and Happy. Vote for Pari-Mutuel Racing.' It is always the same couple and they never look any happier or more secure, but the appeal hasn't failed yet."[35]

If the political implications of the race tracks stopped with the pari-mutuel betting and the direct operations of the tracks, the problem would be serious enough. But it does not stop there. Where horses and dogs race there is a lucrative opportunity for extra-legal

[34] John Strohmeyer, *op.cit.*, p. 40.
[35] Allen, *op.cit.*, p. 46.

betting which does not flow through the pari-mutuel machines and which makes no returns to the state treasury. In short, the bookies move in, and move in they have in Massachusetts. Although the Kefauver Crime Investigating Committee never made an invasion of New England, more recently the Massachusetts Crime Commission submitted a 1,307-page report in which it was charged that a $2 billion business in gambling flourished in the state. A minority report claimed that the total amounted to only $1 billion. The difference is unimportant in one sense: the lucrative nature of the "business" is clear whichever figure is correct. The report charged that there were ties between the gambling interests and other crime, such as prostitution, narcotics, and theft. The police, according to the investigators, know the situation and make no move to stop it. No sooner had the report hit the headlines than there were vigorous denials and challenges to show where action could be taken. Even allowing for some exaggeration, the political influence of the gambling fraternity seems a fact. The original reluctance to pass the laws necessary to establish the investigation and to continue it at later intervals suggests that there are ties between the political world and the underworld. It is not a very pretty picture, to say the least, but whoever tries to unravel the mysteries of the state's politics without considering these influences is bound to end up with only part of the answer.

Precisely what impact these groups have in areas beyond their immediate concerns is difficult if not impossible to say, but that some of the representatives of legal as well as illegal gambling have access to legislators and other officials certainly does not enhance the moral tone of government. To the extent that their influence does come shrouded in secrecy and through back-room dealings, the intelligent and interested citizen is incapable of knowing the source of pressures that affect decision-making. The legitimate importuning of business, labor, and other out-in-the-open groups can become mysterious enough without the addition of underworld characters who thrive on anonymity. Perhaps equally as serious as the regrettable lack of public intelligence of what is going on is the fact that many legislators who are not themselves bought off or in any way brought under the influence of these interests do not know which of their colleagues is in reality an agent for some hidden group.

Sobering as the influence of these hidden and half-hidden groups unquestionably is, the impression should not be left that the legis-lature is a den of vice. One of the toughest and ablest reporters in Boston told me that the extent of bribery and official misdealing was at a minimum on Beacon Hill. He went on to say that there was more influencing of legislators' votes through governmental patronage by party leaders and the governor than through any of the interest groups, covert or overt.[36] The General Court, for all the tarnish that some unscrupulous influences may have put upon it, remains a reasonably responsible even if somewhat conservative body.

[36] In an interview with W. E. Mullins, July 6, 1955.

CHAPTER 7

---- ★ ----

RHODE ISLAND: ONE-PARTY FAÇADE
AND TWO-PARTY REALITY?

RHODE ISLAND adds another variant to the kaleidoscopic picture of New England politics. While it shares many of the constitutional and political traits found throughout New England, its political pattern is unique, for here as nowhere else in New England the Democrats have the dominant position. The Democrats have occupied the ascendant position for a generation, and yet Rhode Island is not functionally a one-party state. The Republicans are not squeezed out of the race entirely; through their hold on the state Senate they are active participants in making public policy.

Prior to 1932 the state was even more Republican than it is now Democratic. The public policy implications of this abrupt turnabout are significant. Where the Republicans had represented the business interests, as they still tend to do, the Democrats take the liberal welfare-state line. Unhappily the change in control did not greatly alter the dominant political practices. The outgoing Republican organization, based largely on rural machines, was changed for a Democratic organization based on city machines. The corruption that had disfigured the state for so long—Lincoln Steffens called it "A State for Sale"[1]—went on as before.

Two general characteristics have forced Rhode Island into the kind of political alignment it has. First, it is one of the most heavily urbanized states in the nation. Almost eighty-five per cent of its citizens are city dwellers, and nearly half of the employed persons are engaged in manufacturing, a higher percentage in manufacturing, in fact, than in any other state. Second, Rhode Island has a higher proportion of immigrants and their second- and third-generation progeny than any other state. The particular ethnic groups that have flooded into Rhode Island in such great numbers are those

[1] Lincoln Steffens, "Rhode Island: A State for Sale," 24 *McClure's Magazine* 337-353, Feb. 1905.

172

which have tended to cast their lot with the Democratic party—the Irish, Italians, and French-Canadians particularly. Such industrialized urban centers with heavy proportions of foreign-born groups were made to order for the appeals of the New Deal. It is no coincidence that the dividing line between the old and new regimes in the state is the year 1932, when Franklin D. Roosevelt became President. The handwriting had been on the wall for some time, but the cataclysm of 1932 served to hasten the consummation of the inevitable take-over by the "New Yankees."

Rhode Island Republicans:
The Palmy Days

What happened on election day of 1932 was the very thing the conservative interests of the state had long feared and staunchly defended against by every means available. For more than a century conservative political leaders had devised legal stratagems to exclude the immigrants from the right to vote. As early as the second and third decades of the nineteenth century the Democratic party began appealing to the disenfranchised, and over the years it won considerable support from the immigrant groups on this basis. The suffrage question is not an issue of the remote past in Rhode Island. As recently as 1928 the issue of full suffrage was still being debated, and only in that year was the unrestricted right to vote in city council elections granted to those without property. Naturally deep resentment and bitterness were engendered by the long exclusion of so many people from full citizenship. Some attention to this suffrage battle of more than a century's duration is necessary to explain the character of Rhode Island politics today.

Roger Williams started the colony on a democratic basis, but aristocratic elements soon began taking over the government. In 1724 the first property qualification for suffrage was provided in a statute. Such barriers to voting were not uncommon in the colonies, but the Rhode Island restriction was among the more severe and it lasted longer than any other. Partly out of a desire to maintain the restricted suffrage, those who could vote—comprising, it is said, as few as one in fifteen inhabitants in 1832—repeatedly refused to consider replacement of the Colonial Charter of 1663 long after Rhode Island had become part of the United States. As other states wrote new constitutions and as universal manhood suffrage became

173

more and more common throughout the country, Rhode Island's stubborn refusal to consider change only increased in pressure. Eventually this culminated in the so-called Dorr War (which wasn't really a war; total casualties, one innocent bystander killed).[2] The attempted *coup d'état* frightened the ruling aristocrats into producing a new constitution in 1842. It provided that non-property owners could vote if they paid taxes of at least one dollar a year, but this was qualified in that it applied only to "every male native citizen."[3] Not until the year 1888 was this deeply resented distinction between native and immigrant citizens removed from the constitution and then only at a price. The 1842 constitution had excluded non-property owners from voting for the office of city councillor in Providence. With the new 1888 amendment, however, the exclusion of non-property owners was made to apply for the elections for all city councils.

This was a shrewd move from the point of view of the tight little oligarchy that led the Republican party. In local politics the Democrats might win mayoralty elections but the city councils remained in Republican hands. According to one calculation "nearly sixty per cent of those who could vote for mayor [in Providence] were disqualified in councilmanic elections."[4] Thus the power that the Democrats might have built up through their urban machines was curtailed. Consequently the rurally based Republican party strengthened its hold on the state. Finally in 1928 a constitutional amendment removed the property qualifications for voting in city council elections, a move which in turn augmented Democratic power.[5]

The exclusion of immigrant groups from the electorate down to

[2] See the brief discussion of the battle for suffrage rights in Rhode Island in Murray S. Stedman, Jr. and Susan W. Stedman, "The Rise of the Democratic Party of Rhole Island," 24 *New England Quarterly* 329-341 (Sept. 1951), at pp. 337-339. See also Chilton Williamson, "Rhode Island Suffrage since the Dorr War," 28 *New England Quarterly* 34-50 (Mar. 1955). On the Dorr uprising and its political implications, see Edward Field (ed.), *State of Rhode Island and Providence Plantations at the End of the Century: A History*, Boston, 1902, Ch. 20.

[3] Rhode Island constitution, Art. ii, Sec. 1.

[4] Stedman and Stedman, *op.cit.*, p. 339. Between 1896 and 1906, they estimate, the average vote for mayor was 20,435 but for the aldermen only 8,163. *Ibid.*

[5] See the constitution of Rhode Island, Art. xx. This amendment, however, continued the property qualification as a condition for voting "upon any proposition to impose a tax or for the expenditure of money in any town, as distinguished from a city. . . ." Thus in the town meeting or local referenda on fiscal matters in the towns the non-propertied citizen continued to be disenfranchised and for that matter he still is.

1888 presumably helped the Republican cause, but probably the party could have maintained power without this restriction, since it was riding high on the wave of favorable opinion resulting from the Civil War. From the time the Republican party took the reins of government from the faltering hands of the old aristocracy in 1856, it kept a grip on the state down to 1932. Brief Democratic interludes were insufficient to break the hold of the GOP. During the 76 years between 1856 and 1932 Democrats occupied the governor's chair for a total of only eight years.[6]

Often boss-ridden and corrupt, the Republican party was the representative of business interests and rural Yankees. The career of Rhode Island's most famous boss, General Charles Brayton, is a gaudy illustration of the kind of power the party had and how it was used. Brayton, who had been a general in the Civil War, had been a minor figure in the party with minor patronage appointments prior to his emergence as party mogul late in the nineteenth century. Blind during the latter years of his rule, he nevertheless operated the government of the state with a sure hand. He had an alliance with powerful Senator Nelson Aldrich, but in matters of internal politics he was by and large on his own. Since Brayton occasionally had trouble with "his" governors, he had a law passed in 1901— commonly called the Brayton Law—by which the Senate, if it did not approve of a governor's nomination to any post, could substitute its own choice for the job. The governor also lacked the veto power then. Prime authority rested with the legislature—that is to say, with Brayton.

Brayton's control over the party and the government was reinforced in two ways. He had the support of the big money in the state and he had a faithful organization with which to discipline the recalcitrant. According to Lincoln Steffens, Brayton controlled legislators by advancing them "to judgeships and other political jobs, threw them law business and, if they were not lawyers, contracts and other business. He had pull enough to get men jobs with his client corporations."[7] If his orders were disobeyed, the "word" would be

[6] Democratic victory years were 1887, 1890, 1902, 1903, 1906, 1907, and 1922. In the latter election the term was two years; in all earlier elections the term was only one year. (Two-year terms were initiated in 1912.) In the gubernatorial elections of 1889 and 1891 Democrats had pluralities only and the Republican candidates were chosen by the Republican legislature.

[7] Lincoln Steffens, *The Autobiography of Lincoln Steffens*, New York, 1931, p. 466.

passed down and only rarely would the offender be able to with-stand the disciplinary action. As "counsel" to such corporations as the New Haven and Hartford Railroad, the Rhode Island Company (street railways), the Providence Telephone Company, and other such large corporations wanting favors from the state, Brayton had ample money with which to work. Cash was put to work in a most undignified manner in elections. It bought votes. Governor Garvin (a Democrat) told the General Assembly in 1903 that something ought to be done. "That bribery exists," he said "to a great extent in the elections in the state is a matter of common knowledge. No general election passes without the purchase of votes by one or both parties. . . . Many assemblymen occupy their seats by means of pur-chased votes. . . . The money paid to the voter [is not called bribery] whether two, five, or twenty dollars, [it] is spoken of as 'payment for his time.' "[8]

When we think of the notorious machines of the past, we usually think of those operating in the big cities—New York, Philadelphia, or Chicago, for example. We are inclined to forget that in the heyday of bossism there were some powerful machines based on the votes and support of countryfolk. Rhode Island Republican candidates got a good proportion of their vote from the cities, but the machine depended upon the organizations of the small towns. Brayton could count on the apportionment of the legislature to give predominant authority to the small towns; accordingly, when picking the chair-men of committees, he gave the choice positions to the rural legisla-tors. "Almost all the chairmen were from the country towns," says one account, "because these were the 'old codgers' the General trusted. He didn't have much use for city slickers, who were likely to be Democrats anyway."[9]

One episode of the General Brayton era is particularly revealing. A presumptuous Republican governor had the temerity to say during a campaign that, if reelected, he would do all in his power to "drive from the State House the criminal boss who has contaminated that place and prostituted the affairs of the people."[10] His Democratic rival for the governorship in that campaign (1906) was making an even more vigorous attack on Brayton, and was directing a collateral

[8] Quoted by Lincoln Steffens, *Autobiography*, p. 468.
[9] David Patten, "Our Rhode Island," *Providence Journal*, Feb. 13, 1956.
[10] *Ibid.*

attack on the favoritism shown toward the utilities in the state. Partly through some maneuvering between Providence Democrats and Brayton and partly, no doubt, due to the attack on Brayton himself, among other factors, the Democrat won. Things began to look ominous when the Democratic governor won reelection in 1907. Brayton dismayed some of his followers but consolidated his position ultimately by running a French-Canadian candidate for governor in 1908. Aram J. Pothier, born in Quebec and an immigrant to Rhode Island at the age of 18, had previously been accorded the honor of the lieutenant governorship in 1897. By nominating Pothier for governor, Brayton played a trump card: he divided loyalties within the Democratic camp. The continued dominance of the Democratic party by Irish politicians had already produced grumbling among Franco-Americans, and the nomination of Pothier postponed the consolidation of the ranks of the immigrant groups.[11]

Rhode Island Republicans: Playing Second Best

Between 1900 and 1930 the Republicans won 17 of the 22 gubernatorial elections with an average of 54.2 per cent of the major party vote. Between 1932 and 1956 the party won only one gubernatorial contest (1938) and averaged 44.5 per cent of the vote. This might seem to put present-day Rhode Island into the category of the one-party states, but Rhode Island does not resemble a one-party state in its political practices nearly as much as Maine, in which the Democratic party over the last quarter-century has had more success in electing governors than the Republicans in Rhode Island. This is analysis by voting statistics alone. Thanks to the warped apportionment of the Rhode Island General Assembly, the Republicans are very rarely left out of the policy-formation process. Nor are they negligible opponents in the races for major state offices. The Republican threat is sufficient to worry the Democratic front-runners;

---

[11] Pothier proved to be unusually popular as a vote getter. He won the governorship in five successive elections between 1908 and 1914. Then in 1924 he returned to bail out the Republicans, after a Democrat had been elected in 1922. He won handily in 1924 and stayed in the governor's office until his death in 1928. Pothier was not a rabble-rousing radical. As a banker and industrial promoter, he was dependably conservative. It should be noted that from time to time there have been deep rivalries in the Catholic Church of Rhode Island between Irish and French-Canadian clerics and laymen. While these disputes have no direct bearing on politics, the indirect implications are obvious.

consequently both the legislative arena and campaigns reflect an atmosphere of competition between the parties that is utterly unlike the processes of the one-party state.

By virtue of the apportionment of the Senate, the Republicans most of the time have a veto on legislative policy decisions. In 10 of the 14 elections between 1930 and 1956 Republicans have won a majority of the Senate, and in the four remaining elections the Democrats got control only through the tie-breaking vote of the lieutenant governor (in 1934, 1948, 1950, and 1954).[12] Each of Rhode Island's 39 towns is entitled to one senator, regardless of its population; when a town has more than 25,000 voters, it is entitled to an extra senator. In no case, however, may any one town have more than six senators.[13] By this reckoning two cities have more than one senator (Pawtucket with two and Providence with five), but the catch is that there are 13 of the 39 towns which have less than 5,000 population each. Taken together these 13 towns have 3.7 per cent of the state's total population, but they elect just under 30 per cent of the Senate.[14] Since most of these small towns are consistently, and one might almost say permanently, Republican, the Democratic chances for control of the Senate are slim indeed.

The usual majorities of the Democratic party in the state at large are more accurately reflected in the House, where Democratic control has been the rule since 1930.[15] The House is based upon population with the exception that each town must have at least one representative and that no town may have more than one-quarter of the membership of the 100-member House. This discriminates against Providence (with nearly a third of the population), but the

---

[12] Following the 1934 election the Democrats managed to gain a tie only by the dubious process of invalidating the election results in two districts where the Republican candidates had apparently won. By quickly unseating the two Republicans and replacing them with their Democratic opponents, a majority was attained. (See below, pp. 191-193.)

[13] See Rhode Island Constitution, Art. vi, Sec. 1 and Art. xix (1928 Amendment).

[14] In fact, all towns under 10,000 population (in all, 22 towns as of the 1950 census), combined have 12.1 per cent of the population but elect exactly one-half of all the senators. In 1951 these 22 towns sent 19 Republicans and 3 Democrats to the Senate, and in the remaining larger towns and cities the Republicans were on the other end of a 19-3 split, with the consequence that there was a tie for Senate control: 22-22.

[15] In the 1938 Republican sweep the Democrats did lose control of the House, but since the 1920's Democratic majorities have been common there.

cities are so overwhelmingly Democratic that the slight favoritism for the small towns becomes insignificant.[16]

The organization of the Republican party reflects the legislative apportionment from which the party benefits. The Republican State Convention, for example, is composed of six delegates from Providence and two each from the other 38 towns, thus weighting the balance in favor of the small towns even more than in the Senate.[17] The convention names the state's delegation to the national party convention and writes the platform, and therefore is not too important a body. Actually more important than the convention is the state central committee, which formally endorses candidates for all statewide and congressional offices prior to the primary. This committee, like the convention, is set up to favor the rural areas. Its membership is comprised of two members from each town, except for Providence, which sends one member for each of its 13 wards. This leaves the Providence Republicans much underrepresented.[18] The structure of both the convention and the state central committee not only reflects the rural orientation of the party but also is suggestive of one of the greatest divisive forces in the party—the urban-rural split.

A coterie comprised of senators from small towns and town leaders who back them constitutes the hard core of the party's leadership. They have power because they can control the largest bloc of Republican official strength—the Senate. Other Republicans may resent the hard-shelled Protestants who dominate this wing of the party, but virtually no Republican would consent to altering the apportionment of the Senate in any way that would relinquish this hold. In one sense the small-town Senate bloc is a millstone around the party's neck; in another sense it is the party's last impregnable bastion of power. Often conservative in the extreme, the Senate bloc embarrasses the remainder of the party by its refusal to accept more

[16] In the analysis of legislative apportionment by Dauer and Kelsay, *op.cit.*, the Senate was listed as the 45th in degree of inequality of population per district, whereas the House ranked 28th or near the median for all states.

[17] David, Moos, and Goldman, *op.cit.*, p. 104.

[18] There is an added contingent of "at-large" members on the committee—15 in 1957—and they are coopted by the committee itself. The at-large members in 1957 included only two additional Providence residents. See *Providence Journal-Bulletin Almanac, 1957*, pp. 271-272. Except for the at-large members, the personnel of both the convention and the state central committee are chosen by local party committees in each town and city.

or less liberal legislation, which in the view of urban and more progressive Republicans is necessary if the party is to win over urban Democratic and independent votes. The Senate bloc is also largely Protestant and Yankee, and so long as the reins of party leadership are in their hands, the urban group of Republicans has a difficult time in currying favor with the urban ethnic groups who have no particular love for the Yankees.

There is also reason to believe that a good many of the Republican small-town contingent have at times lined up with the Democrats. The urban groups have done this too, but many of the small-town group have stayed in office for so long and have established such firm ties with those constantly in power that patronage offers and other favors have cooled the ardor of some members of the Senate small-town faction. On innumerable occasions in American politics the offer of jobs, contracts, and other favors—if handled right by the majority—has made a minority group less than zealous in its efforts to supplant the majority. Clearly there has been a great deal of this double-dealing between Democrats and Republicans in Rhode Island.

The Democrats point out that they are merely giving a fair break to the best man, regardless of party affiliation. In some respects this is no doubt a factor in deciding who gets appointments. But for a party in a dominant position, as the Democrats are—and furthermore one operated as a tightly controlled and patronage-conscious machine—the temptation to use patronage for lessening the threat to jobs must be great. Shortly after a bright and upcoming Republican Senator, Joseph R. Weisberger, had been appointed to the bench, public statements at a political meeting highlighted the patronage point.[19] Bayard Ewing was being congratulated on the occasion of his being elected Republican national committeeman, and one speaker told the gathering, "if the new committeeman con-

[19] Weisberger was thought to be a political threat because he was young, a good talker, and had a liberal record as a senator. Moreover he was a double danger because he could establish easy contacts with two different ethnic groups. A Jewish father bequeathed him his name, but an Irish mother gave him his Catholic religion. Although the Jewish population of the state is not very large, his contact with the Jewish community plus the fact that he was an officer of the Knights of Columbus had some Democrats afraid that he might make a stab at higher things than the Senate. His appointment to the bench at the early age of 35 took care of the problem. See *Providence Journal*, Feb. 15, 1956.

tinued to fight Democrats as stubbornly as he had been, 'Mr. Roberts [the Democratic governor] will offer him a job.' "[20]

One of the leaders of the small-town Senate bloc is George D. Greenhalgh of Glocester (population of 2,682 in 1950), who has been in the Senate since 1935. A conservative and professional politician, Greenhalgh has been the minority party member of the Commission on Horse Racing and Athletics since its creation in 1946. The job pays $6,500 a year. (There is no ban on holding both legislative and administrative positions in Rhode Island.) As a leader of the small-town bloc and as a canny politician, Greenhalgh is often the man with whom the Democrats deal when seeking to resolve their problems with the minority party. Greenhalgh is not on the best of terms with the element of the Republican party representing the urban and suburban areas. During the 1955 session, for example, he boycotted the Republican caucus for weeks, ostensibly because the Republican membership had refused to support unanimously a decision reached in caucus, but apparently his anger was directed at Weisberger and the more liberal element in general rather than being aroused over a breach of custom. In the course of a bitter contest for the election of a new state Republican chairman in 1957 there were thinly veiled accusations that Greenhalgh and his candidate for the state chairmanship (Herbert B. Carkin) had conspired with the Democrats. A telegram sent to an anti-Senate faction meeting said: "Watched Senator George D. Greenhalgh . . . warmly, in fact violently, embrace his benefactor J. Howard McGrath, when they met in Washington [at the 1957 inaugural]. Wish every Republican in Rhode Island could realize that this physical embrace is symbolic of the position of many so-called Republicans who still play follow-the-leader with Thomas Paolino [recently elected by the General Assembly to the Supreme bench, having been Republican national committeeman]. . . ." The telegram went on to say that President Eisenhower had won the state in spite of the "dubious attachment and activities of Mr. Carkin and many of his supporters."[21]

Whatever the truth of the accusations of complicity with the Democrats on the part of the small-town Senate faction, ample basis for

---

[20] *Providence Journal*, Feb. 16, 1956. Ewing's reply was that "there is no job within Governor Roberts' power to give that I would take if offered it." The crowd cheered.

[21] See the story in the *Providence Journal*, Jan. 25, 1957.

conflict between the two factions would still exist. There are often considerable policy differences between the two groups, as I have indicated. Indeed at the close of the 1953 session, the state central committee issued a blast at the dominant group in the Senate which sounded more like one party condemning another than intra-party invective. The committee claimed the "Old Guard Republicans," naming Greenhalgh and Donald A. Kingsley (majority leader that term) specifically, had "run out on" the Republican platform. The party had suffered through their obstructionism, said their opponents on the state committee.[22] In an apparent effort to win back some lost ground, the state chairman announced he would appoint a committee to draw up a legislative program for the party in a forthcoming special session.

The conflict between these two groups is an interesting and revealing instance of the interplay of constitutional and political realities. The constitutional mandate for small-town overrepresentation—originally established for political reasons—stands both as a blessing and as a barrier to the Republican party in the state. Insofar as it has given tenure and power to "unrepresentative" legislators, it has been an invitation to disaster. Such legislators are relatively unconcerned with the party as a whole; their concern is for their own reelection and the best deal they can wangle for themselves from the majority party and from interest groups who need their support. The interests they work with are mainly the business groups in the state, but their very cooperativeness with such groups in using a senatorial veto on legislation proposed by the Democrats is made to order for Democratic propaganda. In a democratic political system one of the salutary forces is the fear of the next election day; insofar as any powerful group need have no particular fear of retribution on election day the chances for its going astray are multiplied. Thus, while it is true that the party has gained by having some power to threaten with, it is also disadvantageous that that power should be held by a permanently fixed minority without particular fear of defeat.

Unquestionably the fortunes of the Republican party had to de-

[22] See *Providence Journal*, May 12, 1953. One committeeman summed up their report this way: "Who is running the Republican Party? The official party convention which adopts the party platform or 28 Republican senators who get together sixty days a year?"

cline under the impact of the Depression and the "liberation" of immigrant groups who had been denied full rights for a century. Whether the bottom need have fallen so completely out from under the Republican party after 1932 is a question no one can answer with assurance, but one may speculate that the very maldistribution of legislative seats may have done as much to hinder as to help the party's fortunes. The party has not been without able leaders. But many of those leaders have not been able to move to the fore past the Senate bloc, and particularly has this been true of Catholic politicians and members of ethnic minorities. The leadership element of Yankees has always tossed some patronage to minorities—beginning with Brayton's promotion of Governor Pothier—but in general the contemporary leadership has been unwilling to accept, for example, the Italians as candidates for high office. Even though grudgingly, Democratic leaders had nominated Italians for statewide office as early as 1930; not until 1944 did Republican leaders extend such recognition.[23] The difference between the parties in terms of ethnic and religious followings is illustrated by the makeup of the delegations to the national conventions of 1952. The Republican delegation was comprised of five Protestants and three Catholics; the Democratic delegation of 19 Catholics and one Protestant.[24] The Democratic delegation is not very accurately "representative" of the actual distribution of religious memberships in the state, but it is obvious that the disproportionately non-Catholic control of the Republican party is not politically helpful where the population of the state is nearly two-thirds Catholic.[25]

The Republican party cannot win elections by depending primarily on the small-town vote. Rhode Island is virtually a city state, and any party failing to reflect this fact does so at its own peril. It is quite possible, however, that the Republican party is now under-

[23] Benjamin Cianciarulo was named speaker of the House as a Republican in the 1920's, but the Republican party refused to give him or any other Italian nominations for higher offices. Cianciarulo switched to the Democrats later and was given an appointive job by them. In 1934 an Italian Republican was nominated for secretary of state, but this was the lone exception to the rule of exclusion. After 1944, however, an Italian has always appeared somewhere on the Republican state ticket, but by this time the Italians in the Democratic party had their sights on the gubernatorial nomination (which they got in 1946).

[24] See David, Moos, and Goldman, *op.cit.*, pp. 110, 117.

[25] The official *Catholic Directory* indicates that the proportion of Catholics in the state is about 61 per cent of the total population. *Op.cit.*, p. 572.

going something of a renaissance which may bring it back into real contention for power precisely because it is beginning to recognize the demographic facts of life. Migration to suburbia and social mobility have put politics in a new light for many second- and third-generation descendants of the foreign-born. Where their families could never consider voting for the party of the mill owners, the younger generation now find that party more to their taste. They are not mill hands as their parents were; they are frequently white-collar workers and often are desperately anxious to lose whatever stigma that may have become associated with "foreignness." Rebellion against the Democratic party has been one of the ways of asserting a complete break with the past.

There were other factors than this involved in President Eisenhower's success in the metropolitan areas in 1952 and 1956, but this was one important factor. It helped him to win 51 per cent of the two-party vote in Rhode Island in 1952 and 58 per cent in 1956. In 1956 the Republican party for the first time ran an Italian-American for a high office—the governorship. Christopher Del Sesto, a Democrat ten years earlier, was the Republican nominee, and he won an actual majority of all the votes cast for the office. Undoubtedly the fact that President Eisenhower was running strongly helped Del Sesto, but equally if not more important than either of these facts was Del Sesto's Italian background. Del Sesto got a boost from Italian-American neighborhoods, normally solidly Democratic. The Republican party, by challenging the Democrats in the field of ethnic political maneuvering, had won an apparent victory. But the victory was more apparent than real, for through the invalidation of some absentee ballots Roberts, not Del Sesto, was declared the winner. Republican leaders are jubilantly certain that this "disenfranchisement" of some 5,000 voters has made enough voters angry to put their candidate in the governor's chair in 1958. That remains to be seen. But there is no doubt that Del Sesto's strength at the polls has established him as the most powerful figure in the party. In a knock-down and drag-out fight for the control of the party organization shortly after the election, Del Sesto's candidate for state chairman ousted an incumbent chairman backed by the small-town Senate faction. For the moment the urban-liberal wing of the party is in control, and if that wing of the party can win the election and solidify its position, a new day may be coming for the Republican party in Rhode Island.[26]

Prediction of easy sledding in the Republican party in Rhode Island in the near future is, however, a risky venture. Several things stand in the way. The traditional alignment of the voters is unquestionably with the Democrats and only the most unusual circumstances seem to change their voting habits. The state is, as we have said, highly industrialized and by now is accustomed to welfare state operations in considerable degree. Should the Republican party win the governorship and the General Assembly, it would have considerable difficulty in enacting a liberal program, since the party still gets its money and much of its backing and influence from conservative business interests. The latter would not be likely to convert to liberalism for the sake of combatting the Democrats. Finally, the small-town Senate faction would still have power through its control of the Senate. Any Republican governor would have to deal with them if he wanted his program passed.

Before reaching the conclusion that the 1956 election was the turning point of Rhode Island's contemporary political history, it would be well to recall the events of the interim Republican administration of 1939-1941. That administration suffered from deep internal divisions in the ranks of the party and, while that alone cannot be cited as the reason for failing to maintain an advantage gained through the 1938 election, it certainly was an important contributing factor. The election of William H. Vanderbilt, scion of the famous Vanderbilt clan and among the wealthiest men in the country, as governor was attributable in part to the nationwide decline of the Democratic party in the 1938 election, but more important was the situation the preceding Democratic governor had allowed himself to get into. An encounter between the governor, Robert Quinn, and Walter O'Hara, a race-track operator and factional opponent of the governor, had led to charges of bribery, libel suits, and ultimately martial law to close the track operated by O'Hara. The repercussions of this affair helped put Vanderbilt in the governor's chair.

[26] The new day came—or at least a day of revenge. Del Sesto beat Roberts notwithstanding the Democratic tide of 1958. His margin was so close (51 per cent) that he failed to take in with him majorities in either house of the General Assembly or any Republican statewide elective officer.

Vanderbilt was young, only thirty-eight, idealistic, and determined to make a good record for the party. He was backed, however, by the urban elements of the party and soon won the bitter opposition of the small-town regulars. One of his bitterest legislative battles was over the creation of a civil service system for the state. The oldtimers from the Senate faction wanted nothing to do with it. Vanderbilt turned to the press and radio to attack them. "These men [the Republicans who were opposing him] were elected on a platform of civil service," said Vanderbilt. "Now they are going to renege. You, the voter, must remind them of their promise and let them know that it means political suicide to block it."[27] The pressure was great enough to force the civil service bill through, but Vanderbilt won no lasting political friendships with the professionals of his party.

In an effort to ban dual job holding (the practice of simultaneously holding legislative office and serving on administrative boards) Vanderbilt was defeated soundly in the General Assembly, but he steadfastly refused to appoint legislators to salaried jobs.[28] With moral indignation Vanderbilt refused to give the names of state officials to the New England Race Track Association, which had requested the list from him for the purpose of extending free passes to the race track. He replied, "I do not wish to be a party to the distribution of race-track passes to state officials."[29] However, in the course of the bitter struggle within the Republican party, Vanderbilt resorted to hiring a private detective agency to tap some telephone wires for him. He denied that he had placed taps on the telephone of his own attorney general, but the charges were serious enough to bring a complete investigation by a young United States attorney for Rhode Island, J. Howard McGrath. "The result of this episode," said one account, "was to open the governor's office to McGrath."[30] This is an exaggeration of the reasons behind Vanderbilt's downfall, although the incident did not help his chances in 1940. Franklin Roosevelt won 57 per cent of the vote in the state that year, and Vanderbilt was not given much help by the Old Guard wing of his own party. The hopeful interlude was over.

---

[27] Quoted from Thomas E. Murphy, "Rhode Island's Vanderbilt," 51 *Current History* 50-52 (Oct. 1939) at p. 50.

[28] *Ibid.*, p. 51.   [29] *Ibid., loc.cit.*

[30] Henry H. Smith, "With Howard, Howard Comes First," 173 *Nation* 421-423 (Nov. 17, 1951) at p. 421.

In short, the divisions within the Republican party are and have been for a long time deep and debilitating. The position of the party has produced a defeatist attitude among many Republicans, and many able newcomers to politics have cast their lot with the Democrats simply because it was the dominant party and the chances for advancement seem best there. Moreover, it seems undeniable that some Republicans have been willing to sell out the party's chances for their own personal gain. The squabbles between the urban and rural wings of the party have prevented an united front that might have won them elections.

There is thus a kind of bifactional division in the Republican party—an urban and a rural wing. Contests between them for control of the party machine are often vigorous, to say the least, and much dirty party linen gets a public washing. Notwithstanding the factional schisms, the party organization is not powerless and insignificant. The state central committee has the power to endorse candidates for the state ticket, and occasionally it can influence the distribution of patronage. It is not uncommon for the committee to use its power to urge policy enactments and to crack down on rebels with disciplinary action. Indeed, the fact that the factions do struggle for control of the committee suggests that it has political significance.

Traditionally the Republican central organization has been strong, although this is not nearly so true now as before the fall of the party in 1932 when the Democrats took over. The loss of the governorship implied a loss of state patronage which had been a prime means of keeping control over legislators. Thus in recent years the small-town Senate bloc lost control over the central party organization, but their actions were beyond the power of the state central committee to control. Still, the fact remains that the party is reasonably well integrated from top to bottom. Perhaps this is partly due to the fact that the state is so small. Sectionalism has not been great enough to form nuclei for counter-organization. Moreover, political leaders on the local level can know and be in frequent contact with leaders at the top of the party. In party financial matters there appears to be reasonably close cooperation between the upper and lower levels of the party.

Finally, and perhaps most important, the party organization built up its strength in the absence of a primary, which undoubtedly enhanced the power of the top organization. Practicing politicians in Rhode Island, like their colleagues in most areas, had no love for the primary, and it is perhaps but a reflection of the strength of the organization that the primary came to Rhode Island next to last of all the states (only Connecticut held out longer). Even when the primary law was passed in 1947, it was cast in such a form as to keep its impact at a minimum. The law permits the state central committee to endorse candidates for each statewide office and for congressional seats; at lower levels the town committees perform a similar function for local offices. The candidate given the endorsement gets first place on the ballot, and beside his name goes an asterisk to indicate his having been blessed by the leadership. From the organization of the primary in 1948 to 1956 no endorsed candidate for statewide or congressional office in either party has failed to win a primary election.

The Rhode Island primary has apparently already fallen into disuse—at least where top-level jobs are concerned. Table 20 indicates this.

Contests for nomination for the General Assembly are equally sparse. In the three most recent elections (1952, 1954, 1956) there were contests in only four of the 44 Senate districts in the first two years and eight in the latter year. Similarly in the House of Representatives nominations there were few contests. The House has 100 members but there were only 11 contests in 1952, three in 1954, and seven in 1956.

Unlike certain other states, where in recent times, as compared with half a century ago, there has been a sharp drop in the proportion of candidates put up for the legislature, the parties in Rhode Island continue to nominate candidates for every or nearly every seat in the General Assembly. In 1952, for example, the Republicans (notwithstanding their minority position) named a candidate for every House and Senate seat, although in one case the town committee did not nominate, and the state central committee used its power to choose a candidate. In 1954 there were no vacancies of nominees left by any town committee, and only one was left vacant in 1956. If the hypothesis is correct that the primary has tended to wither the local party organizations since the locus of power is shifted from the party organs to the electorate in what amounts to an election before the election, then Rhode Island stands as an exception. Local

TABLE 20

Republican Primaries for Major Offices, 1948-1956

	OFFICE CONTESTED AND VOTE RECEIVED			
Year	*U.S. Senator*	*Governor*	*Lt. gov.*	*Sec. of state*
1948	*Hazard: 31,421	*Ruerat: 29,607	*Meunier: 33,513	*Carrellas: 27,887
	Jackvony: 10,477	Archambault: 18,572	Colagiovanni: 13,034	Burns: 17,719
	Sundlan: 9,811	Windsor: 3,136		

Attorney gen'l.	*Treasurer*	Congress (First dist.)	Congress (Sec. dist.)
*Murphy: 33,926	No contest	No contest	*Paolino: 11,013
Abedon: 13,963	"	"	Kelly: 8,404
			Thompson: 5,286
			Moses: 1,045

1950 No primary for any office; all uncontested.

1952 No primary for any office, except Congress, Second District:
*Watts:
9,644
Nelson
1,150

1954 No primary for any office; all uncontested.
1956 No primary for any office; all uncontested.

Source: Data from *The Official Count of Ballots Cast* for corresponding years. Prepared by Rhode Island Board of Elections.
* Indicates the endorsed candidate.

organizations remain alive and active even though in some cases they represent areas where they are overwhelmingly in the minority.

Patently the present form of party primary has had no great impact on the internal politics of the Republican party. There are those who argue that this lack of effect stems from the favored position given the endorsed candidate, but this seems doubtful. When primaries are called, the electors have ample opportunity to ignore the asterisk and vote for whomever they prefer. The tradition of the strong party, the hold that the party organizations have on the decision-making machinery and more particularly over the avenues of political advancement are so complete that rebel forces are discouraged from resorting to primary contests. Against such counter-currents factionalism has not flourished.

Rhode Island Democrats: The "New Yankees" Take Over

The last-ditch resort and high-handed tactics seem almost natural to Rhode Island politics. A certain amount of bitterness in the politics of any of our states can be anticipated, but bitterness backed up with nearly or actually rebellious force is hardly customary. Yet such extremes are endemic in Rhode Island policies. True, there has been only one armed attempt at a *coup d'état*—and that unsuccessful—but near *coups* and violent wrangling have characterized the state's politics. Riots, exile, legislative fistfights, stolen elections, disregard for the spirit and the letter of the constitution—all these and more have been features of Rhode Island's political history.

Bitter-end conservatives of the dim past set a pattern which their more liberal successors have followed with appalling faithfulness. Reactionaries made Rhode Island the last of the states to alter a pre-Revolutionary charter, while the community became more and more deeply and bitterly divided on the question of revision. Hence the Dorr Rebellion. Textile-mill owners imported European and Canadian laborers to work at substandard wages in their mills. Worker antagonism toward the well-to-do entrepreneurs of the mills was almost unbounded, and conversely the aristocratic and wealthy ruling elite thoroughly distrusted the political good sense of their imported minions and therefore refused to extend the suffrage right to them. No state outside the South did so much to restrict the right to vote as did Rhode Island.

The Democratic party early became the spokesman for the under-dog and disenfranchised immigrants and offered a nucleus for counterorganization against the oligarchic element which ran the state. Even as extremes were used to prevent immigrant-worker groups from entering political affairs, so the Democratic party was ready to use extremes to accomplish the goals of the depressed groups. In 1922, for example, a Democratic governor and lieutenant governor were elected, but the party failed to carry the Senate. With the cooperation of Lieutenant Governor Felix A. Toupin the Democratic minority staged a 41-day "debate" on the adoption of Senate rules. Toupin developed an inability to see any Republican when he got to his feet, and the Democratic harangue went on week after week. The purpose was to force the Republicans to vote on three Democratic platform measures: eliminating property qualifications for voting, redistricting the Senate, and calling a constitutional convention. Eventually the Republicans consented to vote on the bills, and with their majority naturally defeated all three proposals.

During the following session of the legislature in 1924 the tensions were perhaps even greater than before. Acrimonious debate on one occasion turned into a full-fledged riot "when Senators and spectators engaged in a battle which brought sheriffs and police to quell the disturbance."[31] This particular session began on June 17 and was not adjourned for fifty-three hours. On June 19 a "gas bomb" was released in the chamber. So noxious were the fumes that five Senators collapsed; adjournment was the only recourse. The Democratic senators went on demanding redress of their grievances and the Republicans were unwilling to concede, so on June 22 the Republican senators took voluntary exile in a Massachusetts hotel, and the Democrats, lacking a quorum to do business, had to give up. As a result the session failed to pass an appropriation act. Twenty-three banks advanced $400,000 to tide the state over. Another probable result of the unruly session was the defeat of several Senate Democrats at the 1924 election and the reelection of all thirteen Republican senators who sought reelection. The Democrats also lost all major state offices as Aram Pothier was recalled from retirement to save the day for the GOP.

Even more dramatic and more significant were the events of January 1, 1935, when a *coup d'état* reminiscent of Latin American politics took place. Democratic Governor Theodore F. Green had won the 1932 election, but the hands of the Democrats were securely tied during his first term by the Republicans who retained both houses of the General Assembly. Republican leaders had the infamous Brayton Law to depend on to keep their men in administrative positions, regardless of the wishes of the Democratic governor. By simply allowing the governor's nominations to lie on the table for three days, the Senate could appoint whomever it liked to any position the governor had suggested filling. Thus the Republicans held nearly all administrative and judicial positions. The Democrats decided to do something about the situation.

[31] For a brief account of this engagement see the *Providence Journal-Bulletin Almanac, 1953*, p. 18.

The election of 1934 returned Governor Green to office and the House of Representatives was safely Democratic, but in the Senate the Republicans appeared to have a two-seat majority. Immediately after the Senate convened, the lieutenant governor proceeded with swearing in the newly elected senators, but he refused to swear in two presumably elected Republican senators from Portsmouth and South Kingston. This made the lineup 20-20 between the parties. A tie-breaking vote by the Democratic lieutenant governor allowed the appointment of a committee to recount the votes of the two senators who had been denied the oath of office. There having been no previous contest on these two close elections, the ballots were not sealed, so the committee proceeded to review the ballots, threw out several that were "defective," and reported back that the Democratic candidates had been elected by pluralities of 10 and 24 votes. It took the help of some state troopers to produce two Republican senators to comprise the necessary quorum but with the escapees returned the Senate duly swore in the two "new" Democratic senators.

With a clear majority thus assured, the Senate then concurred with the House in the removal of all members of the Supreme Court, all of them Republicans. (No Democrat had served on that bench for sixty-three years!) A new court was promptly appointed consisting of three Democrats and two Republicans. Then within minutes many state boards and commissions were abolished, and some eighty governmental units were reorganized into eleven departments under the control of the governor. There being no Civil Service Law protection, the consequences for office-holding Republicans were what one might expect. Few survived the house-cleaning operation.[32]

A few months later, Governor Green, speaking to the General Assembly, reminded them of Roger Williams, founder of the state, who, he said, had established among other "principles of democratic government," the "right of rebellion." "American democracy itself owes an enormous debt to him," the governor went on. "And in our State's history there have been many times when that spirit of dissent and rebellion has shown forth. These times stretch from the colonizing days, through the foundation of the Republic, to present period of reorganization and readaptation."[33] Newspaper commenta-

[32] For a complete account of these events, see Zachariah Chaffee, Jr., *The Constitutional Convention That Never Met*, Providence, 1938.
[33] *Annual Message of Theodore Francis Green*, Jan. 1936, p. 26.

tors around the country used harsher language than "reorganization and readaptation" for what had happened in the first weeks of 1935, but the governor was unquestionably correct that their moves were in keeping with the spirit of Rhode Island "dissent and rebellion."

Evidence that the tempestuous spirit of Rhode Island state politics lives on today is to be found in the election dispute of 1956, referred to earlier. The contestants were Governor Dennis J. Roberts and Christopher Del Sesto. Roberts had come to the governorship in 1950 from the office of mayor of Providence, and the consensus is that he is due to be promoted to the Senate when U.S. Senator Green finally retires. The chance to run for senator, however, demands that the hopeful keep his political lines intact, and no position is better for that purpose than the governorship.[34] Retaining the governorship was all-important to Roberts, a lifelong politician. As he approached the election his chances seemed reasonably good. His ability as an administrator is generally recognized, and he had kept himself clear of scandal. There was some grumbling about his administration and more about the long tenure of the Democrats, but this had all been heard before without harmful results.

But that was without reckoning on the Republican candidate, an Italian-American. Ironically it was Roberts, who, as boss of Providence Democratic politics, helped to decide that it would be John O. Pastore and not Del Sesto who would be promoted to the state ticket in 1944. Both Senator Green and Governor McGrath favored Del Sesto, then a Democrat, but Roberts wanted Pastore for the job. Roberts was then in the navy, but he drove from Washington to Harrisburg, Pa., with Senator Green to confer with Governor McGrath, then attending the annual governor's conference. As Samuel Lubell tells the story, "Their first opportunity to talk was on Decoration Day, as the governors toured the Gettysburg Battlefield. While Leverett Saltonstall, then governor of Massachusetts, was delivering a memorial address, the three Rhode Island politicos exchanged whispers and agreed on Pastore as lieutenant governor."[35]

[34] It would be rash to predict an early vacancy in the Senate, however. Senator Green was born in 1867, just two years after the end of the Civil War, but he continues to be sprightly and active. In 1937 the late Zachariah Chaffee, Jr., wrote that, "it is not unfair for ambitious Rhode Islanders to foresee an early Senate vacancy, for Senator Green has lately passed the Scriptural time-limit of seventy years. . . ." *State House Versus Pent House*, Providence, The Book Shop, 1937, p. 8.

[35] Samuel Lubell, "Rhode Island's Little Firecracker," 222 *Saturday Evening Post* 31 ff. (Nov. 12, 1949) at p. 178.

Del Sesto was by no means without political experience. As a Democrat he had been "state budget director, state finance director, a member of the staff of the chief accountant of the Federal Securities and Exchange Commission, a special assistant to the United States Attorney General in the Anti-trust Division of the Department of Justice, and during World War II, state director of OPA in Rhode Island."[36]

Del Sesto attributed his split with the Democratic party to his attack on OPA, the controls of which he thought "should be removed as soon as possible. I was practically read out of the party."[37] One may speculate, however, that the Harrisburg meeting may have had a good deal to do with the decision to switch party allegiance. Whatever the reason he became an asset to the Republicans. After an unsuccessful bid for the mayoralty of Providence in 1952, he sought but was denied the nomination for governor in 1954; he came back to win it in 1956, the first Italian-American so honored by the Republican party.

When the voting machine results were counted on election night, Governor Roberts had a slim lead of 190 votes. This did not include the civilian absentee ballots; when these were added in, Del Sesto took the lead by 226 votes. Subsequently the votes of "shut-ins" were added and Del Sesto's lead shot up to 934. At about this time, Governor Roberts said, "Let me emphatically say that I will accept the governorship again only if it is the clear expression of the will of the people of Rhode Island as determined by their vote and under no other circumstances."[38] Slowly the count of servicemen's absentee ballots came in and Del Sesto's lead shrank but did not disappear. In mid-December he still led with all votes counted by 427 votes.[39] When interviewed for an article in the *New York Times*, it was his not unjustified assumption that he was to be the state's next governor. "I have two jobs," the *Times* quoted him as saying, "to direct the operations of the state and to supervise the operations of the Republican party in the state."[40]

He was not to be governor in 1957-1958, however. Roberts resorted to the courts to have the votes of the civilian absentees and

[36] *New York Times*, Dec. 18, 1956.   [37] *Ibid.*
[38] *Providence Journal*, Nov. 28, 1956.
[39] See *Providence Journal*, Jan. 2, 1957 for a summary of the vote count.
[40] *New York Times*, Dec. 18, 1956.

shut-ins invalidated. The contention was that those ballots cast before election day were not valid because a statute permitting the casting of these ballots "on or before" election day was unconstitutional. (Roberts himself had signed the statute in question.) The Constitutional Amendment authorizing absentee ballots was said not to permit casting ballots prior to election day. Not until 3:00 p.m. of Inauguration Day did the Supreme Court announce its decision. By a three-to-one majority the court ruled that only the 648 absentee ballots cast on election day were valid. Even if all these went to Del Sesto, Roberts still had a slim plurality of 63 votes. The court declared him the winner.[41] To say the very least of this maneuvering, Roberts was reelected by something other than the "clear expression of the will of the people," which he had said would be his only grounds for continuing as governor.

It does not excuse the skulduggery of the Democrats to say that their Republican predecessors, when in undisputed power, performed similar acts, but it may help to explain their tendency to resort to such tactics. The bitterness engendered by the earlier deprivations and discrimination against minority groups so divided the community that the restraints that might normally apply were often disregarded. Driven to desperation, at least in their view, the Democrats resorted to methods that seemed justified to redress old grievances. The Roberts-Del Sesto fiasco may seem to be a simple case of risking all to hold onto a job in pure and simple selfishness, but it would be unwise to conclude that this affair is entirely apart from the standing traditions. Roberts dared do what he did and others had the temerity to support him not only for the sake of patronage and party loyalty, but also out of the long habit of taking whatever steps seem necessary to revenge old wounds.

One goal the Democrats have long sought to improve their political position has been consistently denied them—a constitutional convention. This was among their objectives in the 1923-1924 dis-

[41] The court majority was comprised of two Democrats and one Republican. (The latter being Thomas Paolino, appointed with Roberts' approval a year before.) The dissenter was a Republican justice, Harold Andrews, who agreed that the court interpretation of the law was correct but held that Roberts' challenge was not timely. Governor Roberts' brother, Thomas H. Roberts, the remaining member of the panel, did not participate in the case. See the opinions as reprinted in the *Providence Journal*, Feb. 14, 1957. The official election returns give Roberts a plurality of 711 votes since the 648 valid votes could not be identified, and thus had to be disregarded. See the *Official Account of Ballots Cast*, 1956, p. 26.

putes, and it was again sought in 1935-1936. In the latter case they were denied the chance to call a convention because at first some small-town Democrats refused to go along with the party, and later when a majority had been mustered to pass a bill for a convention, the electorate rejected it at the polls.[42] On subsequent occasions when the Democrats have had control of the Senate through a tie resolved by Democratic lieutenant governors, efforts to get a convention bill passed have always foundered when one or more small-town Democrats absent themselves from the vote. It has been contended that the leading Democrats really do not want a convention to change the apportionment of the Senate, even though they claim this is among their most ardent desires. The contention is that they are happy to have a conservative Senate dominated by Republicans to kill off the bills they send from the House. Thus the Democrats can appear to be radical enough to attract votes, and sure at the same time of putting the stigma of anti-labor or anti-welfare on the Republican party as a whole. Whether Democratic leaders actually have such mixed motives in their demands for a convention, no one can say with certainty. But there is no doubt that they do use the conservatism of the Senate both to bury really unwanted bills and as a propaganda measure once the bills are killed.

The Politics of Nationality

When Al Smith ran for the presidency in 1928 he unleashed a powerful force for the Democratic party. As an Irish-Catholic and former poor boy from the streets of New York, he became the symbol of success for millions of Catholic immigrants and their descendants. His candidacy brought lower-income Catholic voters to the polls in unprecedented numbers. Only once prior to 1928 had Rhode Island voted for a Democratic presidential candidate (in 1912, when Wilson won a plurality but not a majority of the votes cast). The Al Smith campaign carried Rhode Island even if by a scant margin. Whereas John W. Davis had won but 38 per cent of the vote in 1924 in the state, Smith bettered this by 12.5 percentage points to win with 50.5 per cent.

The fact that Smith was a Democrat helped to cement a tie be-

---

[42] The vote against the convention was 100,000 to 88,000 for it. There is no initiative process in Rhode Island through which a convention referendum could be called.

tween the immigrant groups and the Democratic party. Most of the Irish had long since cast their lot with the Democrats, but many Italians and French-Canadians had had Republican leanings earlier in the century. For the French-Canadians this is at least in part explained by the candidacies of Aram Pothier and Emery San Souci, who between them occupied the Rhode Island governorship for eleven of the first twenty-eight years of this century.

The proportion of foreign-born and their first- and second-generation descendants in Rhode Island is probably larger than in any other state.[43] As of the 1950 census 49 per cent of the population of Rhode Island was "foreign stock" (that is, foreign-born plus native-born of mixed or foreign parentage), which ranked the state fourth among all states in this respect.[44] Politicians in Rhode Island are alert to every nuance of ethnic group politics. Indeed, the State Board of Elections prepared in 1954 an elaborate breakdown of the ethnic groups in every voting district in the state. By an examination of the names on voting lists a tabulation was made of the ethnic character of the voters, classifying them into ten different categories. Table 21 indicates the ethnic distribution of the whole state electorate and selected cities and towns.

In both parties the sub-leaders of the party particularly are comprised of a polyglot mixture of ethnic group representatives. This, of course, is a reflection both of the top leadership's effort to attract the favor of the members of the ethnic group and the inexorable demands of the ethnic group leadership for "representation" in the party. Where these leaders are at times locally selected, there is practically no alternative but that an Italian, an Irishman, or a French-Canadian must have the job in question, local concentrations of particular ethnic groups being so great.

As might be expected, the concentration of the "newer races," to use James Curley's term, is greater in the Democratic party than in the Republican. This is demonstrated by the distribution of names

[43] This is a reasonable assumption not a statistically verifiable fact, since there are no census data recorded beyond the first and second generations—that is, the foreign-born and their children. Yet the assumption would seem correct since the proportion of these two categories continues so high in the state and the state had more foreign-born and second-generation stock than any other state in 1920. It follows that the third generation too must be proportionally large.

[44] Only New York, Massachusetts, and Connecticut had higher proportions of foreign stock, and in any event not much greater. See E. P. Hutchinson, *op.cit.*, p. 29.

TABLE 21

Ethnic Distribution of Names on Voting Lists in Rhode Island, and in Selected Towns, 1954

	English	*Irish*	*French*	*Italian*	*Port.*	*Polish*	*Jewish*	*Germ.*	*Armen.*	*Misc.*
State	29%	20%	17%	16%	4%	3%	3%	2%	—1%	4%
Bristol	41	15	6	25	38	–	—1	6	–	1
Central Falls	14	14	51	2	3	3	–	–	–	2
Charlestown	75	7	7	3	–	–	—1	–	–	4
Cranston	32	20	6	25	2	2	3	3	1	7
Johnston	22	12	10	47	1	2	–	2	–	4
Pawtucket	30	22	24	6	3	5	–	2	1	7
Providence	21	26	7	27	1	2	8	2	2	3
Woonsocket	6	11	65	5	—1	6	1	—1	—1	4

Source: Data from *Survey of Rhode Island Electors*, 1954, compiled by State Board of Elections. Even granting that the process of identifying the ethnic derivation of names is subject to error and at best is somewhat unscientific, the general distribution must not be greatly in error. Naturally the data are even more impressive as to concentration of certain groups when the breakdown is by voting districts varying from a few hundred to roughly a thousand voters.

of members of the General Assembly, election to which is a fair sign that the individual has achieved at least a minor position of party leadership. As for the other states of New England the comparison in Table 22 is between the years 1900 and 1950.

TABLE 22

Ethnic Distribution of Members of the Rhode Island House of Representatives, 1900 and 1950

	DEMOCRATS				REPUBLICANS			
	1900		1950		1900		1950	
	Number	*Per cent of Dems.*	*Number*	*Per cent of Dems.*	*Number*	*Per cent of Repubs.*	*Number*	*Per cent of Repubs.*
Yankees	8	66.8%	15	22.1%	56	93.4%	27	84.4%
Irish	2	16.6	23	33.8	0	0	3	9.4
Italian	0	0	9	13.2	0	0	1	3.1
Fr. Canad.	2	16.6	15	22.1	4	6.6	1	3.1
Portuguese	0	0	3	4.4	0	0	0	0
Jewish	0	0	3	4.4	0	0	0	0
	12	100.0%	68	100.0%	60	100.0%	32	100.0%

Source: Data taken from the *Rhode Island Manual* for 1900-1901 and for 1951. Comparable analysis for the Senate produced similar results, although varying in details. In identifying the names, the brief biographies of each legislator contained in these volumes were of assistance, since they listed birthplaces and often membership in ethnic groups, such as the Sons of Italy, the Ancient Order of Hibernians, etc.

198

The heavy foreign-born population of the state has many political implications; three of the most significant are the boosting of the Democratic vote during the last quarter century, the tendency of ethnic groups to back one of "their own kind" even to the extent of ignoring party affiliations, and the tendency for ethnic group blocs to cause disruption in the party organizations. Some brief analysis of each of these points is necessary to grasp the character of Democratic politics in Rhode Island.

It is not difficult to find the consequences of the various forms of discrimination against the foreign-born in Rhode Island. In addition to the partial denial of the right to vote, the practices of the mill owners toward their employees, most of them imported to work at low wages in their textile factories, inspired a deep and rankling hatred for the upper classes, the monied interests, and the Republican party. Even now, says one able observer of Rhode Island politics, in many of the poorer Italian wards of Providence, the very mention of "mill owner" is enough to bring a stream of invective.[45] The same thing is true in such a city as Woonsocket, probably the greatest concentration of French-Canadians outside Quebec. (Recall that Table 21 showed only 6 per cent of the voters of Woonsocket had English names, whereas 65 per cent bore French names.)

One analysis of the votes of Rhode Islanders in the 1948 presidential election indicates the kind of impact that ethnic factors have on politics. Murray S. Stedman and Susan S. Stedman found a correlation between the proportion of foreign-born population in towns with the Democratic voting tendencies of those towns in the 1948 election. By ranking the towns according to percentages of Democratic vote and comparing this with a ranking by percentages of foreign-born, a coefficient of correlation of .88 was attained.[46] Like all statistical correlations, this one does not *prove* the Democratic tendencies of the foreign-born groups, but corroborating evidence

[45] David Cameron, formerly a political reporter for the *Providence Journal-Bulletin* and presently a member of the editorial staff of these papers. Cameron's reporting on Rhode Island politics has to some extent been specialized in ethnic group influences. Through his kindness the present work has the benefit of much of his painstaking research.

[46] The rank-correlation method was explained above in Chapter 3, pp. 63-64. Murray S. Stedman and Susan W. Stedman, *op.cit.*, pp. 333-334. A parallel investigation by the same method of correlation between tenant occupancy of homes (reflecting economic status) and Democratic voting percentages for 1948 produced a lower, but still significant correlation. *Loc.cit.*

strongly suggests that the statistical inference is not incorrect. Analysis of the 1956 presidential election in which President Eisenhower swept the state indicates the same general kind of distribution found by the Stedmans for 1948. Stevenson won or came close to winning only in those towns and cities with the heaviest foreign-born population, although the Republicans made inroads into former Democratic strongholds.

A second impact of ethnic factors on politics is the tendency for members of an ethnic group to desert their party allegiances and swarm in to vote for one of "their own kind." This undoubtedly happens, but the inferences that have been drawn from this tendency by practicing politicians have not been universally valid. In too many cases the politician has concluded that the important thing is to get a balanced ticket with names of each ethnic group displayed to attract the attention of every ethnic group sizable enough to warrant recognition. The assumption apparently is that the name is what counts. One can point to innumerable cases in which the name beginning with "O'" or ending in "o" or "ski" appeared to make no great difference to the voters to whom it was offered. Party allegiance is often stronger than ethnic ties, so that a candidate outside the ethnic group still wins. Although it is difficult to prove this point conclusively, it would appear that the pull of ethnic group affiliation is strong only when the candidate has some other attraction to the voter. When the candidate has a reputation for honesty, ability, or when he espouses popular causes (the categories are not mutually exclusive by any means), then the candidate drawn from the group in question will be likely to win votes regardless of party alignment; otherwise, he may produce no noticeable shift in the voting habits of the group. If the candidate, in short, becomes the symbol of success to the people of an ethnic group, he will win votes from them over and above the customary pull of his party. Just another Irishman, Italian, or French-Canadian probably will not.

Both John O. Pastore and Christopher Del Sesto were well known when they ran for office; both were widely respected as Italian-Americans who had gone far. In Pastore's case the pull of his Italian background was undoubtedly the factor that let him scrape by a fairly close election in 1946, a notably bad year for Democrats everywhere. (Pastore's plurality went from 22,429 in 1946 to 73,615 in 1948.) Notice in the statistics below the difference between J. Howard McGrath's 1944 vote when he ran for governor and Pastore's running for the same office in 1946.[47]

	McGrath (1944)	Pastore (1946)	Dif.
In 34 Italian districts	64.2%	69.9%	+5.7
In 31 Irish districts	69.1	59.8	−9.3
In 17 French-Canadian districts	72.7	60.1	−12.6
In 6 Yankee districts	43.4	34.8	−8.6

It is interesting and revealing to compare the percentages of the vote in the state's most predominantly Italian districts for Pastore in 1946, when he first ran for governor, and those received by Del Sesto in his 1956 bid for the same office. Pastore carried all but three of these 34 districts and his vote ranged from 41 per cent in the lowest to 93 in the highest, with the median being 74 per cent. Del Sesto carried 14 districts with his vote ranging from 31 to 71 per cent; the median of the districts was 49. For a Republican candidate to fight to a standoff in these districts was, of course, a considerable victory in itself. Normally all these districts are heavily Democratic, and it is obvious that many normally Democratic Italians deserted their party for Del Sesto.

How many normally Democratic voting Italian-Americans went all the way and voted for the whole Republican slate and how many split for Del Sesto alone it is impossible to tell, but some indication of the cutting can be found by comparing Del Sesto's vote with that of his running mate in predominantly Italian districts of Providence. Running with Del Sesto was William Broomhead, seeking the lieutenant governor's post. (Broomhead is a Yankee whom Del Sesto subsequently helped become state chairman of the Republican party.) Table 23 indicates the variance between the votes received by the two Republicans.

That such political figures as Pastore and Del Sesto can make voters abandon their customary voting habits not only has an impact in the voting booth but it also has a significant impact on political organization. Maneuvering to get a balanced ticket can result in neglect of simple considerations of ability in the search for the right "come-on" to minority groups. Slate-making is rarely one of the

[47] These data were prepared by David Cameron of the *Providence Journal-Bulletin*, and through his courtesy are used here. McGrath ran against a Yankee of Scotch background, and Pastore ran against an Irishman.

TABLE 23

Ticket-Splitting in Italian Wards of Providence, 1956

Repres. dist.	Voting dist.	Per cent for Del Sesto, R. (for gov.)	Per cent for Broom-head, R. (for lieut. gov.)	Difference
6	3	55%	44	—11%
7	1	50	42	—8
7	3	49	43	—6
8	2	50	42	—8
8	4	50	40	—10
12	1	54	40	—14
12	2	45	32	—13
13	2	36	28	—8
13	3	39	31	—8
13	4	46	27	—19
14	2	40	31	—9
15	3	48	37	—11
16	1	47	39	—8
16	2	53	40	—13
18	2	50	43	—7
18	3	49	43	—6
24	4	36	35	—1

more becoming facets of American politics. Territorial balance as well as ethnic balance can lead to disregard for virtue as well as ability. But the fact remains that powerful blocs—or what in some cases only appear to be powerful blocs of voters—demand that this or that place on the ticket be given to a particular ethnic group. In one sense nominating responsibility is transferred from the party to the ethnic group leadership, and the latter are often more interested in their own prestige and power than in the party, public policy, or any other element of responsibility.

As ethnic groups develop political consciousness, they are certain to make demands on the political parties. In Rhode Island Irish leaders have dominated the leadership ranks to the exclusion of others, and more recently arrived ethnic groups have resented this. Irish dominance is in part a simple consequence of the earlier arrival of the Irish and their earlier entrance into political life. The predominance of the Irish in Democratic politics is hardly unique to Rhode Island, nor even to New England, but in Rhode Island and the other New England states it seems to be especially resented since other ethnic minority groups are so numerous and politically potent. At the present time the state chairman of the Rhode Island Democratic party is of Italian derivation and one United States Senator is also Italian, but the dominant political power remains in the hands of Irish politicians.[48]

Democratic Party Organization:
Warfare of Machines

With patronage to dispense and nearly unshakeable local machines to depend upon, the Democratic organization is a powerful weapon of political control. While there is no single dominating boss sitting at the apex of this Democratic power pyramid, there is a small clique who make the important decisions of party strategy. Among the most powerful of them, and probably the most powerful single figure in the last analysis, is Governor Dennis Roberts. Senators Green and Pastore also wield some power in the party's inner councils, as does Frank Rao, the state chairman, to a lesser degree, but Roberts is apparently the most powerful man in the party.

Roberts' authority is based upon his control over the Providence Democratic organization, a power he did not relinquish when he ceased being the city's mayor and became governor. An executive assistant to Roberts when he was mayor has since been made mayor—Walter H. Reynolds—with Roberts' backing. Completely loyal to Roberts, Reynolds was one of the few top-rung Democrats in the state who publicly approved Roberts' appeal to the courts when the voters denied him reelection in 1956.

The importance of city machines to the Democratic party could hardly be overemphasized. They not only help to provide the votes with which the party stays in power, but they also form a tightly organized series of lower echelons to the state organization. While it is true that some fierce battles can at times break out between these city organizations, the promise of state patronage and the

[48] At present, for example, the Democratic state committee has 40 members with Italian names, but there are 83 with Irish-sounding names. Sixty-eight other members have various other ethnic backgrounds. It is the contention of the Italians and other groups that the Irish have more than their fair share; if the jobs were meted out in terms of ethnic proportions, this would indeed be the case. For the list of members see *Providence Journal-Bulletin Almanac*, 1957, p. 270.

threat of discipline from the state organization keeps the lower organizations in line.

The ghastly affair of the declaration of martial law against a race track's operators in 1937 illustrates the bitterness with which factional rivalries can be fought. The governor, Robert E. Quinn, had had to compete for succession to the governorship in 1936 against Thomas P. McCoy of Pawtucket, a city immediately adjacent to Providence. An ally of McCoy's, Walter E. O'Hara, was a textile manufacturer with an interest in horse racing which led him to acquire a controlling interest in the Narragansett Racing Association. O'Hara and Governor Quinn got into one bitter argument after another. Finally the governor accused O'Hara of defiance of the state horse-racing regulatory agency. When O'Hara did not meet the governor's demands, martial law was declared by Quinn and a detail of seventy-five soldiers surrounded the race track to see to it that it did not open for racing. Amid charges and counter-charges, libel suits and counter-suits, this comic opera continued from October 17 to November 12, 1937. O'Hara at one point said that Quinn had been bribed with a $20,000 check to prevent him from taking actions inimical to the race track, a charge he subsequently withdrew when under threat of a libel suit.[49] A story written for the *New York Times* by a Boston newspaper editor put the situation this way: "Is not the struggle fundamentally a row between two factions of the Democratic party, one led by the governor, the other by Mayor Thomas P. McCoy of Pawtucket with whom Manager O'Hara is allied? . . . The public believes that the real stake is the domination of the state."[50] The public seems to have decided that it was a maneuver for the domination of the state, for apparently one of the chief causes for the election of a Republican administration in 1938 was the Quinn-O'Hara-McCoy scandal.

But this affair is hardly typical of the political in-fighting in the Democratic party in the state. The power of the state organization to punish by denial of nominations for high office and the denial of state patronage is too great for any local organization or faction to withstand for long. The organization of the Democratic party in

[49] See the lively analysis not only of the facts but also of the legal implications of this affair by Zachariah Chaffee, Jr., *State House versus Pent House*, Providence, 1937. "Pent House" in the title refers to an apartment O'Hara had built for himself over the grandstand of the race track.

[50] Cited in Chaffee, *op.cit.*, p. 15.

Rhode Island is nearly one integrated machine from top to bottom—from the state committee to the smallest local committee.

Rhode Island's 1947 primary law appears to have had no greater effect on the Democratic than on the Republican party. As with the Republicans, the primary started off with a number of contests for nomination with primaries being held in 1948 for four of the seven statewide and congressional offices: attorney general and treasurer and both congressional seats. (The first two officers were not being sought by incumbents but the congressional seats were.) All endorsed candidates were nominated with heavy majorities. Down to and including 1956 there has been only one other challenge of a Democratic endorsee for high office: a challenge to Governor Roberts in 1952 which he defeated, 35,490 to 3,483.[50a] Nor have there been many contests for nominations to the Senate or the House of Representatives. Table 24 shows the number of challenges in the three most recent elections.

TABLE 24

Challenges in Democratic Primaries for General Assembly
of Rhode Island, 1952-1956

| Year | SENATE | | HOUSE OF REPRESENTATIVES | |
	Number challenged	*Number running*	*Number challenged*	*Number running*
1952	5	44	16	99
1954	7	43	23	99
1956	11	44	20	100

Although the number of challenges for seats in the General Assembly has been somewhat higher in the Democratic than in the Republican party, the proportions are not very high in either case. Woonsocket, by the way, has regularly contributed nearly half of the Democratic primary contests for House seats with 8 contests in two of these elections and 7 in the third. In the Democratic party as in the Republican a full slate is presented regardless of the hopelessness of some districts.

[50a] The 1958 campaign proved to be an interesting exception. Hopeful that Roberts had been weakened by the 1956 election, Lieutenant Governor Armand H. Cote challenged him in a primary. Cote got 44 per cent of the vote. The endorsed candidates for Lieutenant Governor, Secretary of State, and Attorney General were also challenged and all won with better margins than did Roberts. See *Providence Bulletin*, Sept. 18, 1958.

By all evidence there has been a strong Democratic organization for many years, but one feature of strong party organizations in some areas does not occur here—the ladder of ascent to the top positions. There is no recognized succession of offices that lead to the governorship, for example. The last three governors came from these positions: McGrath, U.S. attorney for Rhode Island; Pastore, lieutenant governor; Roberts, mayor of Providence. Advancement appears to depend on the political strength and popularity of the candidates rather than on any automatic rotation process. The only possible exception to this may in fact not be a real exception: that the office of United States Senator is the next step beyond the governorship. Senators Green, McGrath, and Pastore went from the governor's office to the U.S. Senate, and Roberts presumably anticipates being the next to do so. But this is less of an indication of an automatic process than of the fact that the governorship implies political prestige and power. Such power can be converted into votes for state committee endorsement, or, in the days before the primary, votes in a party nominating convention.

Once a Democrat lands one of the elective administrative jobs in Rhode Island, his expectations for job tenure are excellent. Undisputed retention of the offices of lieutenant governor, secretary of state, attorney general, and general treasurer seems to be the rule. As of 1956 the incumbents in these offices had an average tenure of 9.5 years, one of them having served since 1941, and the shortest tenure was 7 years. These offices are filled through careful balancing of the ticket, and once "in" an incumbent acquires a vested right to the job. Given the strength of the party organization and the disciplinary weapons that may be directed at all challengers, there are few aspirants to contest renomination in the primary.

The Party of the Left

Because of the extent of industrialization and the heavily urban character of Rhode Island, it is no surprise that the Democratic party in its appeal to the voters and in its legislative actions often takes the liberal-welfare-state line. It is true that many of the more radical proposals made by the Democrats are made tongue-in-cheek, with the hope and near-assurance that the Republicans will veto them in the Senate, but the record of the party over the last generation has generally been acceptable to the liberal-labor groups and anathema to conservative business interests.

In one recent session of the General Assembly the parties were battling each other and yet trying to compromise on which bills would be given approval by both Houses and which would be scuttled. A Senate rule permitted the Democratic minority to petition bills out of committee for debate on the floor—thereby to try to embarrass the Republicans who sought to bury them, of course—and they did in fact petition out seven measures for public defeat. "It was reported that the Senate Democrats," said the *Providence Journal*, "first talked about petitioning 36 bills out of committee, with the governor's consent, including . . . [several] bills that are virtually certain to be enacted anyway. . . ." GOP leaders in conference with the governor were reported to have said that if the Democrats did petition out all these bills, "the Republican Senate Finance Committee would recommend passage of many other big spending bills that the state administration doesn't want, and it would be up to the Democratic House to take the rap for killing them."[51] Governor Roberts admitted the conference with the Republicans about the bills but he "didn't recall any conversation like that." In any event, the Democrats petitioned out only seven bills and not thirty-six, and the Senate did not force the Democrats to "take the rap" for killing the bills.

In spite of some Democratic double-dealing with liberal legislation and the conservatism of the Republicans who most often control the Senate, the Democratic party has put through a considerable number of progressive bills. Rhode Island, for example, was the first state to pass an "off-the-job sickness benefit" plan for employees. Its unemployment compensation program is liberal and very inclusive, and very costly to the industrial taxpayer.[52] Only Alaska has an equivalent rate. The workman's compensation plan is liberal too. The state program for aid to the indigent is relatively generous. According to one analysis of tax payments, Rhode Island had a higher proportion of taxes being paid by business and a lower proportion being paid by individuals than in any other New England state.[53]

Indeed it has been contended that the failure of Rhode Island to attract new industries to replace the failing and departing textile

[51] *Providence Journal*, Apr. 30, 1953.

[52] Rhode Island's law does not provide an incentive tax reduction for employers with low unemployment rates. *All* employers now pay the maximum.

[53] See *The Economic State of New England*, Report of the Committee of New England of the National Planning Association, New Haven, 1954, p. 628.

mills can be attributed in part at least to the liberalism of Rhode Island's laws. A lengthy report in the *Providence Journal* quoted one industrialist who was *not* planning to enter the state: "Whoever was responsible in the last 25 years—and I don't care who—your laws are loaded with 'snuggle the voter' legislation that would cost us more than where we are located now, or are likely to go."[54] Another said, "Industry steers clear of states run by 'machine' politics." The latter is an amusing statement if one recalls the cooperation of businessmen with some of the most corrupt political machines in the history of the country—including the Aldrich-Brayton machine in Rhode Island. Nevertheless, it is probably true that in today's competitive struggle for industrial location, the recent history both of machine politics and of liberal-welfare legislation does retard Rhode Island's chances for gaining new sources of employment. If so, this is an interesting twist on democratic practices. Presumably the Republican party has not been able to win public approval in the state in part because of a refusal to sanction liberal legislation in behalf of the workingmen of the state; conversely, the Democrats have remained in power partly because they did espouse just such legislation. The very fact that the Democratic party acceded to the presumed desires of the people now results in disadvantageous economic consequences for the people themselves.

[54] *Providence Sunday Journal,* "What's Wrong with Rhode Island?" May 12, 1957, Finance Section, p. 8.

CHAPTER 8

---- ★ ----

RHODE ISLAND: POLITICS ON
THE SEAMY SIDE

RHODE ISLAND cannot match the flamboyant and flagrant corruption that has flourished in Louisiana, but it does offer a formidable challenge.[1] It has the dubious distinction of being the one state lacking any kind of Corrupt Practices Act dealing with election expenditures. Louisiana, Nevada, and Delaware have virtually no controls on campaign finances, and several other states might as well not have the laws on their books for all the attention that is paid to them, but Rhode Island legislators have simply refrained from enacting any laws on the subject.[2] There are laws covering ballot frauds in Rhode Island; unfortunately for the voters of the state, they are more frequently needed than used. Year after year there are frauds committed in state and local elections, and the malefactors often go scot-free.[3]

Rhode Island's race tracks are the ultimate source of much of the corruption in the state. Tieups between legislators who receive special favors from race-track operators are frequently reported in the press, but to show associations which arouse suspicion and to prove that a legislator was "bought" are two different matters. The majority leader of the House, James H. Kiernan, has for many years been an attorney for one of the race tracks. One cannot conclude from this fact alone that the actions of the majority leader on race-track

---

[1] Key in his *Southern Politics* said that "Few would contest the proposition that among its professional politicians of the past two decades Louisiana has had more men who have been in jail, or who should have been, than any other American state" (at p. 156).

[2] See the *Book of the States, 1956-1957*, pp. 82-83 for comparative data on such requirements by the states.

[3] In 1955, to take a random year, there were at least three instances of election fraud that led to prosecutions. See the reports in the *Providence Journal* for May 11 (West Greenwich), Sept. 17 (Pawtucket), and Sept. 24 (Providence). In the latter case, the story reported the conclusion of the case with three men convicted and sentenced to five years' imprisonment for frauds in a special election on July 12, 1955. Both Republicans and Democrats were involved in the various frauds listed here.

issues are influenced thereby, but at the very least there would seem to be a serious conflict of interests. Similarly, many legislators have been in the employ of the race tracks in such jobs as clerk at a betting window. Often it has been shown that these legislators and other paid staff members of the legislature were recorded as "present" in the House of Representatives while in fact they were working at the tracks. When on one occasion a reporter found fourteen state legislators working at the tracks while being reported "present" in the General Assembly, there was no great outcry. "Perhaps in any other part of the country this doubling of jobs would have been viewed as a terrible scandal," the reporter wrote later. "But when our newspaper story broke, no public official, including the governor, had a word of criticism about the practice."[4]

On one occasion I witnessed an interesting scene in an anteroom off the House chamber in the state capitol building in Providence. At the close of my interview with a prominent member of the House, a second legislator walked into the room and began discussion of a bill he was about to introduce, which would have severely restricted one particular kind of business. The younger man asked the more experienced legislator whether the bill ought to be introduced since it seemed rather harsh on the companies and ultimately did not have much chance of passage. "Well, put it in," was the reply. "You never can tell what the companies might do." Then with a wink in my direction, he said, "They will be around to see you."[5] Whether this was the introduction of what is sometimes called a Mae West bill ("Come up and see me sometime"), one cannot be certain. But it had many of the earmarks of an attempt to get a payoff for the retraction of a potentially injurious bill. Reporters around the state house claim that such bills are not unknown in the annals of Rhode Island politics.

These various forms of bribery and corruption—to which may be

---

[4] John Strohmeyer, "Yankee Morals and the $2 Bet," 213 *Harper's Magazine* 36-42 (July 1956) at p. 39. See also the stories in the *Providence Journal* for Mar. 25, 1953 ("Seven R.I. Legislators Employed in Lincoln Downs Mutuel Dept.") and Apr. 23, 1953 ("Three R.I. House Attachés Are Paid by State, Employed at Lincoln"). The managing director of Lincoln Downs insisted that he saw no impropriety in hiring legislators. "They are not asking for any favors. They just do their jobs. We don't ask them for any favors." *Providence Journal*, Mar. 25, 1953.

[5] The persons involved in this conversation are left nameless here, since the language was ambiguous enough to permit many interpretations, and there is no desire to accuse anyone on such scanty evidence.

added instances of contract manipulation and other forms of peculation—present a sordid picture. Unquestionably there are far more
honest than dishonest politicians in the state, but the bad apples
in the barrel are what give it the distinctive odor.

V. O. Key in his analysis of one-party politics in the South made
the observation that the loose factionalism of the one-party system
tended to encourage the boodling game, since there was no sense of
responsibility toward an organization, with a hope to stay in office
beyond the immediate term. The greater the degree of anonymity,
the greater the temptation to favoritism toward individual contrac-
tors, liquor dealers, etc. This, as Key himself points out, is not an
invariable rule.[6] And as our earlier analysis pointed out, Vermont,
most distinctly a one-party state with visible but not invariably distinguishable factions, has almost no corruption. But Rhode Island,
which I have described as "not functionally a one-party state," does
have a great deal of corruption. That a great many Rhode Island
politicians have gone astray does not prove that its party practices
fall into either the one-party or the two-party category. The interesting thing, however, is that much of the reported corruption in
Rhode Island comes from the cities and small towns that are predominantly one-party. Where the machines have built themselves
so strong a base of power that they are virtually beyond challenge,
they are able to cover up and conceal the activities of individual
members. In one case, for example, the city of Pawtucket held its
records on tax abatements in secrecy for years, despite the clamor
of the newspapers to see them. Only after the question had ultimately
gone to the United States Supreme Court did the newspapers get to
examine the records.[7] Strong one-party centers are possible in any
state, of course, regardless of the kind of competition that may develop between the parties at the state level. Within those centers
corruption may be practiced with protection. (Boston, for example,
is a one-party enclave within a two-party state, and the extent of
corruption there has been legendary.) Rhode Island as a small state

---

[6] Key, *Southern Politics*, p. 305.

[7] See the *Providence Journal*, Dec. 3, 1951 for a summary story. In another instance the Pawtucket City Council refused to suspend the liquor license of a man
friendly to the organization who had been convicted of selling liquor to minors.
See the *Providence Journal*, Mar. 9, 1957. In 1953 Governor Roberts asked for
legislation to provide for an annual audit of all local government finances. It was
on the list of defeated major bills when the session ended.

has comparatively few local governments (county government does not exist at all), and in most cases the cities and towns are either decidedly Democratic or Republican in their political tendencies. In a large proportion of the local governments cover-up operations are conceivable if not in fact always present. Needless to say, members of the local city or town council often are promoted to the state legislature. There, too frequently, the habits of old continue.

The Legislature: Party Battles
and Public Policy

As in Massachusetts and Connecticut, the public policy battles in the Rhole Island legislature are fought out between the parties. Interest groups make their special pleas as to any legislative body, but in Rhode Island even more than in Massachusetts the pleaders turn to the party leaders for help. Here too the subsurface political maneuvering on major issues is hidden behind closed doors, but it is apparent that those behind the doors virtually always include those high up in the party hierarchy. The governor, the state chairman of both parties, and the formal legislative leaders control the legislature.[8] Conflicts may arise, and members of the General Assembly may at times upset the plans of the leadership, but in the vast majority of the cases the final word rests with the leaders.

Party unity in the legislature is greater in roll-call voting than in either Connecticut or Massachusetts. Analysis of the roll calls of three sessions of the General Assembly indicates a remarkably high degree of party cohesion. In Rhode Island a roll call is not automatic on all bills, as in some states, but a roll call can be demanded by one-fifth of the membership present. In the last of the sessions noted below, the Democrats controlled both houses, and thus the challenge of the roll-call demand by the Democrats was not so frequent.

Throughout the three sessions the majorities of the two parties took opposite positions on 92 per cent of all issues in the House and on 89 per cent of the questions in the Senate. (There were five unanimous votes in the House and eight in the Senate.) The distribution of the roll calls which produced party votes in Rhode Island

[8] An indication of the governor's position is evidenced by the infrequency of gubernatorial vetoes. Between 1938 and 1948, for example, an average of 9 bills per session was vetoed. (Data from R. I. Legislative Reference Librarian, State Library.) An average of about 350 bills per session passed both houses.

TABLE 25

Party Cohesion in the Rhode Island General Assembly,
1931, 1937, 1951

	1931		1937		1951	
	Senate	House	Senate	House	Senate	House
Total number of roll calls	51	67	45	29	12	14
Parties on opposite sides (as %)*	94.2%	97.3%	87.0%	86.3%	75.0%	78.6%
Average Democratic† index of cohesion	99.3	100.0	93.8	96.5	94.5	99.0
Average Republican index of cohesion	95.3	98.0	89.0	95.0	95.0	100.0
Party votes (as % of all roll calls)‡	92.4%	97.0%	80.0%	55.0%	75.0%	78.6%

* The percentage of all roll calls on which majorities of each party took opposite sides.
† This is an average of the indices on all roll calls on which the parties took opposite sides.
‡ The percentage of all roll calls on which the parties disagreed and on which at least 80 per cent of each party voted alike.

differs considerably from the distribution in Massachusetts, where labor, election, taxation, and appropriations questions were among the most contentious issues.[9] Table 26 indicates the nature of the bills on which the Rhode Island parties divided.

What conclusions are to be drawn from the fact that questions of broad policy significance are less numerous than such matters as town charter revisions and discussions over adjournment or some detail of the Senate or House rules? Does this mean that the parties do not really draw their swords on such matters as labor law or business regulation? Such a deduction might seem warranted by the statistical data, but the observed facts other than statistical results of roll-call vote analysis belie this interpretation. Since the Senate is so often in the control of the Republicans, compromise is mandatory if the Democrats are to get their administration program passed. Once the compromise is made and the bill agreed upon in some form, the need for a roll call has vanished. Bills which are not wanted by the majority parties of either House often fail to get to the floor for a vote. They get pigeonholed and die in committee. There are means for forcing bills out of committee, but they are not used very frequently.

[9] See Table 19, p. 154.

TABLE 26

Issues Producing "Party Votes" in the Rhode Island General
Assembly, 1931, 1937, 1951*

	Number	Per cent of all party votes
Local matters	50	27.0%
Legislative procedure	27	14.6
Liquor and crime control	25	13.5
State administrative	17	9.2
Business regulation	11	6.0
Elections	11	6.0
Taxation	6	3.2
Appropriations	5	2.7
Welfare, health, and education	5	2.7
National questions (resolutions to Congress, etc.)	5	2.7
Judicial and legal	3	1.6
Labor	3	1.6
Veterans affairs	1	.5
Civil service	1	.5
	185	100.0%

* This table isolates those roll calls on which the parties opposed each other with at least 80 per cent of each party standing together. This is arbitrarily called a "party vote." Here both Senate and House roll calls are combined. In all there were 218 roll calls of which 185 produced "party votes."

It should also be noted that in many cases the votes called "legislative procedure" are often actually concerned with substantive policy questions. Frequently a move to adjourn or to recess is actually intended to forestall a vote. In 1937, for example, the Democratic minority in the Senate made five successive motions to adjourn on March 19 when the governor's appointments to the judiciary were before the chamber for consideration. With each motion for adjournment four Republicans joined the 15 Democrats in voting "yea," but ultimately the 21 Republicans who voted "nay" had their way.

Nor is the number of roll calls on local matters a source of surprise, given the nearly complete control that the legislature has over local government. Although subsequent to the sessions recorded in Table 26 a home rule amendment was adopted, the legislature at that time had complete control over local government activities.

When a municipality wished to make a change in its charter, or when it wished to float bonds in excess of three per cent of the town's assessed valuation, its only recourse was to request permission from the legislature.[10] Thus a large proportion of the bills presented at any session of the legislature are local in nature, and this is still the case notwithstanding the passage of the home rule amendment. The latter does permit towns to adopt charters of their own choosing and forbids the legislature from passing any act which would "affect the form of government of any city or town."[11] Power to pass legislation affecting municipal "property, affairs, and government" was retained by the General Assembly, although any such act must have the approval of the electors of the city in question in a referendum.

So jealous are the members of the General Assembly of their power to control local government that they have found ingenious ways of hampering the operations of the home rule amendment. This they did in cooperation with local political organizations that were resisting local groups striving for improvement of local government. One particular dodge involved the election of officers under home rule charters. Among the provisions of charters overwhelmingly approved in various cities in 1953 were non-partisan election provisions. Almost no professional politician takes a kind view of non-partisan elections, so when a legal question was raised as to the validity of the elections under the new charters and the courts ruled that they were in fact invalid, the "new officials" of the cities found no help forthcoming from the legislature.[12] The General Assembly adjourned without taking clarifying action and not until a special session almost six months later was the matter resolved.

The desire to retain legislative controls over municipal government has several reasons behind it. First, the legislator is apt to be a prominent member of the local party organization, and as such control over the form and the actions of local government is of prime

[10] See constitution of Rhode Island, Art. of Amendment, xxviii, adopted June 28, 1951. The bonding control was left unchanged by the amendment.

[11] *Ibid.*, Sec. 4.

[12] The Supreme Court ruled in an advisory opinion that power to control elections was retained in the legislature, notwithstanding the home rule amendment's grant of authority to adopt local charters and laws "relating to its property, affairs and government." Voters in Pawtucket, Woonsocket, Newport, and Central Falls had approved the new charters, but were left in a state of suspended animation before they got started. See *Providence Journal*, May 15, 1953.

importance to him.[13] Second, local legislation can be a powerful source of discipline. By holding off local legislation which a member needs passed—or alternatively by threatening to pass unwanted local bills—the member can be brought to heel. Local legislation is also frequently a useful trading item to help get other legislation passed. Local legislators can sometimes be convinced to go along with totally unrelated bills as the price of passage of a bill for his town.[14]

The high degree of unity of the parties in the legislature is a consequence of many varied factors. The lack of sectionalism to produce splits within the party is one important consideration. Also, to a considerable extent the Democatic party is the urban party and the Republican the party of the small town and the suburban area. Each tends to represent distinct kinds of constituency, and therefore there is greater likelihood of getting agreement within the party.[15] The party organizations are strong enough to discipline the dissenter. He may be denied advancement, patronage, or other favors the party grants to the faithful. Recall that there is no ban on the holding of more than than one job—a legislator can hope for appointment to a commission while serving simultaneously as a senator or representative. As for the aspiring lawyer there is always the prospect that the governor may pick him for a judicial post. Such hopes and fears help produce party unity.

[13] Some indication of the Rhode Island legislators' reluctance to accept innovations in municipal government is found in the fact that the *first* Rhode Island municipality to inaugurate a city manager system did so in November of 1953. The adoption was by way of the Home Rule Amendment. See *Providence Journal*, Nov. 23, 1953. In other states, of course, the manager system has long flourished.

[14] The following brief excerpt from a news story illustrates the point: "Stymied in the Republican-controlled Senate corporations committee is the [Providence] bill calling for a $3,500,000 bond issue for reconstruction of the Providence sewerage treatment plant. On the other hand, the Democratic-controlled House corporations committee is keeping a firm grip on several measures wanted by Republican communities, among them a Cranston measure providing a $2,500,000 bond issue for school purposes." *Providence Journal*, Mar. 19, 1953. The story also cited seven other bills tied up waiting to be "swapped."

[15] This is suggested in part by the differences in the occupational distribution of legislators from each party. Republicans in general came from the wealthier districts and have more connections with business than the Democrats, while the latter are more likely to be wage workers. The following is summarized from the occupational data included in the biographies of House members in the 1953 session. (See the *Rhode Island Manual*, 1953, pp. 471-495.) The percentages represent proportions of all Democrats and of all Republicans in the House.

	Democrats	Republicans
Business, banking, managers and manufacturers	20.7%	34.7%
Wage workers, labor leaders, and sales clerical	38.0	13.3

The legislative leaders in both Houses are respected, feared, and followed by the membership. In the House, the speaker, Harry F. Curvin of Pawtucket, is as formidable a figure as was the awesome Speaker Cannon in the early years of this century in Congress. Curvin appoints committees and designates their chairmen and with the help of a few others he controls their actions. While presiding, Curvin has been known to gavel the House into adjournment rather than to allow a roll call that has been demanded. Reporters say that when challenged on one of his rulings, Curvin never fails to get the support of the chamber—or at least of the Democratic members, which is sufficient. The speaker does not feel called upon to leave the rostrum to enter into debate. On one occasion when I was observing the House in action, a bill passed granting rights to a retired teacher. Once the bill was safely passed, a Republican rose to needle the majority by saying that the bill ought to have passed six years ago. Without waiting for any other member of the party to answer, Curvin proceeded to give the party's reply from the rostrum and in no uncertain terms. In the course of about two hours' observation, there were three conferences at the rostrum where the speaker made recommendations to committee chairmen on which bills to advance and which to hold over or recommit to committee. Conferences at the rostrum are not uncommon in state legislatures, and in themselves they imply nothing special, but in the instances mentioned it was obvious that Speaker Curvin was in effect giving orders and that they were being carried out.

Curvin has been in the House since 1931 and has been speaker since 1941. A power in Pawtucket politics, he was the city's director of public safety from 1937 to 1946 and later became the city director of public works. Neither of these jobs is lacking in patronage opportunities for an ambitious politician to build up a political following.

The second most powerful figure in the House is the majority leader, James H. Kiernan. Although he was born in 1884 he remains spry and nimble-witted. An able speaker and master of invective when the occasion calls for it—as the occasion often seems to do—Kiernan has been in the House since 1915.[16] He became

---

[16] Interestingly Kiernan as a professional politician is also apparently a professional joiner. He lists 14 different organizations to which he belongs, ranging from the Sixth Ward Democratic Club to the Ancient Order of Hibernians and the Rhode

majority leader in 1935 and has continued in that job except for one term when the Republicans controlled the House and another when he served as speaker. An attorney from Providence, Kiernan has the closest ties with the Providence Democratic machine and is its leader in the House. With but one interruption he has been chairman of the powerful Judiciary Committee since 1935. In cooperation with Speaker Curvin, Kiernan controls virtually all the time of the House.

In the Senate, where the Republicans have a majority most of the time, the leadership comes from the small-town senators to whom reference was made earlier. George Greenhalgh is perhaps the most powerful of these leaders, having served continuously in the General Assembly since 1927. (He was in the House at first and then went to the Senate in 1935.) Between 1942 and 1946 he served as state chairman of the party, and since 1939 he has been either chairman of the powerful Senate Finance Committee (which handles both taxation and appropriations) or the ranking Republican member of that committee.

The Republicans have a policy committee comprised of important senators, a few representatives, the state party chairman, and a few members of the state central committee. How smoothly this committee functions—or indeed whether it functions at all—depends upon the control of the state central committee. If the small-town block has clear control of both the Senate and the state central committee, the policy committee works well, but at other times when the urban wing of the party gets control of the central committee the policy committee is likely to be less effective. At such times the small town senators are likely to begin bargaining on their own with the Democrats.

In both Houses of the General Assembly caucuses are held regularly, although they are more frequent in the Senate than in the House. Breaking with the decision of the caucus is not a common practice; normally a decision made there sticks. The leaders of each party negotiate and compromise with each other and then the results are taken to the caucus where support is lined up—often after the most strenuous argument.

Island Driving Club. See his biography in the *Rhode Island Manual*, 1953, pp. 482-483.

Although the pay for serving in the General Assembly is negligible ($300 a year), this fact does not seem to dissuade members from serving there for virtually a lifetime. It is frequently argued that one of the reasons for the great turnover of state legislators is that the pay in nearly all states is insufficient remuneration for time spent. Undoubtedly this is a valid argument in many cases; legislators in many occupations cannot afford to continue to serve since to do so means family hardship. But in Rhode Island, although the pay ranks with the worst in the country, the members do come back year after year. Table 27 indicates this tendency.

TABLE 27

Tenure of Members of Rhode Island General Assembly, 1953 Session*

			TERMS OF SERVICE			
	First	*Second*	*Third*	*Fourth*	*Fifth to ninth*	*Tenth or more*
Senate	12	3	12	4	12	1
House	35	4	16	4	34	7

* The 1953 session had a larger than average number of first termers since the 1952 Republican presidential victory had helped carry in several Republican first termers. In a similar count of legislators serving in 1950 there were 6 first termers in the Senate and 15 in the House—that is, less than half the number in 1953. See Belle Zeller (Ed.), *American State Legislature*, New York, 1954, p. 67.

The longer than average tenure of Rhode Island legislators may possibly be accounted for by the fact that there are very close ties between state and local politics in the state. To be a legislator is often the means to acquiring local jobs and local political power. Moreover, the absence of any restriction on holding both legislative and administrative jobs opens to some members state jobs with a good salary to supplement their low legislative income. There is no doubt that some of the members of the General Assembly find ways to make money on the side through their legislative connections. This is certainly the case with those employed by the race tracks. How many others find similar paying positions it is impossible to tell.

Even though the proportion of legislators with long experience is higher in Rhode Island than in most states, the efficiency and orderliness of the General Assembly leaves much to be desired. It is sometimes argued that experience is a prerequisite to legislative efficiency, and my experience as a first-term state senator certainly indicated the truth of this contention. But there is no assurance that acquired experience must necessarily produce effectiveness and rationality in policy making. Experience for a legislator in some cases leads only to more refined means of bargaining and dealing for personally desired ends. Unfortunately for Rhode Island, too many of the latter type of experienced legislators seem to come to Providence annually.

Any legislative body can err in expressing its meaning in the statutes it produces, but in recent years there have been some classic cases of poor draftsmanship in Rhode Island. Perhaps the most dramatic was the mixup that resulted in the disenfranchisement of nearly 5,000 voters in the 1956 election. The ambiguity in the home rule amendment which resulted in a lack of authority for cities to arrange their own elections is another example. Beyond these errors of legislative drafters and the committees that let them get by, there are other serious deficiencies. To list a few will illustrate the point.

First, the legislature has insisted upon retaining the power to settle claims against the state. Governor Pastore refused to tolerate the practice of giving an extra $1,500 a year for serving on the claims committee, and for years claims piled up while the legislators maneuvered to regain their old perquisites. In 1952 both parties pledged in their platforms to transfer to the superior courts the authority to settle claims, but in 1953 both the Democratic House and the Republican Senate ignored the platforms and reconstituted the claims committee.[17]

Unlike the practice in Massachusetts, for example, where bills must be reported out of committee prior to the close of the session, the committee in Rhode Island can and does bottle up unwanted bills to avoid debate on them. This, of course, is not unusual, nor is it indefensible in many respects. But where the parties get together to mutually cover up and evade issues, the practice of burying bills has unfortunate consequences. In many cases the parties flagrantly ignore their campaign pledges. Pledges for correction of faults in workmen's compensation law, to provide for a one-day primary (instead of separate days for each party), and to revise the rules of the General Assembly were made in 1952, and all were ignored by both parties in the ensuing session. Said the *Providence Journal* in

[17] See *Providence Journal*, Apr. 19, 1953.

an editorial on the question of rules revision: "For years the rules have been such that a handful of men, in control of key committees and working behind closed doors, can dictate what legislation shall be passed and what shall be killed, leaving the rank and file of the members of both branches to play the role of dummies. The rules . . . have made possible the holding back of bills and their wholesale dumping in the chaos of all-night sittings, to be passed or killed by groggy legislators who know little or nothing of their import."[18]

The session-end rush in the General Assembly is almost invariably a time for ramming through ill-thought-out bills. In one 22-hour stretch in 1953 the legislature passed 177 bills and killed 17 others; in 1956 just shortly before the adjournment day 100 bills were passed in one sitting. Even granting that many of the bills passed were routine and insignificant, it is not within the realm of possibility for legislators to consider seriously that many bills in so short a time.[19]

Finally, it is of some significance that very few bills are given public hearings in Rhode Island. It is possible that the requirement that every single bill be given a hearing (as is the rule in Connecticut) goes too far in that no useful information is forthcoming in many hearings. But on the other hand the hearing can serve a salutary purpose in alerting the public to questionable bills, and valuable information can come from such a forum. It is true, of course, that when there is enough "demand" a bill will be given a hearing in Rhode Island, but the demand does not often arise.

Pressure Politics: Labor's Near Triumph

In discussing the politics of the one-party states of northern New England, emphasis was placed on the under-dog position of labor unions. In general, unions there have scant access to legislators and

---

[18] *Providence Journal*, May 10, 1953. No doubt the view of the editors that rules revision would cure the problem is too sanguine a hope. Rules less than political traditions and customary practices account for the methods of a legislature. There are ways to avoid the restrictions of rules in most cases, and when they are circumvented—given a strong enough desire to get around them—about the worst that can happen is embarrassment. The unwritten rules of traditional practice are more significant in most cases than the written rules. In fact the rules now provide for discharging a bill from a committee when a minority of the Senate (15 out of 44) or a bare majority of the House petitions for discharge. That they do not often use this device is not the fault of the rule but of the men—if "fault" it is. See Senate Rule 12 and House Rule 30, in *Rhode Island Manual*.

[19] See *Providence Journal*, Apr. 25, 1956.

political leaders. While not shut out of the policy process entirely, labor in those states lacks sufficient numbers and political strength to be an important consideration in political struggles.

But this is not the case in Rhode Island. There, not only is labor's influence a vitally important element in the legislature but—more importantly to legislators and other politicians—labor counts in elections. It would be wrong to say that labor unions get anything they want. Even when the Senate is not dominated by Republicans there are strong counter-pressures against labor's demands. Yet in the long run labor's political effectiveness in the state has been great enough to give it some of the most liberal labor legislation in the country.

It is no accident that the president of the state AFL has also been the state director of the Labor Department.[20] Nor is it without significance that Senator Frank Sgambato, sometime Democratic chairman of the Senate Labor Committee, is an AFL organizer. (Several members of the House are also organizers or officers of unions.) Over the years many labor union officials have been appointed to patronage positions in state government.

Perhaps one of the best illustrations of labor's role in deciding public policy is the recent issue over the establishment of a 90-cent minimum wage for intra-state workers. The many-sided controversy transpired during the 1956 session of the legislature. No one was satisfied with Governor Robert's original proposal of an 85-cent minimum. Labor said it was too low; management said it was too high. The latter cited the 75-cent minimums then in force in the neighboring states of Connecticut and Massachusetts and urged the legislators not to put them at a competitive disadvantage.[21] One of labor's strong arguments was the fact that the Eisenhower administration had recently approved a $1 minimum for inter-state workers; they saw no reason to discriminate between intra- and inter-state labor.

---

[20] Relations are not always harmonious between the CIO and the AFL in the state, and the director of the Labor Department, Arthur Devine, has at times been accused of not dealing squarely with the CIO in affairs before his department. See, for example, the caustic exchanges concerning a jurisdictional dispute involving an Atlantic and Pacific Co. bakery. See *Providence Journal*, Feb. 11, Mar. 8, and Mar. 18, 1957. In an editorial the *Journal* accused Devine of not trying to settle the dispute because of his partisanship toward the AFL, which was being contested by an independent union backed by the CIO.

[21] See story of hearing held on the bill, *Providence Journal*, Mar. 29, 1956.

In due time the Democratic House passed a bill providing a $1 minimum, and the decision was left up to the Senate, particularly when the governor also came around to backing the House bill proposed by the CIO. At one time a Republican senator had introduced a $1 minimum bill in the Senate, but that senator (Weisberger) had since been appointed to the bench, and there was no Republican backing for his bill. This, Democratic orators took particular pains to emphasize. In the Senate on April 26 there was a field-day of maneuvering on the bill with labor leaders making every effort to play off the two parties against each other.

In caucus it developed that three Democratic senators would vote against a $1 minimum wage, so the CIO lobbyists sought out Republicans to see whether enough support could be gained there to get the bill through the Senate. State CIO president, Thomas F. Policastro, "engaged Bayard Ewing, Republican national committeeman [not a member of the legislature but significantly present], in serious conversation for many minutes, reportedly promising CIO support in November for Republican senators whose votes for a dollar minimum would overcome the Democratic defections. Mr. Ewing, it was reported, avoided a deal but told Mr. Policastro he was free to try to win over Republican senators on an individual basis."[22] Ultimately two Republicans did support the $1 minimum, but this was not enough. Nineteen Republicans and three Democrats enacted the 90-cent compromise over the objections of 18 Democrats and 2 Republicans. The House accepted the compromise and the governor signed it. The Senate chairman of the labor committee, Frank Sgambato, called it, "the best we can get," but he was ready to accept it as "the only statutory 90-cent minimum in the United States."[23]

The pressure in the minimum-wage dispute came from small businesses as well as the larger ones, and they were not without effect on Democratic legislators who might be expected to go "down the line" for labor. The defections were few, however, for the political power of labor in this highly industrialized state is naturally feared and respected. One of the Democratic senators who aban-

[22] *Providence Journal*, Apr. 27, 1956.
[23] *Ibid.* The bill covers about 85,000 workers. Included are all employers of more than three employees. Hotels, laundries, and restaurants are included, although some of these businesses are excluded from minimum wage provisions in some states.

doned the CIO had that organization oppose him for reelection in 1956. He lost.[24]

The general favoritism of the Democratic party towards labor has produced reciprocal aid for the party in its state campaigns. In many instances the labor unions contribute heavily to campaign finances and send out campaign workers to assist, both of which actions are doubtless more effective than labor's endorsements, which normally go to the Democrats too. In a radio interview Policastro of the CIO once said that labor should not be too tightly tied to any party. He granted that labor's ties with the Democrats had been strong but said this was so "because the labor movement generally has been helped much by the Democrats." Labor would be "happy" to endorse any "truly liberal" Republican who ran, he said, but "Christopher Del Sesto . . . was not acceptable to the CIO because Mr. Del Sesto had made some 'nasty cracks' about organized labor during the years he served as state OPA director."[25]

Any impression that the only pressure politics played in Rhode Island involved labor would be sadly in error. The full range of special interests make their pleas. The Associated Industries of Rhode Island, local affiliate of the National Association of Manufacturers, is a strong organization with close relationships with the Republican party, even as labor sticks by the Democrats. Insurance companies, public utilities, and banks in the state are also well represented in the halls of the legislature not only by lobbyists but by legislators connected with these businesses. These latter groups, along with the farm interests, are primarily connected with the Republican party. These groups depend upon the Senate Republican bloc to protect their interests.

Other groups are influential from time to time but do not affiliate themselves with either party with any regularity. Among these groups are the sports fishermen, commercial fishermen, automobile dealers, liquor store owners, and various professional groups. It is not uncommon for interest groups to hire many lobbyists from scattered local areas so that they can approach legislators in their home towns as well as in the capital. In one instance the insurance interests sponsored a series of "seminars" around the state to which

---

[24] Senator Thomas D. Santoro of Westerly. The Eisenhower landslide was equally if not more significant in his defeat, however.

[25] Reported in the *Providence Journal*, Feb. 2, 1957.

legislators were invited. These sessions included fancy dinners and were aimed at the passage of legislation to bar the sale of automobile insurance by the automobile dealers.

One of the more significant interest groups in the state are the various race-track associations. Mention has already been made of some of their methods of generating favorable attitudes in the legislature, but hiring legislators is not their only means of promoting their interests. Their contributions to charity help them to keep on the right side of the electorate. They help legislators, besieged for patronage by their constituents, by passing out race-track jobs to those approved by politicians. In campaign time there is no doubt that a good deal of money associated with the tracks comes into the coffers of both parties.

All these interest groups direct their attention toward the party leaders and depend upon their contacts with the party influentials to produce results. It is true, of course, that interest groups do work on committee chairmen to report out or not report out bills they are interested in, but the wise lobbyists know that one of the most important considerations in nearly any legislative battle is what the governor, the party chairman, and a handful of party legislative leaders want done.

Conclusion: Party Competition and Public Policy

The great benefit of a two-party system is that the parties think of themselves as continuing organizations, nearly as worried about the next election as the present one. The threat of the ballot-wielding public affects the organization rather than merely threatening individual politicians. Thus the idea is that greater responsibility results as the parties seek to keep their houses in order while meeting the demands of the public at least so far as the demands are identifiable.

The contention here has been that Rhode Island is functionally a two-party state, notwithstanding the strong position of the Democratic party over the past generation. But the extent of corruption, of disregard of the public interest and of public demands would make it appear that the two-party ideal is not approximated in Rhode Island. Why?

Several observations need be made in this connection. First, the majority party has not been wholly unmindful, nor for that matter has the minority, of the needs of the urban-industrialized society that is Rhode Island. The social welfare and labor legislation passed in the last two decades has met with public favor, and in that respect the parties have acted responsibly. Action in behalf of the under-privileged elements of society is not a common feature of the typical one-party state. More often than not, the dominant political interests of such states are so closely tied in with industrial and business interests that the rank and file of the public gets scant protection from the government. This is not the case in Rhode Island.

Yet the fact does remain that in many matters the political system of Rhode Island results in denial of many clearly spoken public demands. Favoritism and disregard for common political honesty have often disfigured the actions of leading politicians in the state. Why has not the fear of reprisals produced greater respect for the public interest?

As noted previously, the overwhelming proportion of the state's population lives in one-party areas—areas that are nearly as one-party as Mississippi on election day. The habits and practices of these areas carry over into state politics. Significantly, the Democratic party, while perhaps challenged at times by the Republicans, has had things its own way long enough to become somewhat calloused in its attitude.

Traditionally the political practices of the state have not been of the highest order. Those who now bribe, cheat, and ignore the canons of public responsibility are following a tradition that was well established before they were born. What has "always been," even when it is nefarious, tends to establish a pattern of expectations not only for the perpetrator but for the public who more or less "expect" such behavior and do not become as outraged as they might were their expectations different.

It is also significant that Rhode Island has been a relatively disorganized society. Tremendous waves of immigrants poured into the state prior to World War I and most of them adjusted themselves in time to the new civilization, but there were many who resisted assimilation. Others developed a bitter hatred of the mill owners and autocratic elements that ran the society. To those who struggled for power from the bottom of the pile the rules of propriety could be set aside for the sake of goals important to them—an opportunity to participate in government and have a better life economically. Social disorganization of this sort is likely to produce demagogy, extremist actions, and generally irresponsible politics. It would seem that this has been a contributing factor in the Rhode Island situation.

Finally, the possible advantages of two-party competition have been lessened by Republican political leaders who have "played it patsy" with the Democrats for their own gain. While the Republican party has kept a toehold on power through the apportionment of the Senate, the representatives of the party have thereby been minority representatives without any great feeling of responsibility toward the Republican party as a whole and certainly not toward the total electorate. The constitutional anchor of Senate control has served thus both to keep the party in business and to make it less than responsible.

Conceivably the near future may hold out new hope to the Republican party. If it can win some state elections and build up an organization with which regularly to threaten the Democrats in the state, a new brand of politics may come to the state. Fear of real competition in state elections and an opportunity for the parties to compete as relatively cohesive but opposed units could perhaps in time eliminate some of the less admirable traits of the state that has for its motto the single word "Hope."

CHAPTER 9

————————— ★ —————————

CONNECTICUT: THE POLITICS OF COMPETITION

FEW STATES, and certainly none in New England, have equalled the closeness of party competition in Connecticut during the last generation. Since the end of the 1920's both major parties have had to approach each election with trepidation, for victory has usually hung by the balance of a few thousand votes. Fear of ballot-box retribution for party indiscretion has therefore become one of the most signally important forces in Connecticut politics. If, as most scholars in the field of democratic political theory agree, party competition is necessary to party responsibility and party responsibility is conducive to democratic government at least in a large society, then the Connecticut system of government offers an interesting and perhaps revealing specimen for study.

The potential significance of this competition is heightened by the organizational strength of the two parties. Traditionally the parties have tended to be tightly organized, with relatively great internal unity and concerted leadership. This has not always been the case; as in any human institution, Connecticut parties have faced the vicissitudes of internal squabbles. But the general trend has been toward organizational strength to such an extent that the habits of politicians are adjusted to the acceptance of leadership. The kind of maverick spirit that spawned the Non-Partisan League in the West simply has not existed in Connecticut, or, if it has been the credo of some political figures, they have been few and relatively unimportant.

Connecticut does not, however, offer the perfect model for the democratic theorist. The parties are strong and are pushed into relatively responsible behavior by the fear of the next election, but there is one major impediment to the achievement of the ideal of the theorist. This is the apportionment of the House of Representatives. The one-tenth of the people who live in the smallest towns have half the representation in the House, with the obvious consequence

Dem, concentrated in cities & among ethnic minorities

of inordinately great political power for this small segment of the population. Nearly 90 per cent of these towns are regularly to be found in the Republican column on election day, which means that regardless of the success achieved by the Democratic party in contests for other offices it can never control the House of Representatives. Thus a veto is conferred upon the rural-small-town element. The veto is often used irresponsibly by Republican small-town forces and the Democrats often make equally irresponsible use of it by intentionally forcing the use of the veto on issues that they do not want to see passed but want to appear to support. To the extent that the small-town Republicans disregard the threat of statewide election majorities ultimate responsibility by the parties is made difficult.

The existence of this virtual veto power on all policy enactments—accompanied by the great strength of the small towns in the Republican party state convention, a key party instrumentality—has not become an absolute block to responsibility, however. The veto is used to force compromises, and at times actually it defeats the will of the rest of the state, but the power is circumscribed by the traditional and widely accepted authority of the party leadership in matters of legislative policy. Consequently neither in the party organization nor in the legislature has the small-town element wrought the havoc on the party that a similar element does in Rhode Island.[1] Connecticut has escaped many of the possible disadvantages of a minority empowered to gainsay the decisions of a majority.

The Tight Rope of Competition

Before the Al Smith campaign of 1928 and the Wall Street crash of the following year helped to bring to fruition political potentialities dormant in Connecticut politics, there had been little competition between the parties. These events brought the underdog Democrats within striking distance of the theretofore nearly invincible Republican party. From the early days of the Republican party right down to 1930 only the most drastic circumstances interfered with the GOP's control of the state. The party had three strong points: conservative traditionalism, the backing of a growing manufacturing element, and the popular distrust and dislike of the Democrats born of the Civil War. By subtle combination of the fears and

[1] See Chapter 8 on Rhode Island.

aspirations expressed in these sources of strength, the Republican party built up a formidable machine.

In earlier times the conservative traditionalism of the state had been devoted to such ends as the preservation of the established position of the Congregational church, the property and power of the quasi-aristocracy, and the Royal Charter of 1663, which remained in force until the present constitution was adopted in 1818. By the time the Republican party emerged from the ultimate wreckage of both the old Federalist and Whig parties, the manufacturing interests of the state were growing. The national Republican party carried high the banners of protectionism for American industry, and Connecticut's dominant politicians found it natural to stick with the party. For Connecticut was early committed to manufacturing industry. Since the state lacked raw materials with which to build a strong economy, the most important natural resource became the resourcefulness of the Yankee inventor and manufacturer. Agriculture declined sharply after the coming of the canals and railroads which brought grains to the East at a price the Connecticut farmer could not possibly meet. After centuries of valiant struggle with rock-strewn soil—to which the picturesque miles of stone fence are mute testimony—farmers quit the land in increasing numbers. They moved to the cities to work in factories or took off to become Western pioneers. The Connecticut worker was often as devoted to the high tariff position of the Republican party as was his boss. Together they gave solid backing to the party. The vigorous protest of the Western and Southern farmers of the late nineteenth century that culminated both in the Populist movement and the agrarian radicalism of William Jennings Bryan had nothing but adverse effect on the chances of the Democratic party in Connecticut. Where before 1896, when Bryan first ran, some of the small towns retained their Jacksonian leanings of pre-Civil War origins, they now deserted the ranks of the Democrats to join their brethren in the Republican party.[2]

---

[2] Lane Lancaster once wrote that "Some of the staunchest Republican magnates in Connecticut towns today are the sons and grandsons of men who were Democratic mayors and legislators in the pre-Bryan days." See "The Democratic Party in Connecticut," 17 *National Municipal Review* 451-455 (1928). Further evidence of the Democratic leanings of some of the farmers pre-1896 is found in the fact that the *only* times since the Civil War the Democratic party has controlled the House of Representatives—which requires, of course, majorities in many small towns—were in the sessions of 1873, 1874, and 1876. Clearly the Free Silver and Free Trade policies of Bryan buried the Democratic party even deeper than had the

In short the story of Connecticut politics from the Civil War era down to the New Deal was the story of the Republican party. In the long 72-year period from 1858 to 1930 Republicans occupied the governorship for almost 56 years. And in the 15 gubernatorial elections between 1900 and 1928, Republican candidates won all but two. (The average Republican percentage of the two-party vote for governor during that period was adequate but not overwhelming—55.8 per cent.)

The politics of the post-1930 era are in stark contrast with those of the preceding 30 years. Competition brought new vigor to both party organizations, through an intensification of campaigning effort. The new fighting spirit not only struck the state headquarters of each party but went down to the lowest echelons. Few are the regions of the state without some kind of more or less active party organization for both parties. Given the political geography of the state— with overwhelming majorities for the Republican party in most of the more than 100 small towns—there is more extensive Republican than Democratic activity. Yet some kind of Democratic organization exists in every town in the state. In both parties the interrelationships between the top and bottom sectors of the party are so close that local organizations are kept active for reasons of patronage if for no other reason.

The closeness of the competition between the parties in the contemporary period can be illustrated in several ways. The governorship, for example, which had been a near Republican monopoly before 1930, has since then been almost evenly divided between the parties. In the 12 gubernatorial elections between 1930 and 1956 Democrats have won seven times to the Republicans' five. The average Democratic percentage of the two-party vote in these elections has been a scant 49.9 per cent. Table 28 illustrates the alternation between the parties and the narrow margins of victory in most elections. In ten of the 12 elections the margin of victory was less than 25,000 votes and in three the margin was less than 3,000.[2a]

---

waving of the Bloody Shirt after the Civil War. For the earlier history of the Democratic party in the state, see the excellent work of Jarvis M. Morse, particularly his *A Neglected Period of Connecticut's History: 1818-1850*, New Haven, 1933.

[2a] The 1958 election, which took place after these lines were written, may seem to some to be an exception to or even a reversal of the generalization about close competition, for it was an overwhelming Democratic landslide. Abe Ribicoff won reelection as governor with a quarter-million majority (unofficially 63 per cent of the vote). But like the Eisenhower sweep of 1956 in Connecticut it was an aberration, not a repudiation of the point made above. See footnote on p. 269 for amplification.

CONNECTICUT

TABLE 28

Percentage of the Two-Party Vote Won by Successful Gubernatorial
Candidates in Connecticut, 1930-1954

Year	Victor	Per cent of two-party vote
1930	Democrat	50.6
1932	Democrat	51.0
1934	Democrat	50.8
1936	Democrat	57.4
1938	Republican	50.3*
1940	Democrat	51.0
1942	Republican	52.4
1944	Republican	51.6
1946	Republican	57.4
1948	Democrat	50.1
1950	Republican	51.0†
1954	Democrat	50.2

* The vote for the Republican candidate in 1938 actually combines his vote on the Republican ticket with the 3,046 votes he received under the Union party label. Without the latter help he would have narrowly lost the election to Governor Cross, then seeking a fifth term.

† In 1950 the term of office was changed to four years. At the termination of the present term in 1958 Democrats will have served 16 years in the office to 12 for Republicans.

Other offices than the governorship have been subject to equally keen rivalry. (See Table 29.) It is true, however, that there has not been a consistent alternation between the parties. In the Franklin Roosevelt era the Democrats had an edge, and now in the Eisenhower era the Republicans have been winning most elections. Yet neither party in either period has been able to relax its vigilance—the opposition is always too close for comfort. Notwithstanding the statistical edge in recent years for the Republicans, the leaders of *both* parties talk in private of the possibility of establishing one-party dominance for their side. Republican hopes, of course, are based not only on President Eisenhower's two sweeping victories in the state but also on the fact that he carried so many others into office with him. (In 1956 the Senate was won by the Republicans 31 to 5, the widest Republican margin since the 1920's.) Democratic leaders on the other hand are encouraged to believe that the reelection of Governor Ribicoff in 1958 could become the basis of long-run Democratic control. "If we can put Ribicoff back in again," said one high

Democrat in a burst of testimonial-dinner enthusiasm, "we can make Connecticut as Democratic as Rhode Island."

TABLE 29

Indices of Party Competition in Connecticut Elections, 1930-1956

OFFICE OR MAJORITY CONTROL	ELECTION OR CONTROL WON BY	
	Democrats	*Republicans*
Presidential electoral vote	3	3
U.S. Senate elections	5	5
Elections to U.S. House of Representatives	32	51*
Control of Connecticut Senate	7	5†

*The Republican edge in elections to the U.S. House of Representatives is not the inconsistent factor that it appears to be, for in the 14 elections the Democrats won a majority of the votes cast for Congressmen in the five districts on six occasions to the Republicans' eight. Some gerrymandering and urban concentration of "wasted" Democratic majorities account for the disparity in numbers of Congressmen elected.

† In two of the 14 Senatorial control contests, the Socialists of Bridgeport held the balance of power between the parties (in 1935 and 1939). In both instances they joined with the Republicans to organize the Senate.

The Bases of Political Balance
Between the Parties

Whether the competition of the last quarter century can be maintained in the future it would be hard to say. After all, few states have truly competitive politics. As the product of a delicate social, economic, and political balance, competition between parties is more accidental than the product of human design. Factors apart from the internal politics of Connecticut helped materially to produce a new political alignment for the state after 1930. The depression and strong appeal of the Democratic party program during the New Deal period naturally had a powerful impact on state politics. But the impact of these events was far from uniform from state to state. In the heavily Democratic and Republican states it did not have too much effect on party alignment, and not much more on the structure of state parties. Thus in northern New England the depression and New Deal may have led to some new thinking about public policy and to some changes of orientation within the dominant Republican party, but, sheltered behind the imposing and consistent majorities of hereditary Republicans, the dominant politicians of these states saw little reason to change. Even occasional Democratic victories in

Maine and New Hampshire had little effect. Not so below the upper border of Massachusetts. In the three southern New England states, new political systems evolved.

The balance of power that was created in Connecticut at this time was the accidental result of dispersion of different kinds of communities in the state. Connecticut is divided like Caesar's Gaul into three parts—the larger cities, the rural small towns, and the new suburban retreats. There is very little political sectionalism in the state in the sense that one region is the target of common antagonism by the rest of the state—as is the case with Boston, Providence, New York City, Chicago. It is a small state (53 Connecticuts would fit into the borders of Texas!) and the largest urban concentrations are scattered around the state, as are the rural towns and the suburban localities. The fundamental alliances and cleavages of Connecticut politics are based not on antagonism toward any region but rather on the relationships between the three fundamental demographic divisions: rural, suburban, and urban.

Republican party strength is drawn mainly from the rural small towns, the new and ever-growing suburban communities, and the upper income and upper social strata of the cities. The greatest support for the Democratic party comes from the cities and particularly from the urban labor elements and the "foreign-stock" population. These sources of respective party appeal go far to explain not only the character and policy orientations of the parties but the fortuitous balance between them as well.

The small towns of Connecticut are predominantly of old Yankee stock. Conservative and respectable, they are now reduced to a minority status in the very land of their ancestors. At the time of the 1950 census 11.3 per cent of the state's population lived in 103 towns with less than 5,000 population. Into most of these towns in the last generation have come some of the escapees from the discomforts of city living, but the commuter population has in general not taken over the political machinery of such towns. The old Yankee stock in most instances still has dominant control of both the town government and the local Republican organization.

Many of these small towns have declined in population in the course of the last century, as agriculture failed to provide a decent living. "The more enterprising sons of rural families left the old homestead to search for greater wealth or excitement elsewhere, and this exodus caused once-flourishing towns to degenerate into feeble hamlets of the present day, where travellers can see countless hollows in the ground, overrun with weeds or lilacs, where once were cellars stored with vegetables."[3] Even the recent building of highways, beckoning the commuter farther into the hinterland, has not stemmed the decline in population in many of these towns. Ten of the 22 towns in Litchfield County in the northwestern corner of the state now have fewer people in them than they had in 1900, and in many cases even more precipitous reductions in population took place in the preceding fifty years.[4] But thanks to the apportionment of the House of Representatives, these towns have not lost their political importance even though much of the population may have left.

The extent of Yankee control over the political machinery of these small towns is amply illustrated by checking the names of the members sent to the House from the towns under 1,000 population. In the 1949 House, for example, these towns (23 in all) sent 32 members to the House, of which 25 had names of English origins. By contrast, the Democrats in the House that session, most of them from urban centers, had only 25 per cent of their number with recognizably English names. It is also interesting to note in 1956 that 20 of the Republican town chairmen of these towns had Yankee names and only three appeared to be non-Yankees.[5]

Perhaps an even more significant fact about these small towns is their constant support of the Republican party. In that same 1949 session, 28 of the 32 representatives of the smallest towns were Republicans. In 1951 the representatives from the 100 towns under 5,000 population were comprised of 122 Republicans and 23 Democrats. Figure 11 suggests the wide dispersal of Republican communities. In the 1948 election for governor, the Democrats won a slim majority of the total vote, but the Republican candidate won 104 of the 169 towns by at least 55 per cent of the vote.

Except in the largest cities and the smallest towns the size of population is not indicative of the party tendencies of the com-

[3] Jarvis M. Morse, "The Rise of Liberalism in Connecticut 1829-1850," (Connecticut Tercentenary Series), New Haven, 1934, p. 9 (pamphlet).

[4] Robert G. Burnight and Nathan L. Whetten, "Studies in the Population of Connecticut, Population Growth, 1900-1950," Storrs Agricultural Experiment Station Bulletin 228, Storrs, Connecticut, 1952, p. 22. See also *Connecticut State Register and Manual*, 1956, "Population of Towns of Connecticut 1774-1950," pp. 276-281.

[5] See *Register and Manual*, 1956, pp. 432-436.

munities, as Table 30 suggests. At the two extremes of size, however, there is a marked difference in party allegiance.

TABLE 30

Republican Percentage of the Two-Party Vote Cast in Gubernatorial Elections, 1946-1950: By Towns Grouped according to Population

Size of towns*	Number of towns	Republican percentage of two-party vote 1946	1948	1950
Over 100,000	4	48.1%	40.6%	40.5%
25,000-99,999	19	60.9	51.7	53.3
5,000-24,999	46	59.7	52.3	54.6
0-4,999	100	67.0	62.4	64.0
Whole state	169	57.2	49.8	51.0

* Based on 1950 census data.

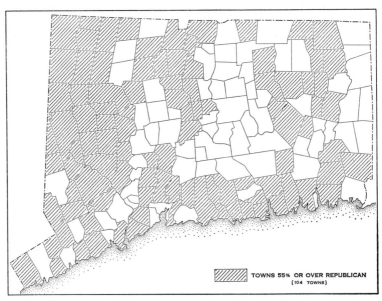

TOWNS 55% OR OVER REPUBLICAN
(104 TOWNS)

11. Areas of Republican Strength in Connecticut, 1948

Of the utmost importance to the creation of the balance between the parties has been the development of the suburban areas clustered around the cities of the state and spreading outward from New York City. The population of these suburban areas is comprised of many different kinds of people—the old residents, in some instances the workers in small plants in some of these towns, and refugees from the larger cities. Some of the latter are factory workers whose skills demand wages sufficient to permit the purchase of a home in suburbia, but more numerous by far are those with white-collar, professional, and managerial positions. The relative wealth and social aspirations of the latter groups incline them toward Republicanism. They comprise a counterbalance to the majorities the Democrats regularly get in the cities, for if the Republicans had to depend on their small-town majorities and their vote in the larger cities, Connecticut would be a Democratic one-party state.

The greatest concentration of suburbanites is in Fairfield County in the southwestern sector of the state adjacent to New York City. From the discomforts of New York to such towns as Greenwich, Stamford, Norwalk, Westport, Darien, and other smaller places in the county have come thousands of "Exurbanites," to use A. C. Spectorsky's term.[6] There on the New Haven railroad line they can commute, albeit with some inconvenience at times, to their employment in New York. Every day some 10,000 use commuter tickets to get to New York. The county has considerable industry and one of the largest industrial centers in the state, Bridgeport, lies within its boundaries, but the county is nevertheless consistently Republican on election day. In 1930 a Democrat won the congressional election in the Fairfield County district, and in the Democratic sweep of 1936 another Democrat won that seat. But this feat has never been repeated.[6a]

All suburbia is not in Fairfield County. Surrounding most of the cities of the state are other retreats from urbanization. Although not as fashionable as some of the Fairfield County communities, such

---

[6] A dispatch to the *New York Times* (Aug. 10, 1957) told wistfully of the changing character of Fairfield County:

"A century-old dairy farm—one of the few remaining in lower Fairfield County—fell victim today to the onrushing suburbs. It lies a scant half mile from the busy Merritt Parkway and a five-minute drive from downtown Stamford. Its peaceful-looking ninety acres are as restful to the eye as a Vermont picture postcard. But for some years it has been neither peaceful nor restful to James H. Finch, its owner.

" 'There's just too much traffic and too much noise,' he said. 'The cows don't like it. It makes them restless. Why even the neighborhood kids tease them. Throw rocks at them and break down fences and all.'

" 'And help? Can't get any hired hands around here. Sure, they send them up from the city but they stay a few weeks and are gone. This isn't the country any more.'

". . . The auctioneer had a few words to say before getting down to business. 'Folks,' he declared gravely, 'strange things are happening to farming today—and this is one. Communities grow and the farmers have to move on.' "

[6a] At least not until 1958. See footnote on p. 269, below.

places as West Hartford, Wethersfield, Hamden, Groton, and Milford turn in equally impressive Republican majorities. (These five towns gave the 1954 Republican gubernatorial candidate a 15,000 majority, and 61.2 per cent of their combined vote.) It is difficult to identify precisely the towns that are predominantly suburban, but at a rough estimate they must have a quarter of the state's population.

Although the Republican party normally gets only a minority of the vote from the urban industrial centers of the state, that minority is large enough to be an important contribution to their total vote. In most of the cities there are large ethnic minorities, and all have Republican as well as Democratic leaders among them. In some local elections in even the largest cities, normally Democratic in state and national elections, Republican candidates of Italian extraction often win the mayoralty races. (For example, a Republican, William C. Celentano, was mayor of New Haven for several terms in the post-World War II years.) To attract the support of ethnic minorities the Republican party, since the 1920's, has usually put some non-Yankee on the state ticket. Thus Francis A. Palloti served as secretary of state from 1923 to 1929 and as attorney general from 1939 to 1945. Since 1946, candidacy for treasurer has been reserved for Italians only and the post for congressman at large has become a Polish preserve. Only once has the party named a non-Yankee to run for the governorship. Lieutenant Governor James C. Shannon succeeded to the governorship in 1948, and got the party nomination that same year. He lost the election to Chester Bowles. For other statewide offices the Republican party has named more than a dozen non-Yankees since 1940.

The ethnic minority influence in the Republican organizations of the cities is illustrated by the fact that as of 1956 in the 16 largest cities only seven of the Republican town chairmen had Yankee names. Exactly the same number have names of Italian origin. Another indication of the non-Yankee inclinations of urban Republican organizations is found in the Senate of 1957 after the sweeping victory of the party in the preceding election. The Senate represents—in some respects overrepresents—the urban population of the state. When a state election is very close, the Democrats usually win control of the Senate, as they did in 1954 when they controlled it 20 to 16. But the 1956 sweep reduced the Democratic membership to a mere five senators. Of the 15 Republicans who replaced the Democrats of the previous session only three appear to have Yankee names. Otherwise there were five with Italian names, three Irish, two Jewish, and one each of Polish and French-Canadian backgrounds.

There is another urban element of importance to the Republicans—the business leadership and the upper social strata in general. The "best" neighborhoods are regularly Republican. Democratic bankers and moguls of industry and insurance exist in Connecticut, but it takes diligent searching to find them. The financial contributions to the party by these well-to-do Republicans are more crucial perhaps than their votes, but in so close a party balance every fragment is significant.

Democratic support is concentrated in the cities of the state, although in a few smaller manufacturing communities and among ethnic minorities all over the state the Democrats have been generally popular for at least a generation. The primary dependence of the party is on the larger urban centers, however. Hartford, New Haven, Bridgeport, and Waterbury have nearly one-third of the population of the state. From these cities regularly come sizable Democratic majorities to offset the Republican majorities of the small towns and the suburban regions. It is not in the big four cities alone that the Democrats win majorities. According to the Census Bureau's categories there are 20 urban localities with over 10,000 population in the state, and in most gubernatorial elections the Democrats carry all but two of these cities. The two exceptions are Stamford and Norwalk, which have urban centers but outlying areas of suburban character. In 1948, for example, Chester Bowles carried all of them except Stamford and Norwalk, and averaged 56.5 per cent of the two-party vote cast in all 20 cities.

The explanation of the Democratic tendencies of these cities is found primarily in the same basic three factors to which we have referred in discussing the urban population of the other New England states: industrialization, ethnic minorities, and Catholicism. The presence of large ethnic minorities is an important factor. As of 1950 Connecticut's population was 14.9 per cent foreign-born, and another 33.2 per cent of the people were the second-generation sons and daughters of foreign or mixed foreign and native parents. There are great concentrations of them in the 20 cities with over 10,000 population. In New Haven, for example, as of 1940 "approximately three-fifths" of the population were "immigrants and their children. The Italians were the largest of the immigrant groups, with the first and second generations comprising nearly 27 per cent of the city's population."[7] The immigrant and second-generation population are not in the larger cities alone—they are widely scattered around the state. Many, in fact, are farmers in the small towns. Many live in the smaller cities and villages and work in manufacturing industry. This is particularly true in eastern Connecticut, where until recently textile mills were numerous. Several of these towns, as Figure 12 indicates, have high proportions of foreign-born population and are Democratic in their voting tendencies.[8]

In Connecticut as in the other New England states the tendency for ethnic minorities to be Democratic is illustrated by the ethnic distribution of names of members of the legislature. In Table 31, however, the data need to be considered with reservation since the apportionment of the House tends to emphasize the Yankee-dominated small towns. The general conclusion that ethnic minorities are more Democratic than Republican is valid, but the degree of concentration in the Democratic party is not quite as great as Table 31 might suggest.

Since the ethnic groups that are most numerous in Connecticut are also those from largely Catholic countries—particularly Italy, Poland, and Ireland, the three most numerous ethnic groups in the state—it is not surprising to find that the cities in which they are congregated also have more Catholics than Protestants. The ties between the Democratic party and the Catholic Church have been

[7] Jerome K. Myers, "Assimilation to the Ecological and Social Systems of a Community," 15 *American Sociological Review* 367-372 (1950) at p. 367.

The 1950 census shows a smaller proportion of "foreign stock" than in 1940, due to the decline in immigration and the deaths of older immigrants who came to Connecticut in the early part of this century. In New Haven, the proportion of "foreign stock" is now "down" to 52.5 per cent and in Waterbury, 57.7; Hartford, 53.6; Bridgeport, 55.3. In New Haven the "foreign stock" of Italian derivation is now only 22 per cent of the population. (See Bureau of the Census, *1950 Census of Population*. "Nativity and Parentage of the Foreign White Stock" (Series P-E, No. 3a). The political implications of ethnic associations do not end with the second generation; at least a third and perhaps more of New Haven's population is of Italian background.

[8] Such eastern Connecticut towns as Thompson, Putnam, Killingly, Plainsfield, Voluntown, Sprague, and Griswold (reading down the eastern border of the state) are either mill centers (Putnam and Killingly) or have high percentages of foreign-born. For details on foreign born in towns, see Nathan L. Whetten and Henry W. Riecken, Jr., "The Foreign-born Population of Connecticut, 1940," Storrs Agricultural Experiment Station Bulletin 246, Storrs, Connecticut, 1943 (pamphlet).

close over the years partly perhaps as a consequence of the Irish tendency to back the Democratic party even before the Civil War. A long line of Irish Catholics have been chairmen of the national Democratic party, and the candidacy of Al Smith further cemented

TABLE 31

Ethnic Distribution of Members of the Connecticut House of Representatives, 1901 and 1951

	DEMOCRATS				REPUBLICANS			
	1901		*1951*		*1901*		*1951*	
	Num-ber	*% Dems.*	*Num-ber*	*% Dems.*	*Num-ber*	*% Repubs.*	*Num-ber*	*% Repubs.*
Yankees	45	86.5%	24	27.6%	197	98.0%	160	84.2%
Irish	7	13.5	30	34.4	3	1.5	9	4.7
Italian	0		13	15.0	0		8	4.2
French-Canadian	0		6	6.9	0		3	1.6
Jewish	0		3	3.4	0		6	3.2
Polish	0		11	12.7	1	.5	4	2.1
	52	100.0%	87	100.0%	201	100.0%	190	100.0%

the tie. Most Democratic leaders in Connecticut come from the larger cities and therefore most of them are Catholic, for the pre-dominance of Catholics in the local Democratic parties make Yankee-Protestant Democratic leaders a rare phenomenon. There is no Democratic monopoly of support from Catholics, but the tendency of the Catholic population has been decidedly toward the Democrats.

Finally, it is significant that the labor movement has been closely allied with the Democratic party. While there is no evidence that the leaders of unions can "deliver" the votes of the more than 300,000 workers who are union members in the state, it is not unimportant that most union leaders are Democrats. Through contributions to Democratic campaign chests, propagandizing for Democrats at union meetings and in some labor publications, and by providing corps of campaign workers at strategic spots, the unions make a considerable contribution to the Democratic cause. Even, however, if the union leadership were not active politically, the fact that there are more than 400,000 people engaged in manufacturing in Con-

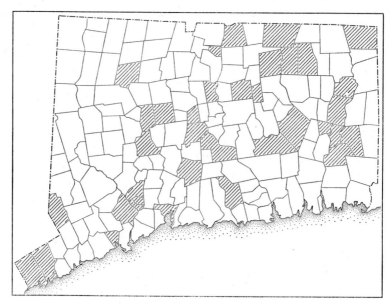

12. Towns with 20 Per Cent or More Foreign-Born Population, 1940

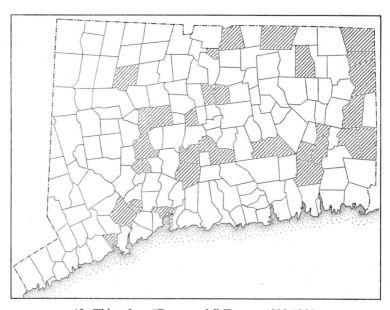

13. Thirty-four "Democratic" Towns: 1930-1954

necticut is politically significant. (That is, about one-fifth of the population.) At least since the beginning of the New Deal, the majority of the wage earners in the United States have been inclined toward the Democratic party. The voting behavior of working-class wards in Connecticut indicates that this state has been no exception.

Thus a delicate balance of forces has preserved for a quarter of a century the competitiveness of Connecticut parties. One can easily conjure up any number of forces that might disrupt that balance. If a number of large industries employing great numbers of militant workers—for example, the steel workers—were to come into the state the Democratic party might pull ahead. Should there be a great expansion of automation to redouble the proportion of white-collar and technical employees, who in search of respectability moved into the suburban Republican communities, then the Republican party could perhaps reassert the one-party dominance it once held. Serious scandals in either party or national events that might have a deep effect on state politics—any of these factors could upset the scales. Should the balance somehow be broken, the character of Connecticut government would certainly be changed, for the pressures of competition have induced a considerable degree of responsibility in Connecticut government, as the ensuing discussion of party strength and legislative operations will indicate.

Organizational Strength of the Republican Party

We are accustomed to calling by the name "political party" institutions of vastly different character. The monolithic parties of the Communist world with their rigid discipline and heavy ideological cant are a far cry from the splintered, localized, and ideologically diverse institutions that go by the same name in the United States. Were we to prepare a spectrum on which we placed parties by the degree to which they have ideological unity and discipline, Russia's Communist party would rest at one end of the line (along with the Nazi party), and American national parties would be near the other. Europe's Socialist parties would be somewhere in the middle, perhaps, and both major parties of England would be, among the democratic parties of the world, well to the unity-discipline side of the line. The party systems of the American one-party states with their factionalism that virtually supplants the party organization as such would be situated near or in some cases beyond the American national parties on the weakness side of the scale.

Connecticut's political parties would have to be located somewhere near the British parties. Less given to ideological unity and less disciplined than British parties, they are nevertheless utterly unlike the American national parties and are far stronger than the party organizations in most American states, including those of many two-party states. The parties of Connecticut exert great authority as instruments of government; they are not mere shadow organizations for the sake of convenience and custom. Factional differences exist in both parties, of course, and there is more localism than one finds in British parties, but traditionally the party leadership in Connecticut is expected to use disciplinary action against recalcitrants, to take the responsibility for forming party policy both in political campaigns and in the legislature, and most importantly to control nominations to high office. This is achieved with a certain amount of compromising, bargaining, and with some participation of the rank and file of the voters who consider themselves Republicans or Democrats. But the party membership participation is at a minimum in Connecticut compared with states which have developed the party primary. Characteristically Connecticut was the last of the 48 states to adopt the primary in any form, and when it was introduced in 1955 it was fashioned so as to preserve the dominant position of the party leadership.

The obvious strength of Connecticut party leadership is the product of many historical and other factors. But it is axiomatic that the leadership would not have much power were it not for the fact that there is relatively broad agreement on policy questions among the elements that comprise each party. Deep divisions would promote factionalism rather than sustain a strong leadership. Fairly broad agreement would seem to be a *sina qua non* for strong leadership. Thus in the heyday of one-party Republican control the conservatism of the business leadership of the state fitted well with the generally conservative outlook of the small-town Republicans who held so much party strength. Today there is general agreement on a somewhat less conservative position between the suburban-business and small-town Republicans. Disagreements do arise between these elements, and when they do the leadership is reduced to compromising and bargaining between the influentials rather than actually "controlling," but these occasions are the exceptions.

The traditional respect and deference paid to Republican leadership and the power which it has long wielded must in large measure be attributed to the phenomenal success of a political boss. There does not seem to be any other way adequately to explain the continued unity and strength of the Republican party organization during the second and third decades of this century. While in other states—and particularly in the one-party states—the political empires of dominant political bosses and their organizations were being hacked down by various reforming drives, the Boss of Connecticut, J. Henry Roraback, held fast. For a quarter of a century he not only saw to it that he did not preside over the liquidation of the Republican empire in the state; he made it a stronger machine than it had been when he took command in 1912. With consummate political acumen he fashioned an unbeatable combination: rural organizational strength, businessmen's money, conservative governmental policy, and a tight political organization. Until the depression, he ruled what was virtually a benevolent dictatorship. In many respects the Roraback machine was comparable to the Byrd machine in Virginia—efficient, conservative, penurious, and in absolute control. "Not only did he have a dictatorial hold on the government of the state but he was also a member of the Republican National Committee, controlled the Connecticut delegation at the national convention and dominated the representation of Connecticut in Congress."[9] As in so many bossed systems there is much hearsay evidence that Roraback during intermittent periods of his rule developed a "double machine"—i.e., a cooperative agreement with Democratic politicians to pass them crumbs of patronage in return for playing dead on election day.

It seems appropriate to review briefly the Roraback career in Connecticut government, for it was in the powerful machine which Roraback built up that the present-day Republican party had its beginnings. He not only proved that the elements of the party could pull in harness, but demonstrated the need of firm hands on the reins. More importantly, he shaped a pattern of expectations that helped his successors to maintain control over the party.

[9] E. E. Schattschneider, *Party Government*, New York, 1942, p. 179.

Roraback entered politics in his small adopted home town of North Canaan in 1894 when he organized a group of young Republicans who helped to put the town in the Republican ranks. Within five years he was a member of the state central committee. After devoting most of his time during the ensuing decade to lobbying for railroads and other business interests, he emerged as chairman of the state central committee in 1912, a post he retained for the next twenty-five years.

His power was not political alone, however, for he sensed the possibilities of water-power development and bought extensive water rights in Litchfield County. Gradually he extended his holdings and ultimately became president of the Connecticut Light and Power Company, the leading utility in the state. He was at the time of his death president of five lesser utilities, a director of four insurance companies, and director of at least one bank.[10]

Roraback was a consummate political strategist. For example, he himself drafted a statute creating the Soldiers', Sailors' and Marines' Fund just after the close of World War I. Politicians at that time feared that the homecoming soldiers might create a political problem, so they were thus placated. Significantly, the aid to indigent veterans was to be distributed by the newly organized American Legion, as indeed is still the case.[11] A less subtle or more effective way of attracting the political support of an interest group is hard to imagine.[12]

Roraback was able through his control over the party organization to keep the business interests happy, and by doing that to keep

[10] *Connecticut Register and Manual*, 1937, p. 409. A first impression is that it is unusual to see a state document print a biographical sketch in memoriam to a departed political leader who has held no official governmental post, but on second thought it is probably appropriate, for Roraback's powers were greater than many who held the highest offices in the state.

[11] *Connecticut State Journal*, June 1937, p. 59. The *Journal* is not an official publication but a magazine devoted largely to Connecticut politics. In a series of articles beginning in the June 1937 issue, old friends of Roraback wrote of their associations with him. The articles, unsigned, ran intermittently through 1943. See also the discussion of Roraback's career in Raymond E. Baldwin, *Let's Go into Politics*, New York, 1952, pp. 49-54. Baldwin was House majority leader during Roraback's time, and later became governor, U.S. Senator, and is presently on the bench of the Supreme Court of Errors. He is not, by the way, related to "Cappy" Baldwin, the present state chairman of the Republican party.

[12] The interest from the fund was to be turned over to "the treasurer of the American Legion, who shall disburse the same" to aid needy veterans. See *General Statutes of Connecticut*, Revision of 1949, Sec. 2957-2960.

money flowing into the party coffers. There were then as now tensions between the rural-organization strength of the party and the urban interests, but Roraback was able to coalesce the two to form a powerful political force. (Fairfield County and other suburban regions began to exert significant political influence only toward the end of Roraback's reign.) Some contend that Roraback was nothing more than a front man for the various utilities, insurance companies, and manufacturers who through him got what they wanted out of state government.[13] Undoubtedly much of his power was based upon his contacts with these powerful interest groups, but he must have been a pretty dangerous front man, for he was no one's fool. Even if it is true that the moneyed interests dictated some politics to Roraback, it was he who called the signals and in the minds of the politicians he was clearly the Number One Man.

Although Roraback was rarely seen around the State House, his influence on the legislature and in administrative offices was overwhelming. He chose to conduct business from the Allyn House in Hartford, but his lieutenants were ever-present in the halls of the legislature. The story is that every day after the close of the legislative session, one of these lieutenants brought a box filled with bills for Mr. Roraback's perusal. The next morning the subordinate would return with the "word" on each bill. By such means he managed to control legislation—some of it favorable to the utilities in which he was personally involved. (Eminent domain rights could be had for the building of dams, for example.) Appointments to such bodies as the Public Utilities Commission were cleared with him, and the choice of the chairmen of important committees in the House and Senate was largely a Roraback decision.[14]

Some old-time politicians claim that in this era it was possible for groups to buy bills by paying the proper persons—though that person was not J. Henry Roraback. He had an absolute rule that none of his men were to touch any state money, although, apparently,

[13] Carl Clyma, political reporter for the *New Haven Register*, claims this was the case.

[14] In the House the speaker is formally responsible for the appointment of committees and the designation of their chairmen. On one occasion a speaker was uncertain whether to appoint a particular businessman-legislator to the chairmanship of the tax-writing Finance Committee. After conversation with Roraback, the speaker is said to have reported: "J. Henry says he's well up in manufacturing circles and knows his stuff. That's all right with me." He got the chairmanship, of course. See *Connecticut State Journal*, Jan. 1943, p. 12.

whatever could be gained otherwise was fair booty. That there was some crookedness is indicated by the fact that two of his lieutenants were indicted for frauds and one of them, Harry McKenzie, was sentenced to prison for participation in the infamous Waterbury scandal.[15]

To challenge Roraback on any serious matter was to invite sure and devastating retribution, for his control of the party machinery was such that the unfaithful could be cast into outer darkness beyond the confines of Republican sunlight. Even obstreperous Republican governors were subjected to this treatment. In 1922 a gala celebration was being held in Hartford for Republicans to keep their spirits high in the then current campaign. No less a figure than Vice President Calvin Coolidge was to be a speaker. In charge of the program, Roraback invited Republican town chairmen from all over the state and dozens of minor figures in the party sat on the platform with the notables of the evening. But the Governor, Everett J. Lake, was not even invited. Denied renomination by Roraback for refusing to agree with the Boss on several matters, Lake was being punished in this petty way as well. Governor Lake sat alone in the balcony unnoticed.[16] Lake's successor as governor was also unable to get along with Roraback and was likewise denied renomination.[17] One Roraback governor, sharply criticized in an editorial, complained to the editor, whose reply was: "I have as much right to my opinion as you have to J. Henry Roraback's."[18]

The use of such strong disciplinary power required a tightly knit party organization—one in which the lower levels of party command were active but closely bound to the central leadership. Roraback as a political strategist was able to integrate the Republican organization as no one man before him had ever done. Nor has any since had so compliant and coordinated an organization to work with. Whether it was a governor or a legislator from a small town who

[15] A monumental piece of municipal corruption which cost the city of Waterbury some $3,000,000. A Democratic city administration, headed by Mayor Hayes, who was concurrently lieutenant governor of the state, collaborated with various Republicans to mulct the city of vast sums of money. Hayes also went to prison.

[16] See the story in the *Hartford Times*, Oct. 25, 1922.

[17] Governor Charles A. Templeton. Denial of renomination was not evidence of any practice of holding governors to one term, for the governor before Lake and the one who followed Templeton both served three terms each.

[18] Quoted in Jonathan Daniels, *A Southerner Discovers New England*, New York, 1940, p. 188.

crossed Roraback's path, the Boss was able to command sufficient support from the organization to punish the offender. To deny re-nomination to either the highest or lowest officials, it was necessary to have the cooperation of local leaders, so the connections between the state leadership and the local leadership were crucially important. By judicious use of patronage and other rewards and punishments, Roraback got ample local support.

The state convention was all-important in the party organization, and Roraback's genius was never more apparent than in his control of these biennial gatherings. The convention nominated the slate of statewide elective officers. There being no primary, the convention consequently made the most important decisions within the power of the party. The opportunity to attend the convention—or more accurately to control a local delegation—was considered a significant political function.

The Republican convention was then (and still is) apportioned so as to favor the small town. The convention in fact simply doubles the General Assembly—two delegates for each representative and senator. The apportionment of the House (with 279 members compared with 36 in the Senate) grants virtual equality to each of the 169 towns (each has at least one member and none may have more than two, regardless of size). Thus the large cities have not much more political weight when convention votes are counted than some small hamlets of a few hundred. The four largest cities of the state (with one-third of the state's population) get about six per cent of the convention representation. Thus the convention is a gathering of the 169 local Republican organizations without much distinction made as to size—at least in convention voting. This equality of small town and large city naturally enhances small-town power, and Roraback, as a small-town man, got on well with the rural Yankees who dominated the small-town organizations.

The multiplicity of local organizations, all on roughly equal footing in the convention, played into Roraback's hands in another way. Centers of opposition were hard to develop, for there were no great blocks of convention votes from any one center that could be used as a bargaining device. He had power, prestige, and patronage to encourage local organizations to go along; dissident elements found it difficult to amass sufficient factional strength to combat his influence with widely scattered local bosses.

The very extensiveness of Roraback's power contributed to his ultimate decline in authority, for it helped bring the Democrats into office. In 1930 the Democrats, partly out of desperation, nominated Wilbur L. Cross for governor. Having spent his life as a scholar, teacher, and dean of the Graduate School at Yale, Cross knew something of power politics, but in his campaign he seemed attractive as a completely "unbossed" candidate. There were other important factors in the election—the depression being the main one, no doubt—but the vigorous attack on Republican bossism undoubtedly combined with Cross's prestige to help produce an upset Democratic victory. Then on the swell of the New Deal tide, Cross remained in office for eight years. Roraback had to find new ways to deal with a new political situation.

A staunch conservative at heart, Roraback had no truck with the liberal legislation being demanded to meet the crisis of depression, but he could and did compromise and drive patronage and other political bargains with what power remained to him. And even in the days after Cross came to the governor's office, Roraback was far from powerless. He retained his hold on the Republican party. He still controlled the House of Representatives. He managed to control the Senate for most of this time as well, either through outright Republican majorities, bargains reached with dissident Democrats, or deals with the Socialists from Bridgeport who held the balance of power in the Senate in 1935.[19] In time Roraback found he could compromise and negotiate with Governor Cross, and all important legislation from 1931 through 1937 was in some degree the result of compromise between these opposing leaders.

Continued Democratic victories and the exigencies of government with divided party control began to disrupt the smooth-functioning machine that Roraback had developed. When the glue of patronage had been available to cement fissures in the party front,

[19] Bridgeport Socialists are a unique breed. They are followers of Jasper McLevy, Socialist mayor of that city from 1933 to 1957. Mr. McLevy is a Socialist in name only; his policies are soundly conservative. The advantage originally of the Socialist tag was that it was neither Democrat nor Republican, both of which terms were in disrepute following local scandals in Bridgeport before McLevy came to power. In the 1935 session the Socialists drove a bargain with the Republicans whereby they were promised local legislation for Bridgeport in return for voting to allow the Republicans to organize the Senate. When on the 110th ballot for clerk of the Senate the Socialists voted with the Republicans, the Democratic senators shouted "Deal, deal!" See *Hartford Courant*, Jan. 11, 1935.

the capacity of the boss to hold the party together had been phenomenal. Now, however, what patronage there was produced as much squabbling as party harmony. Many Republicans were beginning to demand a more bold and progressive party program to meet the challenge of the Democrats. When the 1936 campaign was lost (the fourth in a row) Roraback's authority began to slip. He had been ill for some time and newspaper reporters commented on the almost careless attitudes he assumed in the 1936 convention. Some of his political friends actually deserted him; a few declined invitations to his Harwinton lodge, an unthinkable affront in days gone by.[20] His oldest cronies did not desert the great boss, and he remained a figure of great respect and power in the party until he gave the political world his last great surprise: he committed suicide in May 1937.[21]

No successor to Roraback as state chairman has held anything like the power he had. Powerful figures have arisen in the party since 1937, but none has been able to assert one-man dominance. Following a wild scramble for control of the party after Roraback's death, leadership gradually devolved upon several prominent Republicans and so it remains today. Collegial leadership, of course, cannot provide the unity of purpose and the decisiveness of one-man control, but it would be an error to assume that the post-Roraback Republican party leadership has been weak. The membership of the leading clique has shifted over the years as factional battles have been fought and uneasy truces and alliances worked out. But those who have occupied the topmost positions in the party have continued to control nominations, party strategy in campaigns and in the legislature. The role of the present state chairman illustrates the character of present-day Republican leadership.

Clarence "Cappy" Baldwin has been state chairman since 1950. A long career in politics has fitted him to fill the role of negotiator

[20] See the *Connecticut State Journal*, Feb. 1942, p. 29. Roraback's famous lodge had been the site of three brief vacations for Calvin Coolidge during his tenancy in the White House.

[21] There was no suggestion at that time that he had chosen death because of impending scandals. Within a year widespread scandals were revealed that involved some of his former associates and subordinates, but there was never any evidence that Roraback had personally been involved in any of them. Although he unquestionably advanced his personal fortune through legislative manipulations, he was never shown to have been involved in bribery or other such finagling. The presumption is that his decision to die was related to poor health.

with rural politicians and legislators and leaders of both parties. Resident of a small town on the periphery of New Haven (Woodbridge, which is gradually becoming more a suburban than a farming town), he calls himself a farmer. Baldwin is a member of the Board of Directors of the Connecticut Farm Bureau Federation, but in reality he is more a professional politician than anything else as his present and former political jobs indicate. Among other things he has been twice a member of the House of Representatives, once a state senator, once the clerk of the Senate (after having been a senator), and for a short time he was an assistant to Harold Mitchell, whom he succeeded in the state chairmanship.

Baldwin is "primus inter pares," the first among the leaders, not the whole show by himself. A quiet man with a good memory for political facts, a reasonably able strategist, he has managed to retain his hold on the top organizational job in the party notwithstanding the sometimes shifting sands of factionalism in the party in recent years. In an interview in 1951 Baldwin told me he did not expect to be able to hold onto the state chairmanship. "I'm not the type to push people around," he said. In 1958, however, he is still in the saddle.[21a] Although he is sometimes just the spokesman for group decisions, he cannot be discounted as a neutral force. He can and does give the clearance a piece of legislation may need to get through the House of Representatives, and he can effectively bottle up legislation. Authoritative announcements of party policy come from Baldwin on all manner of public issues ranging from the size of the budget or highway bonding issues to "official" attacks on opposition politicians. He is more likely to be the spokesman when a Democrat is governor than when one of his own party occupies that office, but in either case his public expressions are taken seriously. He sits in on legislative conferences between party leaders seeking to iron out necessary compromises on legislation. As party chairman he takes the lead in organizing the state campaign, and for the most part the campaign is run from his headquarters in Hartford. He is a key figure in every state convention.

The conduct of the state campaign illustrates the degree of centralization in the party. Finances are handled on a "United Drive" basis. The finance committee of each town collects what it can and the proceeds are turned over to the State Central Committee for "approval." Baldwin estimates that about one-third of the funds re-

[21a] See footnote on p. 269, below.

ceived from all sources by the state organization is returned to the towns to meet their budgets. The state organization thus has a complete record of all contributors to the party and early in the campaign sends to local committees the names of all previous donors. Sending money back and forth between town and headquarters involves extra bookkeeping, no doubt, but it permits an unusual degree of centralized control of party finances.

The gubernatorial and senatorial campaigns are largely conducted out of the state office. There programs and schedules are coordinated, the speech-writing done, and policy decisions made. The finances of these campaigns are also handled through the state committee. In the 1956 campaign, for example, Senator Prescott Bush, reported a *total* expenditure of $304.61! (His opponent, Congressman Thomas Dodd, reported having spent $92,300.) Bush's expenditures were, of course, met by the state committee, which reported total expenditures of $246,981.

There is opposition within the party. Baldwin, as state chairman, has to deal with political leaders some of whom have considerable power and prestige. Factional organizations of continuous and identifiable character are not common, however. Opposition frequently rises and from time to time may seem formidable, but it usually dissolves before long. Some of this opposition comes sporadically from figures sometimes called "county leaders" who try to pull together the local organizations of a county to create a basis for political maneuvering. But the maneuver rarely works. The eight Connecticut counties are unlike the counties of the West or South, for they have virtually no functions left to perform. There is practically no county consciousness. The town is the significant political subdivision—to it go the powers of government below the state level and accordingly there also are the political organizations of significance. Thus a county leader setting out to organize factional strength must deal with a group of independent organizations, not a unit that itself is a basic political subdivision, as is the case of most counties outside New England. In any event, the prestige and power of the state organization is such that the county leaders face a difficult task.

The only exception to the characteristic weakness of the county organizations is the powerful and relatively cohesive group in Fairfield County. William Brennan is the acknowledged head of the organization, and although he has often cooperated with the remainder of the party leadership, he has frequently been the focal point of dissident strength. Brennan, a professional politician who even looks like the stereotyped professional, is a ubiquitous figure around the legislature during the biennial sessions. His power is partly the consequence of the suburban character of Fairfield County. One of the most constant sources of friction in the party is the suburban-small-town rivalry. Capitalizing on this, Brennan has been able to build up a strong organization partly on the argument that Fairfield provides the votes and therefore ought to have more of the party's plums. Evidence of the distinct character of the Fairfield organization is found in the fact that it is the only county to collect and disburse separate campaign funds. By pulling together all or most of the convention votes of the county to wield as a unit, Brennan has some basis for bargaining in the inner councils of the party. He, along with others, has helped to force greater recognition for Fairfield County. (Three of the four men who have run for governor on the Republican ticket since 1938 have been from the county—or if one counts separate gubernatorial candidacies seven of eight have been from Fairfield County.)

In 1952, after being pushed into it by Governor John Davis Lodge (brother of Henry Cabot Lodge of Massachusetts), Baldwin set forth to trim Brennan's power. There was great personal animosity involved, particularly because Brennan had been among Lodge's earliest supporters. He had promoted Lodge both for the office of Congressman from the Fairfield County district and for the governorship which he had won in 1950. But Lodge was displeased with some of the maneuvering in which Brennan had been involved and accordingly Baldwin commandeered the convention votes necessary to replace Brennan as Republican national committeeman. This led to a rather intense battle in the party. When the dust had settled, former Governor James Shannon was the new national committeeman and Brennan was forced to go to the convention as a Fairfield County district delegate.[22]

Other illustrations of the significant strength of the state leadership could be cited almost indefinitely. In other states it is not customary for the party chairman in the course of a battle for delegates

[22] For a review of the infighting of 1952, see David, Moos, and Goldman, *op.cit.*, pp. 128-138. Brennan resigned as county leader after the 1958 fiasco. See footnote on p. 269.

for the presidential nomination to send out a letter to local party organizations explicitly endorsing one of the two major contenders. Most state chairmen remain neutral or work covertly for their choices, except, of course, where a favorite son is being promoted. But in contravention to the customary practice elsewhere, Baldwin sent out a letter to each of the 169 town chairmen asking specifically for support for a pro-Eisenhower delegation to the 1952 convention. Meade Alcorn, then one of Hartford County's most prominent leaders and chairman of the Eisenhower clubs of the state, was said to have instigated the letter. The Taft forces were said to have expected the state leadership to be neutral, but this anticipation was badly in error. Lodge, Baldwin, and Alcorn were solidly behind Eisenhower and therefore employed the weapons at hand to achieve their purpose.[23]

Undoubtedly one of the most important reasons the Republican (and, for that matter, the Democratic) organization remained so strong was that—at least until 1955—the state had no party primary law. One can turn this fact the other way to argue that there has been no primary because the parties were strong. But whichever way one chooses to look at the fact, it was a signally important contribution to the power of the leadership. In the absence of a primary the opportunity for political advancement lay with the organization, not through independent appeals to the electorate in a primary election. Local organizations had reason to exist even where there was little hope of winning an election for their party, for there were state conventions biennially in which important decisions were made. In contrast to many states in which the primary has been employed, there has been no appreciable withering away of the party organizations in local areas. The demise of local organizations probably cannot be laid solely at the door of the primary, but it is undoubtedly an important factor, as pointed out above in Chapter 3.[24] Suffice it

[23] Alcorn became national committeeman in 1953 when Shannon was appointed to the bench. The story was that Lodge was set to appoint Alcorn to this job in 1952, but was persuaded not to when objections were made that Brennan, a Catholic, should be replaced with a Catholic. Alcorn's power in state politics has not been diminished by his appointment as national chairman of the Republican party. Only recently the Republicans of Hartford County have organized a Republican association more or less along the lines of Brennan's Fairfield County organization. Through that, Alcorn may be expected to keep his hand in Connecticut Republican politics.

[24] See pp. 55-56.

to say that the evidence in Connecticut would suggest that in the absence of a primary, party organizations have continued to be alive and active. In 1954 there were nominations for the House by both parties in all towns, except that in two towns the Democrats endorsed Republicans and in one the reverse took place. (Contrast this with the data on Ohio, Missouri, or New Hampshire, p. 56.)

The tendency for local organizations to nominate candidates for the legislature is but one evidence of the continued activity of local organizations. There are others: in 1956 every one of the 169 towns had local party officers. Having officers does not necessarily mean anything is done politically; there is a wide range of activity among local organizations, and some which may appear to be alive are nearly moribund. But even in the smaller communities the Democratic organization usually puts on some sort of campaign, and in the larger cities the Republican party often matches or even at times surpasses that of the Democrats.

In 1955 a party primary law was passed after a long and bitter struggle. Characteristically the primary preserves the power of the party organizations. The caucus in the small town continues to exist, and the state convention will continue to nominate in effect if not in law. The actions of the caucus and the convention are now called endorsement, and if there is no challenger seeking to compete with the endorsee there is no primary at all. Even more significant, in the conventions to nominate persons elected from districts of more than one town (or for statewide offices) it is necessary for any challenger to garner at least 20 per cent of the delegate vote in order to challenge the winner of the endorsement. No other candidate can enter the race, and the primary is held only if there is a formal filing by the challenger with a number of signatures to attest his support. (A filing fee is required and is returned to the challenger only if he gets at least 10 per cent of the primary vote.) The rash predictions at the time of the passage of the act that this would spell the end of parties in Connecticut were, like the premature death notices for Mark Twain, "greatly exaggerated." The ambitious will still move ahead in politics *within* the organization. They will not try to sidestep the leadership through appeals to party members in primaries. Some will do this, of course, and no doubt some will be effective in a limited way, but the likelihood is that the organization will maintain its hold on the situation. Unless the primary is vastly altered (and one session has now gone by since its passage without serious change in the law) there is a strong presumption that the party organizations will remain strong.[25]

Democratic Party Organization: the Dominance of City Machines

In the Republican party the intra-organizational strength lies with the small town, although the greatest electoral strength lies elsewhere. In the Democratic party a simpler system applies: both electoral strength and organizational power are in the larger cities. The greatest bulk of political power in the party comes from more than a dozen predominantly Democratic cities. The four largest cities, in fact, tend to dominate the party, since they have large blocs of convention votes with which to attract still more votes by making alliances with other cities. As in the Republican party, the key to the party organization is control over the convention.

Unlike the Republican convention, the Democratic convention gives great strength to the cities. The apportionment of the convention allows each of the towns two delegates, with one extra delegate for each 2,000 votes cast in the preceding presidential election. The small towns consequently have a slightly greater proportion of the total convention membership than they would be entitled to under a straight proportional representation of Democratic voters, but they are overshadowed by the cities in the convention. The size of the convention changes with the size of the presidential election vote, but in general the convention has about 800 delegates. The Democratic cities referred to above have about 35 to 40 per cent of the total membership, and the four largest cities go into the conventions with about 150 delegates between them.[26]

Most of these city Democratic organizations are tightly led, and

[25] It is significant that more than a decade's operation of a somewhat similar primary in Rhode Island has not materially altered the strength of either state party organization.

[26] The present apportionment dates from the 1954 convention. Prior to that, each town had been entitled to one delegate for each 1,000 votes and one for each member of the House of Representatives. Thus the new system increased the representation of the towns with only one representative (61 small towns) and proportionately reduced the city apportionment. But the convention had become so large as to be unwieldy (about 1,500 delegates). The revision benefited the small towns somewhat but not enough to upset the advantage of the cities.

257

some are under the personal domination of bosses. Although there are rivalries and dissension in all these organizations, in most convention battles the top men of the city machines usually manage to present a solid front for bargaining purposes. With their local power and patronage, the city bosses cooperate with the state leaders only as it seems convenient. State party leaders, therefore, have to deal with a dozen or more city bosses backed up by blocs of convention votes, not scattered and isolated small delegations such as those of the Republican convention. In the conventions of both parties there are coalitions made for bargaining purposes, but it is harder to hold together perhaps 25 or 30 separate Republican town delegations necessary to create a significant bloc of votes than to hold the votes of a single Democratic city.

The localized power of the city bosses has necessarily made the Democratic party a somewhat less centralized organization than the Republican. Where the isolation of local organizations has played into the hands of Republican state leaders, the concentration of votes—both popular and in conventions—in Democratic cities has made for greater dispersion of power in the Democratic party. In matters of party finance, for example, there is far less central control in the Democratic party. Town organizations raise their own campaign funds and almost never pass along any of it to the state organization. On the contrary, the state chairman usually gives some money (about one-eighth of total state collections) to local organizations late in the campaign, although this is normally concentrated in districts with close senatorial races.

Still, the fact that the Democratic party is so much an urban party has tended to build up the power of the state leadership in another way. The similarity of outlook of the urban areas—most of them being industrial cities with strong labor unions and relatively radical policy demands—has created a basis of agreement on policy. Granting that there are often vigorous disagreements on policy questions within the Democratic party, most candidates and party leaders at both state and local levels have found it expedient to espouse a liberal policy. The differences in outlook and interests that tend to pull apart the suburban and rural elements of the Republican party are not so significant in the Democratic party. Indeed, it appears that in recent years most of the small-town and suburban Democratic organizations have assumed more doctrinaire liberal attitudes than the urban elements.[27]

Particularly since World War II the Democratic party has turned toward liberalism; during the same period the party has become more and more united. Other factors than liberalism have been involved in the increasing unity, but a look at the party factionalism of the 1930's suggests that liberalism is a factor of some significance. The hold-over leaders of the Democratic party from the 1920's were inclined to be fairly conservative. During the New Deal period, when radicalism was characteristic of the urban areas especially, the unwillingness of party leaders to be more bold was a source of disruption within the ranks. Several conservative businessmen served as state chairmen during this period and in combination with the conservative Governor Cross aroused considerable antagonism in the party. Governor Cross, for example, once proposed an income tax to meet a fiscal crisis, but he offered it with the greatest reluctance. He wanted a tax, he said, "with less generous exemptions in the lower brackets than are allowed by the Federal income tax."[28] He also suggested that all New England be consolidated into one great state, thereby eliminating the "enormous cost of six annual sessions of Legislatures which never adjourn until they are compelled to by law. What a racket! Millions of dollars which we now waste every year might be saved merely by uniting under the banner of one State and placing in the Governor's chair a man like Calvin Coolidge who never let loose a nickel unless he had to."[29]

Roraback's fine hand was unquestionably involved in some of the

[27] It may seem paradoxical that the suburban Democratic elements stand to the left of the urban Democrats, but there is a plausible explanation. In a great many of the small towns and suburban localities, the newer commuting element has taken over weak Democratic organizations. In many of these places the Democratic organization is more a debating society than a serious contender for public offices. At the same time, however, many are building up hard-working organizations that get all the results conceivable out of their communities. The intellectual cast of their leadership has, however, inclined them toward rather uncompromising liberalism.

[28] *Hartford Courant*, Feb. 4, 1937. Cross was essentially conservative, although he did occasionally come out with liberal proposals. His Yankee background and rural Tolland County upbringing shine through his autobiography, *Connecticut Yankee*, New Haven, 1943. In 1935 Cross proposed a sales tax with which the conservative Republican leadership was in agreement. But to a man the Democrats in the House voted against it, and with Republican dissenters they defeated the bill.

[29] *Connecticut Yankee*, p. 374.

disunity of the Democratic party in those days. Democratic politicians who had played ball with the Republican boss in the old days did not lose the habit overnight. Said the *Waterbury Republican* in a 1933 editorial: "The sell-out of the old-guard Democratic Senators to the Republican machine serves at least one useful purpose. It puts in high relief for public inspection a practice that has hitherto been kept pretty well under cover. For years it has been known that the old guard leadership of the Democratic party has worked hand in glove with J. Henry Roraback, but while the Democratic party was in the minority in both the houses of the legislature, the practice was not obvious. . . . With Democrats in control of the Senate, it is impossible for the old-guard to keep its traffic from being conspicuous."[30]

The present prestige and power of the Democratic leadership differs markedly from that of Governor Cross's day. The party was badly shaken by the scandals of 1938 and the subsequent loss of the governorship. After several years of vacillating leadership, John Bailey emerged as state chairman in 1946. Bailey, undisputed leader of the party in Hartford,[31] has gradually and steadily increased his power until he is now the most powerful Democrat in the state. He came to the job of chairman after a background of experience with state government, although he had never held an elective office. As a young lawyer (he graduated from Harvard Law School in the same class with Governor John D. Lodge, subsequently a bitter enemy), he worked in the Young Democratic movement. In 1933 he was made a municipal judge in Hartford, one of the beneficiaries of the notorious sell-out by the Spellacy Democratic group. He subsequently was clerk of the Hartford Court (1935-1939) and was again judge in 1939-1941. In 1941 he became secretary to the Legislative Council, and two years later became statute revision commissioner. Independently wealthy, he has devoted his life to politics, for which he is singularly well-equipped.

Few men know more than Bailey about the intricacies of the Con-

---

[30] *Waterbury Republican*, Feb. 8, 1933. This blast followed a sell-out by which three Democratic senators voted with the Republicans to divide the local judgeships that year. This was reported to have been engineered by the late Thomas Spellacy, then Democratic leader of Hartford and influential lobbyist and attorney for the Standard Oil Co. Two members of Spellacy's law firm got court appointments.

[31] Shortly before being chosen state chairman he had lost control of the Hartford organization, but he soon regained control of Hartford.

necticut legislative politics. Like most politicians who move into the front ranks, he has a remarkable memory, and can, when it has some bearing on a pending question, recall details of legislation passed or debated twenty years previously. He has the strategic capacities to handle the intricacies of political combat whether within the Democratic party or against the Republicans. During the tenure of Republican Governor John Lodge he kept up a steady stream of attack on the administration and on the governor himself. It was he who pinned the label "Silent John" on Lodge—this being an allusion to his unwillingness to take stands on issues. Bailey criticized the vacations which at times kept Lodge out of the state; he took advantage of a Lodge campaign slogan "The Man You Can Trust" to emphasize every failure of the Republicans to live up to any detail of their campaign oratory. Then, in a complete reversal of tactics, he uttered almost not a word during the 1957 session of the legislature. At this point a Democrat occupied the governor's chair (Ribicoff) and the Republicans controlled both Houses of the legislature, so Bailey tried to stay entirely out of the picture. "Why should I say anything? It would just force the Republicans to focus on me. The last thing I want is to unify them. The more divided they are the better off the Governor is. So I stay completely in the background."

Bailey's aim is political advantage and to accommodate this end he can get along with the liberals and the conservatives alike. During the tenure of Governor Chester Bowles he fell into line with the liberal policies the governor desired. No other Connecticut governor in this century has espoused a more consistently progressive program than Bowles, who fought for low-cost housing, improved labor laws, improved mental health facilities, and governmental reorganization.[32] Bailey supported Bowles completely. The Senate was pulled into line behind the Bowles's program largely through Bailey's persuasiveness. The next Democratic governor, Ribicoff, is far more moderate in his political position. There has been as much grumbling about his conservatism as there was about Bowles's liberalism, but Bailey has given Ribicoff exactly the same kind of support he gave Bowles. He was entirely in accord with the first speech of the 1954 campaign, for example, which was given by Ribicoff in Greenwich,

[32] Bowles initiated the most ambitions study of Connecticut government ever made. He got approval from the Republican House for a Commission on State Government Organization, whose *Report* (Feb. 1950) proposed bold changes in Connecticut government.

heartland of suburban Fairfield County. There Ribicoff came out forcefully in opposition to a state income tax. This, of course, appealed or was supposed to appeal to the refugee New Yorkers who come to Connecticut in part to escape New York state income tax.[33]

In the years of his incumbency as state chairman, Bailey has never been seriously challenged for his job. During the first years of his chairmanship he had to accommodate his role to the powerful position of Senator Brian McMahon, who had originally picked Bailey for state chairman. McMahon was extremely popular throughout the state. In the 1950 election, for example, Democratic Senator William Benton was elected by the narrow margin of 1,000 votes and Bowles lost the governorship by 17,000, but McMahon won by more than 50,000. Bailey never was in direct conflict with McMahon; each operated in his own sphere. With the untimely death of McMahon in 1952, however, Bailey emerged as the single most powerful Democrat in the state.

This does not make Bailey a Roraback by any means. The structure of the party forces him into alliances with various city bosses. Prominent among them is John Golden, boss of New Haven and the Democratic National Committeeman. Golden, suave Irish politician from the second largest city in the state, has complete control of his organization. On occasion Golden will appear in Hartford during legislative sessions to consult on policy questions, but like most of the Democratic city bosses he does not concern himself with a wide range of legislative questions. Anything that affects the political machinery of the party or local legislation for New Haven will bring Golden into legislative affairs, but otherwise he is little involved. In all battles for nominations or questions of state patronage, however, Golden is an influential figure.

Others with whom Bailey has to deal are the leaders of Bridgeport, Waterbury, Middletown, New London, and others. Bailey grants patronage to tame some of them; others he chastises by refusing patronage. The boss of Middletown, John Tynan, for example, is presently motor vehicles commissioner. Mayor Edward Bergin of Waterbury is sulking in his tent as of 1958 because he did not get

---

[33] Many Republicans now complain that Ribicoff has stolen one of their most tried and trustworthy political arguments. "How can you say you're against the tax, when all anyone will say in reply is that 'So is Abe.'" The reference is to Abraham Ribicoff, of course. The comment was made by a prominent young Republican gubernatorial hopeful.

the "recognition" he desired. Attilio "Pop" Frassinelli, boss of Stafford Springs, is now food and drugs commissioner. Cornelius Mulvihill of Bridgeport served both as state senator and as motor vehicles commissioner during the Bowles administration. T. Emmet Clarie, of Danielson in eastern Connecticut, serves as a liquor control commissioner. C. John Satti, secretary of state, 1935-1939, boss of New London, is out of favor with the state leadership at present and accordingly has been refused patronage for his area. (Satti's wife, Mrs. Dorothy Satti, was removed as national committeewoman in 1956 in a move widely assumed to be a slap at Satti.) Douglas Bennet, one-time executive secretary to Governor Bowles, is the leader of the small towns of the 20th Senatorial District in New London County, and has considerable standing with state organization—the only example of a small-town Democrat given such recognition.[33a] Bennet's group has been given considerable patronage since 1955, partly in recognition of a strong organization that pulled more Democratic votes than was anticipated in both the 1954 and 1956 elections, and partly, no doubt, to further chastise the Satti organization, which is next door to the Bennet district. Further examples could be cited, but this sampling illustrates the range of political influentials with whom Bailey operates.

The Democratic alliance with labor is at once a blessing and a curse. Labor leaders assist the Democrats in political campaigns year after year, but their interests transcend the party as such. As with the business groups supporting the Republicans, there is an implied *quid pro quo* attached to their support. Old-line politicians are suspicious of labor leaders and tend to resent their role in the party even if they are happy enough to have the votes that labor organizations may help produce. In state conventions, labor leaders play a role similar to that of national labor leaders in the Democratic national convention. Aligning themselves with the more liberal element, they often make demands for specific nominations and, while the regulars are often loath to concede to labor's demands, they are also apprehensive about refusing.

The battle of the 1954 convention illustrates the intra-organizational power of labor as well as the influence of another important facet of Democratic operations—the power of ethnic minorities.

[33a] Bennet withdrew from the 20th District leadership in 1958, but the district organization remains strong and favored.

Labor wanted Chester Bowles as the gubernatorial candidate. Bowles would have been glad to have the nomination to try to avenge his loss to Lodge in 1950, but most party leaders were frightened at the prospect of putting up a loser, so Bowles was shunted aside in favor of Abraham Ribicoff. At this point the labor leaders and other Bowles adherents demanded the nomination of Joseph Lyford for congressman at large. This might have been a reasonable enough choice for the office, for Lyford was young, able, articulate, and liberal, but there was a snag. For more than a decade the nomination for congressman at large had been reserved for those of Polish descent.[34] When labor's demand became known throughout the convention hall and the hotel lobbies, battle lines began to be drawn. An open contest was averted by a compromise which named a woman of Polish background for the office of secretary of state (largely reserved for women since 1938) and Lyford for congressman at large. But the Polish leaders were not satisfied; they had not proposed Mrs. Zdunczyk and were angry that they could not choose their man to oppose Republican Antoni Sadlak, who had been congressman at large since 1947. Labor had won the immediate contest, but the campaign was yet to be run.

Predictions that there would be a widespread revolt of Polish Democrats were heard on all sides. The custom of nominating representatives of certain ethnic groups to specific office had become so well established, it was said, that this breach would hurt the party. Many politicians were already upset that for the first time in the history of the state a man of the Jewish faith was running for governor. An Italian had been chosen for the treasurer's spot, as custom decreed, but the candidate was not well known and the general feeling was that his primary recommendation had been that he came from the New Haven area. There was not a single Yankee on the state ticket, except for Lyford, and he was thought to be more a liability than an asset—at least in the view of many regulars.

As it turned out, Lyford was in fact the low man on the statewide Democratic ticket, but the reasons for his being there were far more complicated than the commonly given one that tradition was flouted by not nominating a Polish candidate. In the first place, he did not trail by much. His total vote was just one per cent less than the

[34] Only three times since 1932 had non-Polish candidates been nominated for this office by the Democrats, and the Republicans had not deviated once since 1938.

average vote for other members of the state ticket (459,500 votes average; Lyford had 455,800). Labor worked hard for Lyford and there was not much overt opposition from Polish Democratic leaders, although not many were very helpful either. However, many old-line Democrats refused to help him, some of them virtually refusing to let him into certain towns to campaign. Lyford also took an unequivocal stand against Senator Joseph McCarthy and McCarthyism. Among Democrats to whom the late senator was hero rather than villain, this did not do Lyford any good, although his attack may well have brought some compensating votes his way.

As elsewhere, Lyford did tend to trail the ticket somewhat in the areas where Polish ethnic groups are concentrated, but the extent of his deficit even there was not great. There are eight town and cities where the Polish vote is supposed to be important (and demographic data tend to sustain the common impression.) Lyford's average deficit in these towns was about 1.1 per cent compared with the rest of the ticket.[35] This would seem to suggest there was not much opposition to Lyford from voters of Polish extraction. A more precise picture, however, may be seen by examining the voting data for three wards in New Britain which are heavily populated with the Polish minority. In Table 32 Congressman Sadlak's capacity to pull votes away from Democratic candidates in heavily Democratic wards is shown to be less than overwhelming. In each of the four elections examined, he drew more votes than the Republican gubernatorial candidate, and he did better against Lyford than any preceding candidate. Compared, however, with the vote-getting power of candidates like Del Sesto and Pastore in Rhode Island, Sadlak's margins are not impressive.

The trends in the two parties as regards the strength of the central organizations are roughly opposite. The Republican organization of necessity is weaker than it was under Roraback, although it still exerts considerable power. The Democratic organization, weak and

[35] The eight towns and the respective percentages by which he trailed (—) or led (+) the average of the remainder of the state ticket are as follows: Plymouth (—2%); Salem (—1%); Suffield (—3%); Burlington (+7%); New Britain (—1%); Montville (—.03%); Thomaston (—1.1%); Meriden (—1.2%). The towns are listed here in the order of descending percentages of Polish foreign-born persons in the population as of 1940. The procedure was to calculate the average vote carried by the statewide ticket not including Lyford, then to compare his vote and the average. Notice that in Burlington he led the average somewhat. In Montville and Thomaston he got slightly more votes than Mrs. Zdunczyk.

divided—without the traditional history of organizational strength of their opponents and faced with independent local organizations—has nevertheless become more and more centralized in the last decade. This is partly due to the personality of John Bailey, but the

TABLE 32

Polish Ethnic Influence in Selected New Britain Wards in
Elections for Congressman at Large, 1948-1954*

Year	Sadlak (R.) per cent of combined vote of wards 8, 9, 10	Democratic candidate	Sadlak's per cent of combined vote of wards compared with Repub. governor's per cent of same
1948	23.6%	Trotta (Italian)	+ 1.6%
1950	25.3	Bogdanski (Polish)	+ .1%
1952†	29.5	Pribyson (Polish)	+ 1.2%
1954	28.5	Lyford (Yankee)	+ 1.9%

* The combined vote of the three wards ranged between 12,000 and 16,000 votes.
† In 1952 there was no gubernatorial race and therefore the comparison is with the candidates for the state Senate. Neither of these was Polish.

necessity of facing a highly centralized and powerful enemy at every state election has also made the need for centralization apparent. Without a state election victory, patronage is scarce, so concessions are made for victory's sake. In some cases there is clearly no choice; Bailey has the power necessary to have his way.

The Decline of Corruption: A Consequence of Party Competition?

Fortunately Connecticut politics have been free of corruption in recent years. In the legislature, in administrative offices, in the state and local police forces, there have been few instances of bought-off officials who covertly do the bidding of bookies, gamblers, or others in need of "protection." There has been no clamor for official investigations of corruption such as those in Massachusetts, Rhode Island, or New York. There have been cases of doubtful manipulations of minor offenses in local courts—reducing motor vehicle charges to lesser offenses to prevent the loss of operator's licenses, for example, and in one case conviction for improper collusion between a legislator and a manufacturer, but these are the exception. A term in the Senate, where I observed legislative operations as closely as possible, left me with the conviction that legislation by bribery is uncommonly rare. Why this happy state of affairs?

If the existence of a one-party multifactional situation has often led to the "ins" taking advantage of the situation to get while the getting is good, having no particular concern for the next faction to acquire office, is it possible that the existence of party competition has tended to keep Connecticut politicians on the straight and narrow path? Has the screening of politicians by the parties before they reach positions of leadership tended to sift out those of dubious character?

The skeptic may ask, though, about the scandals of 1938. The revelations at that point were certainly shocking enough. A Democratic lieutenant governor who was simultaneously mayor of Waterbury was revealed to have been in collusion with other officials of the city and some cooperating Republican politicians in the process of stealing some $3,000,000 from the city. One of Roraback's lieutenants was involved in this affair, and he testified that he had received $14,600 as a "lobbyist" for Waterbury in 1935 and 1937. He also admitted receiving $6,900 from the McKesson-Robbins drug company (the officials of which were then under indictment for false statements regarding company assets involving some $18 million.)[36] In all, Harry McKenzie, the Roraback subordinate, said he had been paid $50,000 as a lobbyist during the 1935 and 1937 sessions. At the time the Waterbury trial was going on (both McKenzie and the mayor were sent to jail) the papers were running at least three other stories on governmental scandals. One involved the Merritt Parkway, then being built. Bogus real-estate companies had been formed to buy land one day, sell it to the state the next for a considerable gain, and then go out of business—with government agents taking a percentage, of course. Another affair involved the building of a state police barracks, and a third the embezzlement of $150,000 in the state national guard.

The corruption had been nicely bipartisan, and the retribution by the public was equally bipartisan. In the 1938 election both major parties ran without prestige. Jasper McLevy, the "Socialist" mayor

[36] See the *Hartford Courant*, Dec. 17, 1938.

of Bridgeport, ran for governor, and his whole campaign was an attack on the corruption of the major parties. Even the "Socialist" label did not prevent his amassing the largest vote a third-party candidate had received in at least a century. He won 166,000 votes or 26.3 per cent of the total vote cast. Raymond E. Baldwin, who ran as the Republican candidate, did not even carry a plurality in his own home town (Baldwin, 40 per cent; Cross, 19 per cent; Mc-Levy, 41 per cent). In Stratford, where his popularity had previously been high enough to send him to the House of Representatives with 60 and 63 per cent of the vote in two elections, Baldwin now lost, although he eked out a narrow victory in the state as a whole (2,688 votes).

There has not been another major scandal since the debacle of 1938. One affair involving a bill regulating fireworks led to prosecution after the 1951 session, but there was no indication that there had been widespread involvement of political leaders. It was apparently the work of one man, a small-town Republican legislator who got a provision into a statute limiting the permissible size of firecrackers, that gave a virtual monopoly to a company for which he had been an attorney.[37] After a complete investigation, the legislator was indicted, prosecuted, and convicted.

Party competition cannot be the sole reason for the relative absence of skulduggery since 1938. Corruption does occur in states with competitive politics, as it has in the neighboring states of Massachusetts and New York. But in both these states there are large metropolitan centers that attract criminal elements who seek to protect their "business" by buying protection from crooked officials. Significantly also both those states have race tracks—as do Rhode Island and New Hampshire, both of which have considerable corruption—which happily Connecticut does not have. Someone proposes race tracks in virtually every session of the Connecticut legislature to help to meet the revenue needs of the state—or at least that is what the sponsors always say—but the proposition never gets far. One of the reasons for the continued refusal to give the race-track

---

[37] The common size for large firecrackers was one-half inch by two inches, but the Backes Company in Wallingford, Connecticut, happened to make theirs seven-sixteenths of an inch by two inches. The legislator finagled the committee to change the maximum size to agree with the specifications of the Backes firecracker, without indicating to them or the cooperating state police, who were technical advisers to the committee, that this worked so neat an advantage for the Backes firm. See the *Hartford Times*, July 6, 1951.

interests a start is the realization of what they have done to the political morality of other states. The case against the race tracks made by political leaders over the years has emphasized this point, and there is no particular reason to believe they are not serious in their warnings.

Fear of the repetition of the scandal of 1938 still has its effect on state politics. This alone may not account for the prevailing happy state of affairs in Connecticut, but it seems logical to assume that it is an important contributing factor.

A Note on the 1958 Election

After this chapter was in page proof, the 1958 election occurred, taking so many people by surprise that perhaps a footnote of commentary is in order on how this event fits or fails to fit my generalizations about Connecticut politics.

It was, of course, a shocking surprise. Governor Ribicoff won 63 per cent of the ·gubernatorial vote, sweeping the whole state ticket, all Congressional candidates, and majorities of both houses of the General Assembly into office. Winning the House was downright stunning—that had last happened in 1876.

The explanation is easy—in retrospect at least. Ribicoff, a moderate and enormously popular governor, in rolling up a quarter-million majority pulled a tremendous number of voters away from their normal allegiances. (He actually won majorities in 119 of the 169 towns.) In Connecticut ticket-splitting is difficult and, as with Eisenhower's 1956 sweep, the anonymous offices went with the visible ones. The national Democratic trend helped, of course, and to top it off a badly divided Republican party was running an uninspiring Taft-faction candidate—Fred Zeller. Zeller was the victor over John Alsop (of the Lodge "Modern Republican" faction) in the state convention, but it was truly a pyrrhic victory.

I cannot believe the election connotes any basic change in Connecticut politics. Within a week strong forces in the Republican party began pulling the organization back together; old leaders are resigning and being replaced. The Republicans are looking forward to the 1959 legislative session in anticipation of making a record for 1960. The close Democratic margin in the House (141-138) assures trouble which the Republicans will exploit fully. Connecticut's close party competition, in short, did not end November 4, 1958.

CHAPTER 10

★

CONNECTICUT: LEGISLATIVE POLITICS
AND PARTY COMPETITION

THE ultimate significance of any party system lies in the impact it has on the making of public policy. Parties are fascinating objects of study; they are interesting as instruments by which and in which men struggle to satisfy their ambitions for power or preferment, but the effect of the party on the laws of society is the aspect of lasting importance. Naturally the policy role of the party depends in good part on the internal character of the party. Whether parties affect the outcome of contests over policy only nominally or substantially depends upon, among other factors, the leadership, the cohesion, the factionalism, the centralization of parties.

But other factors than party structure and leadership condition policy influence of party. Some governmental systems permit a wider range of influence than others. The parliamentary system, by fusing the executive and legislative powers, enhances the role of party particularly where a two-party system prevails. The American presidential system (and in effect this prevails at the state level too) is far more restrictive. The independence of the executive offers a complication unknown to the parliamentary system. Precise and detailed constitutions presided over by courts armed with judicial review constitute a formidable barrier to the party. American parties must operate within the framework set by the past and sealed in a constitutional compact.

Even within these constitutional and institutional boundaries state political parties can be significant formulators of policy. Connecticut parties certainly are. And there is no better place to examine the governmental role of parties than in the General Assembly. While the General Assembly has far less power than a parliament, it is not circumscribed in so detailed a fashion as are many if not most state legislatures. There is only a slight exaggeration in the comment of the 1950 Commission on State Government Organization that "In our State Government, all roads lead to or from the General As-

270

sembly." If the legislature is the crossroads of Connecticut government, the parties and their leaders seem to hold high and strategic
ground controlling the crossroads. Or, as a reporter wrote in 1950,
"The legislative process in Connecticut has been supplanted by a
system wherein government by caucus and decisions by party leaders
dominate."[1] A key element in this party operation is the system of
apportionment.

Connecticut Legislative Apportionment: Republican Blessing, Democratic Curse

The method of apportioning the House of Representatives results in granting majority control over that segment of the government to a small minority of the people who live in the small towns.
This apportionment is detailed in the constitution, which means in
effect that it cannot be altered without the consent of the very group
to which it grants a privileged position. (A constitutional amendment requires majority approval by the House in one session, two-
thirds approval by both Houses in the following session, and then
public approval in a referendum. There is no possibility of initiat-
ing an amendment through popular means.) Conservative interests
have not been blind to the advantage implied in the apportionment,
and for centuries they have protected their favored position. The
apportionment system is not the product of just yesterday's decision—it originated in 1662 under the Royal Charter granted
by King Charles II.[2] The 1818 constitution provided that all existing towns should continue to have equal representation, but any
new towns were to have but one and not two representatives. Subsequent amendments provided that any town with more than 5,000
population could have two representatives,[3] but no town, regardless
of its size, has more than two. Thus there are now 59 towns of

---

[1] Carl Clyma, *New Haven Register*, May 28, 1950.

[2] The 1662 Charter provided a lower House, the representatives of which were
not to exceed "twoe Persons from each Place, Towne or Citty." But the original
constitution of the colony—the Fundamental Orders of 1638-1639—provided for
representation in the legislature according to population. The three original towns
of Hartford, Windsor, and Wethersfield were to "send four of their Freemen as
their deputies to every General Court . . . ," and as new towns were added to the
polity "they shall send so many deputies as the Court shall judge meet, a reasonable
proportion to the number of Freemen that are in the said Towns . . ." (Section 8
of Fundamental Orders). Thus the Charter initiated the virtual equality of representation town by town, not the democratically drawn original constitution.

[3] Amendments xv (1874) and xviii (1876).

the 169 with only one representative; this is something less than a grave injustice in view of their lack of at least 5,000 people to be represented.

Rural over-representation is scarcely a novelty in American state government, but the Connecticut House is the worst of them all. In one recent study of all state legislatures, all the Houses were ranked according to the extent to which small minorities can elect a majority, and the Connecticut House of Representatives ranked 94 in a list of 94 chambers. The ratio between the smallest and the largest district was one to 682.3 (Union with 261 persons compared with Hartford, 177,397 as of 1950). A minimum of 9.6 per cent of the population is able to elect a majority of the chamber.[4] By contrast with the United States Senate, where equal unit representation also prevails and with which the town representation system of Connecticut is often compared, the widest ratio of smallest to largest is one to 93—Nevada compared with New York. Whether or not the Connecticut system is "wrong" depends upon one's assumptions. Those who seriously contend that the towns merit roughly equal representation see no injustice in the disproportionate representation, for in their view it is not people so much as towns that are being represented. Their contention that the towns have august historical standing is well founded. So too is their argument that the towns play an important governmental role. But these two considerations do not add up to a status of independence comparable to that of the states in a federal system with which they make comparison. In constitutional law the state has a status that has never even been seriously claimed for the towns. In fact, the constitution of the state by the 1874 amendment, which grants an extra representative to a town when it reaches the 5,000 population mark if it had had only one representative theretofore, belies the straight town representation argument and introduces the idea of population as one of the criteria of representation.

The political implications of this apportionment system are easily gleaned from Table 33.[4a] The righthand column, which indicates the party affiliations of members of the different population groups, tells the story. It is this which produced the strange results in the 1936 Democratic landslide. That year the Democrats collected 1,238,072

[4] See Dauer and Kelsay, op.cit.
[4a] But see footnote on p. 269, above, for an exception to the rule.

votes for members of the House to the Republicans' 368,816. But the Republicans elected 167 members to 100 for the Democrats!

Representatives from the small towns have made their apportionment advantage pay off in many ways. By compromise and threat they manage to warp the state grants to towns in such a way as to favor their interests. Urban and suburban legislators are often faced with the simple alternatives of having no grants or allowing the small towns to have the lion's share, and although most of the revenue comes from the urban areas, the need for assistance is felt to be so great that concession after concession to the small towns

TABLE 33

Apportionment of the Connecticut House of Representatives*

TOWNS		APPORTIONMENT			PARTY AFFILIATION
Number	Size of population	Per cent of total state pop., 1950	Number of seats	Per cent of all Repre- sentatives	Number of group's seats held by Republicans, 1955 session
23	0-999	.8%	32	11.5%	81.3%
43	1,000-2,499	3.7	58	20.8	88.0
35	2,500-4,999	6.2	53	19.0	80.0
25	5,000-9,999	9.0	50	17.4	68.0
20	10,000-24,999	13.5	40	14.3	50.0
19	25,000-99,999	36.6	38	13.6	50.0
4	100,000 and over	30.2	8	2.9	0.0
169		100.0%	279	100.0%	68.5%

* Proposals to alter the apportionment of the House have been legion. At least five major drives to call a convention to revise the constitution have had as a major objective the revision of apportionment. In 1902 a convention was called but its apportionment plan was rejected by even the supporters of revision, having been the product of a convention composed of one member from each town. (See *Constitutional Convention Journal*, Hartford, 1902.) The Bowles-appointed Commission on State Government Organization proposed that the apportionment be changed to one member from each town. (See their *Report*, p. 54.) Fortunately this proposal has never had much backing since it makes the situation slightly worse than it is. Since 59 towns have only one representative, the larger cities now have a comparative advantage over them which the one-member-per-town plan would eliminate. The towns under 5,000 would then elect 60 per cent of the House rather than the present 51 per cent. A study unit report to that same commission suggested a district system which joined the towns together for representation purposes, but this is not a very popular idea. Still another proposal which retains representation for each town but reduces the size of the House somewhat, while giving either party an outside chance to win control of it, is discussed in an article by Duane Lockard, "Constitutional Revision in Connecticut: Notes on a Stumbling Block and a Proposal," 27 *Connecticut Bar Journal* 163-169 (1953).

is made. One example of this is the formula for state aid to education. Said one critic of this system: "One thing can be seen shining through [the education grants] like a Theseus' thread. That is the plain intent to give preference to the small towns, or, as it is more euphemistically put, 'to equalize educational opportunities.' "[5] The impact of this on local finance is made clear by calculating the grant on a per-capita basis (calculating by town not student population). Those towns with less than 500 population received $27.19 per capita for education in 1948-1949, but the largest cities (over 100,000) received only $3.95.[6] Still, some reasonable argument can be made that the smaller communities have special educational problems. Whether these problems are as serious as those of the burgeoning suburbs is doubtful, but some rational argument can at least be made. No conceivable defense is even offered for the warped grants by the state for town highway assistance. Table 34 indicates the ridiculous extremes to which this is taken.

The House is supposed to represent towns and the Senate in Connecticut is designed to represent population. Here the Democratic party has the advantage, although the extent of malapportionment is negligible compared with that in the House. Occasionally the Democratic party can carry a majority of the Senate, even though the state ticket goes down to defeat. This happened in the 1950 election, for example, when 19 Democratic senators represented fewer people than the remaining 17 Republicans. (The average population of the Democratic districts was 49,500 and for the Republican, 62,600.) The ratio of the largest to the smallest district

[5] H. LeRoy Jackson, "Who Pays the Piper? The Fiscal Side of the Public Schools," 24 *Connecticut Bar Journal* 191-205 (1951) at p. 205. The formula, revised in 1955, provides the following allotments on a per pupil basis:

Average daily membership of students	Amount of grant per student
0-100	$120
101-200	110
201-300	100
301-400	90
401-500	80
501-600	70
all additional over 600	55

(See *1955 Supplement to Connecticut General Statutes*, Sec. 973d.)

[6] Calculated from a table prepared by the state tax department showing all allocations for state aid as of fiscal year 1948-1949. This was under the formula before the 1955 revision and therefore makes the situation slightly worse than it is at present.

TABLE 34

Per-Capita Grants by State to Towns for Education and Highways

Population group	Average of towns per-capita education grant 1948-1949	Average of towns per-capita highway grant 1948-1949
0-500	$27.19	$66.97
0-999	22.52	42.42
1,000-2,499	14.53	18.21
2,500-4,999	11.10	9.97
5,000-9,999	8.50	9.53
10,000-99,999	5.70	2.17
100,000 and over	3.95	.51

is 5.1 to 1, a far cry from the ratio in the House. Among the upper chambers of the country Connecticut's ranked 17th in the analysis involving the minimum percentage of the population able to elect a majority of the chamber.[7]

The greatest disadvantage in the Senate apportionment is for the growing suburban areas. The larger cities, particularly New Haven, contain some of the smallest districts, and the three largest districts are in suburban areas of Fairfield and Hartford counties. Democratic leaders adamantly refuse to consider revision of Senate apportionment until something is done about the House, and since that is not likely to come about their advantage is temporarily secure.[8]

Apportionment in both Houses thus contributes to an endemic problem of American state government: divided party control of executive and legislative branches. More often than not, a Connecticut governor faces a legislature at least half controlled by the opposition party. For Democratic governors a friendly legislature is virtually out of the question since there has not been a single Democratic majority in the House since 1876.[8a] Since 1930 even Republican governors have enjoyed Republican leadership of both

[7] Dauer and Kelsay, op.cit.

[8] Apportionment of the Senate may be changed only in the session "next after" the decennial census. In 1951 the Democratic Senate refused to compromise with Republican leaders on reapportionment so the issue died. Then in 1953 the Republicans controlled both Houses and proceeded to carve out new districts much to their advantage. The Supreme Court of Errors invalidated the redistricting act, however, since it was not an act of the biennial session "next after the census." (See Constitution Article Third, Sec. 5.) If the Republicans gain control of the Senate in 1961 presumably a thorough revision of the districts will be forthcoming.

[8a] See footnote on p. 269, above.

Houses during only three sessions (1943, 1947, and 1953). Thus the apportionment helps to force a kind of coalition or government-by-compromise system. Each side normally has its means of vetoing the plans of the opposition, and therefore the means of forcing compromises and bargaining. The introduction of the four-year term for the governor now makes it possible to elect Democratic governors who in the third and fourth year of their terms may face a legislature dominated in both branches by Republicans. (Such was the case with Governor Ribicoff after the 1956 election.) Out of the bargaining and haggling that result from this divided control come some of the more disgraceful scenes of Connecticut politics.

Toward the end of a legislative session, confusion reigns supreme as the atmosphere begins to resemble an oriental bazaar rather than a serious agency of government. Evasion of responsibility, slipshod legislation, and transferral of the power to legislate to a handful of leaders are all characteristic of the last weeks of every session. This atmosphere is made worse by the mandatory adjournment of the legislature after the passage of five calendar months. As the Cinderella hour draws nearer, the pressure increases to get legislation through both Houses or conversely to see to it that some bills do not get through. Often minor matters so dominate the attention of leaders and many rank-and-file members that important legislation is neglected. Bargains are struck to get local bills passed (often concerning picayune town or city powers) and even matters as important as the biennial budget, tied up by disputes between the leadership of the two parties, may fail to pass before the witching hour. This happened in 1955, for example, in one of the most disgusting scenes in Connecticut political history. Lobbyists ran through the halls and both chambers in the last days of the session, beseeching leaders to clear or condemn certain bills. Legislators ultimately lost control of the situation as hundreds of bills were passed in the last few hours. Often half a dozen more or less related bills were passed in one voice vote, the bills being identified only by their numbers. The whole process was accomplished with such speed that no member had the opportunity to find out what the subject of the legislation was, let alone the content of the bills. The responsibility for enactment or rejection was passed to half a dozen or fewer leaders in each party, as the membership, dazed, unspeakably tired, and confused, watched with amazement. Many of them were horrified at the state to which things had come, but each was unwilling to call a halt to the orgy and thus incur the responsibility for having to call a special session to do in more rational fashion what was then being done with recklessness. Someone should have begun a debate on one of the bills and tied up the proceedings until midnight and a mandatory adjournment hour to force a special session, since in the end a special session was required in any event to straighten out the mess.[9]

The debacle of 1955 was not typical of all end-of-session rushes; it was worse than any in the memory of reporters or veteran politicians. The reaction to it was great enough to force rules changes to try to prevent such developments in the future, but it is not likely that altering the rules will have much effect. Procedural change, after all, strikes at the symptoms rather than the cause of the malady, for the basic cause is the divided responsibility with powerfully led political parties. Each side wants to get legislation favorable to its interest backing; each wants to strengthen its hand for the next election. And each has the power normally to hold off passage of opposition bills through control of one or the other of the two Houses. So the pressure grows higher by the day as haggling continues on both fundamental and insignificant bills. Neither side in 1955 would concede to the other on certain points, and the resulting procrastination led to the last-night mayhem. As long as the parties remain powerful and divided control continues to be the custom, last-night pandemonium can be expected in the future.

Evidence of Party Power in the General Assembly

There are essentially two tests of the extent of party influence in a legislative body: the character and conduct of the party leadership

[9] Entirely unknown to all but two or three members, so far as I have been able to discover, a bill passed that last night of the 1955 session which increased the tolls on the Merritt Parkway but simultaneously *exempted legislators* from paying any toll at all. We had debated the bill to increase the tolls earlier and knew the need for it and there was general agreement that the step was necessary. What we did not know was that in the Finance Committee the House chairman had engineered the exemption for legislators. As a legislator from a small Fairfield County town, the House finance chairman disliked having to pay tolls to get to Hartford to do state business, so the exemption was slipped in without the realization of the members. Had they read the bill, they would have seen it was there in plain sight, but under the circumstances who had time to read bills? We were trusting our colleagues and our leaders not to pull any tricks, and in this case we were misled. Needless to say, the privilege was repealed in special session later, but not until the prestige of the legislature had gone down a few notches lower than before.

and the voting behavior of the membership. In Connecticut the party leadership is the real leadership of the legislature. Party chairmen are almost never absent from the halls of the capitol. Majority and minority leaders, and a handful of other influential party faithful, are the key members of the legislature. It is they to whom deference is paid; it is their opinions the newspaper reporters seek; it is they to whom the interest groups turn when they want action. Only the naïve fail to recognize the importance of the party leadership in Connecticut.

Some evidence of the power of the leadership is to be found in the roll-call votes of the legislators themselves. As Table 35 below indicates, the members of both parties in the legislature stick together in most roll-call voting. In the period 1931-1951, for which detailed analysis of all roll calls was made, there were relatively few unanimous or near-unanimous votes of the whole membership (7.3 per cent of 348 Senate votes and 3.3 per cent of 148 House votes); rather, legislators tended to divide according to party affiliation.[10]

The majorities of the two parties were opposed to each other 83.5 per cent of the time in the Senate and 80.7 per cent in the House. Table 36 indicates the distribution of these roll calls according to the extent of cohesion within the party membership.

Among the 496 roll-call votes of the eleven sessions there were 341 or 69 per cent which not only had the majorities of each party opposed but furthermore had at least 80 per cent of the members of each party voting alike. It is revealing to see the kinds of issues on which the parties stood so firmly opposed. Party cohesion on matters of routine—the election of a speaker, for example—is not very significant, but cohesion on broad policy issues suggests a party role of more than nominal importance.

Table 37 indicates that the one issue that brought more cohesion than any other was the question of patronage. This is a somewhat ambiguous piece of information, however, since 52 of the 63 roll calls on patronage deal with three dissident Democrats in the Senate, and as the judgeships in question came before the Senate,

[10] These figures exclude 110 marathon votes in the Senate at the opening of the 1935 session, when the Socialists held the balance of power and the two major parties were jockeying for control. To have included these votes—on which the two parties consistently voted solidly in opposition to each other—would have meaninglessly inflated the extent of apparent cohesion.

TABLE 35

Party Cohesion in the Connecticut General Assembly, 1931, 1937, 1951

	1931		1937		1951	
	Senate	House	Senate	House	Senate	House
Total number of roll calls	22	20	18	13	8	4
Parties on opposite sides (as %)*	84.6%	95.0%	66.6%	92.4%	50.0%	75.0%
Average Democratic index of cohesion†	99.0	80.8	92.0	87.6	100.0	66.6
Average Republican index of cohesion	99.0	90.8	88.4	85.0	100.0	66.5
Party votes (as % of all roll calls)‡	86.4%	85.0%	44.5%	69.2%	50.0%	50.0%

* The percentage of all roll calls on which majorities of each party took opposite sides.

† This is an average of the indices on all roll calls on which the parties took opposite sides.

‡ The percentage of all roll calls on which the parties disagreed and on which at least 80 per cent of each party voted alike.

TABLE 36

Distribution of Roll Calls, Connecticut General Assembly, 1931-1951, According to Index of Cohesion of Party Groups in Senate and House

INDEX OF COHESION	HOUSE				SENATE			
	Democratic		Republican		Democratic		Republican	
	#	%	#	%	#	%	#	%
90-100	112	75.6	83	56.0	190	54.5	234	67.2
80-89.9	12	8.1	25	16.9	25	7.2	39	11.1
70-79.9	4	2.7	11	7.4	22	6.3	22	6.3
60-69.9	8	5.4	8	5.4	54	15.5	9	2.6
50-59.9	4	2.7	5	3.4	15	4.3	9	2.6
40-49.9	4	2.7	2	1.3	11	3.2	7	2.1
30-39.9	0	.0	3	2.1	6	1.8	14	4.0
20-29.9	1	.7	10	6.8	15	4.3	5	1.4
10-19.9	3	2.1	0	.0	3	.9	7	2.1
0-09.9	0	.0	1	.7	7	2.1	2	.6

the remaining Democrats forced an individual vote on each judgeship rather than letting the slate of appointments pass in one vote, as was customary. If the roll calls in this marathon are excluded from the calculation, the percentage of patronage votes becomes 3.7 per cent instead of 18.5 per cent.

TABLE 37

Issues Producing "Party Votes" in the Connecticut General Assembly, Eleven Regular Sessions, 1931-1951*

Subject of vote	Number	Per cent of all "party votes"
Patronage	63	18.5%
Labor	40	11.7
Welfare, health, and education	32	9.4
Procedural questions	31	9.1
State administration	27	7.9
Regulation of business	24	7.0
Judicial and legal	24	7.0
Local	20	5.9
Taxation	19	5.6
Appropriations	10	2.9
Civil service	8	2.3
Constitutional revision	7	2.0
Elections	6	1.8
Liquor and crime control	6	1.8
National questions	6	1.8
Other	18	5.3
	341	100.0%

* This table isolates those roll calls on which the parties opposed each other with at least 80 per cent of each party standing together—in short a "party vote." Here both Senate and House roll calls are combined.

More than half of the issues which produced "party votes" were concerned with substantive policy questions and not the kind of legislation that would affect the organization of the parties. Such matters as patronage, election laws, and support or attack on a governor's administration are preeminently the kind of issue that brings party unity for self-protection. Yet labor, welfare, business control, and state fiscal matters produced more party votes than the matters of strictly party organizational concern.

Roll-call voting data can be misleading. They need corroborating evidence and careful interpretation. Taken alone, the voting data can suggest more or less leadership influence than was actually present. In the case of the House Republican leadership, the data understates the extent of party leadership influence, since the leadership during these twenty years never lost control on any significant roll call, although some members may have voted contrary to the leadership's desires. The effectiveness of the House Republican leadership illustrates the point. In the period from 1931 to 1951 there were four sessions (1931, 1939, 1945, 1949) when the Republican leadership never once failed to push through any bill put to a record vote.

The effectiveness of the Republican leadership is also shown by examination of the bills which they *could not* put through the House when put to a roll call. Between 1931 and 1951 there were 148 roll-call votes in the House, and of all these (if we exclude for the moment bills on which the party did not exert pressure—women jury service, birth control, gambling and horse racing) there were only seven bills on which the Republican leaders either needed Democratic help (one bill) or failed to carry enough Republican votes to win. (Even so one of these losses was recouped the next day after some intensive campaigning for support.)

On the other hand, the roll-call voting data for the earlier part of the present two-party era of Connecticut politics overstates the effectiveness of Democratic leadership in the Senate. In that period Democratic leaders were not so effective as the Republican leadership in the House, although the data alone do not suggest much difference. In more recent years, however, the Democrats in the Senate have been an extraordinarily cohesive group. In some sessions there has at times been only one or two instances where even a single Democratic senator has deserted his party colleagues. Indeed in 1951 not a single Democrat deserted his party colleagues on any roll call of the session. The caucus of senators, which takes place daily, is the scene of some protracted disputes and debates on bills, but when the senators leave their caucus to come to the floor it is rare indeed for the disputes of the inner chamber to be brought out in Senate debate and rarer still for members to desert in a roll call.

In the daily caucus—to which is normally devoted far more time than that spent on the floor of the Senate—the procedure is to review the day's calendar of bills and to come to agreement on the party stand on all bills. All senators attend their respective caucuses, as do the state chairmen of the parties. Each senator is responsible for bills being reported out of his committees (those over which he is Senate chairman). As the list of bills is read off by the majority leader, the senator from whose committee the bill came will briefly outline its intent and implications. This may be only a cursory comment on insignificant bills or a lengthy analysis in other cases. Discussion among the senators as to the bill and the appropriate position for the party to take on it may occupy minutes or hours. By custom any senator may by simple request have any bill held over for consideration another day. After about three requests to "hold" a bill, those interested in its passage will call for a decision. Usually a vote is taken and the dissenters will agree to go along. On some bills, however, no agreement can be reached and each senator goes his own way. On administration bills more formidable pressures are involved.

The governor, if he is a Democrat, may send an appeal for support. This is normally delivered by Bailey, who can be a very persuasive pleader. He does not demand that the bill be accepted—in the course of a five-month session and two special sessions I never once heard a "demand" from Bailey—but he *is* a convincing advocate. By patient explanation of the circumstances surrounding a bill, analysis of the interests backing it, and the probable loss or gain implied for the party, he can inveigle support where none seemed possible. Bailey says of himself that he is "just a messenger boy from the governor," but this scarcely does justice to his importance in the caucus room. He is, of course, a liaison between the governor and the Senate Democrats, but his prestige and ability to help or restrain the ambition of the aspiring politician play no insignificant role in his pleas for support on legislation.

It is always easier to kill legislation than to get it passed. In most cases to kill it only necessitates that the committee chairman be persuaded to keep it in committee, since there is no requirement that a bill ever be reported out. (About 25 to 30 per cent of the roughly 3,000 bills presented in any session never get out of committee.) Connecticut along with only two other states (Maine and Massachusetts) uses joint committees. There are always more House members on the committee than Senate members, but either half of the committee can decide not to give joint approval to a bill. If this happens, the bill is then reported only to the House which will pass it; then it must go to the Senate or House half of the committee before being reported to the floor. On contentious bills to which the chamber has strong objections, this is often the final resting place. (The House leaders often refuse to allow bills calling for a constitutional convention to come to the floor; similarly, the Senate Democrats have bottled up bills to reapportion the Senate.)

Bills can be killed even though they may get out on the floor. Without roll calls—and there is no constitutional requirement that there be a roll call on any ordinary bill—many bills are quietly recommitted or scuttled. A good example of this process took place on the last night of the 1951 session. An enterprising Democratic senator from Middletown (Edward Opalacz) had scurried around recruiting Republican backing for a bill concerning the police department of Middletown. He had helped get several Republican's pet bills through the Senate, and in return he built up enough pressure to get the House chairman of the Cities and Boroughs Committee to release his bill to the floor of the House. To have it released from committee was tantamount to passage—there was no dissenting voice when the vote was called for. When the Republican leader in Middletown, who was significantly present for the closing hours of the session, heard that the bill had passed he immediately contacted Baldwin, the Republican state chairman. Baldwin immediately located the House chairman of Cities and Boroughs and had the bill "recalled" from the House for "reconsideration" by the committee. Since the recall came at about 10:00 p.m. with mandatory adjournment scheduled in two hours, there was, of course, no intention to reconsider the bill. The leadership had intervened to kill a bill which was not unreasonable or damaging in any way. The effort to evade the power of the state chairman had ended in complete failure.[11]

The power of the leadership can be used in innumerable ways. It can be employed, for example, to break deadlocks as well as to make them. During the 1955 session the two Houses had come to

[11] I used up much energy that evening chasing after Senator Opalacz and thus the story is based on both personal observation and the lengthy article in the *Middletown Press*, June 5, 1951.

stalemate over two education bills. The Democrats wanted one bill but were lukewarm if not opposed to another which the Republicans wanted. (Involved were bills concerning the entrance of the state into the New England Regional Compact on Higher Education and the plan to create a state medical school in Hartford.) It appeared that both bills might fail for lack of a compromise. Bailey suggested that I see the House chairman of the Education Committee who could in turn get in touch with Meade Alcorn, Hartford County Republican leader, to arrange for a swap. Bailey said, "If Alcorn agrees to go for this, there won't be any trouble. His word is good." The suggestion worked like a charm; within two days both bills were on their way to safe passage.

It would be wrong to assume that the political leaders are omnipotent. They are utterly unable to get some bills through and they cannot stop others. The passage of the party primary law in 1955 is a case in point. With very few exceptions party leaders in both parties were opposed to the idea of a primary. Why should they want one? As things stood, Connecticut was the only state without a primary in any form, which simply meant that it was easier for the bosses to choose candidates in convention without outside interference. Yet by luck, maneuvering, and the misfiring of some time-tested methods for killing a bill, the primary bill did become a law. Some Republicans were won over to the primary when they realized it might be a weapon to use against William Brennan, who, they feared, might win party control in the next convention. Many Lodge-Baldwin faction Republicans abandoned their long-standing opposition to the primary on this ground. Probably the law would never have passed, however, had it not been for the misfiring of the "improve-it-to-death" weapon. This technique involves the amendment of a bill in one chamber so as to "improve" it (by making its restrictions more rigorous or its terms more inclusive), always in the hope that the other side will not accept the changes. Then the last side to pass the bill can piously point to their "record" of having passed the "best" bill which the other chamber defeated. In just this manner the primary bill made five trips between the two Houses before it was passed in the same form by both.

In the final stages of this long-drawn-out battle there was no place left to hide: further amendment would have made it obvious to everyone that the leaders were only seeking to kill the bill. When the bill came before the Democratic caucus for the last round, Bailey, who had never liked the idea and had used all his wiles to defeat it in some fashion, now reversed his field and argued for it. It took some pleading to get previously committed Democratic senators to change their minds, but the argument that the party could not afford to be charged with wrecking the bill had its impact. In the end only five Democratic senators voted against it.[12] The identification of the party with its legislative record put the leaders in an embarrassing spot. In the end their fears of the primary were overcome by their greater fear of retribution at the polls.[13]

Connecticut Interest Groups: Competitors for Political Power

While all the available evidence indicates the crucial role of party in determining legislative policy in Connecticut, this does not mean that the interest groups do not contribute importantly to legislative end results. Connecticut has the usual complement of interests that send lobbyists to the legislature to press for their special concerns. In an average session 300 to 350 lobbyists will register with the secretary of state to ply their special trade, and their sponsors report payments of more than $100,000 for the five months' work. Former legislators are in demand as lobbyists; many of them earn as much as $10,000 for services rendered during the brief session

[12] *Connecticut Senate Journal*, Part II, Special Session, June 1955, pp. 44-45.

[13] By the time the final vote was taken, the primary law had been considerably watered down by compromising amendments. At various points in the long committee consideration of the bill the respective party chairmen had been important contributors of suggestions for change. As chairman of the Elections Committee during this battle, I had a ringside seat for an exciting affair. A majority of the Democratic members of the committee really wanted a primary to pass and therefore Bailey's suggestions were not always accepted. On the other side, the House chairman of the committee occasionally held up joint consideration of the bill pending clearance with Baldwin. Both sides of the committee had mixed roles: at times they worked more as a committee unit than as Republicans and Democrats; on other occasions the compromises demanded by the respective leaderships became the uppermost consideration. On the committee there were some members devoutly attached to the idea of a primary and others were lukewarn or opposed. In general the proponents of the primary were most defiant of the leadership; the opponents were the most compliant supporters of the leaders. The maneuvering of many members of the committee was an important element in the eventual success of the bill, and to them a considerable amount of the "credit" for the bill must go. But every member of the committee was conscious of the power of the leadership and *all* were in varying degrees influenced by leadership demands.

of the legislature. One former speaker of the House returned in the session following his term as speaker to earn $11,850 working for thirteen different clients including farm groups, breweries, and other businesses. Legislative experience is doubly useful to the lobbyist: he is not only thoroughly familiar with the intricacies of the legislative process but also has friendly contacts with party and legislative leaders.

There are four significant aspects of interest-group operation in Connecticut. First, many groups have special connections with one or the other of the parties, giving them what one may call "built-in" access to the party's leaders. Second, there is relatively little effort on the part of interest groups to persuade legislators to form a majority for specific bills; the interest-group attention is concentrated on the party leaders. Third, the parties rely on the pressure groups almost as much as the latter on the former to accomplish their legislative ends. Fourth, the parties are so powerful that they will occasionally discipline an unruly interest group.

Certain groups have such close relations with one of the two parties that access to the party leadership is assured. The clientele of the interest group are often so predominantly members of the party that the group virtually becomes an appendage of the party. Thus the Farm Bureau Federation, the Grange, the Connecticut Manufacturers Association, and the insurance lobby are all closely allied with the Republican party. Similarly, the labor unions and various reform groups have their ties with the Democratic party. The "built-in" position of the interest group is, however, a somewhat mixed blessing. The favorable attitude of their "own" party's leaders is useful, but legislation must be pushed through *two* Houses and this can cause difficulty when the two Houses are controlled by different parties. Negative action is relatively simple: the allied party rejects the bill and that is usually the end of it. But positive action requires some maneuvering and bargaining.

Labor and the Democratic party offer a good example of the problems of the built-in pressure group. Over the last quarter century labor has usually managed to have one of its organizational leaders in the Senate on the Democratic side, where they have either presided over or been the minority member of the Labor Committee. There—in consultation with the party leaders—the Democratic labor position is worked out. When the Democrats have both the governorship and the Senate, the problem of the labor lobbyists and "their" senator is to convince the House Republican leadership that their bills should be considered. Labor leaders frankly say they normally have little trouble convincing the Democratic leadership to go along. Indeed one of labor's difficulties is to get the Democratic Senate to slow down so as not to prevent the House from being presented with a *fait accompli* unacceptable to them. "Credit" for legislation being so important, Republican House leaders do not fancy the idea of helping the Democrats cement their labor attachments.

On the other hand, the interests of labor are not those of the Democratic party except incidentally. Labor leaders have a home constituency of union members who want results in the form of legislation. Or, if the union membership itself is not especially aware of the intricacies of labor legislation, there are competing labor leaders who would like to replace those in the saddle of leadership at any given moment. Thus the leaders are forced to make it appear that great results follow from their lobbying endeavors. Consequently when the Democrats have no majorities in either House and a Republican governor is in office, labor tries to convince the Republicans that now is the time to make hay while the Democrats are away. They have had considerable success with this tactic. On many occasions when a Democratic Senate has proposed labor legislation it has failed to get anywhere with the Republican House, but two years later, when the Republicans had undisputed control of both Houses, precisely identical legislation has been passed.

Much the same situation prevails with the farm group-Republican alliance; Republican leaders can normally be counted on to come to the farmers' aid, but convincing the Democrats is sometimes a tough proposition. A 1951 battle concerning reorganization of the Department of Agriculture illustrates the point. One prominent Republican did rise in the House to object to the provision in the bill which gave the farm organizations virtual control over the membership of the governing body of the department, but the Republican organization as a whole backed the bill and accordingly it passed the House. Senate Democrats adamantly refused to accept the bill, claiming that it was improper for the governor to be forced to choose members for the Board of Agriculture from a

287

list composed by the farm groups. Lobbyists for the Connecticut Milk Producers Association contacted a Democratic dairy farmer representative and tried to talk him into pleading their case with one or two Democratic senators. It was their hope that with these defections they could get a majority for the bill in the Senate. It is doubtful if the tactic would have been successful even if it had been tried, but the test never came, for the Democratic farmer shared the dislike for the implications of the bill and refused to intercede.[14]

The deep commitment of the built-in pressure group to one party thus makes it difficult at times to make contacts with the opposition party leaders. One senator, who served two terms as a Senate Democratic leader, reported he was never once approached directly by lobbyists from farm interest groups. The farmers rely on Republican senators, Democratic farmers, or they work through the Republican leadership to bargain with Democratic leaders.

The second important characteristic of interest-group operations in Connecticut is that they devote very little effort to building up majorities for their legislation by direct contact with legislators. There is, of course, much effort to contact individual legislators, but this is commonly aimed indirectly at the caucus decision. The customary volume of pleading communications, hallway conversation, and other forms of entreaty are involved, but instances of specific effort to get legislators to ignore the caucus and the party leadership to ram a bill through are rare indeed. A good illustration of this process is the effort by domestic insurance companies to achieve reduction and final elimination of a tax on their net premiums first levied in 1935. In 1955 one of the longest and bitterest battles of the session was fought over the proposed reduction of this tax, but the insurance lobbyists never once approached me to plead their case. They did work with two Democratic senators who were employed in the insurance business, but otherwise they did not make much effort to win away Democratic votes by direct pleading. Year after year they had conducted these negotiations through the leadership and never before had they failed to achieve some reduction of the tax. The grave illness of one Democratic senator at the time the bill came up, plus the defection of one

---

[14] The background for this story came from several interviews with Ralph V. Reynolds, Democratic representative from the small town of Coventry during the 1951 scssion.

member, reduced the Democratic majority to a single vote—that of the ill senator, who rested in the governor's office between roll calls on amendments to the bill during what turned out to be a day-long filibuster. But the lines held and at 9:30 p.m. the bill was finally defeated. Anxious as the companies were to be rid of the tax, they had not sought to proselytize Democratic senators except in a very general way. The customary means of getting legislation were adhered to even under this much pressure.

A third facet of pressure politics in Connecticut is that the parties are nearly as apt to use the interest groups to achieve their ends as are the interest groups to use the parties. Often the party leadership will ask for pressure to be applied on particular bills, sensing that a political gain can be had by the enactment of specific bills but needing help to popularize the idea. The Democrats, for example, wanted low-cost housing in 1951, but there was not much vocal demand for it. Of course, the Democrats, since they controlled the Senate, could easily pass the bill there, but little credit would be forthcoming if the bill were to die in the House. So with the avid cooperation of several interested groups they raised a hue and cry for housing and eventually forced the Republican leaders not only to accept the bill but to abandon a pay-as-you-go demand and accept a $50,000,000 bond issue for state-sponsored housing.

Fourth, the parties will occasionally discipline unruly pressure groups. This may well be nearly unique in American politics, but it does happen at times in Connecticut. The built-in pressure group is subjected to a certain amount of such retaliation, but this is usually done by the party to which the group has no particular attachment and the anticipated damage is negligible. The clientele of the group is already dominantly committed to the opposition party, and the loss of votes, particularly among the smaller groups, is not expected to be enough to cause concern.

More significant are the instances of disciplining of groups not closely allied with either party. In two fairly recent cases, the Democratic party has cracked down on groups which had tended to oppose them in previous campaigns. One case involved the dentists. The dental group had proposed a bill in 1949 to prohibit dental laboratories from providing false teeth directly to patients. They insisted that the laboratories should not issue dental plates without a dentist's prescription, ostensibly because harm might be done to the patient. Some cynics suggested the dentists were also concerned over the loss of fees. In any event, lobbyists with liberal expense accounts did manage to get the bill through both Houses in 1949. Then Governor Chester Bowles vetoed the bill. In retaliation the dentists set out to help to defeat Bowles in 1950 with advertisements, letters, and considerable private conversation against him. No one can say how much effect their campaign had, but Bowles did lose the election. The dentists then came to the next session in 1951 asking for the same legislation again, but Democratic leaders, far from being frightened, announced publicly that they were going to kill the bill. One Democratic leader said in a hearing that the dentists were going to be taught a thing or two about politics since they appeared so anxious to get into the game. Some Republicans began to work for the bill in the House, but there was considerable rank-and-file Republican objection—from members who apparently felt, as Governor Bowles had, that this was a special-interest bill likely to work a hardship on a poor man in need of new teeth.

Much the same kind of situation occurred with the sportsmen of the state. Their organization had unofficially opposed Bowles in 1950 because he refused to support their demand that all money from hunting and fishing licenses be used to replenish game animals rather than to have any of it spent on the administration of the Board of Fisheries and Game. In 1951 to return the kindness Republican leaders put a bill through the House carrying out the sportsmen's desires. Democratic members jeered at the Republican leadership for letting half a million dollars be shifted to the state exchequer in this fashion when supposedly there was a drive on to save revenues. Accordingly when the bill came to the Senate it was defeated—and largely because of the provocation from the campaign opposition of the sportsmen.

It is true that these rejections of special-interest bids came less from distaste as such than from anger at being opposed in the election campaign. Yet the fact remains that the bids were rejected—an unorthodox action for an American political party.

There are always special-interest bills before the legislature on which the party leaders take no stand and on which the caucuses of the two parties may be divided. There are so many state statutes which regulate professions and businesses that groups must organize to defend their interests. It is common for such groups to attempt so to rig the law as to trim down or eliminate competition. Insurance agents try to deprive automobile dealers of the sale of auto insurance. Civil engineering firms have to fight individually licensed engineers who want to exclude their organized competitors. Large garages try to keep gas stations out of the repair business. Liquor distributors oppose liquor distillers; one kind of oysterman is against another; liquor stores and drug stores that sell liquor battle over the legal closing time. In short, an endless array of economic interests combat each other—and all in the name of free enterprise, public health and safety, or fair trade.

It is unfortunately true that this particular sort of legislation often brings out some of the least noble traits of legislators. The lawyer, insurance man, druggist, real-estate dealer or automobile dealer who is a parttime legislator is not always scrupulously careful to separate his two roles. There is no bribery involved in this process in Connecticut—at least none that I ever detected. But the clear conflict of interest between the individual's role as business or professional man and his duty as a legislator for the interests of the community can become a source of what ought to be, but usually is not, embarrassment.

Party Power in the Legislature: Some Reasons Why

It is far easier to prove that the party leaders have arrogated to themselves the major power over legislation in the General Assembly than it is to say why they have been able to do so. A great many factors, including the fact that it has become a custom for parties to exert great authority, are involved. The following are among the most crucial: (1) Broad areas of ideological agreement within both parties. (2) The competitiveness of the two parties. (3) Local legislation used as a lever to bring the member into line. (4) Great turnover of legislative personnel. (5) Aspirations of members and discipline combined with strong party organizations.

1. *Ideological similarities.* The degree to which any group can be held together in its actions depends partly upon the area of agreement prevailing within the group. Sharp differences of opinion such as those disuniting the parties in Congress obviously reduce the influence of the group. The gulf between the Southern conservative congressmen and the Northern liberals in the Democratic party is

so wide that party cohesion is the exception rather than the rule. But in Connecticut there is no group to compare with the Dixiecrats among Congressional Democrats and no LaFollette-Norris element among the Republicans. The suburban-rural-business components of the Republican party are all generally conservative in their outlook, and the urban-ethnic minorities-labor constituent parts of the Democratic party are generally liberal. Differences and disagreements do arise within both parties as we have noted—the interests of labor produce separatist tendencies at times and so do those of suburban Republicans. But the general agreement in both parties overshadows the disagreements, making it possible to weld the party-in-the-legislature into a working group.

These similarities of outlook within each of the parties is suggested by the occupational pursuits of legislators from each party. The proportion of businessmen and farmers among Republican legislators is greater than among Democrats and in the last two decades about three-fourths of those who would be classified as wage workers were elected as Democrats. An analysis of the occupational-party distribution of the members of the House in four sessions indicated these proportions:[15]

Per cent of members who were Dem.	*Per cent of lawyers who were Dem.*	*Per cent of farmers who were Dem.*	*Per cent of wage workers who were Dem.*	*Per cent of businessmen who were Dem.*
32.1%	35.0%	20.0%	77.0%	29.5%

There are, of course, farmer Democrats and laboring Republicans in the General Assembly, but the general distribution of these and other groups is consistent with the known sources of strength of both parties, and accordingly this tends to heighten the intra-party agreement.

2. *Party competition.* As has been amply illustrated, the competition between the parties is fierce and close in Connecticut. Appeals by the leadership to the patry members in the legislature to work for the party's record in anticipation of the next election do not always produce the desired results, but most of the time this tactic will work. To win elections is to acquire patronage and political

[15] The sessions analyzed were 1931, 1933, 1949, 1951. Roughly similar distributions prevailed in the Senate during the same period, except that the smaller membership there tends to exaggerate the tendencies.

initiative, and if nothing else, most of the members of the legislature are politicians who want party victory for personal, prestige, or ideological reasons. This kind of appeal reaches even those who have no fear about their own reelection since they come from safe constituencies. The rural Republicans in the House, for example, do not have to fear that their towns will be swept by the Democrats. That they or some other Republican will come to the House the next session is as safe as any political prediction can be. To win personally is not enough, however. The leadership is often able to talk the rural element into accepting labor or welfare legislation which they dislike, and the persuasion behind this is that the party cannot stay alive by allowing the Democrats to sequester all the favor of the urban groups.

3. *Local legislation.* In common with most New England states, local government powers are granted through specific legislation passed by the legislature. The movement for "home rule" by which the municipality can undertake to frame or amend its own charter, widespread in other parts of the country if not always totally effective, has made little headway in New England. The resistance to home rule in Connecticut has been overpowering. This stems partly from local political organizations that fear the invasion of the city-manager plan. The local custom of turning to the legislature even for the most picayune matters is so ingrained that even the local officials who might be expected to want change have not demanded home rule with any consistency or persistence. But another reason for the retention of local special legislation is to be found in the use of this legislation as a means of holding legislators in line.

In the 1957 session a statute was finally passed which may provide a workable means of avoiding constant appeals to the legislature by municipalities. The form of the 1957 statute still permits local legislation but only at the request of local officials or by local petition signed by 10 per cent of the voters.[16] It is highly probable that this loophole will continue the flow—although reduced in number—of local special bills. In many cases the town fathers will think it simpler to continue old habits than to go to the difficulty of having a commission draft the change and of holding a referendum for its

[16] See Section 19 of Public Act 465 of the General Assembly, Session of 1957.

approval. In any event it is now for the first time practicable to use local means to accomplish local charter changes. Supposed home-rule statutes passed in 1951 and revised in 1953 intentionally set the hurdles for local initiative so high that successful local action was virtually impossible.[17] If the town fathers want to keep the local initiative, they have but to avail themselves of the opportunity. The lack of such an opportunity in the past has made some major headaches for legislators, for they often found that their local bills were bottled up by the leadership and held in committee as the price of regularity on other legislation.

This comment by a former House member illustrates the *modus operandi* used to exact support for legislation: "Every year I went up there [to Hartford], there was some pressing local matter that had to be cleared through the General Assembly. At first I gladly went along with the leaders and got the bills I needed for my home-town organization; later I had no choice—they owned me. Either I went along with their legislative program or my own bills would never get passed. I finally raised hell. Of course, I haven't been back since."[18]

Local legislation has also been used to put pressure on the opposition party as well as by the party leaders to put pressure on their own members. The local bills of key members of the opposition are sometimes held as bargaining bait to get more significant legislation passed by the other House. Although most local legislation involves no great analytical effort on the part of the Cities and Boroughs Committee, the local pressures (from local Democrats, for example, who do not want to see Republican representatives from their town

---

[17] The 1951 law required the approval of a majority in a referendum, but a minimum of 51 per cent of the voters had to vote on the question. Since in most local elections only 30 to 35 per cent of the electorate vote, even unanimous approval would have defeated the proposal. In 1953 the hurdle was lowered slightly by requiring that the majority approving had to constitute 26 per cent of the electorate. Neither of these laws was used much by local governments. The 1951 law was tried in four communities, never successfully; the 1953 revision was used at least four times, once successfully. In some instances the majorities in favor were as high as three-to-one, but the required minima were not met and therefore the action failed. (See Duane Lockard, "Home Rule for Connecticut's Municipalities," 29 *Connecticut Bar Journal* 51-60, 1955.) The new law requires simple majority approval in a general election when the local referendum is on the ballot or a majority equal to at least 15 per cent of the voters in a local or special election. (See Section 5 of Public Act 465, of 1957.)

[18] Since this former legislator is still an active politician it is probably wiser not to reveal his name.

make certain changes), and the political bargaining over their bills always delays the mass of local legislation until late in the session. In the neighborhood of 20 to 25 per cent of the bills presented in any session are local in nature. An analysis of the 1949 session indicated that "of the 911 bills passed . . . , 451 were passed between May 31 and June 8, and of those 291 or 64 per cent were special legislation."[19] Some of the special bills referred to in this report did not concern local government, but probably at least two-thirds of them were local. (Others concerned corporate charters, claims bills and other such special bills.) Some aspects of this bargaining and pressure process are kept quiet; both sides are using the same weapon and therefore each hesitates to toss the first accusation. In a burst of frankness the Democratic majority leader in the Senate in 1949 made a public announcement of his intentions: "Until the Republican House shows a willingness to consider some of the governor's program, we do not intend to pass private pet bills of individual Republican members."[20]

Local legislation often seems to the average member of paramount importance. To get authorization for a local waterworks or permission to borrow more money to expand school facilities may seem more crucial to the local representative than most items of general legislation. His standing in his own community and with his local party may depend far more on his success in getting local bills through than on how he votes on tax or appropriations measures. How much the new home-rule statute will eliminate this form of pressure on the member remains to be seen. But there is no doubt that in the past it has been a powerful force for getting party unity.

4. *Legislative personnel turnover.* Disciplined and unified party operations in a legislature are possible without a high turnover of legislators, as the evidence in Rhode Island and Massachusetts indicated. Nor does rapid turnover contribute to party cohesion when other conducive factors are not present—as the histories of the three northern New England states indicate. But apparently when other conditions are right for strong party leadership in the legis-

[19] Reese Harris, Commission on State Government Organization Survey Unit 17, "Legislative Report," p. 31 (unpublished manuscript in Hartford State Library).
[20] *Hartford Courant*, May 1, 1949. The list of bills mentioned included several corporation charters, private group charters, one agriculture bill, and several local bills.

lature, the fact of high turnover helps to strengthen the hand of the leadership. This seems to be the case in Connecticut at least.

Turnover is very high in the General Assembly. Over the period from 1931 to 1951 the average turnover in Connecticut was about one-half of the membership in each session. Using the proportion of first termers as an indication of turnover, the average percentage of first termers in the House in that period was 45.0 per cent and in the Senate 57.3 per cent. To judge from data collected by Professor Charles S. Hyneman, Connecticut has about as high a turnover of legislators as any state, if not higher. Hyneman found that in ten legislatures for the period 1925-1935 the average percentage of first termers in the lower chambers was 39.6 and for upper chambers, 20.3 per cent.[21] The fact that Connecticut has such closely competitive politics might lead one to expect that the relatively higher rate of turnover was a consequence of more frequent elimination of legislators through election defeats. But such is not the case. In Connecticut the proportion of senators replaced by loss of election was 15.2 per cent in the period 1931-1951 and in the House for five selected sessions in that same period the percentage was 17.3.[22] Hyneman in his analysis of turnover attributed to election defeat only 16.1 per cent of the turnover in lower chambers and 14.7 per cent in Senates.[23] The reasons for such high legislative turnover have to be found elsewhere than at the polls. The ridiculously low pay for legislators ($300 per year and no expenses except for daily travel allowance) is a contributing factor, but an insufficient explanation in itself. As we have noted, the tenure is high in Rhode Island although the legislators receive exactly the same remuneration as their colleagues in Connecticut. Yet in a good many

[21] Charles S. Hyneman, "Tenure and Turnover of Legislative Personnel" 195 *Annals of the American Academy of Political and Social Science* 21-31 (1938) at p. 23. The states analyzed were California, Illinois, Indiana, Iowa, Maine, Minnesota, New Jersey, New York, Pennsylvania, Washington. In none of these states was the percentage of first termers higher than in Connecticut, except that in the lower Houses of Indiana and Maine the percentage was somewhat above the average in Connecticut. In no case was the Senate turnover greater than in the House, except, of course, in Connecticut, where the turnover in some years amounted to more than two-thirds of the membership.

[22] The elections analyzed were 1933, 1939, 1943, 1947, and 1951. The 1947 election was selected as one in which the extent of legislative turnover was excessive; the others were more "normal." Yet even in that year the percentage of Senate turnover due to election was only 32.0, and for the House 17.6 per cent.

[23] *Ibid.*, pp. 26-27.

cases it is clear that legislators find the penurious income a handicap. In most cases legislators actually cannot break even financially for the period of the biennial session of five months duration. Loss of time from business or other occupations more than offsets the legislative pay plus travel expense. To many members who serve, the pay is a matter of no particular importance, but to others it is reason enough to give up public service.

Another contributing factor is that in many Senate districts there is a fairly rigid custom that the nomination for the Senate should be rotated from town to town with each election. This is a custom that at times can be broken by a prominent legislator, but in many districts there have been no repeaters for decades. Finally, many find that serving in the General Assembly is a frustrating experience. Many fail to see the advantage in returning to be a very small cog in a closely geared piece of machinery. There is no doubt that many do fail to return because of the dominant power of the leadership.[24]

The high turnover of legislators undoubtedly enhances the power of already strong leadership. Even a conscientious newcomer can be misled in the confusing welter of complicated legislative process. The leaders have complete familiarity with the intricacies of legislative procedure, know how to speak the obtuse language common to the legislative hall, and can therefore take advantage of the first termer. Not that they always do so. Patient teaching of new legislators by the veterans is an invaluable asset for the ambitious new man. Still, superficial explanations and only half-honest reassurances on complicated but important legislation are often purveyed by the leaders. Even without intent to mislead a newcomer, the veteran leaders have an advantage. The new member arriving in a new and confusing atmosphere is likely to turn to the party leaders for guidance, for they are the most respected and strongest figures to be found around the capital.

5. *Aspirations, discipline, and strong party organizations.* The centralization of Connecticut parties permits the organizational leadership to reward the faithful legislator and to punish the unruly.

[24] High turnover of legislative personnel is no new phenomenon in Connecticut. The state *Register and Manual* for 1887 lists 954 senators who served between 1819 and 1887 and 67.4 per cent of them had served but one year. Only 2.1 per cent had served as long as four years. Until 1876 there were annual elections and annual sessions, and thus the members elected after that time served two years but only one term.

The close contact maintained between the state leadership and local organizations permits the virtual elimination of some recalcitrants from political activity. Even if there is no harmony between state leaders and local leaders, in some cases the ambitious but unco-operative legislator may find his upward path firmly obstructed by the state leaders regardless of local organizational desires. Clearly not all legislators are so ambitious that a future possibility of denial of promotion will constitute a threat for them, but many are. More-over, the ambitious ones are often the most active and influential, for by their ambition they are driven on to work harder and shine brighter than others. With the party organizations as strong as they are in Connecticut the remark once attributed to Speaker Sam Ray-burn is applicable: "Young man," the veteran legislator is said to have told a young Congressman, "if you want to get ahead you have to go along."

At the present time the means of dangling rewards before the ambitious are somewhat more indirect than they were until 1951 when a law was passed forbidding legislators from simultaneously holding judicial or administrative jobs. Before the dual-job ban came into being (and it arrived, like the primary, through the mis-firing of the improve-it-to-death weapon with John Bailey again having to push Democratic senators into accepting the bill and Baldwin and Governor Lodge hammering it through in the House) legislators often went to Hartford with their eyes on specific appoint-ments they wanted to get out of the session. Often the leadership held off until late in the session to get as many concessions as pos-sible before handing out the jobs. Governor Hurley in 1941, for example, made it clear that he would not hand out appointments until action had been taken on his program, and indeed he did not hand out the plums until a riotous last day of the session.[25] The widespread use of direct-patronage encouragement for legislators is illustrated by the fact that 16 of the 26 Democratic senators of the 1949 session were given some kind of job by Governor Bowles.

The enactment of a dual-job ban has not had the decisive impact on the operations of the General Assembly that both the fervent advocates and bitter opponents thought it might have. Jack Zaiman, political writer for the *Hartford Courant*, voicing the dire forebod-ings of opponents of the bill, wrote: "The political system of ad-

[25] See the *Connecticut State Journal*, June 1941, p. 6.

vancing men in party ranks from local levels, up through the legislature, then to various jobs in the government setup . . . is now out
the window. With the political incentive gone, the new legislators
may be of a type who have little or no interest in politics, despite
the fact that politics controls the legislature. Groups and cliques
may spring up, making it extremely difficult to achieve agreements
on legislation."[26] No doubt there has been some alteration in the
kinds of individuals seeking to serve in the legislature—some may
have refused to run because they wished to be a municipal judge
and found legislative service a bar rather than an aid to that ambition. But the change wrought by the ban has not been the fundamental revolution vaguely predicted by Zaiman. The authority of
the party has not been significantly diminished in the three sessions
following passage of the bill. There are, after all, other ways to
satisfy the ambitious desires of legislators than by direct and immediate grants of patronage. The state organization still controls
patronage and there is nothing to prevent a faithful legislator from
being rewarded after the completion of his term. The state organization can have much to say about state ticket nominations and even
nominations in Congressional districts. Significantly too, the organization has other ways of expressing its displeasure toward rebels.

Disciplining legislators is by no means uncommon, although it is
usually not well-publicized when used. The "spanking" process, as
it is sometimes called, has many forms. Denial of promotion to the
ambitious is one. Cutting off the patronage for followers and backers of the recalcitrant is another. Demotion to insignificant positions
in the next session of the General Assembly and systematic exclusion
from the inner circle of decision makers are often used. In many
cases the state organization has close enough contacts with local
town committees to terminate the local career of a member. Naturally where the local organization is controlled by the legislator in
question, the latter form of discipline is unavailable.[27] In most cases,

[26] *Hartford Courant*, June 10, 1951.

[27] The case of Representative E. O. Smith, 85-year-old dean of the House, is a
notable exception to the discipline rule. Smith, first elected in 1933, set himself
an independent course and soon incurred the wrath of the leadership. He voted
with the Democrats almost as often as with the Republicans on whose side of the
House he sat. Plans were made to remove Smith at the next caucus in his home
town. The Republican town chairman, asked if Smith was going to be renominated,
replied that Smith was through. At the caucus, however, Smith *was* renominated.
The chairman shortly after the caucus was asked why he had allowed that to

however, a local organization is anxious to be in the good graces of the leadership and prefers to toss a legislator aside if this seems to be the price of peaceful relations.

One could use any number of illustrations to show how discipline works in both parties. Perhaps the most dramatic case is that of E. Lea Marsh. Bright, energetic, and articulate, Marsh entered Republican politics as a young lawyer and small-town gentleman farmer. He entered the House in 1937 and proceeded to go up the ladder rapidly. In spite of his somewhat progressive views (he was a Willkie delegate to the 1940 Republican National Convention) he got on well with the leadership and in 1945 was made speaker of the House. During that term he had several disagreements with other Republican leaders, one of which resulted in a vigorous speech in caucus defending his position and attacking other leaders during a battle about the distribution of minor court judgeships. Once during that session he left the rostrum and came to the floor of the House to defend a bill opposed by other Republican leaders. The bill concerned soil conservation and partly because it emanated from Washington other Republicans were opposing it as a loss of state's rights. Marsh won the ultimate battle on the bill, but won no great favor with the state leadership or with the Republican governor, Raymond Baldwin. It is said that he wanted very much to get the nomination for lieutenant governor in 1946, but this was denied to him. Some Republican regulars say that Marsh became a "sorehead" when he was refused this nomination; others more friendly to Marsh say the refusal was the first piece of discipline used on him. The convention was not held for a year after the events that had first incurred the wrath of the leaders, however, so the disciplining argument would seem the stronger of the two. Subsequent treatment of Marsh strongly suggests it was the first of a series of retaliatory actions.

Denied a place on the state ticket, Marsh came back to the House

---

happen. "Had to," he said. "If we hadn't, the darn Democrats would have, and they'd have elected him too." Smith has stayed in the House ever since, still with independent ways, although not nearly so "radical" as in his younger days. Significantly, however, for all his experience, acknowledged ability, and undoubted courage, he has never held a position of leadership in the House. He has been House chairman of the Education Committee for many years, but he has never been allowed to go further.

in 1947. Where previously he had been speaker, he was now shunted off into a corner and ignored. He was given no assignment to any significant committee and was made chairman of the least important of all committees, that on Intergovernmental and Federal Relations. In time he organized a band of rebels who needled the leadership whenever possible. Said one reporter of a sortie by the Marsh insurgents:[28]

"G.O.P. legislators who were 'strictly' organization blasted Representative E. Lea Marsh, Jr. with every certain and uncertain term they could get on the tip of their tongues the day he tore the veterans' bonus bill apart on the floor of the House.

"Marsh charged that the measure was 'loosely' drawn and ambiguous, and he set out to prove it.

"The rest of the House just yawned, and when the leaders' whip cracked they passed the bill without a murmur."

In time the very points made by Marsh against the bill turned out to be serious difficulties in the administration of the bonus bill. The state treasurer had to appeal to the attorney general to unravel the ambiguities to which Marsh had pointed.

In 1948 Marsh made an effort to return to the House once again, but reportedly after "advice" from the state leadership he was denied renomination. (And so were several of those who had joined Marsh in heresy in the preceding term.) In that session, to round out the foreclosure of Marsh's political career, he was in effect removed from two non-paying positions he held on state commissions. Of all the myriad recommendations made by the Bowles Commission on State Government Organization, the only ones accepted in the special session following the submission of the report were those which terminated the Mosquito Control Board and the Old Lyme-Saybrook Bridge Commission and placed their functions in other departments. Marsh had been a member of both these commissions! Thus as one politician said: "They buried Lea Marsh and threw away the shovel."

These are Republican examples of disciplinary action, but there are ample Democratic cases to be put beside them. One Democratic legislator who returned to the 1951 session said he had been removed for rebellion and that it had taken him ten years to get back

[28] Frank Wooding in the *Bridgeport Herald*, June 22, 1947.

again. Senator Fred Damiani served in the Senate from New Haven for three terms (1945-1949) but was denied renomination. A combination of reasons was offered for his disappearance: both the local organization and the state leadership were displeased with him and consequently he has never managed to get anywhere in Democratic politics since. One boss said in connection with a senatorial nomination which he controls without difficulty: "You can't trust these fellows. Send them up to Hartford more than a session or two, and they forget the local organization. They don't remember that it was the organization that made them in the first place. That was the reason I didn't let - - - - - have the nomination again; he wanted it, but I wouldn't give it to him."

Discipline may not be brought to bear on every legislator who steps out of line with the state or the local organization or both, but for many legislators it is a fearsome weapon. Its ominous existence in the party armory is not easily forgotten.

Connecticut Parties and Democratic Responsibility

There are few questions one can ask about a political system that are more crucial than this: does the ordinary citizen have means to make his preferences felt in government? Or, to put it another way, do political leaders feel it necessary to respond to such preferences? Naturally there are innumerable difficulties involved in the expression of public desires and equally innumerable means of expressing them. At best a political party is an inexact method of expressing desires and also a more or less inefficient means of carrying them out. In virtually all circumstances where democratic institutions and practices prevail, however, the party is an important means of translating citizen preferences into public policy. There is nonetheless a fantastically wide range of variation in the degree to which parties actually serve this function.

In one-party states, manifestly, the party is a means of expressing the preferences of *some* citizens much more than others. Not only the members of the minority party but the people in general have less direct voice in government under a one-party system. Except where bifactional alignments in a one-party system provide a viable and continuous means of putting pressure on politicians, there is not much to force the dominant leaders of the moment to cut the policy to fit the cloth of public demand.

But where the parties compete with each other, and where they are strongly organized and able to bring intra-organizational pressure to bear on the governmental officials representing the party, then the potentialities for a party contribution to democratic responsibility are greatest. The existence of competition and strong parties do not *per se* imply that the ideal of democracy is necessarily at hand. Personal motives of prominent politicians are inseparable elements of the governmental process. The public cannot be fooled all the time but so much of the public can be kept in the dark on most policy that dominant politicians are ready to gamble even under conditions of dangerous competition. They may have implicitly and ambiguously promised action on a public question, but there are ways of seeming to approve and seek action without actually doing so. Tactically it is often possible to load the blame for inaction on the opposition, or by shrewd obfuscation of the situation to make it utterly unclear who was responsible for the eventual demise or success of a piece of legislation. In short, although competition may force strong parties to seek public approval and put politicians in a pitiless spotlight at times, there are ways to evade responsibility even under the most ideal circumstances.

But the question remains whether such a competitive system as prevails in Connecticut enhances the opportunities for the citizen to get his will expressed. There is certainly no fetish about the sanctity of party platforms in Connecticut. There are innumerable instances of implicitly promising x but in actuality performing y. The party is, as was said before, an imperfect tool. The very fact that the apportionment of both the House and Senate are warped so as to give undue power to minorities automatically gives special preference to the votes of some over those of others.

Moreover, the party comes to have an independent interest role. The desires of those deeply involved in the party become one of the important considerations in the making of policy. If the question is whether to build a new highway, construct low-cost housing, or pay a bonus to veterans, the party *as such*, at least under Connecticut's conditions, has its own interest in the matter. How many jobs will be available? From whom will the money be taken to finance the job? Who will get the credit or blame that will affect the chances in the next election, which in turn will affect the opportunities for more patronage, prestige, and power? The position of the party is almost never a simple matter; it is rather an infinitely complicated question of motives and machinations.

In the final analysis it does seem that the Connecticut political system turns out to be reasonably responsive to public demands. The fear of the next election does not work all wonders, but it works many. The strong parties do more or less force their members in the legislature to stand by the policies of the party. The identification of the party with its record, while imperfect, is great enough to frighten the leadership. In dozens of instances in recent years, matters of grave importance have been decided consistently with what one assumes to be the public will only because the party leaders felt it unsafe to do otherwise. Politicians do not behave responsibly solely out of the goodness of their hearts any more than General Motors tries to build better cars out of sheer altruism. One seeks a payoff in the market, the other at the polls. The important thing is to facilitate the means by which the votes can influence the politician. The methods used in Connecticut, however imperfect they may be, come closer to success in this respect than those of any other New England state.

CHAPTER 11

───── ★ ─────

ETHNIC ELEMENTS IN NEW ENGLAND
POLITICS

SEARCH as you will, there is no other part of the United States with
a larger proportion of ethnic minorities in its population than New
England. The New England that once was—the Pilgrim-Puritan
society of history and legend—is no more, nor has it existed for a
long time. As early as the Revolutionary War, Puritanism was more
a remembrance of the past than an active force in society. When in
the middle of the nineteenth century Hawthorne published *The
Scarlet Letter* in condemnation of the moral decadence of seven-
teenth-century Puritanism, few rose to the defense of the moral
code of the founders. Some traditional Congregationalists defended
the old order on theological grounds, but most readers of Hawthorne's best-known work accepted his strictures without cavil.

In the course of Hawthorne's life, however, New England began
to undergo a change of even greater significance than that implied
in the decline of Puritanism. In his youth (he was born in 1804)
the people of New England were remarkably homogeneous at least
in an ethnic sense. At mid-century one person in ten in New England was foreign-born. Nor were the immigrants of the same ethnic
stock as the Yankees to whose society they came. Increasingly the
immigrants were from Ireland and from Central Europe. Many
were Catholics.

Most New England Protestants took a dim view of this increasing challenge to their orthodoxy. True, Yankee industrialists had
invited the hungry and dispossessed to New England to work in
their factories, but the mass of the workers and farmers were far
from happy about the waves of immigrants. Not only were the
newcomers "different"; far worse, they were cheap labor and a
threat to jobs. Physical violence was not uncommon: in 1834 a
convent in Charlestown, Massachusetts, was burned to the ground
by a howling mob, and twenty years later a Catholic church in

Dorchester was blown up with gunpowder. Economic and social discrimination was prevalent. In the confused political atmosphere of the decade before the Civil War, the anti-foreigner and Anti-Catholic Know Nothing party flourished in New England. The 1854 election in Massachusetts was a sweep for the Know Nothings; they won not only the governorship but all the other state officer elections, and all but two members of the General Court were pledged to this anti-Papist crusade. The following year similar if somewhat less comprehensive victories followed in Connecticut, Rhode Island, and New Hampshire.[1]

But where in 1850 one in ten was foreign-born, in 1920, nearly a quarter of New England's population was foreign-born and another third (actually 36 per cent) had been born of foreign or mixed parentage. The heaviest waves of immigration came into lower New England, but New Hampshire absorbed large numbers of immigrants too, and even Maine and Vermont were not far behind the national average in the proportion of foreign-born population, as Table 38 illustrates.

TABLE 38

Proportions of Ethnic Minorities in New England, 1920 and 1950

| | Per cent of population foreign-born | | Per cent of population born of foreign or mixed parentage | |
	1920	1950	1920	1950
U.S.	14.5%	7.5%	23.9%	17.5%
Maine	14.0	8.1	21.2	25.2
Vermont	12.7	7.6	22.5	18.0
New Hampshire	20.6	10.9	28.4	25.2
Massachusetts	28.3	15.3	39.3	33.4
Rhode Island	29.2	14.3	41.6	34.8
Connecticut	27.7	14.8	39.2	33.3

New England's proportion of "foreign white stock" population (which combines the foreign-born with those born of foreign and mixed parents) is greater than that of any other region. The percentages given below refer to the proportion of foreign white stock in the total population of the regions as of 1950.[2]

[1] See Ray A. Billington, *The Protestant Crusade, 1800-1860, A Study of the Origins of American Nativism*, New York, 1938, p. 388.

[2] Or, one may view the proportion of ethnic minorities in New England this

New England	46.5%	West South Central	9.7%
Middle Atlantic	41.4	East South Central	2.3
East North Central	27.0	South Atlantic	7.4
West North Central	20.9	Pacific	28.7
		Mountain	19.4

New England is of course not the only region of the country with political problems arising out of ethnic heterogeneity. In New York, Buffalo, Chicago—in most of our larger cities—there are heavy concentrations of ethnic minorities to whom politicians make constant appeals. The German in Wisconsin, the Swede in Minnesota, the Czechoslovakian in Nebraska—all get special attention at election time. The New England situation is not unique; it is the same problem accentuated.

Ethnic Groups and Public Policy

What are the political consequences of the ethnic minorities? First, and perhaps the most fundamental fact of all, the nationalities that have chosen New England have been primarily those from Catholic parts of the world. Consequently there are divisions in the society which stem from the philosophic and social differences between Protestantism and Catholicism. One need not subscribe to the sentiment of James Gould Cozzens in his most recent work, *By Love Possessed*, to arrive at this conclusion. There he had one of his characters say: "Yet does any free man, without grief, without shame, without fear, see names so proud a hundred years ago in their birthright of liberty as New Hampshire, Massachusetts, Rhode Island and Connecticut little by little in the last fifty years degraded to designate virtual papal states?"[3]

On many questions of public policy, the two great religious communities, Catholic and Protestant, come into direct and often heated conflict. In Connecticut and Massachusetts the purveyance of birth-control information is forbidden by law. The laws themselves date from Victorian times and were not passed in response

---

way: the region has 12.3 per cent of all foreign white stock in the country, but only 6.2 per cent of the nation's population resides in New England. The data of this table are drawn from a Special Report of the Census Bureau, *Nativity and Parentage*, 1950 Census Vol. IV, Part 3, Ch. A, Table 2. The regions are the standard ones employed by the Census Bureau.

[3] James Gould Cozzens, *By Love Possessed*, New York, 1957, p. 229.

to Catholic political pressure, but no one would deny that today the only reason they remain on the statute books is the support of the Catholic community. Similarly throughout New England various aspects of educational policy are bitterly debated in religious terms. In many matters where the law and public morals become interrelated—and where not infrequently great issues of civil rights are inescapably involved—the religious divisions in the New England states pose grave political problems.

Thus in some respects the fact that so many of New England's immigrants were Catholic is likely to be of greater long-run significance than ethnic factors *per se*. Over time ethnic distinctions and attachments are worn away; religious differences are unlikely to be. When the desire to be socially acceptable comes into conflict with emphasis upon ethnic associations, it is the latter which gives way to the former. Indeed it is the view of some observers that the sense of ethnic identification is now kept alive only by "hyphenate organizations" seeking primarily to serve their own selfish interests by emphasizing ethnic loyalties.[4]

Viewed in historical perspective, the pull of ethnic association is on the decline. One measure is the concurrent decline of the old-fashioned political boss and his kind of political machine which depended so much on the bewilderment of ethnic minorities for votes. A leader like the fabulous Martin Lomasney, for example, was capable of getting "his people" to vote for whomever he chose. Lomasney ran Ward Eight in Boston for decades, emerging as a state political leader in the Democratic party. When his Irish followers were asked by Martin to vote for a Republican—as the dictates of Democratic factional politics sometimes demanded—they trooped to the polls to do his bidding.[5] It is true that such machines rested upon more than mere ethnic loyalty—there was the gift of a Christmas basket to the needy, the hope of some bit of

---

[4] See, for example, Johan J. Smertenko's article, "The Emerging Hyphen" 203 *Harper's Magazine* 63-70 (Aug. 1951). It is, however, a fact of some significance that 25 daily and weekly foreign language publications remain profitable business ventures in New England. See *Ayers' Directory of Newspapers and Periodicals*, 1956, Section on "Foreign Language Publications."

[5] See the short biographical sketch on Lomasney by A. D. van Nostrand, "The Lomasney Legend," 21 *The New England Quarterly* 435-58 (Dec. 1948). For another fascinating picture of the great boss, Lomasney, see Lincoln Steffens, *Autobiography*, New York, 1931, Chs. 36, 37.

patronage, and the social function that the political club performed. But the political club tended to cater to ethnic blocs, partly because of ethnic group colonization of particular areas in the large cities. When the machine had to cater to conflicting ethnic groups—as Martin Lomasney's had to later in his life—some of its effectiveness was lost. The political arrival of the Italians, the Polish, and the French-Canadians threatened the hegemony of the Irish leadership of the Democratic party in the urban areas, and the entry of the newer elements infinitely complicated the process of slate-making and internal party maneuvering. Significantly also in lower New England particularly, the Republican party ultimately has begun to play the ethnic game too. Mere appeal to the Old Sod, the virtues of Mazzini or Pulaski is not enough.

Although a bit more sophisticated now than in the past—as well as less frequent—irrational ethnic appeals have not vanished from the New England political scene. An occasional fervent speech is still made on the subject of Irish independence. Connecticut's Governor John D. Lodge used to good advantage his ability to speak Italian in his campaigning, and his Italian-born wife sometimes did Italian folk-dances at rallies. A two-minute spot announcement on Italian radio programs in the 1950 campaign reminded listeners that "Signor Lodge speaks our language like a native, shares the political principles of the great Mazzini, and has our interests at heart because he is married to one of our people."[6] Some politicians now claim that Lodge overdid the special appeal to Italians; it is their contention that the younger generation resented having their background emphasized. Whether this is wishful thinking on the part of Democratic politicians of Italian derivation, who were smarting over Lodge's success in using their own weapons against them, or whether there is some truth in the supposed backfiring of the Lodge technique, there is no real way of knowing.

Ignorant and irrational appeals to nationality groups continue to be made, although one may doubt the efficacy of many of them. As exhibit number one of the kind of appeal that *ought* not to get anywhere with people of the slightest intelligence, consider this item taken verbatim from the *New Yorker*:[7]

[6] Quoted by Smertenko, *op.cit.*, p. 68.
[7] A letter to the *Boston Herald*, which the *New Yorker* in reprinting labeled "Clear Days on the Historical Scene," June 29, 1957, p. 84.

To the Editor of the Herald:

In reply to Col. Rich's letter which appeared in your paper on May 13, I wish to reiterate what I said on the floor of the House, that the Pilgrims were a band of pirates, political rejects and undesirables. They stole New York City, then New Amsterdam, from the Indians for two barrels of whiskey, then got the Indians so drunk and stole all their women and land. Later on in years when our country became united, the poor Indians could not get any whiskey in bar-rooms because of what your ancestors, the Pilgrims, did to them.

Your ancestors were only too happy to get the help of the Europeans in ridding themselves of the Redcoats, they could not do it on their own, not being real men or soldiers. Your civilization was founded by Italians, French and Germans, who were not among the Pilgrims but who were badly needed to build this country. Later on you needed the Irish to build your homes and educate your children.

Your own people tried to discipline you while in the Old Country, but when failing to do so, the prisons and institutions being full, they sent you to sea, to make your fortune, hoping that you would drown.

Thank God, Michael [sic] Angelo, Leonardo de [sic] Vinci, Dante, Formi [sic] (who enabled the atomic bomb to operate) Caruso, and Perry Como, and many others did not come over on the Mayflower, but were essential to the civilization of the entire world, and respected for their accomplishments, and not for their escapades.

I was very much surprised when the Governor of Massachusetts decided to appropriate $125,000 to entertain the ghosts of the renegades that invaded our shores in 1620. I think they have one specific reason in mind to make this trip to the United States—they were trying to put the touch on Uncle Sam.

I am filing a bill next year, for one half million dollars for the building of three replicas, the Nina, Pinta, and the Santa Maria, and also to build a bronze statue of a great man, Christopher Columbus, which if it were not for him, you would not be collecting a pension today.

I hope, Mr. Rich, that I have made myself clear. If there is anything in this letter that you don't understand, don't hesitate to call me. If I have time, I will be glad to discuss this matter with you.

Representative Chas. Iannello
Assist. Majority Leader

Boston

Such arrant nonsense can only be intended to deceive someone, although who could be taken in by it is hard to imagine. Yet the rantings of a Pitchfork Ben Tillman or a Theodore Bilbo are not far different, and they won support through outrageous remarks that appealed to the hatreds and prejudices of their communities. Is Iannello's denunciation of the second landing of the *Mayflower* any more ridiculous than the "contribution to statesmanship" of Senator W. K. Vardaman of Mississippi, who advocated the repeal of the Fifteenth Amendment? As V. O. Key has said, this was "an utterly hopeless proposal and for that reason an ideal campaign issue. It would last forever."[8]

To what extent are such rantings intended to obscure more significant political questions? In the South emphasis on what W. J. Cash called Negrophobia undoubtedly serves to deemphasize issues. "In part," says V. O. Key, "issues are deliberately repressed, for, at least in the long run, concern with genuine issues would bring an end to the consensus by which the Negro is kept out of politics. One crowd or another would be tempted to seek his vote."[9] The exclusion of any element from voting is not today a factor in Massachusetts politics, but emphasis on the irrational prejudices of ethnic association still serves as an avenue to power without the necessity to consider policy questions in any forthright manner. In any event, whatever the intent, concentration on such irrelevancies does serve to depress the issue content of politics. Deliberate or not, if the irrational appeal opens the way to power, why substitute any more debatable and contestable issue?

Ethnic Group Politics and Parties

Surveying the history of ethnic group politics in New England, one is impressed with the extent to which the particular groups coming to New England were those whose allegiance in recent times at least has been primarily with the Democratic party. The Irish, French-Canadian, Italian, and Polish groups—the most numerous minorities in the region—have been largely Democratic since the 1920's. Certain other ethnic groups—the Germans and the Swedes, for example—have chosen to be Republicans in the main, but relatively few of them came to New England. The rise of the Democratic party from the ashes of defeat and exclusion to competition with the Republicans is inextricably connected with the settlement of the ethnic elements in New England.

Why these ethnic groups have either come to or stayed with the Democratic party is apparently a question of both tradition and

[8] Key, *Southern Politics*, p. 232.
[9] *Ibid.*, p. 131. See also W. J. Cash, *The Mind of the South*, New York, 1941, p. 252.

pocket-book voting. Since the Whigs, the Know Nothings, and the Republicans, who derived largely from the remnants of these earlier parties, were largely anti-Catholic and anti-immigrant, it was natural that the Irish as the first comers turned to the Democratic party. The Democrats made a special appeal to the Irish in these early days, and it paid off handsomely. Later when the Democratic party became more and more urban the leadership element reflected the rise of Irish political leadership in the cities. Irish leaders, of course, never lost an opportunity to cement the ties of ethnic association and party faith. Irish infiltration into the leadership of the party and a general affiliation of the Irish voters with the party served to temper the anti-Catholic and anti-immigrant attitudes of the Democratic party. Consequently, when later immigrants from Catholic countries came into New England the Democratic party had at least somewhat of a head start on the Republicans, who, if not outrightly antagonistic to the newcomers, at least had a record of antagonism to live down.

There were, however, certain negative factors involved. The dominance of the Democratic party by the Irish was no warm invitation to the Italians and the French-Canadians. In most areas the by then well-established Irish tended to be the straw bosses on jobs, to be on the police force, and no less than the Yankees of earlier generations they were now apprehensive about the cheap labor threat. Irish neighborhoods were invaded by the Italians late in the nineteenth and early in the twentieth centuries and there were some vicious brawls growing out of the inability of the two communities to adjust to each other. Thus the entry of these groups into the Democratic party was far from automatic—in various areas both the Italians and the French-Canadians tended to vote with the Republicans.

Yet in the long run the element of economic status in political choice tended to favor the Democratic party. The vast majority of the immigrant population occupied the lowest rungs of the economic and social ladder, and once the Democratic party had taken its trend toward a more liberal position it could make a successful appeal to the working-class ethnic minorities. William Jennings Bryan's radicalism in 1896 irrevocably cut the ties between the Democratic party and the New England small-town population. What few victories the Democrats won in the small towns of New England after

312

the Civil War were now almost unthinkable. But the very emphasis on liberalism with which Bryan sought to win the old Populist vote of the West was to become the salvation of the Democratic party in the East. Bible-quoting, fundamentalist Protestant that he was, Bryan did his bit for the party by helping to win over Catholic ethnic minorities.

The winning over of a group does not mean that it will stay won, as the Republican party discovered in the case of Negro voters who in the course of the New Deal forgot their allegiance to Lincoln. The traditional ties of New England's ethnic minorities with the Democratic party are less significant now than they were a generation ago.[10] The upward social and economic mobility of ethnic minority people has resulted in some desertion of the Democratic party. A young and ambitious Italian-American politician finds the very fact that Italians are not numerous in the Republican party an asset to his career. In the Democratic party his Italian background is no particular distinction; indeed being a Yankee Democrat is more likely to be unique in New England. In the Republican party the aspiring Italian-American may find the dominant leadership of the party not entirely sympathetic to his demands, but often this is apparently outweighed by the mystical hope on the part of the leadership that promoting a "representative of the Italians" may be the key to victory. In short, the once relatively comprehensible ethnic battles *within* the Democratic party have now given way in most of New England to the more complicated double battling of ethnic minorities who have two arenas in which to operate.

The inevitable result is that the parties are weakened as a consequence of ethnic rivalries. In the discussion of New Hampshire, I pointed out how devastating the Irish-French-Canadian conflict in the Democratic party has been. The unfortunate thing is not only that the Democratic party as an institution suffers but that the resultant weakness of the party has a depressing effect on the total politics of the state. Ethnic rivalries have not been quite so crucial

[10] Lawrence H. Fuchs traces this in his study of the 1956 presidential election in Boston. He found that the Irish particularly (more so than Italians, Negroes, or Jews) deserted Adlai Stevenson in 1952 and 1956. In 1956 heavily Irish areas of the city still turned in Democratic majorities, but they were much diminished as compared not only with 1948 but also with 1952. See his "Presidential Politics in Boston: The Irish Response to Stevenson," 30 *New England Quarterly* 435-447 (Dec. 1957).

in the other New England states, but in each state they have been a factor of some importance. In both Maine and Vermont they have helped to keep the Democratic party disorganized and ineffective, although not quite so dramatically as in New Hampshire. In Vermont, ethnic rivalry or no, the Democratic party was destined to be weak. Maine Democratic hopes have not been quite so forlorn as those in Vermont, but clearly the rivalries of the past have helped to postpone the day of two-party politics. In southern New England industrialization and urban growth were such that ethnic conflict could not prevent the rise of the Democratic party. Whether or how long it postponed the coming of two-party politics in those states is difficult to say.

Ethnic competition in the Democratic party is normally between the Irish and the more recent comers, such as the Italians, the Polish, and the French-Canadians. Which of the latter has the strength to fight in a district or state depends upon the demographic pattern. But the group to be fought in nearly every case in the New England states is the Irish, who were well fixed in the Democratic party before the others came. In many areas where the Irish now comprise a scant minority of the population, Irish leadership continues to dominate the Democratic party. In New Haven, for example, the Italians now far outnumber the Irish, but the latter nevertheless keep a stranglehold on the city's Democratic machinery. It is true that an Italian-American has for several years served as Democratic town chairman, but he does not run the party by any means. His appointment in fact is a byproduct of a Republican Italian's winning mayoralty races. John Golden, Democratic national committeeman, remains the top man of the New Haven party. Similarly in Rhode Island, the Democratic state chairman is of Italian derivation, but he is in truth a front man for Irish politicians. "Recognition" is easier to get than power.

In the Republican party, the Yankees are in control and their competitors are mainly the Irish and Italian and Jewish Republicans. Of necessity the Republican party throughout New England has a somewhat split personality; organizational power resides with the small-town Yankees, but deference must be paid to the suburban and urban Republican organizations. The latter particularly are likely to be dominated by non-Yankees. There are too many votes in the urban areas to make it safe to ignore these urban organizations, however uncongenial their leaders may be to the more powerful rural Republicans. Thus in the Republican party the battles tend to be over what concessions are to be made by a dominant Yankee element to the ethnic minorities, in contrast with a somewhat more open battling among ethnic factions within the Democratic party. The strength of the Irish Democratic leaders is not exactly comparable with that of the rural Republican Yankees.

What's in a Name?

In both parties there is a tendency for the formal leadership to lose its control over nominations to the leaders of the ethnic groups. Or, more accurately, this situation exists for both parties in Connecticut, Massachusetts, and Rhode Island and for the Democrats in other states. Very frequently the nomination goes to the man with an "O" at the beginning or end of his name rather than to an individual who might make a good officeholder on other and perhaps more significant grounds. This is comparable to the divisions in a party on a geographic basis. In some states the tradition has it that the attorney general must come from "down state," regardless of other factors that may be involved. Neither form of pressure on the party leadership is likely to emphasize the ultimate rationality of the decisions made.

In the case of ethnic-group struggles for party position or recognition on the slate of nominees, it seems to me that there is an unusual amount of mythology about what might happen on election day. Hard-headed and highly practical politicians are led down the garden path more often than one might imagine by the bogey man of threatened ethnic insurgency. Leaders who customarily take all kinds of risks in a political lifetime seem inordinately frightened by the prospect of mass ticket splitting. This, of course, is part and parcel of the total mystery of election day. The mystifying uncertainty of the electorate's behavior is, as any who will reflect on it for a moment will realize, one of the most powerful if undirected forces operative in a democracy. Money is spent by the bushel in fear of that uncertainty. Compromises that would make Machiavelli blush and forced but heroic actions that the recording angel perforce must put on the positive side of the ledger all result again and again from lack of knowledge of what the voters may do on the first Tuesday in November. But on the ethnic question, how much ground is there for being so frightened? Do ethnic groups really vote as blocs, as their leaders imply, or frankly say they will unless the leaders' demands are met?

One student of the subject, Johan Smertenko, says the answer is "an emphatic No." He said he had "examined the records of more than twenty elections in half a dozen states, with special reference to candidates from minority groups, and I find that in every case statistics controvert the prevalent idea that these groups vote as blocs in support of candidates of their own faith or race."[11] In support of this contention, he cited several situations in Connecticut and New York where it appeared to make little difference whether the candidate was of a particular ethnic derivation. "Obviously," he concluded, "it is no more possible to testify that Patrick O'Rourke, Domenic Mazzarelli, Izac Cohen, Olaf Olsen, and Hans Schmidt did not vote for candidates of their own national origin than that Douglas Scott and Cabot Mather did not split their ballots in favor of Presbyterians and Congregationalists. But it is also obvious that whatever preference voters have given to candidates of their own race or faith is either too slight to be material or is counterbalanced by the prejudices of other voters."[12] He goes on to admit that at times, as Samuel Lubell and others have clearly proved, minorities have voted as blocs on men and issues, but these cases have resulted from old loyalties to basic political ideals and not from mere promotion of men by hyphenated organizations.

Within certain clear limitations, I think Smertenko is correct in his analysis. The data cited in the chapter on Connecticut concerning the Democratic party's decision to run a Yankee instead of a Polish candidate for congressman at large in 1954 is a confirming bit of evidence. Antoni Sadlak, the Republican incumbent, did not do much better against the Yankee in Polish wards than he did against the two previous candidates, both of whom were Polish. (He ran 1.9 percentage points ahead of the Republican candidate for governor in 1954; in the earlier two races he had run .1 per cent and 1.2 per cent ahead.) This, I think, offers a pretty good test case since it follows a bitter battle in the Democratic convention in which the Polish delegation made threats against the party if they did not get their way. In a close election, of course, a 1.9 percentage point

[11] Smertenko, *op.cit.*, pp. 68-69.
[12] *Ibid.*, p. 70.

lead may not be insignificant *if it is a lead throughout the electorate*, but such a lead among a minority group is far less important for two reasons. First, it is intrinsically a small factor in the total vote; second, it may well be offset by other groups who are persuaded to support the man just because he is *not* what the ethnic group insisted that he be.

Another interesting illustration is a recent primary election in Maine. Frank M. Coffin, a Yankee, was opposed in a 1956 congressional primary by a French-Canadian candidate. Clearly Coffin was the more illustrious of the two candidates, and he had the support of Governor Muskie, but he happened to be running in a district where the French-Canadian population was as heavy as it is probably in any congressional district in the country. Yet Coffin won handily, carrying a good many districts where French-Canadians comprised a considerable majority of the voters. On the evening of the primary, when Coffin's victory was obvious from the returns then in, one old-time French-Canadian Democratic politician was brought literally to tears in pride that "his people" had chosen without regard for nationality. "You see," he told a Coffin aide, "we didn't do what the Yankees said we would—we chose the best man, not the Frenchman."

One final example will illustrate a slightly different variant of this point. In Massachusetts, as we have seen, the Republican party has only recently begun to compete with the Democrats by running statewide candidates representative of ethnic minorities. In 1950 and 1952 party leaders backed an Italian candidate, Roy C. Papalia, for the nomination for state treasurer, and in both primaries he was opposed by the same Republican oldtimer, Fred J. Burrell. In 1950, without the benefit of a convention endorsement, Papalia lost the nomination; in 1952 with a formal endorsement he won it. The interesting thing is that Papalia did not get any overwhelming majority in the eight towns of the state with the heaviest Italian population. Indeed he got a lesser percentage from these towns than he did in the state at large.[13] How did he fare in the general election?

[13] The eight towns in question gave him 36.4 and 42.1 per cent of the vote cast for the office in two primaries. These towns all have more than five per cent of their population who were born in Italy. They are in order of descending proportion of Italian-born: Milford, Franklin, Plymouth, Revere, Everett, Mansfield, and Medford. Apparently what he picked up in these towns must have been more than offset by others in the town who cut him.

He was the number five man on a six-man state ticket in the state as a whole, trailing the governor by 92,000 votes out of slightly more than the one million average Republican vote. And how did he fare in the eight towns with the highest proportions of Italian-born? There he was number four man, if we count all the towns together. His vote was 7.4 per cent below the average vote of all six Republican candidates in these eight towns combined.[14] Clearly there was no great desertion of Italian Democratic voters to vote for a Republican compatriot.

Are there, then, no exceptions to the proposition that ethnic affiliation is not a potent political factor? There is a clear exception, and one of some importance. If the candidate is not only an Italian, an Irishman, or a French-Canadian, but also a man who is attractive as a candidate on other grounds, it can make a difference. Moreover, when such a candidate scores a "first," he is likely to be given the benefit of ticket splitting. The candidacies of two prominent vote getters in Rhode Island—Senator John Pastore and Christopher Del Sesto—are cases in point. As the data presented in Chapter 7 indicate, both Pastore and Del Sesto pulled unusually high votes in Italian districts. In both cases these extra votes provided the margins for close majorities for the governorship. Pastore in 1946 could hardly have won without that support and Del Sesto, as the first Republican to win a majority (although not, as it turned out, the governorship) in 18 years, could not have made it without the Italian wards. Pastore was running as the first Italian Democratic candidate for the office, and Del Sesto as the first Italian Republican. Both are men who have considerable prestige and honest ability. They were men with whom the Italian voters could identify themselves with pride. So also with many local candidates of a particular ethnic group; in many cases even a relatively unimportant office may seem an upward step of great proportions to people who long for evidence that they are as good as anyone else but suspect that they are not, having been made to feel inferior in many ways innumerable times. Still, even locally, it is not just the name that counts; it is the name of a person who is respected and admired.

[14] In 1954 an Italian candidate for auditor ran 10.8 per cent behind the average in those same eight towns, and was sixth in the field of candidates on the ticket.

In the final analysis, then, I agree with Smertenko but with the important reservation that all depends on the quality of the candidate involved. If the candidate is good enough to hold his own with other voters, then the fact that he has the right kind of name may be just the added fillip needed for success.

CHAPTER 12

———— ★ ————

PUBLIC POLICY-MAKING AND POLITICAL
PARTIES IN NEW ENGLAND

IT HAS BEEN my contention that the ultimate significance of a state's party system lies in the effect it has on the making of public policy, but the measurement of that effect is no simple undertaking. At best the decision-making process is somewhat obscure, and at worst there is a concentrated effort to confuse the voters as to the realities. The apparent role of the parties and their real role are not always the same thing. To ascertain the realities of who did what and to whom is a challenging task, but one of some merit if the basic proposition about the significance of party systems has validity. If it is true, for example, that the parties often play an important role in determining which interests in the society are to be given a boost and which are to be neglected, then the character of the party system is an important political factor. The party system can play a role of importance in a negative as well as a positive way. Negatively, the party system can result in a confusing and deeply obscure legislative process in which certain interests walk off with all the prizes without the public ever being aware of it. This is exactly what tends to happen under a multifactional one-party system. On the other hand, a party system with highly competitive parties which are reasonably well led and relatively cohesive can result in not only the maximization of the power of the party leadership but at times considerable rationality and responsibility as well.

The policy-making process is so wondrously complex that assessment of the ultimate role of the party system cannot be reduced to objective and unerring procedures. The role of the party is not an isolated factor but one among a vast number of forces. The range of differences in party roles from state to state is so wide that generalization is difficult. The outsider, looking at the legislative-political processes of a state, suffers from the handicap of not being able to

320

get all the necessary information about what went on between the influentials who ultimately make the decisions. He must perforce infer from the outward appearances what *must* have gone on, and this can be a misleading operation. Take the following case as an example of the pitfalls of making broad inferences about a legislative struggle which outwardly appeared to be a party-based decision.

One hot June afternoon during the waning days of the 1955 session of the Connecticut General Assembly, an emissary of the governor strode into the Democratic Senate caucus room. What he saw was a shirt-sleeved, peevish, and thoroughly fatigued group of senators, who for five months had been struggling with a fantastic workload—all of it of necessity done on a parttime basis, since no one can live on the $600 a term paid a legislator in Connecticut. There was no senator present who had not met with rebuffs to more than one of his pet projects, whether picayune or noble. The subject under discussion on the arrival of the emissary was the governor himself. There was general unhappiness that he had not carried the battle to the Republican House of Representatives on many issues which the Democratic senators thought deserved his support.

Into this atmosphere the governor's messenger tossed a bill concerning a state program for the treatment of the so-called "sexual deviate." The governor, he said, had decided to support the bill (sponsored by a persistent Republican House member) and hoped the Senate would pass it. The senatorial response was immediate, noisy, and utterly negative. This absolute rejection of the suggestion was unusual—virtually all the governor's requests for legislation had been accepted and passed in due form by the Senate. Nor was there any substantive objection to the proposal itself; unless I badly misjudge the situation, the same bill presented under more propitious circumstances would not have had any trouble getting Senate approval.

To infer anything about the operation of the parties from this event would be quite misleading. There were no political pressures of the ordinary kind involved: no backroom deals to swap this for that, no pressure group maneuvering, no dictation from a boss decided the fate of this bill. Frustration and fatigue defeated it. It is not my contention that this was a customary occurrence; on the contrary, for purely personal predilections to become so heavily involved in a Connecticut legislative decision is unusual. Still, the example should serve as a warning against over-inferring from such information as one can glean from the outer fringes of a political assemblage.

Even where such adventitious circumstances do not arise, there are serious difficulties in isolating the consequences of political influences. The degree to which the party serves as a link between the governor and the legislature is the product of both the party's effort and the constitutional arrangements within which the party must work. Similarly, the party may serve well or badly as an enunciator of policy for which it assumes responsibility, but if the constitution provides a legislative apportionment which permits a small minority of the people to gain control of the legislature (as is true in both Connecticut and Rhode Island) then is it the failure of the party or of the constitutional system which encourages irresponsibility? If a long ballot facilitates the election of state administrators of the opposite party from the governor, and conflict and evasion of responsibility result, is this the fault of the party system? Or if a governor's council is constitutionally established in such a way as to tie the hands of a governor because the council happens to be of the opposite party (as in Maine and Massachusetts), is this attributable to the party's failure or that of the constitutional system?

If the party has any meaning at all in the making of state policy—and it certainly has in the three southern New England states—then the possibility of having a governor and a legislature of the same party assumes considerable importance. But as the data in Table 39 indicate, it is difficult to achieve that degree of legislative-executive harmony. It is only somewhat less difficult for a Democratic governor to get a friendly legislature in one of the New England states than for the camel to pass through the eye of the Biblical needle. In Connecticut, Massachusetts, and Maine no Democratic governor was so favored by the electorate during the period covered in Table 39; in Rhode Island, where the Democratic party comes uncomfortably close to having a one-party hegemony, Democratic governors have had sympathetic legislatures during only ten of the twenty-four years that Democrats have held the office since 1931.[1]

[1] As V. O. Key has illustrated, this tendency for Democratic governors to be unable to bring in Democratic legislative majorities with them is by no means limited to New England. Analyzing 32 states, he found the "chances were 50-50 that an election would be followed by a period of divided control when the

TABLE 39

New England States according to the Number of Years, 1931-1958,
in Which the Governorship and One or Both Legislative Houses
Were in Control of Opposite Parties

| | DIVIDED CONTROL | |
States	Number of years	Percentage of years
Connecticut	18	64.3%
Massachusetts	18	64.3
Rhode Island	16	57.0
Maine	8	28.5
New Hampshire	0	0.0
Vermont	0	0.0

In Massachusetts, Connecticut, and Rhode Island it is not infrequent
that more Democratic than Republican votes are cast in the legislative elections, although the Democrats wind up without a legislative majority. This is the result of gerrymandering and disproportionate districts. In effect the constitution bars the people from
making an open choice between the parties.

To observe that these constitutional provisions are therefore
essentially *political* provisions and significantly important precisely
because they are political is probably more logical than persuasive
to most Americans, trained from youth to consider constitutional
matters as in some mystical sense supra-political. That such matters
as apportionment are placed at arm's length—well beyond the reach
of urban majorities, for example, to tamper with—is seen less as a
minority-empowering political device than as some immutable dis-
tillation of ancient and therefore admirable wisdom. Yet the harsh
realities of state politics when examined from even the lower foot-
hills of the mountain of objectivity make it clear that here in the
constitutional realm is a major source of limitation on political
parties as rational and responsible contributors to the making of
public policy.

---

governor was Democratic. . . . When a Republican sat in the governor's chair,
only about one out of six elections gave the Democrats a majority in one house
or both houses." The period examined was 1930-1950. See *American State Politics*,
p. 58.

The Variable Impact of Parties
on Public Policy

There are other factors that condition the effectiveness of parties in making policy. The internal structure of the party in a state, the traditions regarding the proper place of party in government, and the degree of competitiveness between the parties are decisive factors. These four forces—structure, traditions, competition, and the constitutional system—vary incredibly among the states, and accordingly the extent of party influence varies as well. In order properly to assess the political processes of state government in America in the broadest sense of the term, it will be necessary to evolve some new approach to the classification of state parties. It is not enough to divide them according to the degree of competition alone, as political scientists have tended to do. The party systems of the one-party states are not all alike, nor are those of the two-party states. The internal structures of the parties within a state can have the most far-reaching implications for the kind of policy orientation of the state government, and accordingly perhaps some such classification as the following may facilitate comparative analysis of state politics.

Broadly, there seem to me to be five types of party system among the forty-eight states. The most significant division is that between the one-party and the two-party systems, but subcategories within each of the two main types are nearly as significant as the major types themselves, as the outline below suggests.

Admittedly there are difficulties in applying this classification to actual parties. Political situations in the states are subject to constant change; what at one point may be bifactionalism may in a few years be altered to one of the other variants of one-partyism, or one party in a two-party state may be rent by factionalism at one point and relatively centralized ten years later. Borderline cases which do not precisely fit the descriptions of the subcategories can be imagined. The criteria are not completely objective; in some cases two observers might disagree as to the niche into which a particular state fits. Nevertheless, it seems to me to be an advance beyond the more superficial typologies depending entirely on electoral data. At least some of the ambiguities inherent in references to the one-

and two-party systems may be obviated by further elaboration of some such classification scheme.

I. THE TWO-PARTY STATES

    A. *Cohesive, strong organizations*
1. Clearly identified and continuous leadership
2. Considerable leadership control over ascent up the ladder of political promotion (i.e., considerable control over nominations in the hands of the leadership)
3. Centralization of party finances and relatively centralized conduct of election campaigns
4. Great party influence in the making of legislative policy decisions (e.g., an influential role for the state party chairman in working out policy in the legislature)

    B. *Splintered, weak organizations*
1. Factional cleavage extensive (e.g., sectional or urban-rural)
2. Personality battles for statewide nominations common; little leadership control over nominations
3. Relatively little leadership influence on legislative policy formation

II. THE ONE-PARTY STATES

    A. *Machine-led; one faction predominant*
1. Clear, continuous leadership
2. Control over nominations and advancement in the hands of organization leaders
3. Considerable influence over legislative policy in the hands of the organization
       a. Dominated by one or two powerful interests (such as those based on a natural resource or an important farm crop), or
       b. A more confusing array of economic powers controlling decision-making

    B. *Bifactional party structure*
1. Two contesting factions with relatively continuous and identifiable leaderships
2. In varying degree some questions of policy transferred to primary contests
3. Moderate to minor legislative policy identification of factions

    C. *Multifactional party structure*
1. Party organizations as holding companies—virtual non-participants in policy-making
2. Factions and their leaderships ever shifting and non-continuous and without clear identification

325

3. Personality conflicts dominate in primaries
4. Policy formation a lottery in which the "haves" use the disorganization of politics to achieve their conservative ends

No effort is made here to classify all the states according to these categories, although from general knowledge many of the states could be assigned without much difficulty. The states of New England, however, occupy only three of the five subcategories listed. Two states (Vermont and New Hampshire) are one-party bifactional, one (Maine) is one-party multifactional, and two states (Massachusetts and Connecticut) are two-party with strong centralized parties. (Massachusetts is obviously in the two-party centralized category where the Republican party is concerned. The diffuse patterns of the Democratic party fit less well.) About the sixth state there may be some disagreement. Rhode Island, to judge from the electoral data alone, would appear to have one-party dominance equal to that of Maine, but the realities of Rhode Island political operations suggest that considerable competition does actually exist, as was pointed out in Chapter 7.

Some Probable Consequences of Competition and Party Structure

How much difference does it make in the long run whether a state has a set of competitive parties or whether one-party dominance prevails? How much does it matter whether the parties are centralized and cohesive or bifactional or multifactional? At times when one is involved in battling within a particular political system for the accomplishment of specific goals—or for that matter when observing with frustration from the sidelines—one is tempted to conclude that in the last analysis none of these factors can matter much. Separation of powers, unwieldy state constitutions, and warped legislative apportionment make it so easy so often for minorities to gainsay the apparent desire of the majority (of which one mystically considers oneself a member, of course) that it almost seems that the existence of two-party competition, for example, can make little difference in the ultimate policy output of a state government.

The common assumption is that the political leaders in a two-party system are more responsible to the preferences of the citizenry whether of high or low status in life, not so much out of principle as out of fear of retribution at the polls. If this is a correct assumption, precious little effort has gone into proving the extent to which the facts bear it out. A decade ago when he published his pioneering work in comparative state politics, V. O. Key observed that one-party factionalism gave a tremendous advantage to conservative interests, which, with the money to spend and with relatively little organized effort, manage to influence government to serve their interests nicely. "The factional system [of the one-party state]," he said, "simply provides no institutional mechanism for the expression of lower-bracket viewpoints."[2] At times the upper economic brackets may accede to discontent to keep rebellious pressure from rising, but in general the conservative elements are aided by the fact that no "continuing competitive groups carry on the battle."[3] To a degree at least the competing groups of politicians within the Democratic and Republican parties do provide this minimal condition. Key then goes on to say that the "great value of the two-party system is not that there are two groups with conflicting policy tendencies from which the voters may choose, but that there are two groups of politicians."[4]

Particularly in view of the fact that the pressures of close competition tend to pull the parties to a median ground where policy differences between them are minimized, the existence of competing camps of politicians becomes the more important. In no other way is there much opportunity for the otherwise preoccupied voter to make his choice a meaningful one. But how does one go about testing the proposition that competitive parties tend to be more responsive to the needs of the have-nots, who after all constitute the most neglected portion of the electorate? What differences in policy orientation among the various states can be attributed to the character of the parties, and which result from other conditions? The area of difficulty here is reduced somewhat, although certainly not eliminated, by restricting the comparisons to one region. The six New England states have a sufficient similarity of heritage, governmental structure, economy, and social composition to make such a comparison possible.

To indicate the differences in policy orientation and political process among the New England states, I have chosen three different

<hr>

[2] *Southern Politics*, p. 309.   [3] *Loc.cit.*   [4] *Ibid.*, p. 310.

types of criteria: first, the distribution of the tax load in the various states; second, the provisions of certain laws providing state services to the people; third, the apparent effects of two-party competition in overcoming the minority-empowering provisions of legislative apportionment.

There are differences in the wealth of these states which affect the ability of the states to provide public services. The proportions of certain groups—such as manufacturing employees—are different from state to state, a fact which undoubtedly contributes to the ease or difficulty in organizing effectively to make demands on government. Table 40 sets forth some of the indices of the economic differences between the states.

It is obvious from Table 40 that the three one-party states are less wealthy than their neighbors to the immediate south, but they are not far below the national average in their per-capita income. In fact, their rank in per-capita income is equal to or above the states of the Southwest and Northwest and considerably above the states of the Southeast. Even Florida and Virginia, the Southeastern states with the highest per-capita income, rank below the average of the northern three states of New England. Notice also that the proportion of the work-force engaged in manufacturing in Maine and New Hampshire does not differ radically from that in the two-party states. The lack of businesses on which to levy taxation can hardly therefore be the reason for the relatively light tax-take from business in these two states. Yet as Table 41 illustrates, these two states do not tax business as heavily as do their sister states.

TABLE 40

Comparative Economic and Cultural Data on the New England States

States	Per cent of work-force employed in agriculture (1950)	Per cent of work-force employed in manufacturing (1950)	Per cent of population urban (1950)	Per cent non-agricultural workers in unions (1953)	Per-capita income (1955)
Vermont	18.2%	24.6%	36.4%	18.9%	$1535.
Maine	9.3	34.2	51.7	21.4	1593.
New Hampshire	6.5	40.4	57.5	24.6	1732.
Massachusetts	1.8	37.4	84.4	30.1	2079.
Connecticut	2.9	42.6	77.7	26.5	2499.
Rhode Island	1.5	44.0	84.5	27.4	1957.

TABLE 41

Business and Death/Gift Taxes in New England States, 1956*

Proportion of total tax revenue from	Conn.	Mass.	R.I.	N.H.	Maine	Vt.
Business taxes	23.8%	28.3%	25.0%	7.9%	12.5%	16.2%
Death/gift taxes	5.4	4.4	3.3	4.5	3.4	1.9
Combined	29.2%	32.7%	28.3%	12.4%	15.9%	18.1%

* Business taxes included here are those which can be identified specifically as being levied on business only. Taxes paid both by individuals and businesses (e.g., motor-fuel taxes or motor-vehicle licenses) are excluded. Taxes included are those on gross and net receipts on insurance and public utilities, occupations, and businesses. See *Compendium of State Government Finances in 1956*, Bureau of the Census, pp. 11-13. This does not include payments by business into unemployment compensation funds, but the exclusion does not distort the relative proportions of business taxation from state to state. The rank order of per-capita payment into these state funds is as follows: Rhode Island, Massachusetts, Connecticut, New Hampshire, Maine, and Vermont. For comparative data see *The Economic State of New England*, New Haven, 1954, p. 628. That committee divided state tax income into three categories as indicated by their data for 1950 taxes given below:

	Conn.	Mass.	R.I.	N.H.	Maine	Vt.
Individual	37	40	23	34	22	50
Business	39	47	50	29	24	27
Paid by both individual and business	24	13	27	37	54	23

Note that more than one-half of the taxes paid by both individuals and businesses in Maine were motor-vehicle and motor-fuel taxes. Hence the figures indicating a seemingly small load on individuals in that state are misleading.

To contend that the lack of business accounts for the small proportion of business taxation in Maine and New Hampshire fails to be convincing since the proportion of business income is patently less in Vermont than in either of these states and yet its percentage of total revenue taken from business is higher than in either Maine or New Hampshire. The tax-take from business in New Hampshire, in fact, is less proportionally than in any other New England state, and yet its economic pattern is not so remarkably different from that of Massachusetts, which gets nearly a third of its revenue from business. (The proportion of manufacturing employees, for example, is actually greater in New Hampshire than in Massachusetts.) The important point is that the average percentage of taxes from business and inheritances combined is just twice as great in the three two-party states as in the three one-party states.

The tax structures of virtually all states are heavily loaded with regressive taxes such as the direct consumer's sales tax and various flat-rate hidden levies on consumer items, and in this respect the New England states are not exceptional. The degree of regressiveness of sales taxes, however, varies considerably from state to state, depending on the extensiveness of the list of tax-exempt items. Connecticut, for example, collects more than a third of its revenue in the sales tax but, as such taxes go, Connecticut's is among the less regressive. Retail-store operators complain of the nuisance created by the wide range of exceptions, but nothing is done to satisfy them. The desire to make the tax more palatable that originally forced the exceptions into the law still operates to keep them in force.

It ought to be noted too as a significant datum of New England tax policy that two states, Vermont and New Hampshire, still rely on the most regressive tax of them all—the poll tax. It does not account for much in Vermont (only 1.5 per cent of general taxation), but in New Hampshire the poll-tax levy brings in 4.2 per cent of tax income (or more than half as much as distinguishable taxes on business).

One striking fact about New England state taxation is that Vermont alone has a graduated personal income tax. Two other states have forms of personal income tax—New Hampshire and Massachusetts. In New Hampshire the tax is not graduated, is levied only on income from intangible property, and brings in but three per cent of total revenue. Massachusetts law is mildly progressive in that lower rates are charged for earned than for unearned income. Vermont's graduated tax produces 19 per cent of total state revenue, and a good proportion of it comes from the relatively well-to-do. Does this, therefore, disprove the hypothesis about the incidence of taxation according to economic status as related to political structure? In my view, it does not. Rather, it reflects a temporary triumph of Vermont bifactionalism. When the income-tax law was passed during Governor Gibson's administration, it was driven through over the protests of Proctor-faction leaders. Gibson in other words had considerable "lower bracket" support, particularly from the relatively poor farm element. Their combined power was sufficient to get a majority in favor of pulling more tax dollars from the upper brackets. Subsequent governors, however much they may have disliked the tax, have for a variety of reasons been reluctant to seek its repeal. Once the state budget had been accommodated to income tax revenue, it could only be replaced, not simply repealed. To get support for new sources of taxation is no easy task. Moreover, Proctor-faction governors have no desire to provide so clear a basis for reuniting the now divided anti-Proctor faction.

In short, the evidence would seem to indicate that the tax structures of the one-party and two-party states are different in precisely the way that Key suggested. The lower element of the economic pyramid appears to bear the heavier burden in Maine and New Hampshire particularly where not only one-partyism prevails but one-partyism complicated by multifactionalism in the one case and vague, shifting bifactionalism in the other. Vermont's situation is ultimately only slightly better. I cannot recall any great liberal acclaim for the tax structures of Connecticut, Massachusetts, or Rhode Island, but the pressures of the have-nots on the political leaders of competitive parties seem to have helped to produce a generally fairer tax structure in those states.

How do the one-party states compare with the two-party states in the other end of the fiscal process—that of distribution of funds for various functions? To test the hypothesis that the less-privileged element are disadvantaged by the non-competitiveness of one-party politics, I examined state efforts to provide certain services to the unfortunate. There is a considerable variation between the one-party and two-party states of New England in this respect, as Table 42 indicates. But it does not follow that the variation is wholly attributable to the presence or absence of party competition. The wealth of the state conditions the extent to which it can be generous to those in need, however serious the need may be. Note, however, that the variations in wealth between the states, at least as measured by per-capita income, are not nearly as great as the differences in the levels of aid offered.

Roughly the same situation prevails among the New England states where workmen's compensation benefits are concerned. Although the data on these benefits are not easily reduced to qualitatively comparative terms (there is difficulty, for example, in comparing a benefit program which allows a specific maximum per week but has a definite limit on the number of weeks of eligibility as compared with one with a similar maximum but an unlimited length of payment), it would appear that in general the most favorable program exists in Connecticut and that the other states have respectively

TABLE 42

New England State Funds for Certain Services
as Percentage of Average for All States*

	Per-capita income (1955) (U.S. = 100)	Aid to blind	Aid to disabled	Old-age assistance	Aid to dependent children
			(Average of all states = 100)		
Connecticut	135	194	259	217	209
Massachusetts	114	201	237	189	189
Rhode Island	106	134	152	122	147
New Hampshire	94	109	147	121	180
Maine	86	62	64	69	70
Vermont	83	59	66	65	66

* All data for services are calculated for 1954 and are drawn from the *Book of the States, 1956-1957*, pp. 324-329. Excluded from the calculations are the federal contributions which are, of course, higher for the poorer states than for the richer.

less attractive programs in the order listed in Table 42. The same rank order of benefits to the worker applies for the unemployment compensation laws, with the exception of Rhode Island, whose program is second in order rather than third.[5]

Another interesting example of the difference between the two types of states is the matter of legislation prohibiting discrimination in employment. All three two-party states were leaders in the development of such statutes, but little has been done in the other three states. Or, more precisely, nothing has been done in Maine and Vermont, and New Hampshire's law applies only to labor unions.[6] (It is a bit hard to believe that the only discrimination practiced is by the unions. It is more than likely that industry's relative political power may have had something to do with the way the act emerged from the legislature.) The existence of greater numbers of Negroes in the lower three states has undoubtedly helped legislators in those states to see the good qualities in such legislation, but this should not be taken to mean that there are no minority problems in the

[5] *Book of the States, 1956-1957*, pp. 408, 431-433. Minimum wage provisions follow a similar pattern: Connecticut, Rhode Island, Massachusetts provide a $1.00 minimum; New Hampshire, 85 cents; Vermont, 75 cents, and Maine, indeterminant.

[6] See the "Check List of State Anti-Discrimination and Anti-Bias Laws" prepared by the Commission on Law and Social Action of the American Jewish Congress, New York, 1953 (pamphlet). See also their "Summary of 1957 State Anti-Discrimination Laws" (mimeo. undated).

upper three states. One indication that such problems exist is that Vermont in 1957 passed a statute prohibiting discrimination in places of public accommodation. Although there are fewer Negroes proportionately in Vermont than in either Maine or New Hampshire, the latter two states have not enacted such laws.

Finally, one of the most significant effects of two-party competition where parties have a reasonable degree of unity is that the party leadership can partially mitigate some of the consequences of legislative apportionment schemes which empower small minorities. As I have said several times earlier, I conceive the apportionment of our state legislatures to be one of the most blighting aspects of state government. But the consequences of the empowering of these special minorities might be a great deal worse in some states were it not for the pressures applied by political leaders fearful of the next election.

In Rhode Island and Connecticut, for example, the results of the rigged apportionment systems would undoubtedly be much worse were it not for the competition between "two groups of politicians" competing under the names of different political parties. In both Connecticut and Rhode Island the small-town Republicans have great authority in the legislatures and state party conventions and they make their privileged position pay off. But they do not make as much of their special position as they presumably might. Part of the reason they moderate their demands is the fact that the legislators from the small towns are pressured by party leaders from urban and suburban areas not to put the Republican party in an impossible position for the next election. Most of the small-town representatives have no particular fears about the next election in their home towns, but that is not enough. To reap the satisfactions of patronage rewards, for example, it is necessary to win the governorship and other administrative offices. If the minority gets in a position where it feels the situation is hopeless—as some leaders of the Rhode Island Republican minority have done from time to time—they may feel that it is wiser to deal with the dominant Democrats on the basis of a kind of double machine than to compromise for the sake of a party program. But so long as there remains hope of victory, the small-town legislators can often be persuaded not to act so as to embarrass the rest of the party.

Perhaps the best proof of this point is to be found on the statute books of Connecticut. The laws of Connecticut are really quite enlightened, all things considered; in many respects the state has been among the vanguard in accepting new and relatively radical programs (as, for example, labor and anti-discrimination laws). But none of those laws ever got on the books without the affirmative vote of most of the rural small-town Republican legislators whose general outlook is hardly daring. They are mostly true conservatives; they will wait awhile, thank you, and would rather not spend the money anyhow. But they voted yes on a good many innovations. Nor did all these laws result from the maneuvering of Democratic governors and a Democratic Senate; many of them came when the Republicans had complete control over both Houses and the governorship. Many a law for which Democrats pleaded in vain when they shared power was rejected only to be passed the next session when the Democrats were out of power entirely. "Let's act now, when there can be no doubt of who gets the credit," is the plea of the Republican leadership. Among others the following acts got passed in just this manner: the first Fair Employment Practices law in the state, minimum wage increases, and the repeal of prohibitory taxes on oleomargarine.

In Massachusetts the apportionment pattern does not enthrone the rustics as it does in Connecticut and Rhode Island. But there is enough gerrymandering of Senate districts to give a pretty important position to certain senators from rural small-town areas. Consequently the leaders of the Republican party and especially the Republican governors use all their wiles to win over senators particularly from the western part of the state. They often cajole them into accepting liberal legislation for the sake of the next election.

In Vermont, New Hampshire and to a lesser extent in Maine, legislative apportionment is such as to reduce drastically the legislative power of urban areas. Many if not most of the critics thus partially disenfranchised are Democratic on election day, which is not much encouragement to Republican leaders to correct the malapportionment. And since Republican candidates can expect to win virtually all statewide elections, there is no leverage for persuading the empowered minority to act so as to avoid retribution at the polls. The transfer of political contests to internal party conflict leaves the urban leaders with less voice and less authority than their counterparts in the three two-party states.

The contention is sometimes made, however, that a vigorous bi-factionalism within a one-party state serves essentially the same function as competition between two parties. The argument is that contests are between Republican factions (at least in New England) rather than between Democrats and Republicans. This, however, assumes that the competing groups of Republicans will have sufficient cohesiveness and continuity to make them comparable to the parties. In order for factions to give the public a reasonable opportunity to choose between them, a minimum of public identification is a logical necessity. But in fact they have no such clarity. The leadership of the factions shifts and changes, and the factions, even more than the parties, come together to win elections and forget common purposes once elected. In the one state in the country where bifactionalism is probably most rigid and pronounced— or was at least some years ago—the bifactional arrangement did tend to serve as a substitute for two-party competition. That state is Louisiana, whose party system was intensively studied by Alan Sindler. Huey Long, Sindler reported, "gave Louisiana a structured and organized politics, a politics that made sense."[7] In Louisiana the factions use a "ticket system" whereby candidates for the legislature and county offices are identified with the prominent statewide candidates as members of the same "ticket" or faction, and thus the voter has some indication of who is fighting whom and, at least in part, for what. It is Sindler's opinion that in the post-Huey Long era Louisiana's bifactionalism is "superior to one-party confusion," but still "considerably inferior to two-party politics, or at least to the claims put forward on behalf of the two-party system in the United States."[8]

If in the considered judgment of an able student of Louisiana's bifactionalism (embellished with the ticket system), even that state fails to produce an adequate alternative to party competition, how can it be contended that the much more confusing and loosely organized systems of the three northern New England states do provide a suitable alternative? None of these states has anything approaching the ticket system. In none are the factions continuous

[7] Alan P. Sindler, *Huey Long's Louisiana, State Politics, 1920-1952*, Baltimore, 1956, p. 282. See also his article, "Bifactional Rivalry as an Alternative to Two-Party Competition in Louisiana," 49 *American Political Science Review* 641-662 (1955).

[8] *Ibid.*, p. 283.

or consistent in their leadership. The facts of New England one-party politics and the quite reasonable analogy with the facts in Louisiana make a mockery of the argument.

Within the factional systems of Vermont, New Hampshire, and Maine certain interest groups have managed to take over the government to a considerable degree. Manufacturing interests, public utilities, and timber companies have tremendous power. When they oppose each other, the normal reaction of legislators is to let the giants resolve their differences among themselves before the legislature ratifies the agreement. But they do not normally oppose each other; on the contrary, they usually seek advantages which are relatively independent of the needs of the other big interests or they join forces to work for mutually beneficial laws. In matters of tax legislation, labor regulation, or natural resources control, for example, the major economic interests of these three states in most cases have a common attitude. Their needs are usually not those of the marginal farmer or the urban worker who, since he has relatively little political power, frequently gets the short end of the legislative stick. On occasion the Farm Bureau in Vermont serves as a counter-force against the marble and granite and machine-tool groups, but it does so only sporadically. And not even this degree of opposition is at all customary in Maine and New Hampshire.

There are, in short, meager sources of "countervailing power," to use J. K. Galbraith's term in a somewhat different manner. At the national level the great corporations are opposed by large and powerful unions. Grazier and timber interests must contend with the conservationists. Clearly the counterbalancing process is less than perfect even on the national level—there are certain interests that are difficult if not impossible to mobilize (consumers, for example) and other interests are such that opposition to them is difficult (veterans, for example). Still on the national level, there are usually countervailing sources of power for the most powerful interests. The same is true in Massachusetts, Rhode Island, and Connecticut. Both manufacturing and labor-union interests are strong. No single interest or small group of interests (such as the combination of pine, power, and manufacturing in Maine) can get control over the legislature. Countervailing power is present to resist any effort to take complete control. The very fact that the economies of these states are highly developed and highly diversified tends to promote a wider control over government.

The diversity or the lack of diversity of economic interests in a state tends to be reflected in the prevailing party system and the mode of its operation. In the first place, of course, it is the diversity in part that creates the atmosphere for two-party competition, and the absence of diversity facilitates one-partyism. In the two-party states the anxiety over the next election pushes political leaders into serving the interests of the have-less element of society, thereby putting the party into the countervailing power operation. Conversely, in the one-party states it is easier for a few powerful interests to manage the government of the state without party interference since the parties are not representative of the particular elements that might pose opposition to the dominant interest groups. The parties do not represent the have-less element for the simple reason that politically there is no necessity to do so.

The Prospects for Party Competition in New England

If the presence or absence of party competition is as important to the political character of a state as it appears to me to be, what, then, are the prospects that competition will be maintained where it exists or be developed where it does not? In one sense, party competition is like good weather—we rejoice in its appearance and lament its absence, but there is not a great deal we can do about it. The habits of generations, the chance dispersal of industry and agriculture, a party's local reputation, and the nuances of constitutional inclusion and exclusion—all affect the chances for the creation or maintenance of party competition. Vermont Democrats will testify, I know, to the difficulties of changing party voting habits. Constitutional provisions can be nearly as difficult to change, partly because they are based upon the same habits as are voting prejudices. A party's reputation once lost is hard to regain, for, unlike a woman fallen from virtue, the opposition party sees to it that the sinner is more to be censured than pitied. And certainly the dispersal of industry and agriculture among the states is not consciously affected in any major way by partisan hopes. Undoubtedly politicians have hopes and fears on the occasion of the arrival of a new industry or when observing the decline of agriculture, but few of the actual decisions to change the economic pattern of a state are motivated by such political ambitions as those involved in the balance of voting strength.

The late Bernard DeVoto once called New England a "finished piece," and he did not mean it sarcastically. He meant that it was economically and otherwise the most mature region in the country and undoubtedly he was correct. But this does not mean that change has ceased in New England. The three one-party states of New England are constantly gaining in industry. Vermont, the state farthest from two-party competition, has had an amazing increase in industry in recent years. Between 1939 and 1956 the proportion of factory workers in Vermont increased by 41.4 per cent, a rate of increase in New England second only to that in Connecticut.[9] Undoubtedly the increasing proportion of industrial workers in Vermont was a contributing factor in the 1954 election, when the Democratic candidate came within 2.3 percentage points of winning the governorship.

In both Maine and New Hampshire there would seem to be possibilities for the development of stronger minority parties which in time might become competitive. Recent elections in Maine have indicated a surprising upturn in Democratic victories, and, while this may be a temporary and passing phase in Maine politics, it may also be the beginning of a new era. The improved organization of the present-day Democratic party in Maine could lead to a substantial change in political climate.[9a]

To judge from the composition of the electorate of New Hampshire, the surprising thing is that the state has not had a more competitive party system. As the three victories of Franklin Roosevelt in New Hampshire indicate, there are a great many potentially Democratic votes. But the emergence of the minority party to truly competitive status is dependent upon three developments which could begin to appear tomorrow or which may be delayed indefinitely: (1) the curtailment of the deep ethnic rivalries within the Democratic party, (2) the curbing of some leaders of the party who have been more anxious to pick up patronage crumbs from the Republican table than to develop a Democratic party, and (3) the refurbishing of the reputation of the Democratic party in

[9] U.S. Department of Labor, *Monthly Labor Review*, vol. 80, p. 285 (Mar. 1957).
[9a] The 1958 election in all three of these states suggests that competition is growing.

the state since the careers of several urban Democratic machines have not done that reputation any good. Competition *could* come to New Hampshire politics without revolutionary change in its social patterns; it is no Mississippi by any means.

In Connecticut and Massachusetts the prospects for the retention of reasonably competitive parties would seem to be good. Since they have been competitive for the last thirty-odd years, clearly the basis for competition exists. Barring some abrupt changes in the economy or population of these states, a prediction that competition can continue would seem about as safe as such predictions can be.

In Rhode Island virtually all signs point toward increasing competition. The Democratic party has behaved badly enough within recent years to encourage considerable disaffection among the voters.

So long as the Republican party was pitifully weak and divided, with many of its leaders playing ball with the dominant Democrats, the voters really had no place to turn. But the recent resurgence of the Republican party as well as the increasing suburbanization of the state's population may well change the whole political system of the state. If the emerging urban and suburban Republican leaders can keep control of the party out of the hands of certain double-machine small-town Republicans, the prospects for competition would seem fairly good.

While I grant that these predictions are scarcely gilt-edged in their reliability, the long-run developments of American society do seem to suggest that the opportunities for competitive parties are increasing. The national culture now conveyed to every home with instantaneous speed has had the effect of eroding away the long-standing sectionalism of the country. As industry disperses across the nation and as cities grow (along with their suburbs) to accommodate the industrial development, the inevitable result is that the insularities of the past begin to recede. Maine and Vermont, like Georgia and North Carolina, have begun to adapt themselves to the demands of industrialization. As the range of similar social and economic problems for all sections of the country becomes wider, the opportunities for two-party systems increase.

If my contentions about the significance of two-party competition have validity, the growth of party competition in the New England states may lead to substantial improvement in New England state government. More competition will ultimately bring more bitter elections, a good many gross exaggerations as to the party "record," and it is likely to enhance the power of certain party leaders. But if it also brings in a little more clarity about who did what and why, if it tears away some of the curtains of obscurity within which one-party politics normally operates, will not the voter have a better opportunity to make his weight felt? Party competition surely does not guarantee that rationality and responsibility will prevail in a state government, but, all things considered, it is apparently more conducive to these goals than its counterpart.

INDEX

Adams, Brooks, 120
Adams, John, 3, 12, 120
Adams, Sherman, 53
Aiken, George, 18
Alcorn, Meade, 255, 284
Aldrich, Nelson, 175, 208
Alexander, Jack, 165n
Alien and Sedition Acts, 12
Allen, Ethan, 12
Allen, Robert S., 166n, 168n, *quoted* 169
Amory, Cleveland, 119
Arizona, 27
Ascoli, Max, 51n
Associated Industries of Maine, 108, 113
Associated Industries of Massachusetts, 165
Associated Industries of Rhode Island, 224
Associated Industries of Vermont, 40
Aswell, J. R. and Michelson, E. J., 168n

Bailey, John M., 260-263, 266, 282, 284, 285, 298
Baldwin, Clarence ("Cappy"), 246n, 251-255, 283, 284, 285n, 298
Baldwin, Raymond E., 246n, 268, 300
Bangor Hydroelectric Company, 114
Barnes, Clarence A., 142-143
Bass, Perkins, 52
Bass, Robert T., 50
Bennet, Douglas, 263
Benton, William, 262
Bergin, Edward, 262
Bilbo, Theodore, 129, 130, 310
Billington, Ray A., 306n
Bishop, Neil, 89
Book of the States, 113n, 149n, 209n
Boston and Maine Railroad, 48
Boston Brahmins, their place in Massachusetts politics, 119-120
Boston Herald, 150
Boucher, Jean C., 115
Boutin, Bernard L., 52n
Bowles, Chester, 19, 238, 239, 261, 262, 264, 273n, 290, 298
Bradford, Robert P., 120, 144
Bradford, William, 144
Branon, Frank E., 30n, 38
Braun, Robert, 84
Brayton, Charles, 175, 176-177, 183, 208
Brayton's Law, 175, 191
Brennan, William, 253-254, 255n, 284
Brewer, Basil, 136, 137

Brewster, Ralph Owen, 50, 85, 88
Bridges, Styles, 47, 49-52, 61n, 67
Briggs, James, 93, 109ff
Broomhead, William, 201
Brown, Fred, 62
Bryan, William Jennings, 230, 312-313
Buckley, Thomas H., 131
"built-in" interest groups, *explained*, 163. *See also* entries under states
Burke, William H., 127
Burlington (Vt.) *Free Press*, 10n
Burnight, Robert G., 235n
Burrell, Fred J., 132n, 140-141, 317
Burrill, Charles L., 132n, 141
Bush, Prescott, campaign finances of, 253

Cameron, David, 199n, 201
Carkin, Herbert B., 181
Carr, John C., 127
Cash, W. J., 311
Cater, Douglas, 50
Celentano, William C., 238
Central Maine Power Company, 84, 108
Chaffee, Zachariah, Jr., 192n, 193n, 204n
Chandler, William E., 48n, 49n
Chapin, Miriam, 9
Charles II of England, 271
Chicago Tribune, 51
Churchill, Winston (American author), 47
Cianciarulo, Benjamin, 183n
Clarie, T. Emmet, 263
Classification of state political parties, 324-326
Clauson, Clinton, 94n
"Clean Waters Act," 109-110
Clyma, Carl, 247n, *quoted* 271
Coefficient of correlation, *explained* 63-64
Coffin, Frank M., 101, 102-103, 317
Commission on Horse Racing and Athletics (R.I.), 181
Connecticut, Chapters 9, 10: Connecticut, absence of race tracks in, 268-269; "built-in" interest groups in, 286-287; business interests in the politics of, 246-247; cities in the politics of, 239-240, 257ff; Commission on State Government Organization of, 261n, 273n, 301; compared with Massachusetts, 124, 127, 157, 162; compared

Lockard, Duane, 1921—. New England State politics. Princeton, N. J., Princeton University Press, 1959. 348 p. illus. 25 cm. 1. New England—Pol. & govt. 2. Political parties—New England. I. Title *Full name*: Walter Duane Lockard. JK2295.A112L6 (329) 59-5600 ‡ Library of Congress